Stone Age Spear and Arrow Points of the Midcontinental and Eastern United States

Stone Age Spear

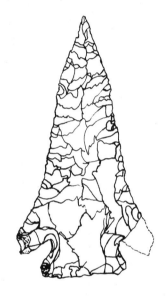

Indiana University Press

BLOOMINGTON & INDIANAPOLIS

and Arrow Points

of the Midcontinental and

Eastern United States

A Modern Survey and Reference

NOEL D. JUSTICE

*This book was brought to publication
with the assistance of a grant from the
Andrew W. Mellon Foundation.*

First paperback edition 1995

Manufactured in the United States of America

Library of Congress Cataloging-in-Publication Data

Justice, Noel D.
   Stone age spear and arrow points of the midcontinental
and eastern United States.
   Bibliography: p.
   Includes index.
   1. Indians of North America—Implements. 2. Projectile
points—United States. 3. Indians of North America—Antiquities.
4. United States— Antiquities.
I. Title.
E98.14J87   1987   623.4'41   86-45399
ISBN 0-253-35406-4   ISBN 0-253-20985-4 (pbk.)

2 3 4 5 6 00 99 98 97 96 95

CONTENTS

Projectile Point Type Descriptions

Figures

Plates

Plates follow page xvi.

Maps

Acknowledgments

While it is impossible specifically to thank everyone who made this work a success, a number of individuals made significant contributions to this effort. James H. Kellar, Professor Emeritus and former Director, and Christopher S. Peebles, Director of the Glenn A. Black Laboratory of Archaeology, were of constant support and ultimately made this work possible by allowing the several years of collections research at the Glenn A. Black Laboratory. I am indebted to them. The Eli Lilly Collection housed at the Glenn A. Black Laboratory provided a major source for illustrations used in this book.

Many individuals and institutions made it possible to study their collections and gave permission to illustrate materials for use in this book. Charles H. Faulkner, Paul W. Parmalee, and Jefferson Chapman at the Frank H. McClung Museum, University of Tennessee, provided specimens from the Eva and Ice House Bottoms sites and other materials from Tennessee. George F. MacDonald and Robert J. Pammett of the Archaeological Survey of Canada, Canadian Museum of Civilization, provided casts of projectile points from the Debert site, Nova Scotia. Peter L. Storck of the Royal Ontario Museum provided casts of Paleo-Indian types from southern Ontario. Richard A. Nolf and Bonnie K. Watkins of the St. Joseph Museum, Missouri, provided casts of projectile point caches from Missouri and Nebraska. Jane Stevenson Day of the Denver Museum of Natural History gave permission to illustrate projectile point types in the J. A. Eichenberger cast series. Lynne Peters Sullivan and Timothy Pauketat at Southern Illinois University at Carbondale, Center for Archaeological Investigations, provided specimens from Crab Orchard sites in southern Illinois. Peter A. Bostrom provided casts of materials from Mound 72 Cahokia site and other materials from his Lithic Casting Lab. Robert E. Funk, State University of New York, Albany, State Education Department, gave permission to redraw specimens published in William A. Ritchie's (1971a) volume on New York projectile points. Gregory Perino granted permission to redraw selected specimens in his latest work (Perino 1985) on projectile points. James B. Richardson III of the Carnegie Museum of Natural History, Division of Anthropology, provided photographs of materials from the Cresap Mound, West Virginia, for illustration. Donald R. Dickson provided drawings of points from Calf Creek Cave, Arkansas. Kent Vickery, Charles R. Lacer, Jr., Tom Fallwell, Nick Nye, Bill Brockman, Benjamin H. and Jack W. Justice, Avery Lewis, George L. Johnson, John Sinclair, D. Brian Dellar, Herbert Sisson, and Donald Champion made specimens or collections available for examination and illustration.

Many people offered their help and insights and I am indebted to them. I would like to thank Lawrence A. Conrad, Patrick and Cheryl Munson, Carl H. Chapman, David M. Stothers, Donald R. Dickson, Gregory Perino, Howard D. Winters, Donald Cochran, Robert Pace, Edward Smith, Brian Redmond, Christopher Baltz, Ruth Brinker, and John W. Richardson for their invaluable discussion and comments.

I must thank those who offered their time and help in the identification of raw material types for projectile points used in this volume. Especially valuable assistance with rock I.D. was provided by John R. Hill of the Indiana Geological Survey and Charles Vitaliano, Indiana University Department of Geology, as well as Jefferson Chapman, Jack Hofman, Peter A. Bostrom, and Kenneth Tankersley.

The artists who helped prepare the hundreds of line drawings and maps used in this volume put in hours of careful work. I would like to thank Kathryn Henke, Rachael Freyman, and especially Jill Harris-Cowan. Additional help with illustrations was given by Patricia Wildhack-Nolan and Karen J. Price. These artists accepted my critiques of flake scar configuration, effective attribute representation, and stylistic matters in good spirit. Kathy, Jill, and Rachael have my appreciation as they took primary responsibility for the majority of the illustrations. Julie Pitzen was a great help with illustrations and preparation of key distribution maps. Kent C. Miller of the Indiana University Audio-Visual Center is responsible for the fine color photos of projectile points.

An invaluable exchange of ideas was provided at a Projectile Point Workshop organized by Kent D. Vickery and held at the University of Cincinnati in 1983. At this workshop I had an opportunity to share typological concerns with James B. Griffin, Howard D. Winters, Bettye Broyles, W. Fred Kinsey III, Mark Seeman, Thomas Genn Cook, James L. Murphy, Alfred M. Lee, Patricia A. Tench, Rebecca A. Bennett, Robert A. DeRegnancourt, Jack M. Schock, and John J. Winsch. It was of great benefit to me.

Last, but not least, I would like to thank my mother and father, sister Rebecca, and brother Joseph for their constant support and inspiration. I must also thank my children Angela, Sarah, and Adam, for that fresh splash of vigor and continuity.

—NDJ

Stone Age Spear
and Arrow Points
of the Midcontinental and
Eastern United States

Plate 1: Paleo-Indian Projectile Points

a. Agate Basin. Wyandotte chert. GBL 21/330. Indiana.

b. Cumberland. Attica chert. GBL 2681/27. Site 12 Al 58, Allen Co., Indiana.

c. Clovis. Wyandotte chert. GBL 1448/421. Southwest Indiana.

d. Folsom base. Allibates. GBL collections. Bell Co., Texas.

e. Clovis. Holland chert. GBL 281/269. Franklin Co., Indiana.

f. Folsom. J. A. Eichenberger cast. Lindenmeier site, Colorado. University of New Mexico collection.

g. Ross County. Flint Ridge chert. GBL 21/302. Delaware Co., Indiana.

h. Clovis. Wyandotte chert. GBL 21/285. Indiana.

i. Plainview. J. A. Eichenberger cast. Texas. Baylor University collection.

j. Cumberland. Fort Payne chert. Tennessee. Specimen 24/103, Frank H. McClung Museum, University of Tennessee.

k. Agate Basin. Muldraugh chert. GBL 14/872. Greene Co., Indiana.

Plate 2: Late Paleo-Indian/Early Archaic Projectile Points

a. Hardin Barbed. Unidentified chert. GBL 21/420. Southwestern Indiana.

b. Greenbrier. Fort Payne chert. Florence, Alabama. Marshall L. Fallwell collection.

c. Scottsbluff. J. A. Eichenberger cast. Saskatchewan. American Museum of Natural History collection.

d. Dalton. Burlington chert. Missouri. Specimen 88/103, Frank H. McClung Museum, University of Tennessee.

e. Beaver Lake. Attica chert. GBL 3304/51. Unknown provenience.

f. Greenbrier. Wyandotte chert. GBL 21/309. Indiana.

g. Quad. Unidentified chert. GBL 21/344. Southwestern Indiana.

h. Hardin Barbed. Bevel resharpening. Attica chert. GBL 177/9. Owen Co., Indiana.

i. Dalton. Serration resharpening. Unidentified chert. GBL 21/419-2. Southwestern Indiana.

j. Beaver Lake. Holland chert. GBL 14/820. Indiana.

k. Beaver Lake. Laurel chert. GBL 21/344. Southwestern Indiana.

l. Thebes. Muldraugh chert. GBL 21/369. Boone Co., Indiana.

Plate 3: Early Archaic Projectile Points
a. St. Charles. Wyandotte chert. GBL 14/927. Rush Co., Indiana.
b. Kessell Side Notched. Paoli chert. GBL 1448/101. Southwestern Indiana.
c. Big Sandy. Fort Payne chert. Eva site, Tennessee. Specimen ST2D:D 504/6Bn12, Frank H. McClung Museum, University of Tennessee.
d. Thebes. Attica chert. GBL 31/106. Fulton Co., Indiana.
e. Lost Lake. Bevel resharpening. Indian Creek chert. GBL 14/871. Greene Co., Indiana.
f. Lost Lake. Bevel resharpening. Liston Creek chert. GBL 31/106. Fulton Co., Indiana.
g. Kessell Side Notched. Unidentified chert. GBL 14/206. Rush Co., Indiana.
h. St. Charles. Flint Ridge chert. GBL 21/431. Unknown provenience.
i. Big Sandy. Muldraugh/Fort Payne chert? GBL 14/927. Rush Co., Indiana.
j. St. Charles. Flint Ridge chert. GBL 14/876. Hancock Co., Indiana.
k. Lost Lake. Haney chert. GBL 1448/68. Southwestern Indiana.

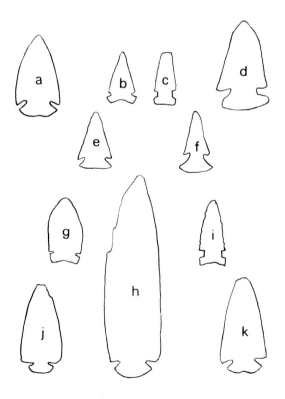

Plate 4: Early-Middle Archaic Projectile Points
a. St. Charles. Burlington chert. GBL 14/206. Rush Co., Indiana.
b. Raddatz Side Notched. Unidentified chert, heat treated. GBL 281/268. Unknown provenience.
c. Charleston Corner Notched. Wyandotte chert. GBL 119/891-2. Unknown provenience.
d. Kirk Corner Notched. Unidentified chert. GBL 21/345. Washington Co., Indiana.
e. Kirk Serrated. Muldraugh chert, heat treated. GBL 285/22-1. Clark Co., Indiana.
f. Kirk Corner Notched. Wyandotte chert. GBL 14/459. Wayne Co., Indiana.
g. Palmer Corner Notched. Unidentified chert. GBL 119/891. Unknown provenience.
h. Palmer Corner Notched. Quartz. GBL 422/80. Georgia.
i. Raddatz Side Notched. Muldraugh chert, heat treated. GBL 14/871. Greene Co., Indiana.
j. Palmer Corner Notched. Wyandotte chert. GBL 1448/50. Southwestern Indiana.
k. Pine Tree Corner Notched. Wyandotte chert. GBL 119/891. Unknown provenience.
l. Stilwell Corner Notched. Burlington chert. GBL 14/823. Indiana.
m. Decatur. Flint Ridge chert. GBL 14/823. Indiana.
n. Decatur. Indian Creek chert. GBL 3921/1. Site 12 Mo 702. Monroe County, Indiana.

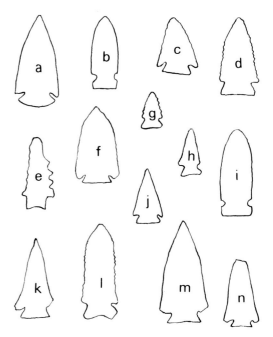

Plate 5: Early-Middle Archaic Projectile Points
a. Stanly Stemmed. Translucent quartz. Ice House Bottom site, Tennessee. Specimen 689/40Mr23, Frank H. McClung Museum, University of Tennessee.
b. Fox Valley Truncated Barb. Unidentified chert, heat treated. GBL 119/891. Unknown provenience.
c. Kanawha Stemmed. Knox Black chert. Ice House Bottom site, Tennessee. Specimen 1479/40Mr23, Frank H. McClung Museum, University of Tennessee.
d. Stanly Stemmed. Vein quartz. Ice House Bottom site, Tennessee. Specimen F195-2/40Mr23, Frank H. McClung Museum, University of Tennessee.
e. LeCroy Bifurcated Stem. Upper Mercer chert. GBL 3645/239. Unknown provenience.
f. Eva I. Fort Payne chert, heat altered. Eva site, Tennessee. Specimen ST2.B 1627/6Bn12, Frank H. McClung Museum, University of Tennessee.
g. Elk River Stemmed. Cobden chert. GBL 4204/2. Site 12 Po 108, Posey Co., Indiana.
h. Benton Stemmed. Dover/Fort Payne chert. GBL 21/367. Boone Co., Indiana.
i. Morrow Mountain I. Knox Black chert. Ice House Bottom site, Tennessee. Specimen 1025/40Mr23, Frank H. McClung Museum, University of Tennessee.
j. Morrow Mountain I. Knox Black chert. Ice House Bottom site, Tennessee. Specimen 462/40Mr23, Frank H. McClung Museum, University of Tennessee.
k. MacCorkle Stemmed. Upper Mercer chert. GBL 3645/222. Unknown provenience.
l. White Springs. Wyandotte chert. GBL 281/264. Franklin Co., Indiana.
m. Sykes. Fort Payne chert? Heat fractured. Eva site, Tennessee. Specimen ST5 477/6Bn12, Frank H. McClung Museum, University of Tennessee.
n. White Springs. Fort Payne chert. Eva site, Tennessee. Specimen B1/6Bn12, Frank H. McClung Museum, University of Tennessee.
o. Eva II. Unidentified chert, heat treated? Eva site, Tennessee. Specimen B 15-1/6Bn12, Frank H. McClung Museum, University of Tennessee.

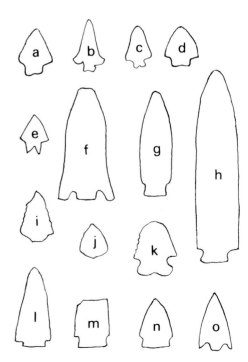

Plate 6: Late Archaic Projectile Points

a. Brewerton Corner Notched. Bayport chert. GBL 13/891. South-central Michigan.

b. Ledbetter Stemmed. Unidentified chert. GBL 119/891. Unknown provenience.

c. Etley. Burlington chert, heat treated. GBL 14/952. Warren Co., Missouri.

d. Pomranky. Bayport chert. GBL 21/357. Indiana.

e. Brewerton Eared-Notched. Jeffersonville chert. GBL 817/92. McCain site, Dubois Co., Indiana.

f. Matanzas. Dupes Folley chert. GBL 5634/57. Unknown provenience.

g. Merom Expanding Stem. Glacial gravel chert, heat treated. GBL 421/302. Indiana.

h. Pickwick. Fort Payne chert. Florence, Alabama. Marshall L. Fallwell collection.

i. Buck Creek Barbed. Wyandotte chert. GBL 304/637. Spencer Co., Indiana.

j. Brewerton Eared-Triangle. Unidentified fossiliferous chert, heat treated. GBL 817/90. McCain site, Dubois Co., Indiana.

k. Bottleneck Stemmed. Burlington chert. GBL 421/263. Morgan Co., Indiana.

l. Lamoka. Liston Creek chert. GBL 2682/8. Site 12 Al 59, Allen Co., Indiana.

m. Trimble Side Notched. Glacial gravel chert, heat treated. GBL 962/8. Crib Mound, Spencer Co., Indiana.

n. McWhinney Heavy Stemmed. Muldraugh chert. GBL 219/4. Elrod site, Clark Co., Indiana.

o. Fulton Stemmed Turkey-tail. Wyandotte chert. GBL 14/823. Indiana.

p. Lamoka. Unidentified chert, heat treated. GBL 13/891. South-central Michigan.

q. Savannah River Stemmed. Quartzite. GBL 242/3. South Carolina.

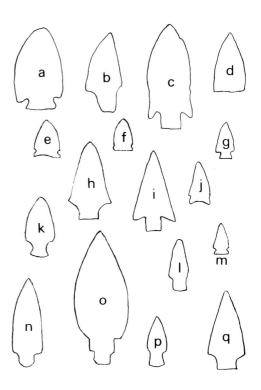

Plate 7: Late Archaic/Early Woodland Projectile Points

a. Adena Stemmed. Wyandotte chert. GBL 14/823. Indiana.

b. Susquehanna Broad. Upper Mercer chert. GBL 10/90. Erie Co., Pennsylvania.

c. Meadowood. double notched drill form; Onondaga chert. GBL 10/49. Erie Co., Pennsylvania.

d. Sedalia. Burlington, fossiliferous chert. GBL 14/928. Rush Co., Indiana.

e. Dickson Contracting Stemmed. Burlington chert, heat treated. GBL 14/823. Indiana.

f. Snook Kill. Bayport chert. GBL 13/891. South-central Michigan.

g. Perkiomen Broad. Onondaga chert. GBL 13/891. Southeastern Michigan.

h. Ashtabula. Plum Run/Pipe Creek chert. GBL 31/106. Fulton Co., Indiana.

i. Fulton (fkrs) Turkey-tail. Wyandotte chert, red ocher stain. GBL 14/912. Marion Co., Indiana.

j. Gary Contracting Stemmed. Novaculite. GBL 3304/282. Arkansas?

k. Cresap Stemmed. Upper Mercer chert. GBL 14/932. Shelby Co., Indiana.

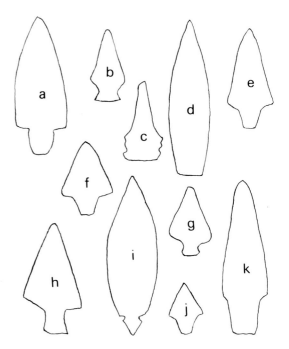

Plate 8: Middle Woodland/Mississippian Projectile Points

a. Chesser Notched. Flint Ridge chert. GBL 14/905. Madison Co., Indiana.

b. Snyders. Burlington, fossiliferous chert, heat treated. GBL 31/106. Fulton Co., Indiana.

c. Hamilton Incurvate. Unidentified chert. GBL 119/891. Unknown provenience.

d. Nodena Banks variety. Wyandotte chert. GBL 119/891. Unknown provenience.

e. Copena. Wyandotte chert. GBL 119/890. Unknown provenience.

f. Levanna. Quartz. GBL 281/268. Northeast U.S.

g. Scallorn. Unidentified chert, heat treated. GBL 3304/454. Unknown provenience.

h. Bakers Creek. Fort Payne chert. Florence, Alabama. Marshall L. Fallwell collection.

i. Steuben Expanded Stemmed. Burlington chert, heat treated. GBL 13/891. South-central Michigan.

j. Nodena Elliptical. Burlington chert. GBL 31/112. Kansas.

k. Lowe Flared Base. Wyandotte chert. GBL 21/345. Washington Co., Indiana.

l. Cahokia. Burlington, fossiliferous chert. GBL 3887/1. Site 12 Po 283, Posey Co., Indiana.

m. Nodena Elliptical. Burlington chert. GBL 31/112. Kansas.

n. Fort Ancient. Paoli chert, heat treated. GBL 422/98. Hamilton Co., Ohio.

o. Morris. Burlington chert. GBL 31/110. Madison Co., Arkansas.

p. Jack's Reef Corner Notched. Liston Creek chert. GBL 14/931. Shelby Co., Indiana.

q. Sequoyah. Burlington chert. GBL 3304/471. Unknown provenience.

r. Morris. Unidentified chert. GBL W11B/1454. Angel site, Vanderburgh Co., Indiana.

s. Robbins. Flint Ridge chert. GBL 134/55. Nowlin Mound, Dearborn Co., Indiana.

t. Copena Triangular. Quartz. GBL 1448/448. Southwestern Indiana.

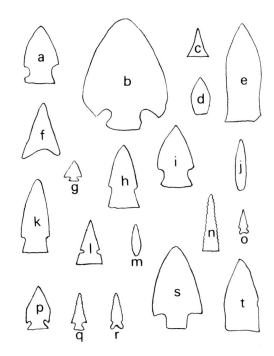

Introduction

Archaeologists have long considered spear and arrow points to be a basic unit of study in research on the ancient lifeways of prehistoric American Indians. These stone tools are commonly referred to as projectile points, although for the layman, the terms spear point and arrow point are more universally known—hence the title of this identification manual. Other terms such as hafted biface and hafted knife have been applied to these forms in recent years, the latter two being an outgrowth of archaeological research into microscopic wear and breakage patterns on the edges of ancient tools. Use-wear analysis has shown that these tools were often used as knives, saws, and many other things besides tips for spears and arrows. For convenience, I have chosen to use the term projectile point or more simply point throughout this book, intending it to cover this large and varied assortment of tools without premature assignment of function; that must remain for researchers to discover. Figure 1 illustrates the basic parts of projectile points.

Unlike many artifacts left behind by ancient peoples, projectile points were made out of durable materials. Flint or chert is the type of stone preferred by Indian hunters of the eastern United States. It occurs in many colors and qualities, and often contains fossils. Obsidian (natural volcanic glass), varieties of quartz, quartzite, and a number of other types of rock were also used. Each of these materials breaks according to the same principle (Speth 1972), referred to as the conchoidal fracture (see Figure 2). They do not readily disintegrate or decay even after thousands of years of being buried in the ground. Thus, projectile points are especially good for study because their shape and characteristics of manufacture still remain much as they were when left behind by their makers. There are literally hundreds of shapes and most were made following specific rules of manufacture dictated by native tradition. Being able to identify particular types of projectile points and recognize methods of manufacture unique to them, one is in a position to organize the remains of many extinct cultures, follow the path of developments, and see significant changes over time.

The raw materials for projectile point manufacture were obtained from stream gravels, eroded areas, and natural outcroppings of rock. Prehistoric quarries are normally identified by the presence of millions of stone chips or flakes broken from blocks or naturally spherical lumps of chert (nodules). This industrial debris is substantial, with hand-excavated

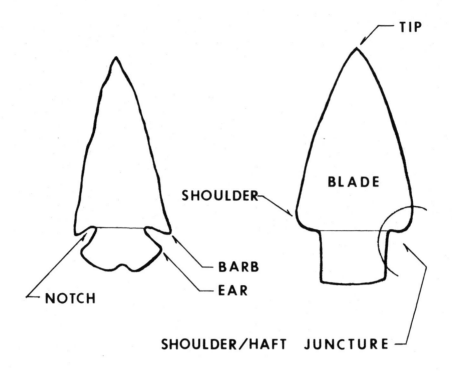

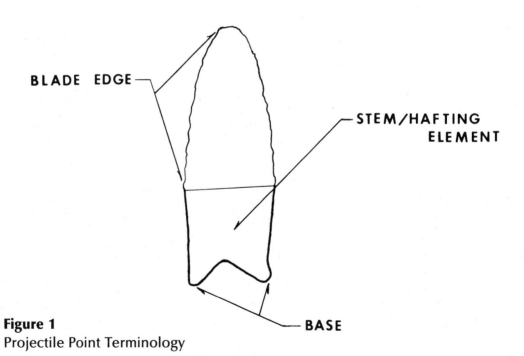

Figure 1
Projectile Point Terminology

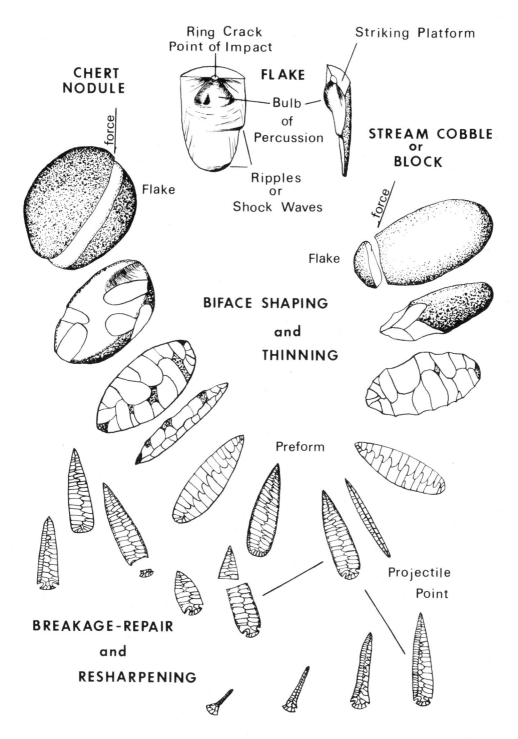

CHERT NODULE

Ring Crack
Point of Impact

FLAKE

Striking Platform

Bulb
of
Percussion

Ripples
or
Shock Waves

Flake

STREAM COBBLE
or
BLOCK

force

Flake

force

BIFACE SHAPING

and

THINNING

Preform

Projectile
Point

BREAKAGE-REPAIR

and

RESHARPENING

Figure 2
The Conchoidal Fracture and Projectile Point Manufacture

pits accompanied by piles of waste debris and flakes discarded from the manufacture of thousands of tools that were transported from the workshop to be used elsewhere (see Fowke 1928). Sources of chert vary greatly in quality and quantity. Inferior grades of chert were often improved by heat treating. Controlled heating causes the molecules of grainy or porous cherts to form stronger bonds and become more like glass in texture and improves the workability and beauty of the stone. Certain cherts that naturally have good fracture properties are often ruined by heating; others significantly improve in quality. Naturally light-colored cherts that have been heat treated often exhibit pinkish and reddish hues due to the oxidation of iron in the heating process, while others become darkened. Heat treated cherts normally have a high luster and also an increased waxy feel (see plates).

The manufacturing strategies used in prehistory varied widely within each time period and from culture to culture. Some basic aspects of stone age industries, however, are universal. Flakes or slabs were struck from blocks or nodules with hammerstones usually of granite or quartzite (i.e., direct percussion). These were then trimmed around the edges to remove irregularities and prepare the edge to withstand the impact necessary to detach sizeable flakes over much of each side. This produced a form called a biface or preform. Additional stages of manufacture would further reduce the thickness and be used to shape all sides of the preform. The first part of the reduction process could be accomplished with stone hammers. The more difficult process of thinning and shaping the biface was accomplished with hammers fashioned from deer, moose, caribou, or elk antler or billets of hardwood. Thus, there are two types of direct percussion flaking: hard hammer (stone) direct percussion and soft hammer (antler) direct percussion. Flakes produced with the hard hammer tend to have large striking platforms and are thick and short. (A striking platform is the area of the biface edge selected to strike that is removed with the detaching flake.) Flakes detached from a biface with a soft hammer tend to have comparatively small platforms, but the dimensions of the overall flake tend to be thin and large. This is why soft hammer direct percussion is preferred by modern flintknappers, as it was in prehistory. Whenever there is good bone preservation at an archaeological site, antler hammers will be part of the ancient tool maker's kit (Seeman 1985). In addition, early accounts of stone tool manufacture by North American Indian groups indicate the use of various applications of antler hammers and antler pressure flaking tools (Powers 1877; Kelly 1928; Kroeber 1961).

The physical properties of hard hammer and soft hammer direct percussion produce different but overlapping effects of the conchoidal fracture. Producing this fracture with a hard object causes an acute and rapid explosion of force away from the point of impact. Using an antler hammer, which is softer and less dense, allows some of the shock of percussion to be absorbed by the hammer and slows the process of fracture. The shock waves flatten away from the point of impact, allowing the detaching flake to compress and bend as it detaches. Chippable stone is flexible as well as brittle. Large points can be made by this method that are quite thin and flat with totally flaked surfaces.

Often the final stage of manufacture of a projectile point involved the fashioning of the stem or notches for tying to the end of a spear, arrow shaft, or knife handle. This is normally referred to as the hafting element. This feature was produced by making notches at the sides on one end of the biface. Notching was accomplished using one of several techniques or in combination. Percussion may be used to start the notch. Pressure flaking (i.e., pressing in on the edge until flake detachment occurs) and indirect percussion (i.e., using a punch and hammer to detach flakes) allow increased control to form the desired notch depth and width. Although these are the basic methods of manufacture, there are a host of prehistoric technologies based on the use of one or more of these techniques with unique strategies of manufacture. There are also many examples of projectile points lacking notches that were clearly prepared for use as cutting tools.

Most prehistoric projectile points were discarded or lost during work and maintenance activities at camps and villages. Because most points were tailored to a particular use, many blades were shortened and narrowed during their use-life by repeated resharpening. However, pristine or apparently unused projectile points occur as well as specimens which were broken or recycled and worn out from repeated heavy use. Like manufacturing stages, resharpening techniques were accomplished in learned and patterned ways, specific to particular temporal periods and prehistoric traditions. While the blades have often been much changed by use and resharpening, the haft elements are typically unmodified from original manufacture regardless of time period.

Any significant change in the type of flakes detached from the edges may indicate resharpening. In other cases, resharpening was carried out using the same basic flaking strategy as that used to shape and thin the blade during manufacture. The later resharpening is recognizable simply from changes in blade form and size. Drills are often finely pressure flaked along the bit and may exhibit wide bases and residual shoulders, indicating considerable careful reduction of the blade to maintain the length. Short blunted blades or hafted scrapers resulted from repeated resharpening of the tip to exhaustion, or the rejuvenation of a blade broken during manufacture or use. A hafted scraper with a beveled end for scraping the flesh from animal hide might be recycled into a spear point or knife by flaking away the bevel to make a new tip, or two smaller points could be fashioned from a large one accidentally broken (cf. Frison et al. 1976). Projectile points were apparently used interchangeably as spear points, knives, saws, and other tools without any modification to the hafting element. By experimental replication of points (Crabtree 1972) and by use of them in controlled work situations, researchers have been able to reproduce manufacturing stages and also match a type of wear pattern seen microscopically with a particular prehistoric work activity (Semenov 1964; Ahler 1971; Tringham 1974; Keeley 1974; Swanson [ed.] 1975; Hayden [ed.] 1979).

The utilitarian nature of projectile points has been discussed. Another very important role was in ritual. Points were made for ritual occasions of all kinds: for burial with the dead for use in the afterlife, as symbols of wealth, status, and prestige, or as part of a ceremonial bundle or cache to be buried as an offering to appease spirits. In ritual contexts, use-wear is seldom seen; if present, it may differ from the kind of wear seen on utilitarian items. Chipped stone forms produced for ritual use are often exceedingly large and made from an unusual or exotic raw material. These often represent superior effort on the part of expert prehistoric artisans to finely shape a work of art.

All prehistoric industries exhibit examples of the craft ranging from poor to finely wrought specimens. However, both ends of this range more or less reflect the application of a single lithic tradition. The qualities shared between utilitarian and ceremonial forms can be observed by comparison of the blade shape, haft element, and especially the flaking pattern exhibited on the faces of preforms and finished points.

Projectile points are important cultural and chronological markers in prehistory. Being the products of particular cultural traditions from specific time periods, they represent fossilized behavior patterns of their makers. Thus, typology (i.e., the classification of projectile points and other artifacts) seeks to identify these patterns (Krieger 1944). They can also be looked upon as the material representation of ancient ideas (Taylor 1948; Rouse 1960; Ford 1954a,b; Steward 1954; Whallon and Brown [eds.] 1982). Specific types were consistently reproduced during a time period because of cultural standards of what constituted a structurally and stylistically appropriate tool. This has been expressed as a mental template in lithic manufacture whereby the artisans envision the finished product as flakes are detached and follow a particular learned strategy to achieve the desired product within a range of limitations of ability, knowledge, and quality of the raw material being reduced. This intuitive sense of rightness and fitness or the "mind's eye" (see Ferguson 1977) is realized within particular technological and cultural regimes which have their own unique parameters of usage and application. Aesthetics must also be considered. Prehistoric tools and especially projectile points are products of ancient art as well as technology.

TYPE DESCRIPTIONS AND TYPE CLUSTERS

The form and flaking characteristics or attributes of projectile points reflect cultural patterns that maintained special guidelines for manufacture. The presence of attributes in particular combinations is what allows us to recognize and classify these forms today. It is important to have some familiarity with projectile point types of every condition from pristine to highly reworked. Figure 3 illustrates the range of particular attributes that are observed within the type descriptions. The individual descriptions concentrate on those attributes critical for identification, and this in turn promotes an appreciation for the variation that occurs within types. Also sometimes named are varieties of a type, each representing some portion of the described range of variation; these are taken into account when applicable. Certain named types refer to essentially the same material. Thus a category of morphological correlates is provided to organize these other named types in a systematic way based on the nature of their respective descriptions.

New type definitions or new names are sometimes proposed that in fact crosscut one or more existing described types and that often fail to discuss how the "new" type can be distinguished from the others already

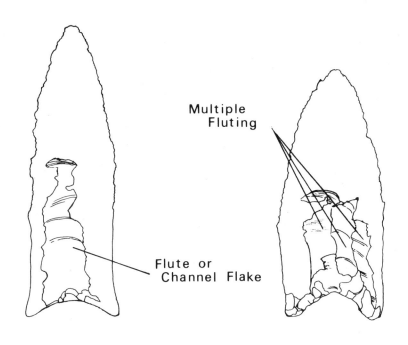

Multiple
Fluting

Flute or
Channel Flake

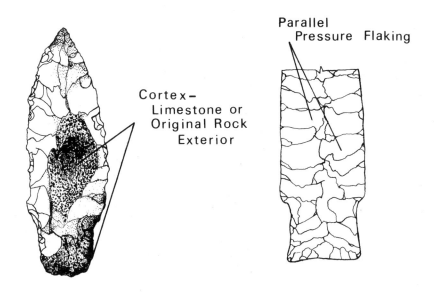

Cortex –
Limestone or
Original Rock
Exterior

Parallel
Pressure Flaking

Figure 3
Flaking Characteristics

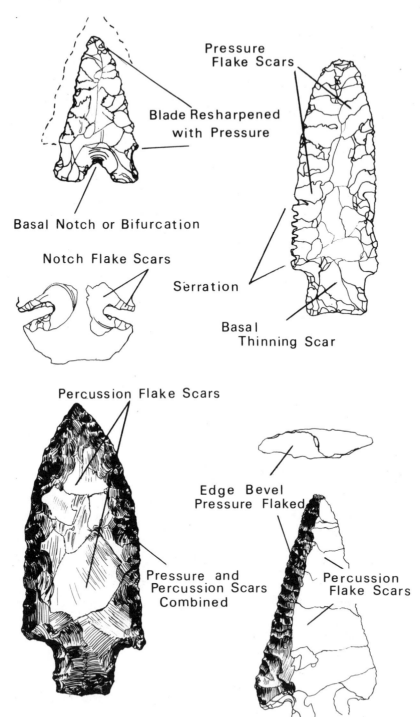

Pressure
Flake Scars

Blade Resharpened
with Pressure

Basal Notch or Bifurcation

Notch Flake Scars

Serration

Basal
Thinning Scar

Percussion Flake Scars

Edge Bevel
Pressure Flaked

Pressure and
Percussion Scars
Combined

Percussion
Flake Scars

Figure 3

in usage. The establishment of a type cluster helps resolve many of the problems of overlapping type definitions. A type cluster is a group of named types which, by definition and illustration, overlap morphologically. Several authors have previously used this approach: e.g., Winters (n.d., 1963), Bacon (n.d., 1977), Faulkner and McCollough (1973). The morphological overlap between types is reflected within the technological attributes of overall form, characteristics of manufacture, and resharpening processes. Because of this, types within a cluster often share the same temporal period, may represent part of an evolutionary trend, or may be within the same cultural tradition or manufacturing technology. But, since the path of prehistoric developments often remains to be discovered, not every cluster can be treated in exactly the same way.

There are several kinds of clusters. Most of the clusters in this manual are named for a well-known point type in the cluster: e.g., the Dalton cluster. Such a name handily connotes a basic form and suggests the kinds of characteristics embodied within the cluster. A second kind of cluster is composed of one broadly defined type plus named types which represent variations or named varieties of this major type. Yet a third kind of cluster contains types that are morphologically similar, although a historical or cultural connection between them may not have been demonstrated; each of the types is often used and potentially misidentified. Other clusters are composed of types which overlap morphologically and appear to represent a technological evolution of a single basic hafting style (e.g., Large Side Notched cluster). A final situation involves a cluster composed of types that are similar, but each has restricted usage over limited geographic areas; thus a morphological and/or temporal designation is offered to name the type cluster (e.g., Terminal Archaic Barbed cluster).

It is necessary to apply a clustering approach in the course of classifying collections. Each diagnostic trait must be weighed against a series of others in order to assess the degree of fit between a specimen and a definition. Whole type descriptions must often be compared and contrasted to others in order to classify many individual specimens. The overall relationship of separate types within a cluster is highly variable depending on the level of knowledge about the lithic tradition(s) that produced each of the types. The temporal and morphological variability within and between clusters can involve a combination of specific attributes shared by projectile point types of different origins and evolutionary patterns as well as types that share much of their existence with others in the same lithic tradition.

AGE AND CULTURAL AFFILIATION

The age and time period when particular types occur in the archaeological record are discussed along with the particular ancient cultures with which they are associated. Age estimates are based on radiocarbon dating or carbon 14. This element is absorbed from the atmosphere by all living things. Libbey (1952) discovered the rate of decay of carbon 14. It is possible to measure the amount of carbon 14 remaining in a piece of charcoal, ancient wood, shell, or bone and calculate the age of the specimen.

Charcoal is by far the most reliable material for deriving an acceptable date. The radiocarbon dates cited herein are based on wood and nut charcoal from prehistoric houses, pits, campfires, or particular cultural deposits or layers of sediment within archaeological sites. All dates discussed are given in years before Christ (B.C.) or years after the time of Christ (A.D.). Radiocarbon dates are statistical averages and necessarily are presented with one standard deviation from the mean; they have a plus and minus factor indicating that there are two chances out of three that the actual age of a sample falls within the given range. Today there are ways to make corrections for certain errors inherent in the procedure, and other factors are taken into account when deriving radiocarbon dates. Regardless of what problems there may be with dates of this kind, after years of applying the technique to a host of archaeological situations we now have a range of complementary dates for similar archaeological phenomena and most projectile point types. Within many regions of the East several culturally and/or geologically stratified archaeological sites have been excavated that provide good chronological control and dated stratigraphic sequences. A series of overlapping radiocarbon dates is usually considered acceptable. Dates falling far outside the expected range, either earlier or later, will be discarded. Archaeological fieldwork in recent years has provided a great deal of new information on the age and chronology of point types. These data are summarized and updated in the present volume.

For convenience of discussion, temporal periods have been given particular names. The Paleo-Indian period lasts at least 2,000 years, from the end of the Wisconsin glacial sequence to about 8000 B.C. The eastern Archaic is divided into Early, Middle, and Late segments. Most projectile point types fit somewhere within the 7,000 years of time represented by the Archaic. Throughout most of the Archaic, the spear thrower or atlatl was probably used to gain added thrust and distance to hand thrown spears. Ground stone atlatl weights or bannerstones were added to this device as early as 5800 B.C. To judge from the atlatls recovered from archaeological sites, they apparently had wooden shafts with carved handles, often of bone, and were tipped with a carved deer antler hook. Weights are commonly of pecked and ground slate, quartz, or other hard stone and are drilled through the center to be placed on the spear thrower along the shaft. Spears were drilled or notched on the end to engage with the atlatl and many were probably fletched much like arrows or darts to increase accuracy over long distance. For most of the archaeological record, the spear appears to have been the principal if not the exclusive weapon or hunting device. Evidence for the use of the bow and arrow in the eastern United States is limited to the Late Woodland and Mississippian periods. The bow and arrow probably appears after 750 A.D. when small and delicate arrow points that compare with those used by Historic Indian groups appear for the first time in the archaeological record.

Several terms repeatedly used in this volume should be defined here. The term *complex* is used along with a particular name assigned by an archaeologist to denote a series of identifiable tool types including projectile points of a particular style which derive from an excavation in which they were apparently associated. Normally, the assignment of a named complex is tentative and awaits further data while serving as a mode of discussion until additional questions can be answered from the archaeological record. The term *horizon* is most often used to recognize the developments of major classes of projectile point types. This term is used to describe particular deposits at archaeological sites recognizing a range of, for example, corner notched projectile point types occurring in a separate segment of a stratified deposit (e.g., Kirk horizon). Horizon is also sometimes used to refer to a wide geographic spread of a particular projectile point hafting mode such as the side notched horizon which is an aggregation of the bulk of archaeological data across a known area of extent. The term *tradition* is sometimes used in a broad sense like horizon. However, a named archaeological tradition is used to refer to identifiable prehistoric cultures that are well dated and occur across a known geographic area. An additional term, *phase*, is often applied with the name of a particularly well-known projectile point style or ceramic style. Since this is one of the strictest archaeological designations of a prehistoric culture, it usually specifies unique artifact traits as well as a geographic and often temporal restriction within the known area and time range of the tradition. The terms horizon, tradition, and phase are thoroughly discussed in Willey and Phillips (1958) and Cook (1976). A final term which is often used in archaeology is *component*. A component is a separate occupation at an archaeological site that is recognizable for its distinctive artifact assemblage or collection, such as a particular projectile point type. In other cases the number and kind of archaeological cultures represented are not determined; thus a range of materials assigned to one temporal period can be considered a component.

PROJECTILE POINT DISTRIBUTION

Since projectile point types represent prehistoric technological and cultural traditions, the tracing of their distributions allows the delineation of the area of influence or trade as well as the range of ecological zones to which they became adapted during their existence. Each type description is accompanied by a discussion of its distribution, including key references to archaeological literature where they are mentioned or illustrated. This provides a basis from which distributional information can easily be researched for cultural traditions cutting across state boundaries and natural areas. A map is also given featuring the geographic extent and important archaeological sites mentioned in the text.

MORPHOLOGICAL CORRELATES OF TYPES AND TYPE CLUSTERS

Previous projectile point descriptions often mention named types which are considered to be synonyms. However, projectile point names are applied in different ways, especially when similar or identical forms are known from different areas and/or associated with different cultural entities. For example, Montet-White (1968) chose to use the general term Mason to refer to contracting stemmed specimens in Illinois which admittedly were essentially the same form which Dragoo (1963) named Adena Ovate-base. However, the latter is diagnostic of the Adena culture, which does not occur in Illinois. To avoid confusion, Montet-White coined a new name for the type in Illinois. In one sense, Mason and Adena Ovate-base are synonymous in that they designate very similar forms. However, on a more important level, these terms refer to archaeological phenomena of quite different value and are not synonymous at all (Cantwell 1980:55). Thus, in archaeology the term synonym has at least two meanings, one that refers only to similar morphologies, and another which follows Webster's definition implying commonality of definition (i.e., same meaning) and usage of two names for the same thing.

Used in the strict sense, synonymity is uncommon in archaeology for reasons of time, space, economy, culture, and historical application of specific terms. Recognizing that there are few exact archaeological synonyms and that similar morphologies referred to by different names can be correlated or "brought into mutual relation" without assuming exact synonymity, the term morphological correlate will be applied here. This is the same basic morphological consideration given to constructing projectile point clusters, which recognizes similar and sometimes overlapping ranges of variation of certain named type projectile points. In all cases, morphological correlates also represent material of comparable age and to a lesser extent cultural affiliation.

Two levels of morphological correlates are used in this volume: morphological correlates of a type and morphological correlates of a cluster. These are placed at the end of the respective type or cluster descriptions. References for each type are provided so that the reasoning behind their respective placement can be traced. Morphological correlates of a type incorporate or share the range of variability recognized within the type description. This section is also reserved for named varieties of a type and other named types that overlap some portion of the variation recognized in the description. It also incorporates certain named types which may overlap one or more described types in the cluster to a slight degree but which share a majority of attributes with the type they are subsumed under.

Named types which by definition incorporate the morphological variability of one or more established types in a cluster are placed at the cluster level of morphological correlates. A case in point is the Faulkner Side Notched type (MacNeish 1948), which by definition covers essentially the entire range of side notched point variations covered by the Large Side Notched cluster. In addition, named types which may be useful subdivisions within the cluster are included at the cluster level if the descriptions lack the degree of specificity to segregate these consistently from the variation already contained in the types presented. By the same token, named types judged to be useful additions to the cluster (i.e., Additional Types) are given with a series of references pertaining to their descriptions and usage in the literature.

The most important aspect of the cluster level is its role in the actual process of classification. Virtually every typologist has faced the problem of classifying specimens that have attributes that overlap more than one defined type. Either the material remains unclassified or classification is made using one of the existing type definitions. In cases such as these, the option to use the cluster level designation, which incorporates the range of variation of a number of types, allows materials to be classified on technological considerations without the need to force specimens into type categories. Consequently, a higher level category (e.g., morphological correlates of a cluster) is available for specimens that would otherwise be unclassified or potentially misidentified. This classification system allows more flexibility, but it also invites the user to become increasingly familiar with the various traits which combine to form the unique types that are critical to understanding prehistory.

Projectile Point Type Descriptions

Clovis Cluster

The Clovis cluster is composed of projectile points exhibiting many subtle variations of a standard lanceolate, narrow-bladed, concave-based, and fluted form. Much of this variation is undoubtedly due to site specific re-sharpening, use, and discard behavior. Thus, certain named Clovis type points are recognizable primarily in pristine form but may lack specific characteristics that enable discrimination of the type in reworked form. Nonetheless, several named Clovis point types do appear to warrant recognition as distinct entities that represent stylistic trends within the Clovis horizon.

CLOVIS

Clovis type projectile points were first recognized at Blackwater Draw (Locality No. 1) in eastern New Mexico (Sellards 1952) and at a number of other sites in that region. These are fluted lanceolate points with parallel or slightly convex sides and concave base. Grinding of the base and lateral edges for hafting is readily apparent (Figure 4). The flutes sometimes extend almost the full length of the point but are usually no longer than one-half the maximum length (Wormington 1957). The manufacturing technology of Clovis points includes percussion bifacial thinning using several methods and pressure flaking. Clovis biface manufacturing, described by Bradley (1982:203–208), involved the production of a few large percussion thinning flakes from opposite margins near the end of the preform on the same face (i.e., alternate opposed biface thinning). These thinning flakes were purposefully terminated at or near the opposite edge in early reduction stages. Later, flakes were intentionally hinge terminated at the midline (i.e., opposed diving biface thinning) at the end of the thinning and shaping stages (see also Callahan 1979).

Multiple fluting of the base is a typical feature of Clovis points. Two types of fluting methods have been recognized. One is the Enterline Fluting technique defined by Witthoft (1952) at the Shoop site. It involved detaching short, narrow flutes near the lateral margins of the base to act as guides for a larger flute detached from the center of the base. The other is the Folsom Fluting technique (Roberts 1935), analyzed and replicated by Crabtree (1966). This technique involved producing a nipple at the center of the base to act as a platform and guide for detaching single flutes on each face. A number of Paleo-Indian base camps in eastern North America indicate a wide range of variation in the fluting process of Clovis cluster fluted points. Extremely long, single flutes on one face will often be accompanied by a short flute on the opposite face, or multiple fluting which may only be apparent on one face. Fluting is sometimes totally lacking on one face. A number of Clovis points have been analyzed and measured within the manufacturing and refurbishing sequences recognized at Paleo-Indian base camps in the East (Byers 1954; Ritchie 1953; McCary 1951; Dragoo 1973; Gardner 1974; Kraft 1973).

Age and Cultural Affiliation

Clovis points are the earliest defined projectile point type of the Paleo-Indian tradition, widespread in North America by about 12,000 to 11,000 B.C., nearing the close of the Pleistocene glacial period (Dragoo 1976a). Radiocarbon dates from Meadowcroft Rock Shelter in Pennsylvania are well in excess of 16,000 B.C. (Adovasio, Gunn, Donahue, and Stuckenrath 1978:643, Table 2; Adovasio et al. 1980: 589). However, these dates have not been accepted. Dates falling between 9000 and 8000 B.C. represent the later phases of the Fluted Point tradition in the Great Lakes area and the Northeast (Gramly and Rutledge 1981: 356–358; Byers 1966).

Knowledge of changing ecological conditions of the late Pleistocene period and numerous finds of extinct animals and the presence of Clovis points in the East have long suggested an association of large elephants and Clovis hunters similar to the well documented mammoth kill sites in the Southwest (Mason 1962). The association has now become a reality with investigations at the Kimmswick site in eastern Missouri near St. Louis. A clear Clovis-mastodon (*Mammut americanum*) association has been documented in pond sediments beneath an early Holocene deposit. Smaller mammalian fauna in the pond sediment and pollen data from this region indicate a deciduous woodland and open grassland environment for the Clovis component (Graham, Haynes, Johnson, and Kay 1981:1115–1116). The environment to the north at the time of the Kimmswick occupation was probably still periglacial with subarctic open parkland flora (i.e., spruce, fir, tundra vegetation) and fauna (Mason 1958; Quimby 1960; Fitting, DeVisscher, and Wahla 1966). Although information about the Clovis economy is still scanty in the East, the developing ecological picture implies a more diverse economy of which the hunting of large animals was only a part. For example, faunal remains from Bull Brook in Massachusetts included caribou associated with Clovis (Spiess and Curran 1985).

In the East, two stratified sites with Clovis components are noteworthy. One is the Thunderbird site investigated by Gardner (1974) in the Shenandoah Valley of Virginia, which provides good evidence of the superposition of living floors and workshop areas related to occupations of Clovis, Late Paleo-Indian, Early Archaic (Kirk), and later side notched projectile point traditions (1974: 13–17). Another has been recorded along the Delaware River in Pennsylvania (McNett et al. 1977). The Shawnee-Minisink site is a multicomponent site with three occupation zones identified. The earliest of these is a Clovis component. This zone is overlaid by a zone of sterile sediment. The site was then reoccupied during the Early Archaic period represented by Kirk Corner Notched and

Figure 4: Clovis Cluster

a. Clovis. J. A. Eichenberger cast. Blackwater Draw No. 1 site. New Mexico. Eastern New Mexico University collection.
b. Ross County. Flint Ridge chert. GBL 21/302. Delaware Co., Indiana. Pictured in Plate 1,g.
c. Clovis. J. A. Eichenberger cast. Domebo Mammoth Kill site. Oklahoma. Museum of the Great Plains collection.
d. Clovis (small). J. A. Eichenberger cast. Blackwater Draw No. 1 site. New Mexico. Denver Museum of Natural History collection.
e. Clovis. Unidentified chert. GBL 22/45. Warren Co., Missouri.
f. Redstone. Wyandotte chert. Warrick Co., Indiana. Courtesy of Donald Champion.
g. Debert. Drawn from cast. Original: homogeneous chalcedony. Debert site, Nova Scotia. Specimen BiCu-1:1883c, Archaeological Survey of Canada, Canadian Museum of Civilization. Ottawa, Canada.
h. Debert. Basal fragment. Drawn from cast. Original: brecciated chalcedony. Debert site, Nova Scotia. Specimen BiCu-1:120c, Archaeological Survey of Canada, Canadian Museum of Civilization. Ottawa, Canada.
i. Debert. Basal fragment. Drawn from cast. Original: siltstone. Debert site, Nova Scotia. Specimen BiCu-1:E/2c, Archaeological Survey of Canada, Canadian Museum of Civilization. Ottawa, Canada.
j. Holcombe. Unidentified chert. Southern Michigan. Redrawn from Perino (1985:186, 4th from left).
k. Holcombe. Wyandotte chert. GBL 21/343. Indiana.
l. Crowfield (Holcombe). Drawn from cast. Udora site, Ontario. Courtesy of the Royal Ontario Museum (c-500).

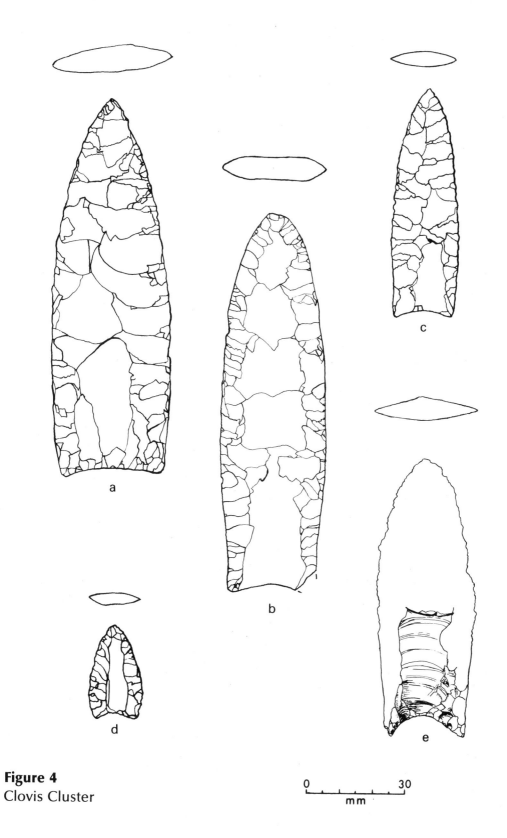

Figure 4
Clovis Cluster

0   30
m m

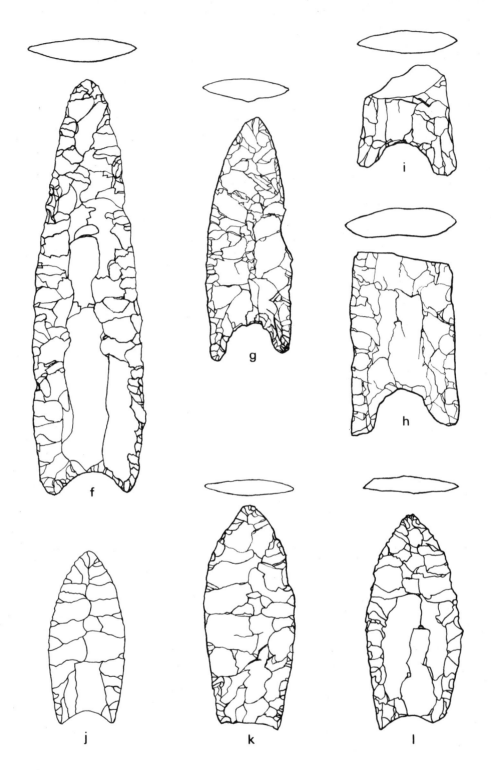

Figure 4

LeCroy projectile points. The latest occupations of the site included both Late Archaic and Woodland material.

Distribution

Clovis points occur over a wide area covering most regions of eastern and western North America (Wormington 1957). In the eastern United States, Clovis points are numerous and recorded within every state (Mason 1962:233). They are identified as far south as Alabama (Mahan 1956) and Florida (Reichelt 1973; Purdy 1981a:4; Waring 1961: 550–552), and occur across the Northeast (Ritchie 1957; Fowler 1954; Roosa 1977:119), in the Great Lakes area (Mason 1958), and along the eastern seaboard (see An Aena Project 1982). Clovis points have been found across Indiana (Dorwin 1966; Justice n.d.), Illinois (Winters 1962; Munson and Downs 1968), Wisconsin (Hurley 1965), Michigan (Fitting 1970), Ohio (Seeman and Prufer 1982), Tennessee (Adair 1976), and Kentucky (Rolingson 1964), to name only a few states.

ROSS COUNTY

This distinctive fluted point style derives its name from Ross County, Ohio, and is described by Prufer and Baby (1963:15). Ross County points represent one of the longer fluted point styles and are wide-bladed in comparison with the general class of fluted points (Figure 4). A major defining characteristic of the Ross County style is the presence of wide, shallow (thinning) flake scars on the blade with short, marginal retouch intruding from the blade edge. The overall lanceolate form noted for Clovis is modified by the presence of a gentle blade recurvature. The type exhibits a flat, hexagonal cross section. Fluting includes multiple and single channel flake scars which were produced by several methods of basal platform preparation. Basal and lateral grinding are present.

Age

These points are not documented from a dated context. However, the type is consid-

Map 1: Clovis—Distribution and Important Sites

ered to date to the same period as Clovis, from about 11,000 to 9000 B.C.

Distribution

Ross County points may have a concentration in south-central Ohio and the surrounding region (Prufer and Baby 1963:27; Dorwin 1966:154). Ross County points are also reported in lower frequency in northern Alabama and Louisiana (Waters 1957), South Carolina (Waring 1961:550–552, Fig. 1a), Kentucky (Rolingson 1964), Virginia (Callahan 1979:3), Missouri (C. Chapman 1975:91, Fig. 4–22; 244, Fig. A6), and Michigan (Roosa 1965:94, Plate 1h). The extent of the northern and western distribution of Ross County is not well known.

Map 2: Ross County—Distribution

Morphological Correlate

Hazel (Van Buren 1974).

REDSTONE

Redstone fluted points (Figure 4) were first recognized along the Tennessee River in northern Alabama (Cambron and Hulse

1969:99). The defining characteristic of these points is the triangular form with the widest margin of the points occurring between the basal ears. The basic triangular outline is accentuated with a straight to slightly excurvate blade. Unlike most Clovis cluster projectile points, the distal end is elongated and acute, rather than abrupt and widened. The fluting technique is variable, with combinations of single and multiple flutes without any noticeable standard of flute length. The base is bifacially retouched following the fluting process and then ground. Usually the ears project markedly from a deep basal concavity which is similar to the Debert point although not as pronounced. Lateral grinding is typical.

Age

Given its similarity to Clovis, the Redstone type is assumed to date within a range of 11,000 to 9000 B.C.

Distribution

The Redstone type is somewhat rare even in the Tennessee Valley in northern Alabama and southern Tennessee where the type was defined (Lewis 1960; Perino 1968a:74). Examples similar to Redstone have been found in Ohio (Prufer and Baby 1963:17, Fig. 7) and Indiana. Present information suggests that the distribution of the type is primarily confined to the South in an area including southern Missouri, northern Texas, and Alabama (Van Buren 1974:197,207).

Morphological Correlates

Mouser, Yazoo (Van Buren 1974).

DEBERT

Debert fluted points (Figure 4) derive their name from the Debert site in Nova Scotia. MacDonald's study (1968:124) of the site concludes that Debert is unique in that it represents the earliest dated Paleo-Indian occupation in a truly periglacial environment.

MacDonald (1968:70–76) presents an in-depth analysis of the manufacturing trajec-

Map 3: Redstone—Distribution

tory of Debert points. The following presents portions of his discussion which exemplify the unique morphological characteristics of these fluted points. Debert points are fluted on both faces. The length of the fluting is directly proportional to the length of the point for all complete specimens from the Debert site. Each specimen exhibits channel flake scars terminating at less than one-half the length. Primary discriminating attributes of Debert points are the exceptionally deep and rounded concave base and the absence of a fluting platform remnant or nipple at the center of the base. In the latter instance, the final fluting blow removed the entire platform. The extreme depth of the concave base accentuates the long parallel-edged ears, which are characteristic of the haft on Debert points.

Age
Debert site radiocarbon dates place this occupation at about 8600 B.C. (MacDonald 1968:143,147).

Distribution
The technological attribute of the removal of the striking nipple with the channel flake in

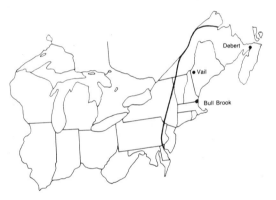

Map 4: Debert—Distribution and Important Sites

a single detachment on Debert points has not been specifically noted at other sites but does occur at Bull Brook in Massachusetts (Byers 1954) and probably elsewhere in the Northeast. The type has been identified in New Jersey (Kraft 1973). The Debert point exhibits morphological characteristics closer to other northeastern types than to western fluted points (MacDonald 1968:78) and appears to have a distribution confined to the Northeast. The deep basal concavity typical of Debert points was reported at the Vail site in Maine (Gramly and Rutledge 1981).

HOLCOMBE

The Holcombe point was first described
from the Holcombe Beach site in Macomb
County, Michigan (Fitting, DeVisscher, and
Wahla 1966; Wahla and DeVisscher 1969). It
is distinguishable from other points of this
cluster in that it is a small, thin, fluted point
with markedly convex sides and sharp basal
ears (Figure 4). Most points are widest at the
point well above the center. Exaggeration of
this trait on certain specimens gives them a
"pumpkin seed" appearance. Sharp contrac-
tion toward the base on Holcombe points results in a very narrow basal width, unlike
that of other Clovis cluster projectile points.
All are well ground laterally and in the basal
concavity. The ears are thin and delicate.
Often one ear is pointed and one is rounded
on the same specimen. About 55 percent of
Holcombe points are fluted. In most cases
the fluting is unifacial and was accomplished
using multiple channel flake detachments. In
cross section, Holcombe points are smoothly
lenticular or biconvex with one face usually
more convex than the other (Wahla and De-
Visscher 1969:109–110). A type similar to
Holcombe has been reported from the Crowfield and other sites in southern Ontario
(Deller 1983; Storck 1984:8–9).

Age and Cultural Affiliation
Holcombe fluted points represent a later
phase in the Paleo-Indian tradition which
correlates with the final stages of the Wisconsin glaciation in the Great Lakes region (Mason 1962:233). A date of about 9000 B.C. was
obtained from a hearth at the Holcombe
Beach site (Fitting, DeVisscher, and Wahla
1966:120). The remains of Barren Ground
Caribou (*Rangifer arcticus*) were identified
in association with the Paleo-Indian occupation, indicating the hunting focus at the site
(Cleland 1965).

Map 5: Holcombe—Distribution and Important Sites

Distribution
Holcombe projectile points occur over much
of Michigan and are thought to correlate with
the distribution of open parkland and open
spruce parkland vegetation zones of the late
Pleistocene period. (Fitting, DeVisscher, and
Wahla 1966:134). The distribution of fluted
points similar to Holcombe includes Ontario
(MacNeish 1952), Wisconsin (Mason 1963),
and Ohio (Prufer and Baby 1963:31–43;
McKenzie 1975:72). This style was also found
in New Jersey at the Plenge site (Kraft 1973:
77, Plate 3). A few Holcombe type points
have also been found in Indiana.

Morphological Correlates
of the Clovis Cluster
Lincoln Hills Fluted (Winters in Conrad
1981:25); St. Louis (Perino 1985:334). Additional types: Anzick (Perino 1985:18); Colby
(Frison 1978:91; 1986:91–96). Refer to Van
Buren (1974) for descriptions of a large
number of Clovis fluted point variations.

Cumberland Cluster

CUMBERLAND

Lewis (1954) recognized this distinctive style of fluted point because its fishtailed appearance and delicate ears are unlike those of the general class of fluted points. The basic shape is trianguloid with marked recurvate edges at the haft, concave base, and basal ears (Figure 5). Maximum blade width occurs well above the haft region. The basal ears are often accentuated due to the incurving blade edges above the ears and deep concave base. Cumberland points are narrow relative to length. Basal and lateral grinding are typical on the edges of the haft. Fluting characteristics relate more to Folsom than Clovis, since the flutes often extend across the entire length of the point. In addition, a platform remnant or nipple is sometimes intact at the center of the base, indicative of the use of the Folsom Fluting technique (Roberts 1935; Crabtree 1966; Roosa 1977a). Cumberland points identified in the Great Lakes region were termed Barnes points by Roosa (1965). The manufacturing sequence of these forms has been studied by Wright and Roosa (1966) and Roosa (1977a,b). Additional comparison is presented by Roosa and Deller (1982:6–8), who note some similarities between Cumberland and Folsom.

Age and Cultural Affiliation
Cumberland points are diagnostic of the Paleo-Indian period in eastern North America from 10,000–8000 B.C. In the lowest cultural level (Stratum 2) in Dutchess Quarry in New York, a single Cumberland point was recovered along with a caribou bone (*Rangifer tarandus*). A radiocarbon date of 10,580 B.C. ±370 was obtained from the bone (Funk, Walters, and Ehlers 1969:20–21; Guilday 1969:17). Unfortunately, the date may not be entirely reliable (see Kraft 1977:268; Kopper, Funk, and Dumont 1980:135).

Cumberland type projectile points are diagnostic of the Parkhill complex in the Great Lakes area thought to date to about 8500 B.C.

(Roosa 1977a:120). Roosa (1965) refers to them as Barnes points. They differ from Cumberland only in size, the latter being somewhat larger (1977a:119). Barnes points are within the range of variation of Cumberland. Parkhill complex camp locations correspond with fossil beach ridges of late Pleistocene age that may relate to Caribou hunting strategies over and above other factors of settlement (see Roosa 1977 a,b; Deller 1979; Roosa and Deller 1982).

Distribution
Cumberland points are common throughout the Cumberland and Tennessee river drainages in Kentucky (Rolingson 1964), Tennessee (Kneberg 1956; Adair 1976), and Alabama (Mahan 1956). Bell (1960:22) observes that these projectile points may occur in highest frequency in this region's valleys and adjacent Highland Rim. Cumberland points have a much wider distribution extending into the northern Great Lakes region. The type has been recorded in Indiana

Map 6: Cumberland—Distribution and Important Sites

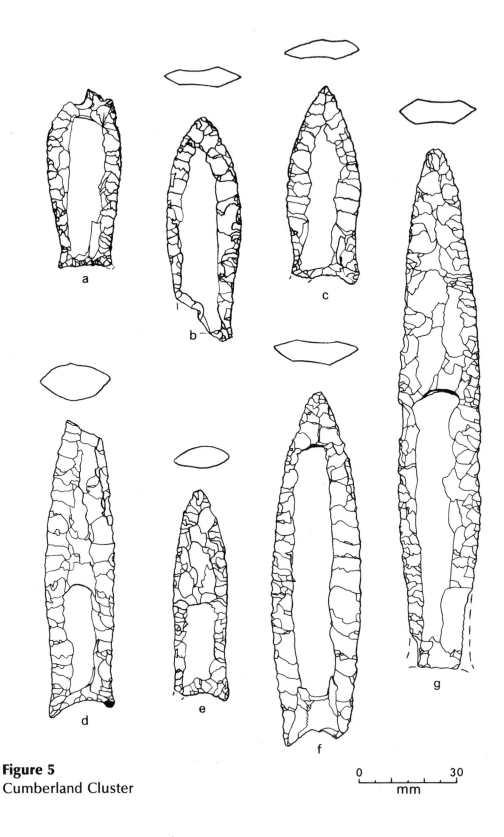

Figure 5
Cumberland Cluster

0   30
mm

(Justice n.d.), Ohio (Prufer and Baby 1963), Illinois (Winters 1959:5), Michigan (Mason 1958:Plate 4,c; Peru 1965:8, Plate 1,g), southern Ontario (Roosa 1977a, Deller 1979), and New York (Funk, Walters, and Ehlers 1969). Apparently the distribution of the type extends sporadically to the west in the Mississippi basin, as it occurs in southeast Iowa (Morrow 1984) and in the Ozark region of Arkansas (Newton 1975:87, Fig. 2).

There appears to be a stylistic variation of the Folsom type which also includes a fishtail typical of Cumberland in the East (cf. Roosa 1977b:352). Particularly notable is the fluted point morphology recovered at the Hanson site (Folsom occupation) in the Big Horn Basin of Wyoming (see Frison and Bradley 1980:50, Fig. 31a). Some of the illustrated specimens are quite close to Roosa's (1965) definition and illustration of the Barnes type and the general morphology of Cumberland. Further research should address this problem and clarify the cultural, temporal, and spatial boundaries now recognized for the Cumberland type.

Morphological Correlates
Barnes (Roosa 1965, 1977a:119, 1977b:352); Jackson, Kuttawa, Inez, Leon (Van Buren 1974).

Morphological Correlates of the Cumberland Cluster
Coxey, Montgomery (Van Buren 1974).

Folsom Cluster

FOLSOM

Folsom projectile points represent an apex in the technique of fluting on lanceolate spear points (Figure 6). Platform preparation using pressure flaking was highly refined, producing a small projection or nipple at the center of the base. This preparation technique aided channel flake production that often extended the full length of the projectile point. A remnant of the nipple may be present on finished specimens. Basal concavities on these points are deep with straight unflared ears extending downward along the lateral margins (Figgins 1934:3; 1935:20–21), although specimens with slightly flared ears also occur (Frison and Bradley 1980:50, Fig. 31). Typical Folsom points exhibit maximum width above the middle of the blade and a "snub-nosed" appearance of the tip, which is actually delicate and sharp as a result of carefully controlled pressure retouch (Crabtree 1966:3). Refer to Crabtree (1966) for a thorough description of Folsom point manufacture based on replication experiments (see also Tunnell 1977; Flenniken 1978; Frison and Bradley 1980; 1982).

Figure 5: Cumberland Cluster
a. Cumberland. Impact fracture at tip. Attica chert. GBL 2681/27. Whiting site, 12 Al 58. Allen Co., Indiana. Pictured in Plate 1,b.
b. Cumberland. Leiber chert. GBL 281/270. Indiana.
c. Cumberland. Wyandotte chert. GBL 21/282. Jefferson Co., Indiana.
d. Cumberland. Fort Payne chert. Tennessee. Specimen 24/103. Frank H. McClung Museum, University of Tennessee. Pictured in Plate 1,j.
e. Cumberland. Wyandotte chert. GBL 21/280. Monroe Co., Indiana.
f. Cumberland (Barnes). Drawn from cast. Thedford II site. Ontario. Courtesy of D. Brian Deller. Royal Ontario Museum (c-501).
g. Cumberland. Recent basal damage. Muldraugh chert. GBL 119/858. Provenience unknown.

Age and Cultural Affiliation
Folsom occupations range in time from 9000–8000 B.C. based on the reviews of radiocarbon dates from several sites (Haynes

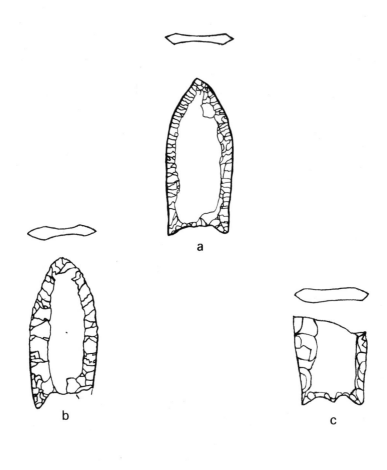

a

b

c

0   30
mm

Figure 6
Folsom Cluster

Map 7: Folsom—Distribution and Important Sites

1964; Judge 1973). This is a well dated Paleo-Indian tradition that endured for a relatively short period of time.

Folsom sites are commonly camp locations associated with procurement and processing of large, now extinct, forms of bison (*Bison antiquus,* etc.) as well as smaller game (Frison 1978; Wilmsen and Roberts 1978).

Distribution
Folsom points are primarily found in the High Plains of the West. They occur over a large area extending from Texas and New Mexico to Alberta, Saskatchewan, and Manitoba (Pettipas 1970). Some of the better known discoveries are Folsom, Blackwater Draw, and Sandia Cave in New Mexico; the Lubbock, Lipscombe, Scharbauer and Kincaid sites in Texas; the Lindenmeier, Linger, and Powars sites in Colorado; and the Machaffie site in Montana (Wormington 1957). Folsom points occur in low numbers east of the Mississippi valley. However, the existence of the Folsom complex in the East is negligible considering the High Plains ecology with which the complex is largely associated in the West. Several authors such as Salzer and Stock (1961), Roosa (1965:95), and Ritzenthaler (1966) have reported finds of Folsom points from southern Wisconsin. Similar material is reported for Illinois generally, and Folsom type projectile points have been found in western Illinois (Conrad 1981:24; Fowler 1954; Perino 1967). The type is also recorded in Missouri (C. Chapman 1975:93) and occurs in northwest Louisiana (Neuman 1984). The use of the Folsom Fluting technique in the manufacture of fluted lanceolate points is relatively common in the

Figure 6: Folsom Cluster
a. Folsom. J. A. Eichenberger cast. Lindenmeier site, Colorado. University of New Mexico collection. Pictured in Plate 1,f.
b. Folsom. Fractured ear. J. A. Eichenberger cast. Folsom site. New Mexico. Denver Museum of Natural History collection.
c. Folsom. Base. Allibates. GBL collection. Bell Co., Texas. Pictured in Plate 1,d.

East although other attributes of these latter forms are often not particularly characteristic of the Folsom type by definition.

Morphological Correlate
Lindenmeier (Van Buren 1974).

Morphological Correlates of the Folsom Cluster
Seymour, Dinnehotso, Doon (Van Buren 1974).

Lanceolate Plano Cluster

PLAINVIEW

The Plainview type projectile point form (Krieger 1947:17–18) exhibits the essential characteristics of Clovis, although fluting is absent (Figure 7). This is a lanceolate form with a shallow concave base and heavy basal grinding. The blade form varies from parallel-sided to recurvate. The flaking pattern ranges from collateral to transverse parallel with an irregular flake scar pattern being most typical (Suhm, Krieger, and Jelks 1954:472; Wormington 1957:264; Bell 1958:74).

Age and Cultural Affiliation
Plainview points are regarded as Late Paleo-Indian or Plano (Jennings 1955, 1974) and relate to a western bison hunting tradition. The type was found in association with extinct bison at the Plainview site in the High Plains of Texas (Sellards, Evans, and Meade 1947). Radiocarbon dates from Plainview, Lake Theo, and other sites indicate an age of about 8000 B.C. (Johnson, Holliday, and Neck 1982:124). Lake Theo is a well stratified site with a Plainview occupation occurring between Folsom and Archaic deposits. Plainview, Dalton, and fluted points are reported from the lowest level at Rodgers Shelter in Missouri (C. Chapman 1975:73; Wood and McMillan 1976). Reagan (1981:18) has suggested that there may be a technological link from Plainview to Dalton.

Distribution
Plainview projectile points are known across the Plains from Texas and as far north as Alaska (Wormington 1957; Wormington and Forbis 1965). The highest frequency of Plainview points occurs in the southern Plains (Wheat 1972:153; Frison 1978:40). Although the density of the Plainview type is low east of the Plains, these projectile points occur over a wide territory. The type is reported from sites in Ontario (MacNeish 1952; Marois 1975), Wisconsin (Ritzenthaler 1966), Missouri (C. Chapman 1975:73, 103), Mississippi (Brain 1970), Kentucky (Rolingson 1964:50, Fig. 34), and Alabama (Cambron and Hulse 1969:22). The type is also reported in Ohio within a class called "Unfluted Fluted" (Prufer and Baby 1963:23, Fig. 12, left). The type is also present in low frequency in Indiana.

Morphological Correlates
Clovis, Unfluted (Cambron and Hulse 1969:22).

Figure 7: Lanceolate Plano Cluster
a. Plainview. J. A. Eichenberger cast. Texas. Baylor University collection. Pictured in Plate 1, i.
b–d. Plainview. Basal fragments. Allibates. GBL collections. Bell Co., Texas.
e. Agate Basin. Muldraugh chert. GBL 14/872. Greene Co., Indiana. Pictured in Plate 1, k.
f. Agate Basin. J. A. Eichenberger cast. Wyoming. Charles Bass collection.
g. Agate Basin. Wyandotte chert. GBL 21/330. Indiana.
h. Agate Basin. Wyandotte chert. GBL 119/862. Provenience unknown.

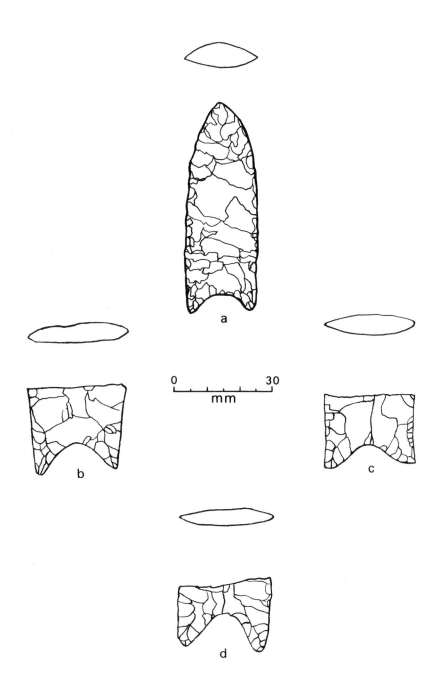

a

b

c

d

0   30
mm

Figure 7
Lanceolate Plano Cluster

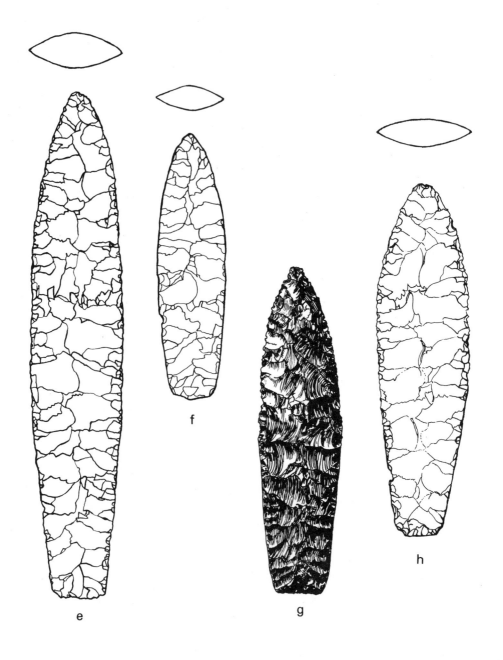

Figure 7

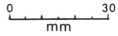

Map 8: Plainview—Distribution and Important Sites

AGATE BASIN

This is a long, slender, lanceolate form with horizontal parallel pressure flaking across the blade and fine marginal retouch along the edges. The type was first reported by Roberts (1943:300) from the Agate Basin site in Wyoming (Figure 7). The blade shape varies from parallel-sided to slightly excurvate. Maximum width of the blade occurs at the midline or between the midline and tip. The cross section is biconvex. In all variations of blade shape, nearly perfect bilateral symmetry is maintained. The blade constricts toward the base in all dimensions, and lateral grinding demarcates the haft region. Basal morphology varies from straight to convex. Certain specimens of the type possess rounded basal features suggesting a nearly bi-pointed appearance. Slightly concave basal edges appear to be fairly common. Agate Basin points with this latter characteristic and sometimes oblique parallel flaking have been designated the Angostura variety (Roberts 1962:91; Munson and Downs 1968:125; Frison and Stanford 1982:Fig. 2.49b, i).

Basal thinning is usually absent since the thickness of the base conforms to the thickness of the haft region as a whole and lateral flaking extends across the haft (Wormington 1957:141, 269; C. Chapman 1975:241). Refer to Frison (1978:159–161) and Bradley (1982:185–186, 194–195) for a further description of Agate Basin points and manufacturing techniques from the type site. There is some suggestion that the flaking technique involved the isolation of striking platforms for individual flake detachments (see Shelley and Agogino 1983), and resharpening is a common trait (Frison and Bradley 1982:194–195).

Age and Cultural Affiliation

The Agate Basin cultural complex begins about 8500 to 8000 B.C. (Irwin-Williams et al. 1973; Frison 1978:31) and persists to about 7400 B.C. (Wormington and Forbis 1965:70; Wychoff 1964:52,103). Agate Basin points are regularly associated with early forms of bison at kill and processing sites in the West (Wheat 1972; Frison 1978), although no Agate Basin kill sites have been found east of the Plains.

The type was recovered from the "Middle Archaic" (mixed?) levels at the Rodgers Shelter in Missouri (Ahler 1971; 1976:134–135). However, Agate Basin was restricted to the lower levels of Graham Cave and Arnold Research Cave, where they were considered to date at least as early as the Dalton period (C. Chapman 1975:105).

Distribution
Agate Basin projectile points occur across the western Plains from New Mexico into the Northwest Territory–Grant Lake Region (Wright 1976; Wormington and Forbis 1965: 20; Frison 1978:31–32). East of the Plains the type has been observed in Ontario (Reid 1980:34), Minnesota (Elson 1957; Quimby 1959:424), Wisconsin (Mason 1963; Ritzenthaler 1967:19), Illinois (Munson and Downs 1968:125; Luchterhand 1970:33; Conrad 1981:44), Indiana (Tomak 1980c:88), Missouri (C. Chapman 1975:241), and Ohio (Prufer and Baby 1963). These forms occur south into Alabama (Cambron and Hulse 1969:5) and north at least into Michigan

(Perino 1968a:2). The type also occurs east through New York (Funk and Schambach 1964:91, Plate 1) to the Plenge Site in New Jersey (Kraft 1973:29–30, Plate 5a; 1977:275, Fig. 1k).

Morphological Correlates
Angostura variety (Hughes 1949:68; Roberts 1962:91; Munson and Downs 1968:125; Cambron and Hulse 1969:5; C. Chapman 1975:241).

Morphological Correlates of the Lanceolate Plano Cluster
Belen (Judge 1973:71); Golondrina (Johnson 1964; Hester 1977:185; Turner and Hester 1985:103–104); McConnell Lanceolate (Prufer 1963, 1975b:315; Murphy 1975:71); Meserve (Turner and Hester 1985:123–124); Russelville (Van Buren 1974:163); Starved Rock Lanceolate (Mayer-Oakes 1951; Conrad 1981:47–48, Plate 5). Additional types: Browns Valley (Jenks 1937:30–33; Ritzenthaler 1967:18; Van Buren 1974:167); Hell Gap (Agogino 1961:558–560; Prufer and

Map 9: Agate Basin—Distribution and Important Sites

Baby 1963; Frison 1974; Bradley 1974:191–197; Frison and Bradley 1982:196); Jimmy Allen (Wormington 1957:145–146); Midland (Wormington 1957:41–42; Wendorf and

Krieger 1959; Agogino 1969; Judge 1970; Perino 1971a:62; Willey (1966:44); Milnesand (Sellards 1955:336–344; Warnica and Williamson 1968:17–19).

Dalton Cluster

BEAVER LAKE

Beaver Lake projectile points exhibit recurved blade edges, concave base, and basal ears (DeJarnette et al. 1962:47; Cambron and Hulse 1960b; 1969). These points compare in overall form to the Cumberland style but totally lack fluting and exhibit only moderate basal thinning (Figure 8). These were previously referred to as unfluted Cumberland. However, Beaver Lake points are usually much thinner in cross section and may possess broader width proportions. The cross section is typically biconvex, sometimes with a median ridge exhibited on one or both faces. Both lateral and basal grinding of the haft region are characteristic. These points were made with a combination of controlled percussion and pressure flaking.

Age and Cultural Affiliation
Beaver Lake projectile points are considered late Paleo-Indian in affiliation. Two Beaver Lake points were recovered from the Dalton Zone (D) at the Stanfield-Worley Bluff shelter in Alabama. The earliest of two radiocarbon dates for Zone D (7690 B.C. ±450) may be too late for Beaver Lake and Dalton points at the site (DeJarnette et al. 1962:85–87). Zone D at Stanfield-Worley also contained a variety of materials including Quad, Big Sandy I, Greenbrier, and other projectile point types, suggesting admixture with subsequent Early Archaic types. A similar situation occurred at the Quad site (Cambron and Hulse 1960a), where most of the types above were associated in a shallow deposit. The age of the Dalton horizon, from 8500 to 7900 B.C. (Goodyear 1982:389–392), is thought to be a rea-

sonable age estimate for Beaver Lake projectile points.

Distribution
Beaver Lake points occur throughout the Tennessee River Valley in northern Alabama (Cambron and Hulse 1960b:11; DeJarnette, Kurjack, and Cambron 1962:47), northeastern Mississippi (Perino 1968a:8), Tennessee (Taylor 1957:85, Fig. 19; Adair 1976:327, Fig. 1), and Kentucky (Rolingson 1964:66). The type may occur over much of the South, since Beaver Lake points have been identified in northern Florida (Bullen 1975:49), South Carolina, North Carolina, and Georgia (Hemmings 1972:100). Beaver Lake

Map 10: Beaver Lake—Distribution and Important Sites

points also occur north of the Ohio Valley in Illinois (Perino 1968a:8), southern Indiana (Cook 1980:373), and Ohio (Prufer and Baby 1963:18, Fig. 8).

QUAD

Projectile points of this type were first recognized at the Quad site in northern Alabama (Soday 1954:9). Quad points are short lanceolate forms with distinct basal ear projections, pronounced basal thinning, and are sometimes fluted (Figure 8). Recurvature of the blade is typical. Basal and lateral grinding is exhibited with lateral grinding usually being more distinct. Flaking patterns range from random to collateral, the former of which is more characteristic (Cambron and Hulse 1969:98). Cambron and Waters (1959:79) note that the flaking quality of these points is comparable to most Paleo-Indian types. These forms are similar to Beaver Lake overall, although Quad points are shorter relative to width and have wide ears and an abrupt stubby appearance at the tip of the blade. Maximum width usually occurs at the base (Bell 1960:80).

Age and Cultural Affiliation
Quad projectile points are Late Paleo-Indian in affiliation. Two Quad points were found in Zone IV at the Hardaway site associated with Dalton and Hardaway Side Notched points. These were considered to date ca. 8000 B.C. (Coe 1964:64–66). The type was recovered within Zone D at the Stanfield-Worley Bluff Shelter (DeJarnette et al. 1962) in mixed association with other early lanceolate forms and later side notched material. However, Quad points were found in good context in lowest level at Graham Cave and were dated to 7744 B.C. ±500 (Logan 1952; Crane 1956:665). Current information suggests that the type dates within the age of the Dalton horizon placed at 8500 to 7900 B.C. (Goodyear 1982:389–392; Walthall 1980:32). In addition, Mason (1962) and Adair (1976:326) suggest that Quad may be an intermediate development from Clovis to Dalton. If this is correct, Quad should occur early in the above temporal range.

Distribution
Quad projectile points are known throughout much of the eastern United States. The type has been found at numerous sites along the Tennessee River in northern Alabama (Waters 1957; Cambron and Hulse 1960a) and Tennessee (Cambron 1958c:80; Adair 1976:327, Fig. 1). The type has been recognized across much of the Southeast from northern Mississippi (Brain 1970:105) to South Carolina (Hemmings 1972:100) and North Carolina (Coe 1964:64, Fig. 56b). To

Figure 8: Dalton Cluster
a. Beaver Lake. Breathitt Formation chert. GBL 422/74. Dearborn Co., Indiana.
b. Beaver Lake. Holland chert. GBL 14/820. Indiana. Pictured in Plate 2, j.
c. Quad. Unidentified chert. GBL 21/344. Southwestern Indiana. Pictured in Plate 2, g.
d. Quad. Wyandotte chert. Site 12 Pe 624. Perry Co., Indiana. Courtesy of Donald Champion.
e. Dalton. Pristine. Burlington chert. Missouri. Specimen 88/103, Frank H. McClung Museum, University of Tennessee. Pictured in Plate 2, d.
f. Dalton. Unidentified chert. GBL 21/419–2. Southwestern Indiana. Pictured in Plate 2, i.
g. Dalton. Bevel resharpening and basal thinning emphasized. Unidentified chert. GBL 21/419. Southwestern Indiana.
h–j. Dalton. Illustrating degrees of resharpening. Unidentified cherts. GBL 21/419. Southwestern Indiana.
k. Greenbrier. Impact fracture at tip. Wyandotte chert. GBL 21/309. Indiana. Pictured in Plate 2, f.
l. Greenbrier. Fort Payne chert. Florence, Alabama. Marshall L. Fallwell collection. Pictured in Plate 2, b.
m. Hardaway Side Notched. Unidentified chert. GBL 421/281. Wayne Co., Indiana.
n. Hardaway Side Notched. Unidentified chert. GBL 21/391. Central Indiana.
o. Hardaway Side Notched. Unidentified chert. North Carolina. Redrawn from Perino (1985:168, middle).
p. Hardaway Side Notched. Jeffersonville chert. GBL 5523/37. Site 12 B 515. Bartholomew Co., Indiana.
q–r. Hardaway Side Notched. Wyandotte chert. GBL 1448/414. Southwestern Indiana.

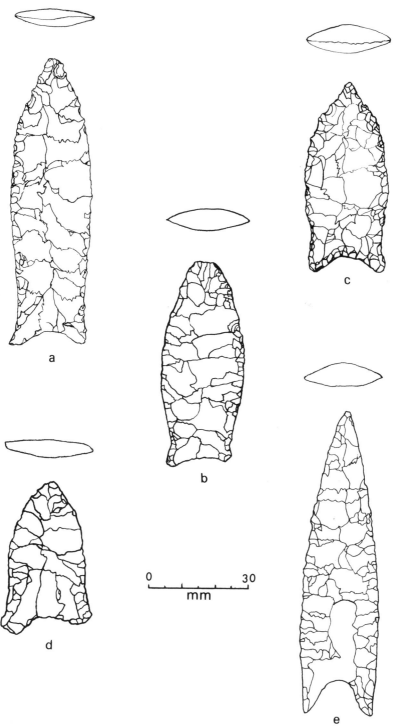

Figure 8
Dalton Cluster

a

b

c

d

e

0   30
mm

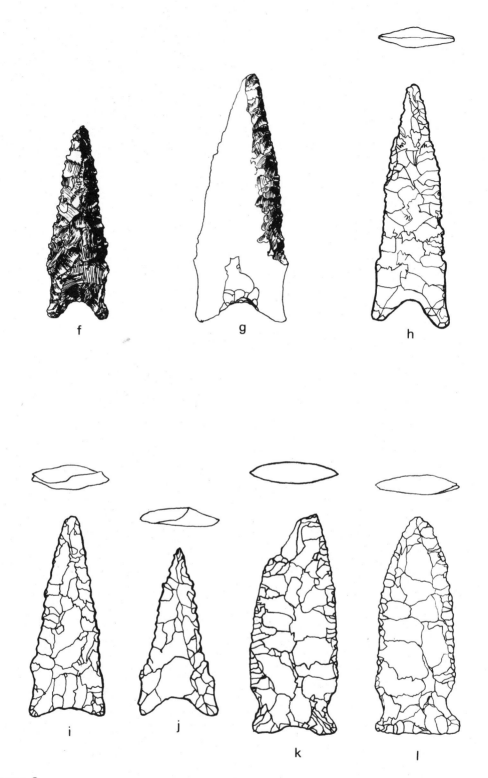

Figure 8

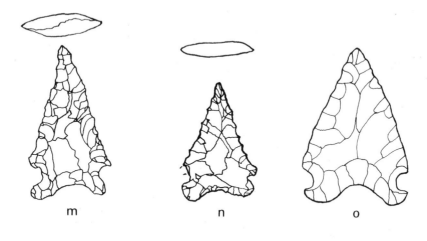

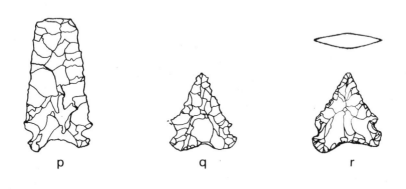

Figure 8

Map 11: Quad—Distribution and Important Sites

the north, Quad type projectile points occur in Kentucky (Rolingson and Schwartz 1966) and southern Ohio (Bell 1960). The type occurs in low frequency in southern Indiana (Tomak 1970:41–42, 1979:85). Five Quad forms were recovered during a transect survey in west-central Illinois (Conrad 1981: 36). These points are rare in Iowa (Morrow 1984). Quad projectile points are apparently lacking or occur in very low frequency in Missouri (C. Chapman 1975:79). However, the type may extend well into the Northeast since similar forms have been reported in Massachusetts and elsewhere (Fowler 1968).

Morphological Correlate
Hardaway blade (Coe 1964:64–65, Fig. 56b; Ward 1983:63).

DALTON

Dalton projectile points were first described by Chapman (1948:13) as lanceolate or trianguloid-bladed points with serrated edges and concave base (Figure 8). The diagnostic attributes of the Dalton haft are the parallel to slightly incurvate lateral margins that are smoothed by heavy grinding. The basal concavity is deep and thinned with one or more thinning flakes detached from a beveled striking platform (Morse 1971a:13). In some cases these flakes extend above the top of the haft onto the blade. Heavy grinding of the base is also typical. Basal ears are distinct and vary in length with the depth of the concave base. The ears flare outward in conjunction with an incurvate lateral haft margin or may project downward with specimens exhibiting straighter lateral margins (Goodyear 1974:19–23).

Aside from a preform stage, Dalton point blades are serrated. The blade shape is initially excurvate (Morse 1971a), but is progressively reduced through repeated dulling and resharpening. Serration or right-hand beveling methods, often in combination, were used for edge rejuvenation. The final result of this process is sometimes a drill-like form with prominent haft region and drastically reduced blade which is very narrow and nearly parallel-sided. Goodyear (1974) presents a thorough study of the use trajectory of Dalton points (Brand site) and the resulting morphological changes from preforms through sawing and scraping edges and burinated tips.

The Meserve type (Bell and Hall 1953) has long been considered an entity closely related to Dalton, the former being defined in the Plains. Many authors have concluded that Dalton and Meserve are one and the same. Hence the names have been used interchangeably (Luchterhand 1970; C. Chapman 1975:245–246). However, a recent article (Goodyear 1982) separates Dalton from Meserve on several grounds. Bell (1958: 52) noted that Meserve is not a common form on the Plains. Goodyear (1982:382–383) suggests that certain forms previously labeled Meserve may in fact represent blade resharpening strategies of a number of Plains lanceolate types such as Plainview and Fredrick. The remaining "Meserve" projectile point samples share the reduction and resharpening strategy defined for Dalton points and therefore indicate a western extension of Dalton (see Myers and Lambert 1983:109–111).

Age and Cultural Affiliation

The Dalton complex (Chapman 1948) is regarded as a technological shift from Paleo-Indian to Early Archaic, dating from about 8500–7900 B.C. (Goodyear 1982:389–392). The Dalton complex includes a type of adz (Morse and Goodyear 1973) and the use of beveling as a resharpening technique which are typical Archaic traits incorporated into a Paleo-Indian tool kit. Associations at a sizeable number of stratified sites demonstrate that Dalton points were manufactured after the time of fluted points and largely prior to the appearance of Early Archaic notched point traditions, although Dalton is a technological link between these traditions. Zone D at the Stanfield-Worley Bluff Shelter, dated within a time span from about 8000–6000 B.C., has often been cited for the time span of the Dalton complex (DeJarnette et al. 1962:87). However, there was no clear stratigraphic division between Dalton, Big Sandy I, and other materials, and the charcoal collected for the dates was obtained from throughout Zone D.

Distribution

The Dalton horizon is present across much of the southeastern U.S. and extends west into the Plains, where it is probably coterminous with the western boundary of the eastern deciduous forests (Myers and Lambert 1983:110). For example, Dalton is present in eastern Oklahoma at the Billy Ross site in the Arkansas River valley (Galm and Hofman 1984), one of several major drainage systems covering the western Plains that flow east to the Mississippi.

A tremendous amount of work has been devoted to the study of Dalton manifestations in northeastern Arkansas. Some of the more notable studies are concerned with settlement distribution (e.g., Morse 1971b; Price and Krakker 1975). Graham Cave (Logan 1952; Klippel 1971) and especially the Rodgers Shelter (Ahler 1971; McMillan 1976) are important in Dalton studies in Missouri. Dalton complex materials are also known from northern Louisiana (Redfield 1970:98, Fig. 1), Mississippi (Brain 1970: 104–105), Alabama (DeJarnette et al. 1962), Georgia (Wauchope 1966: Fig. 235), northern Florida (Goodyear et al. 1983), South Carolina (Michie 1973), North Carolina (Coe 1964:66), Tennessee (Lewis and Kneberg 1958:66; Adair 1976:327, Fig. 1) and Kentucky (Rolingson 1964:41–44).

North of the Ohio Valley, Dalton points are

Map 12: Dalton—Distribution and Important Sites

present although not common in Ohio (Prufer and Baby 1963:22) and Indiana (Tomak 1980c:85). The type is present in southern (Fowler 1959a,b; May 1983:1354) and west-central Illinois (Munson and Downs 1968:125; Conrad 1981:31). The type has also been reported in eastern Iowa (Anderson 1981:15) and Wisconsin (Ritzenthaler 1967:13), indicating that the distribution of Dalton forms may occur farther north within the Mississippi Valley. Data from northern Indiana and Michigan indicate the absence of Dalton in these areas. The Great Lakes area is dominated by Hi-Lo cluster projectile points during the Dalton interval.

Morphological Correlates
Colbert Dalton (DeJarnette et al. 1962); Dalton Serrated (Scully 1951:6); Greenbrier Dalton (DeJarnette et al. 1962); Hardaway Dalton (Coe 1964:64); Holland (Perino 1971a:56; Holland 1971); Nuckolls Dalton (DeJarnette, Kurjack, and Cambron 1962:51–57; Cambron and Hulse 1969: 1975:37–38); Sloan (Morse and Morse 1983:89–95; Perino 1985:356); Vandale (Van Buren 1974:127).

GREENBRIER

The Greenbrier type (Lewis and Kneberg 1960; DeJarnette et al. 1962:56; Cambron and Hulse 1969:66) is a lanceolate-bladed expanding stemmed form that shares characteristics with Dalton and later notched point types (Figure 8). However, the basic flaking style and haft morphology suggest a close relationship with the lanceolate forms of the Dalton cluster. The blade shape is basically triangular and varies from excurvate to straight due to resharpening of the blade edges. Resharpening was typically accomplished at a steep angle, which resulted in bifacially beveled blade edges that may include serration. The manufacturing method appears to have been a combination of percussion and pressure, and pressure resharpening erased portions of the pristine flaking pattern. Cross sections vary from flattened to biconvex. The hafting region of Greenbrier points has been described as broadly side notched, with the notches producing shallow indentations and slightly flaring or expanding stems. The basal ears may vary from being the same width as the shoulders to slightly wider than the shoulders depending on the degree of shoulder reduction resulting from blade resharpening. The basal edge is typically incurvate. Heavy lateral grinding of the haft is typical.

A large number of Greenbrier type projectile points were recovered from the Hester site in Mississippi (Brookes et al. 1975). These represent a wide range of manufacture and resharpening. Various types of breakage and edge wear indicate use as knives and spear points interchangeably.

Age and Cultural Affiliation
Greenbrier points are diagnostic of the Early Archaic period and possibly overlap in time with Dalton and Kirk style points. Greenbrier points were recovered from lower Layer G at Russell Cave in Alabama (Griffin 1974:94) which is dated between 7000 and 5000 B.C. Lower Layer G also produced Russell Cave, Big Sandy, Kirk Corner Notched and Stemmed, Rice Lobed cluster, and other unclassified forms. Greenbrier points were probably no longer in use by ca. 6500 B.C. Walthall (1980:49) observes a considerable overlap in the late Dalton and Big Sandy side notched forms suggesting cultural continuity. It is thought that the Greenbrier type represents an intermediate position in the development from Dalton to the later notched traditions which includes Big Sandy.

Distribution
The distribution of Greenbrier type projectile points appears to be less extensive than Dalton and Hardaway forms in the South. The type is well represented at Late Paleo-Indian and Early Archaic sites in northern Alabama (DeJarnette et al. 1962:56), Mississippi (Brookes et al. 1975), and Tennessee (Lewis and Kneberg 1958; 1960). The type is also recorded from sites in Kentucky (Rolingson and Schwartz 1966: Fig. 56,c), Virginia (Brookes et al. 1975), and in the Ohio Valley. Southern Indiana, Ohio, and Illinois probably represent the northern periphery of dis-

Map 13: Greenbrier—Distribution and Important Sites

tribution for the type. The type appears to occur across the Southeast as it is present in Florida (Bullen 1975:53).

Morphological Correlates
Breckenridge (Thomas 1962:3; Perino 1971a:12); Nansemond (Bottoms 1965; Perino 1985:266); Russell Cave (J. Griffin 1974:36–37); Union Side Notched (Bullen 1975:54).

HARDAWAY SIDE NOTCHED

Hardaway Side Notched points are not to be confused with the Dalton point of the same name. The Hardaway Side Notched is trianguloid in overall form and exhibits a deep concave base and delicate ears with a lateral flare (Figure 8). The side notching is distinct, often being parallel-sided or U-shaped and placed low on the blade. The deep basal concavity, in conjunction with the side notch placed low on the blade, produces distinctive projecting ears. Basal and shoulder widths on these points are comparable. At the Hardaway site, many specimens exhibited a basal

concavity almost notch-like in appearance. Basal thinning was accomplished by the production of broad, shallow flakes that frequently extend a third of the distance up the face (Coe 1964:67).

Age and Cultural Affiliation
Hardaway Side Notched is intermediate in development from Dalton to later side notched types dating from ca. 8000–7000 B.C. These points were recovered from Zone 4 at the Hardaway site associated with Hardaway blade (Quad) and Hardaway Dalton points. Hardaway developed later and lasted longer in the sequence than the latter two forms (Coe 1964). Hardaway Side Notched was recovered from Zone D and later levels at the Stanfield-Worley Bluff Shelter. The type was associated with Big Sandy I and Dalton points, again suggesting an early placement but also indicating a greater longevity of the Hardaway Side Notched form (DeJarnette, Kurjack, and Cambron 1962:82).

Distribution
Hardaway Side Notched points are restricted largely to the southeastern United States (Perino 1968a:30). The type occurs throughout an area including Alabama (DeJarnette et al. 1962), Georgia, South Carolina (Hemmings 1972), and Florida (Bullen 1968:41), to West Virginia (Broyles 1971). A named type that intergrades with Hardaway Side Notched is the San Patrice type, St. Johns variety, which occurs west into Texas and dates to the same time period (Suhm, Krieger, and Jelks 1954:477; Redfield 1970:106). The Hardaway type also occurs in low frequency in the Midwest and the Northeast (Ritchie and Funk 1971; Funk 1977a:23).

Morphological Correlates
San Patrice St. Johns variety (Webb 1946, 1948; Suhm, Krieger, and Jelks 1954:477; Redfield 1970:106).

Morphological Correlates of the Dalton Cluster
Graham Cave Fluted (C. Chapman 1975: 247–248); Green Point (Van Buren 1974:142); Pelican (Gagliano and Gregory 1965:71; Per-

Map 14: Hardaway Side Notched—Distribution and Important Sites

ino 1985:295); Pike County (Perino 1985:
300); San Patrice Hope variety (Webb et al.
1971:11–15); Santa Fe/Tallahassee (Bullen
1975:45–46); Simpson (Bullen 1975:56).

Additional type: Suwannee (Simpson 1948:
11–15; Michie 1970b:31; Goodyear et
al. 1983).

Hi-Lo Cluster

HI-LO

Fitting (1963a:88–90) describes this type
from collections obtained at the Hi-Lo site in
southwestern Michigan (Figure 9). The form
is lanceolate in outline, with a concave base.
Basal modification varies from thinning (i.e.,
with several short and narrow flakes struck
from the base) to fluting. Heavy basal and lateral grinding are characteristic traits. The
lateral haft margins vary from slightly incurvate and expanding to weakly side notched.
The typical haft characteristics are retained
throughout the resharpening process (cf. Fitting 1970:42; Perino 1971a:52), although the
shoulders of these points are often reduced
(cf. Deller 1979:16–17, Figs. 8–9). Left-hand

edge beveling produced by bifacial retouch
is the common resharpening mode, while
resharpening without beveling also occurs.
Heavily resharpened specimens may possess
recurvate or asymmetrical blade shapes. The
resharpening trajectory includes the produc-

Figure 9: Hi-Lo Cluster
a. Hi-Lo. Bayport chert. GBL 13/854. Michigan.
b. Hi-Lo. Attica chert. GBL 14/820. Indiana.
c. Hi-Lo. Muldraugh chert? GBL 2681/30. Whiting site, 12 Al 58. Allen Co., Indiana.
d. Hi-Lo. Drawn from cast. Original, unidentified chert. Southwest Ontario. Courtesy of the
Royal Ontario Museum (c–522).
e. Hi-Lo. Drawn from cast. Original, kettle
point chert? Southwest Ontario. Courtesy of
the Royal Ontario Museum (c–521).

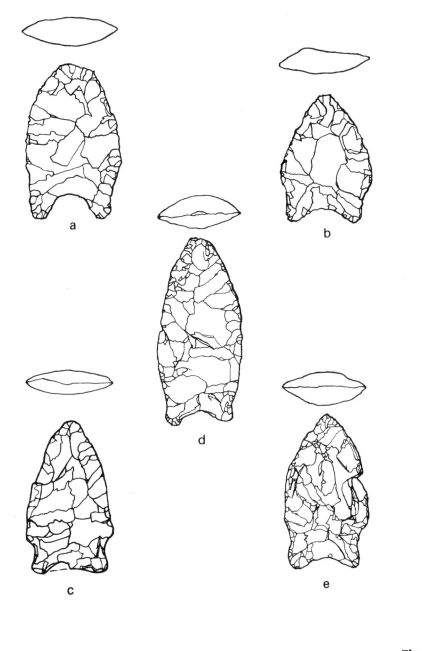

a

b

d

c

e

0   30
mm

Figure 9
Hi-Lo Cluster

tion of hafted end scrapers and other tools made from Hi-Lo points. Hi-Lo preforms exhibit broad, expanding, thinning flakes, and edge beveling and grinding for the preparation of striking platforms. Blade resharpening in the preform stage has also been observed (Ellis and Deller 1982).

Age and Cultural Affiliation

The Hi-Lo complex dates to the Late Paleo-Indian/Early Archaic period in the Great Lakes area. The age of this manifestation is thought to correlate with the age of the Dalton horizon, 8500–8000, B.C. (Ellis and Deller 1982:17). Specific Hi-Lo sites have not been radiocarbon dated. The hunting focus is thought to have been caribou and other species in a periglacial environment. Deller's survey (1979) indicated that former glacial lake beach ridges, such as that found by Fitting, DeVisscher, and Wahla (1966) at Holcombe Beach, were preferred camp sites probably relating to caribou hunting strategies.

Distribution

Hi-Lo projectile points are known primarily in the Great Lakes and adjacent areas. These forms are observed in southern Ontario (Deller 1979; Ellis and Deller 1982), Michigan (Fitting 1963a), west-central Illinois (Conrad 1981:36), northern Indiana (Justice n.d.), and northern Ohio (Prufer and Baby 1963). Fitting (1963b:22) notes that the type occurs west into Wisconsin (cf. Hurley 1965: 84, Figs. 14–16). The western extent of distribution may be represented by the pres-

Map 15: Hi-Lo—Distribution and Important Sites

ence of points similar to Hi-Lo at the Itasca Bison Kill site in Minnesota (Shay 1971:70). In the East, a single specimen was illustrated along with Paleo-Indian material at Bull Brook in Massachusetts (Byers 1954:346, Fig. 91g).

Morphological Correlates

Aqua Plano (Quimby 1960:Fig. 14. Certain specimens referred to by this term are Hi-Lo points. The remainder belong to either the Lanceolate Plano or Dalton cluster in general); Le Roy (Van Buren 1974:128).

Scottsbluff Cluster

SCOTTSBLUFF

Scottsbluff projectile points are distinctive lanceolate straight stemmed forms that characteristically exhibit a transverse parallel flaking pattern across the elongated blades (Figure 10). Wormington (1957:267) presents two types (varieties) which differ only in subtle metric attributes. Type I points possess triangular or parallel-sided blades with weak shoulders and broad stems. The flaking pattern is usually a transverse parallel style but is at times more irregular. The cross section is a symmetrical biconvex shape. Type II are essentially the same except that they have wider triangular blades and have thin lenticular cross sections with more clearly defined shoulders. Both types are subsumed under Scottsbluff as segments of the range of variation. In addition, a Scottsbluff III variant (Satterthwaite 1957:12–17) is also within the range of variation described above (Wheat 1972:141–142). Slight basal ears are present on certain specimens of the type in Wisconsin (Ritzenthaler 1967:15).

Age and Cultural Affiliation

Scottsbluff points, along with Eden points and Cody knives (i.e., a straight stemmed form with an asymmetrical and angular blade), are diagnostic of the Cody complex in the Plains (Wormington 1957). The complex is thought to have existed from 6800–6400 B.C. (Irwin-Williams et al. 1973). A single Scottsbluff point was stratigraphically the deepest diagnostic artifact in the Cody complex zone at the Claypool site in Colorado, where a series of Eden points and Cody knives were represented (Dick and Mountain 1960:226). The Cody complex

economy is known particularly for procurement of early forms of bison such as that found at the Scottsbluff Bison Quarry in Nebraska (Barbour and Schultz 1932) and many other sites in the Plains (see Frison 1976, 1978; and Wheat 1972).

Scattered occurrences of Scottsbluff projectile points are found east of the Plains, although the economy of the people who made them probably differed markedly from the bison economy noted above for the West. Wheat (1972:142) suggests that finds of these points along the eastern margins of the Plains in the tall-grass prairie be separated from the Cody complex and termed the Renier complex. The Renier site itself produced an Eden and Scottsbluff cremation burial (Mason and Irwin 1960:45–46). Although the projectile points from this site are exceedingly long (i.e., 180 mm. based on a reconstruction index), all other essential attributes of the type as defined above were represented (Wheat 1972:142). In addition to the Eden and Scottsbluff points a single Simonsen (Turin) Side Notched point was found (Mason and Irwin 1960). This type

Map 16: Scottsbluff—Distribution and Important Sites

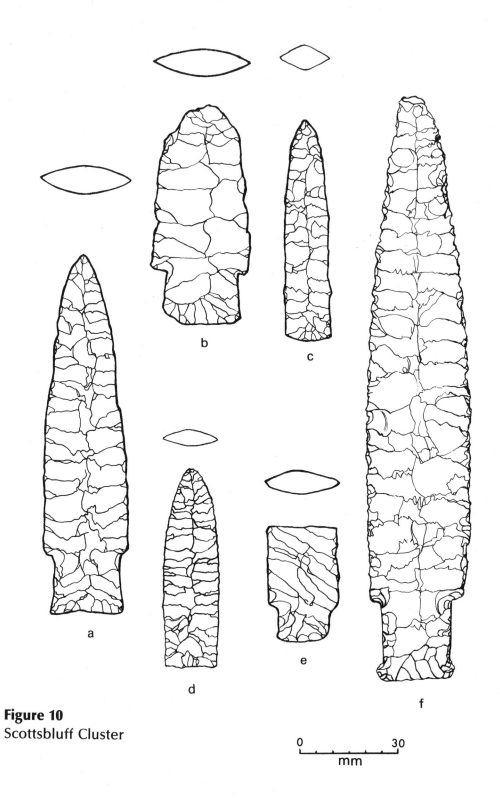

Figure 10
Scottsbluff Cluster

0   30
mm

dates to about 6471 B.C. and is linked with *Bison occidentalis* in western Iowa (Agogino and Frankforter 1960:414).

Distribution

Scottsbluff type projectile points are distributed widely in the Great Plains. The type occurs as far north as Saskatchewan, Alberta, and British Columbia (Wormington 1957:118–123). Within the northwestern Plains, the Cody complex was found to occur from the lower elevations in intermontane basins to the timberline (Frison 1978:34). The type also occurs south and east across Texas (Suhm et al. 1954:478), Arkansas (Davis 1967:3, Fig. 3), Missouri (C. Chapman 1975:103), and northern Louisiana (Webb 1948:231). Scottsbluff points have been found in the Great Lakes area (Mason 1963) at sites in Wisconsin (Ritzenthaler 1967:14), Manitoba (Steinbring 1966:5), and Ontario (Fitting 1970:60–63; Ross 1979:23).

Morphological Correlates

Scottsbluff I and II (Wormington 1957:267); Scottsbluff III (Satterthwaite 1957:12–17; Wheat 1972:141–142); Scottsbluff Eared variety (Ritzenthaler 1967:15); Scottsbluff II Renier variant (Wheat 1972:142).

EDEN

Eden style projectile points (Wormington 1957:124–126, 267) closely resemble Scottsbluff in overall form and flaking quality.

Figure 10: Scottsbluff Cluster
a. Scottsbluff. J. A. Eichenberger cast. Saskatchewan. American Museum of Natural History collection. Pictured in Plate 2, c.
b. Scottsbluff. Unidentified chert. GBL collections. Craighead Co., Arkansas.
c. Eden (short). J. A. Eichenberger cast. Saskatchewan. American Museum of Natural History collection.
d. Eden (short). J. A. Eichenberger cast. Claypool site, Colorado. Bert Mountain collection.
e. Eden. Basal fragment. Allibates. GBL collections. Cochise Co., Texas.
f. Scottsbluff Eared Variant. Drawn from cast. Original, Hixton Silicified Sandstone. Silver Mound, Wisconsin. Courtesy of John Sinclair.

However, Eden points are very narrow and often have only very slight shoulders (Figure 10). In the extreme, these shoulders can be so minute that pronounced lateral grinding may largely account for the juncture between stem and blade which is probably a result of resharpening. Eden points, like Scottsbluff, exhibit collateral or transverse parallel flaking patterns on the blades. However, the narrow width in conjunction with a diamond-shaped cross section and often pronounced median ridges are attributes lacking on the Scottsbluff type. The haft region is characterized by straight lateral margins and a straight to slightly convex basal edge. Full haft grinding is typical. Slight basal ears occur on certain specimens in Wisconsin (Ritzenthaler 1967:16) resulting in an eared variant which apparently does not exist in the Plains.

Age and Cultural Affiliation

Eden points date from about 6800 to 6400 B.C. (Irwin-Williams et al. 1973). Scottsbluff and Eden points, as well as Cody knives, make up the distinct bifacial tool kit of the Cody complex in the West. Subsistence data for the Cody complex in the Plains pertain primarily to bison hunting. The economy of Eden style projectile point makers east of the Prairie is unknown.

Distribution

The Eden type projectile point is essentially a High Plains phenomenon occurring over much of this region from New Mexico into Canada (Wormington 1957; Mason and Irwin 1960:54). The central area of distribution occurs in Wyoming, northern Colorado, and western Nebraska (Wheat 1972:152). In Texas, the type is restricted to the Llano Estacado area (Suhm, Krieger, and Jelks 1954:418). East of the area defined above, Eden points have been identified at the Renier site (Mason and Irwin 1960) and elsewhere in Wisconsin (Ritzenthaler 1967:16). Eden and Scottsbluff projectile points were noted at the George Lake sites at Killarney, Ontario (Greenman 1966:542, Fig. 5). Also, a single Eden point was found at the Sheguiandah quartzite quarry on Manitoulin Island, Ontario (Fitting 1970:61), and this material

Map 17: Eden—Distribution and Important Sites

has been reported along the St. Lawrence Seaway in Quebec (Benmouyal 1978). Ritchie (1940:71, Plate 25, 13–15) mentions a single occurrence in New York of three parallel-flaked points which are somewhat similar to Eden style points. The Plenge site in New Jersey also produced an Eden-like projectile point (Kraft 1973:83). Current information suggests a Great Lake distribution for occurrence of this type east of the Plains.

Morphological Correlates

Eden Eared variety (Ritzenthaler 1967:16); Eden Renier variant (Wheat 1972:142); Kersey (Wheat 1977; 1979:71–97).

Comments

There is little information that would indicate a clear occupation in the East by makers of Eden and Scottsbluff type projectile points, and there are no supportive data for the existence of the Cody complex east of the Plains. However, in Ohio and Michigan there are materials that have been compared to Scottsbluff cluster projectile points that should be noted. Several authors (Smith 1960; Prufer and Baby 1963; Prufer 1963; Pi-

sunyer et al. 1975) discuss archaeological sites in Ohio that have produced assemblages which include stemmed and basally spurred or eared lanceolate points. Among these were true Agate Basin style points and other untyped lanceolate projectile point fragments. Similarities between the stemmed forms and Eden, Scottsbluff, and Alberta points were observed (Prufer and Baby 1963: 20–30, 32–43). Yet this material is problematical as a whole since there is a lack of clear evidence of the highly specialized parallel pressure flaking technology typical of Eden and Scottsbluff points. Such names as McConnell Stemmed Lanceolate (Prufer 1963) or Stringtown (Converse 1973) have been applied to them. These points have only been found at shallow multicomponent sites without datable context. The same is true for the Satchell complex defined in Michigan (Peske 1963) to which this Ohio material has also been correlated.

The Satchell complex derives its name from the Satchell site in the Saginaw Valley where Scottsbluff type projectile points were collected (Fitting 1970:59). The Satchell complex as originally defined was composed of an assortment of cultural materials including those primarily attributable to the Late Archaic period. They were grouped according to the use of coarse raw material such as quartzite, argillite, and other locally available stone. Some authors (Roosa 1966:32–33; Kenyon 1980a,b) have argued that the Satchell complex is entirely a Late Archaic phenomenon. Certain sites regarded as Satchell complex loci have been radiocarbon dated to the Late Archaic period and typologically linked to the Broadpoint tradition (see Simons 1972 and Kenyon 1980a:13, 19; 1980b). However, some of the remaining material may still be regarded as indicative of the Scottsbluff cluster (cf. Griffin 1964:228–229, Fig. 5; Fitting 1970:59) and thereby no longer linked to the Satchell complex which contains diagnostic Late Archaic material.

Surface collections from Indiana have not disclosed Scottsbluff cluster projectile points, and only minimal numbers of Hardin Barbed, a related type, have been found (primarily in the western half of the state). In Illinois, Hardin Barbed projectile points are common and grade morphologically close to the Scottsbluff style. The Hardin Barbed type is most easily differentiated from Scottsbluff by the presence of alternate beveling of the blade edges. The literature search failed to indicate the presence of Hardin Barbed forms in either Michigan or Ohio. In sum, the maximum eastern extent of Scottsbluff cluster forms appears limited to the Great Lakes area.

Morphological Correlates of the Scottsbluff Cluster

Cody Points (Wormington 1957:136; Wheat 1972:142); Hixton (Morrow 1984); Minoqua (Ross 1979:23); San Jon (Wheat 1972:125–155). Additional types: Alberta (Wormington 1957:134; Bell 1960:2; Frison 1978:177).

Hardin Barbed Cluster

HARDIN BARBED

These projectile points were first recognized as a distinct lanceolate and expanded stemmed form occurring in the central Mississippi Valley (Scully 1951:3; Bell 1960:56). Pristine examples are often large and wide-bladed and exhibit a fine overall flaking quality (Figure 11). Basically, this type resembles what has been referred to as Scottsbluff types I and II (Wormington 1957; Mason and Irwin 1960:47; Munson 1967:18; Luchterhand 1970:27–28). Note that the degree of refinement is nearly the same, although transverse parallel flaking typical of Scottsbluff forms is lacking on the blades of Hardin Barbed. Hardin points often exhibit percussion bifacial thinning scars from flakes which were struck from one edge and which cover much of the blade on each face. In addition, cross sections vary from biconvex to rhomboidal since Hardin blade edges were resharpened using a combination of left-hand beveling and serration (Munson 1967: 19). Hardin points possess short downward projecting barbs that flare outward away from the stem without interrupting the fine contour of the blade. The majority of manufacturing and resharpening traits are comparable to types in the Thebes cluster.

The haft element of Hardin Barbed features an expanding stem that varies to nearly straight. Basal edges vary from straight to slightly concave. Hardin Barbed forms exhibit random flake scars on the stem. The terminal notch scar at the blade/haft juncture is often a small semi-circular hertzian cone. Heavy grinding of the basal and lateral margins is typical.

Age and Cultural Affiliation

Hardin Barbed projectile points are diagnostic of the Early Archaic period. The suggested age of these forms is from 8000–

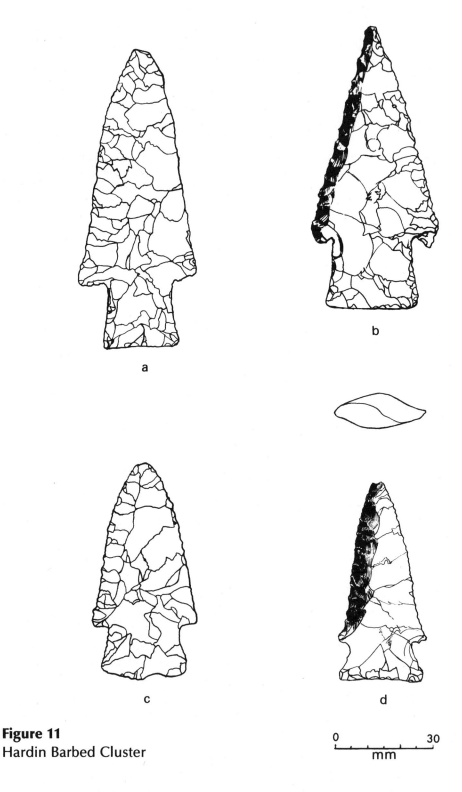

Figure 11
Hardin Barbed Cluster

0   30
mm

Map 18: Hardin Barbed—Distribution and Important Sites

5500 B.C. (Munson 1967:17–18; Luchterhand 1970:10). A single specimen of the type was recovered from the lower levels (levels 5 and 6) of Graham Cave (Logan 1952:34–35, plate 6, g). The morphological attributes of Scottsbluff and Hardin Barbed, and the assigned ages for each type, suggest that there is temporal overlap and morphological intergradation between them. Munson (1967:18) argues that Hardin Barbed is derived from Scottsbluff, and there is good evidence suggesting a local adaptation to the Prairie Peninsula area of central Illinois and west-central Indiana. These forms are concentrated within relict prairie areas almost without exception.

Figure 11: Hardin Barbed Cluster

a. Hardin Barbed. Unidentified chert. GBL 21/420. Southwestern Indiana. Pictured in Plate 2, a.
b. Hardin Barbed. Bevel resharpening emphasized. Unidentified chert. GBL collections. Provenience unknown.
c. Hardin Barbed. Bevel resharpening. Unidentified chert. GBL 31/100. Fulton Co., Indiana.
d. Hardin Barbed. Bevel resharpening emphasized. Attica chert. GBL 177/9. Owen Co., Indiana. Pictured in Plate 2, h.

Distribution

The area of highest concentration appears to be within the Prairie Peninsula region mentioned above (Munson 1967; Luchterhand 1970; Conrad 1981:418). These forms are also present in lower frequency in a wider area which includes eastern Iowa (Anderson 1981:15), Missouri (C. Chapman 1975:246), Arkansas (Redfield 1966), southern Illinois (Butler et al. 1979:35), southwestern Michigan, northwestern Indiana (William L. Mangold, pers. comm.), and western Kentucky (Weinland and Fenwick 1978:189, Fig. 34 f). Faulkner (1968) mentions a single fragmented specimen from the Tims Ford Reservoir in Tennessee. Indications are that the maximum eastern extent of Hardin Barbed points lies within Indiana. A single specimen similar to Hardin Barbed from Early Archaic levels at the Haag site in southeastern Indiana represents a single occurrence in this region (Tomak et al. 1980:35, Plate 1). Bell (1960:56) mentions the presence of Hardin Barbed as far west as Oklahoma.

Morphological Correlates

Hardin Stemmed (Scully 1951:3); Urich (Van Buren 1974:156).

Thebes Cluster

THEBES

Thebes projectile points (Winters 1963, 1967; Luchterhand 1970; Perino 1971a) are medium to large-sized dart points or knives having pronounced side or diagonal notches (Figure 12). The blades are broadly triangular in form with straight to convex edges. Recurved edges occur on resharpened specimens and serration is common. Cross sections are flat or biconvex in pristine condition and rhomboidal in reworked state. The beveled edge is commonly placed on the left side of the blade. Basal edges vary from straight to slightly concave or convex. The edge of the haft element is smoothed with heavily ground facets being characteristic of the basal edge. The notches are broad and parallel-sided, directed inward at a slight upward angle, and are commonly squared at the notch terminus.

This form has also been termed Cache Diagonal Notched (Winters 1963, 1967) and given other names distinguishing the varying morphology of the notch terminus and degrees of reworking of the blade (see morphological correlates). Winters (1963:20) used the term Thebes type cluster to include among others the Cache Diagonal Notched. In all respects, Cache Diagonal Notched is essentially identical to Thebes. Certain examples exhibit expanded notch interiors whereby the notching direction was intentionally split into two directions producing a widened notch terminus. This leaves a characteristic spur at the center of the notch which is often termed the Key-hole notch (Perino 1971a:96).

Examples of the Thebes form have been recognized which carry all essential attributes including beveling yet lack a haft element (see Conrad 1981:90).

Age and Cultural Affiliation
Thebes points are diagnostic of the Early Archaic period dating from 8000 to 6000 B.C.

Klippel (1971:22, 27–28) has reported two dates of 7530 B.C.±400 and 7340 B.C.±300 for a level in Zone IV at Graham Cave containing a Thebes and a St. Charles type point, which secures the age of these forms.

Distribution
The Thebes type projectile point and its variants are quite common across Indiana (Tomak 1970; Cook 1980:446, Plate 17.12), Ohio (Converse 1973; Brose and White 1979) Illinois (Winters 1963; Springer, Karsh, and Harrison 1978), and Missouri (Logan 1952). These forms occur in lesser frequency in Michigan according to Fitting (1970:70, Fig. 22). Mayer-Oakes (1955:81, Plate 30a) pictures two Thebes type points from Pennsylvania, and Holland (1970:85, Plate 15m) has identified Cache Diagonal Notched (i.e., Thebes) in southwest Virginia. By and large the type appears to be scarce in the Upper Ohio Valley and elsewhere in the East.

Figure 12: Thebes Cluster
a. Thebes. Exhibits expanded notch characteristic. Wyandotte chert. GBL 14/820. Indiana.
b. Thebes. Attica chert. GBL 14/820. Indiana.
c. Thebes. Exhibits drastic bevel resharpening. Unidentified chert. GBL 14/820. Indiana.
d. St. Charles. Laurel chert. GBL 14/206. Rush Co., Indiana.
e. St. Charles. Bevel resharpening. Attica chert. GBL 14/68. Decatur Co., Indiana.
f–g. St. Charles. Haft variations. Unidentified chert. GBL 1448/48, 14/820. Indiana.
h. Lost Lake. Wyandotte chert. GBL 14/823. Indiana.
i. Lost Lake. Bevel resharpening. Wyandotte chert. GBL 14/850. Decatur Co., Indiana.
j. Lost Lake. Exhibits reduced blade and steep bevel due to resharpening. Unidentified chert. GBL 14/68. Decatur Co., Indiana.
k. Calf Creek. Wyandotte chert. GBL 30/159. Jefferson Co., Indiana.
l. Calf Creek. Pitkin chert. Calf Creek Cave, Arkansas. Drawing courtesy of Donald R. Dickson.

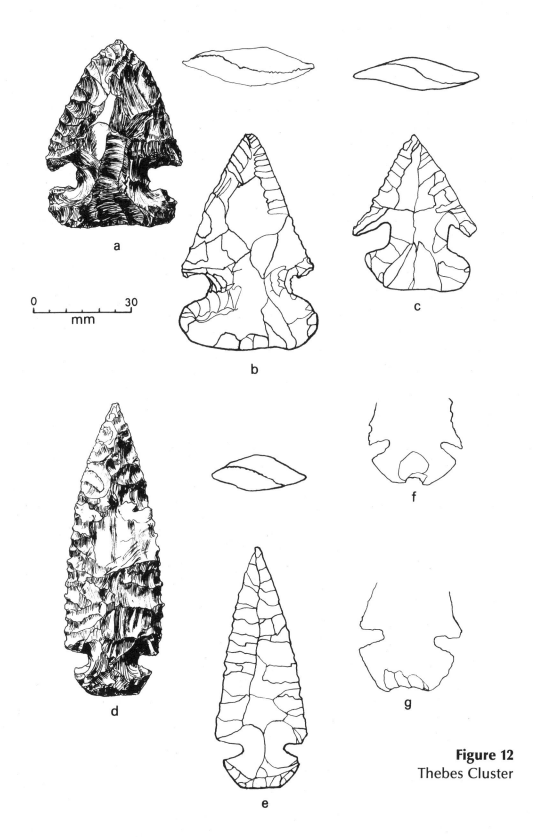

Figure 12
Thebes Cluster

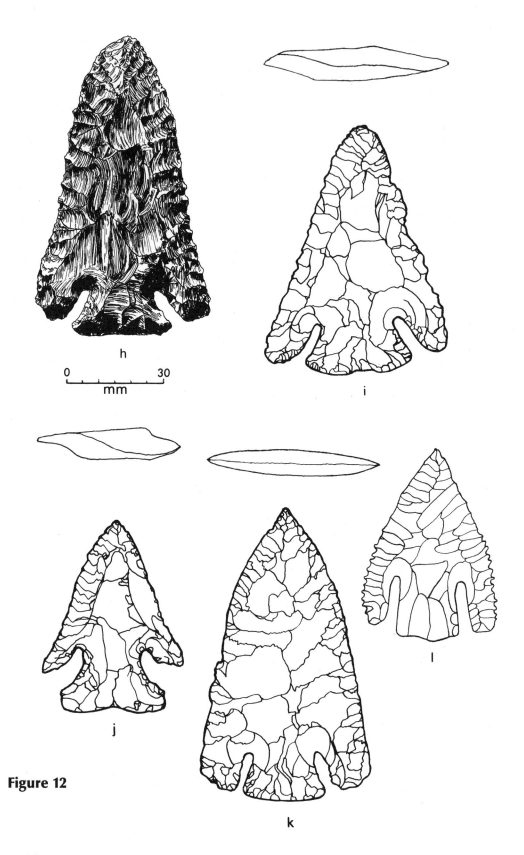

h

0   30
mm

i

j

k

l

Figure 12

Graham
Cave

Map 19: Thebes—Distribution and Important Sites

Morphological Correlates

Archaic Bevel (Converse 1973:23); Cache Diagonal Notched (Winters 1963:25); Expanded Notch Points (Converse 1973:26); Thebes Knives (Perino 1971a:96–97).

ST. CHARLES

The St. Charles projectile point (Scully 1951:4) is a lanceolate and often ovate-shaped corner notched point with a convex base (Figure 12). The pristine blade form characteristic of St. Charles is excurvate and biconvex in cross section and is very well made using refined percussion and pressure flaking. Some St. Charles blades resemble the Agate Basin type in flaking quality and shape. Resharpening of the blade is common, with most reduction on the long axis resulting from the use of pressure flaked serration in conjunction with alternate beveling of the blade edges (Luchterhand 1970; Bell 1960:82). It seldom exhibits a truly flat basal edge; however, two or three flattened facets which may result from grinding or the production of burins may be present as variations in the basal finishing process (Con-

verse 1973:45). Another haft variation is the infrequent occurrence of a basal notch which is shallow relative to the average corner notch depth. The corner notches on these points are finely made with robust hertzian cone flake scars surrounding the notch terminus. These notches are narrow and deep and the edges converge forming a smooth arc. Heavy basal and notch grinding is typical.

Age and Cultural Affiliation

St. Charles points are diagnostic of the Early Archaic period. A suggested age for these forms is from about 8000 to 6000 B.C. (Luchterhand 1970:12). Dates from Graham Cave Missouri for Thebes and St. Charles points ranged from 7530 B.C.±400 to 7340 B.C.±300 (Klippel 1971:22, 27–28; Conrad 1981:80). The lower Kirk levels at Ice House Bottoms in Tennessee were dated to about 7500 B.C.; that is in agreement with the above dates (J. Chapman 1976:5; 1977:166). These levels contained heavily reworked projectile points similar to Lost Lake, Charleston, and Plevna/St. Charles (J. Chapman 1977:51). Recently, a St. Charles point was recovered within early Holocene deposits stratigraphically above pond sediments containing a Clovis and Mastodon association at the Kimmswick site in eastern Missouri (Graham et al. 1981:1115–1116).

Distribution

St. Charles projectile points are widely distributed within the eastern United States (Bell 1960:82). These points are well represented at sites throughout much of the Middle South and Southeast from Kentucky (Weinland and Fenwick 1978:45; Ottesen 1981:381, Plate 2,h) to Alabama (DeJarnette et al. 1962; Cambron and Hulse 1969) and northern Florida (Bullen 1968:42–43). In the Midwest, St. Charles points are quite common outside the Great Lakes region in Missouri (C. Chapman 1975), eastern Iowa (Anderson 1981:18), Illinois (Luchterhand 1970; Conrad 1981), Indiana (Tomak 1970; Kellar 1973), and Ohio (Converse 1973). The type appears to be rare in the Northeast (Ritchie 1961, 1969a), but it occurs in limited

Map 20: St. Charles—Distribution and Important Sites

siderably due to resharpening processes. These shapes range from excurvate to deeply incurvate. In the latter forms, changes in blade shape are due to the use of bevel resharpening which includes serration and results in a drastically shortened blade. Cross sections range from biconvex in pristine condition to rhomboidal in beveled examples. Heavy grinding is present on many specimens at the base which varies from straight to slightly convex or incurvate. The Lost Lake style is similar to the later Kirk Corner Notched type except that the Kirk notch depth is shorter and is straight rather than curved, and bevel resharpening and basal grinding are deemphasized.

Age and Cultural Affiliation

These projectile point forms are diagnostic of the Early Archaic period dating from about 8000 to 6000 B.C. Lost Lake points were recovered in early context at the Stanfield-Worley Bluff Shelter in Alabama. Projectile point forms recovered from lower Kirk strata at Ice House Bottoms in Tennessee included points with heavy basal grinding and beveling which J. Chapman (1977:51) recognized

numbers in the Upper Ohio Valley (cf. Mayer-Oakes 1955), and it has been recovered from sites in West Virginia (McMichael 1965:529–31). In addition, the Shawnee-Minisink site in the upper Delaware Valley of Pennsylvania has produced projectile points that are quite close to St. Charles. These have been referred to as the Kline type (McNett 1985).

Morphological Correlates

Dovetail (Luchterhand 1970:31–32); Ecusta (Harwood 1958:23; Cambron and Hulse 1975:43; J. Chapman 1977:44); Fractured Base Dovetail (Converse 1973:45); Notched Base Dovetail (Converse 1973:38); Plevna (DeJarnette et al. 1962; Cambron and Hulse 1969; Chapman 1975:255).

LOST LAKE

Lost Lake projectile points (DeJarnette el al. 1962; Perino 1968a:50; Cambron and Hulse 1969:46) are generally large forms with deep corner notches that often curve in and up from the edge of the blade (Figure 12). Terminal notch scars exhibit semicircular hertzian cones. The blade shape varies con-

Map 21: Lost Lake—Distribution and Important Sites

as sharing a number of attributes with Lost Lake and Plevna types. In addition, these forms were considered to predate the majority of the types of the Kirk Corner Notched cluster. An age of about 7500 B.C. was secured for the lower Kirk strata (J. Chapman 1977:161, 166).

Distribution

Lost Lake projectile points are known over much of the southeastern United States. These forms also extend into the Ohio Valley. The literature search noted the presence of the type in south Florida (Hazeltine 1983: Fig. 1a), Alabama (DeJarnette et al. 1962), Tennessee (Lewis and Lewis 1961), Kentucky (Schock and Langford 1979b; Ottesen 1981), southern Indiana (Tomak 1980b:2, Fig. 2; Cook 1980:396), Ohio (Converse 1973:25) and West Virginia (McMichael 1965:Fig. 24).

Morphological Correlates

Bolen Plain/Beveled (3&4) (Bullen 1968:42–43); Cypress Creek I (Lewis and Lewis 1961; Schock and Langford 1979b); Diagonal Corner Notched Point (Converse 1973:25); Dover Hill (Tomak 1980b:2, Fig. 2, bottom).

CALF CREEK

Calf Creek projectile points (Dickson 1968) are basically triangular in form and possess deep parallel-sided basal notches (Figure 12). Haft morphology on these points exhibits a straight to slightly expanded stem with straight to slightly convex basal edge. Shoulder barbs extend downward nearly even with the base. Reworking of the blade is accomplished with bifacial retouch or unifacial beveling. Resharpening of the blade was often terminated in line with the notch terminus. Thus, the barbs retain much of their original morphology resulting in an angle formed between the blade and barb. Serration is common along the blade edges and basal and lateral haft grinding is typical (Perino 1968a:14). Calf Creek points are most similar in morphology to Lost Lake (Cook 1980:377). The barbs of Lost Lake, however, terminate in a point, and the notching is accomplished from the corner of the preform and is curved.

Age and Cultural Affiliation

These points are diagnostic of the Early Archaic period dating from about 8000 to 6000

Map 22: Calf Creek—Distribution and Important Sites

B.C. Calf Creek points were recovered from the lowest levels of Calf Creek Cave stratigraphically beneath Rice Lobed and Searcy type points, side noted forms, and other material. This, plus other excavation data, indicates an Early Archaic association (Dickson 1970; Donald R. Dickson, pers. comm.).

Distribution

Calf Creek points have been found primarily in Arkansas, eastern Kansas, Missouri, and Oklahoma (Perino 1968a:14; Dickson 1968, 1970; Donald R. Dickson, pers. comm.). Calf Creek points are rare in Indiana and Illinois. Two specimens were found at sites in the Patoka Reservoir in southern Indiana (Cook 1980:377).

Heavily resharpened Calf Creek points lacking shoulders could be difficult to identify. Projectile points exhibiting the basic haft characteristic of Calf Creek may be included in the Harpeth River type and Harpeth River Rockport variety defined from sites in Kentucky (cf. Cambron 1970; Adair and Sims 1970). However, the Harpeth River type also includes material which is most characteristic of resharpened projectile points in the Kirk Corner Notched cluster. In addition, the Andice and Bell basal notched types described for areas west into Texas (Turner and Hester 1985) include variations similar to Calf Creek, but the relationship of these projectile point types to Calf Creek is not fully understood (Donald R. Dickson, pers. comm.). Further research into the lithic technology and specifically the resharpening strategies of Calf Creek points should clarify the distribution of these projectile points.

Morphological Correlates of the Thebes Cluster

Bristol Diagonal Notched (Winters 1963:25; Denny 1972:138, Fig. 20); Grundy (Morrow 1984); Kline (McNett 1985:95–97, Fig. 6.8a); Ocala (Bullen 1975; Perino 1985:277); Pulaski (Winters n.d.; Holland 1970:91; Conrad 1981:73, 81–82. This type designation overlaps with the Kirk Corner Notched cluster.)

Large Side Notched Cluster

BIG SANDY

The Big Sandy type (Kneberg 1956:25; Cambron and Hulse 1960a:17; 1969:14) is a side notched projectile point with distinctive blade and haft characteristics (Figure 13). The typical blade shape is a narrow and elongated triangle. Cross sections vary from biconvex or plano convex to rhomboid or median-ridged depending on the degree of blade resharpening. Beveling and serration are common resharpening features produced using pressure flaking techniques. The shoulders of these forms may be parallel with the basal ear margins, representing the unmodified preform sides, or nearly exhausted from resharpening.

The haft element of Big Sandy specimens exhibits side notches that tend to be shallow, in that notch width may be greater than notch depth. The notching techniques exhibited vary from indentations produced bifacially following a single inward direction, to those exhibiting a Y-pattern resulting in two notching directions in the interior of the notch. The former notching technique is generalized, resulting in single hertzian cone scars surrounding the notch terminus on each face, or multiple nondescript flake scars. The latter notching technique exhibits dual and overlapping hertzian cone flake scars at the notch terminus, with a weak nipple at the center of the notch. An exaggerated form of this technique occurs within the range of variation recognized for Thebes projectile points (e.g., interior notch direction may split at 90°), hence the terms "Keyhole" and "Expanded Notch" (Converse 1973:26) have been applied to those forms.

The basal edge of Big Sandy varies from nearly straight to deeply concave and is sometimes nearly bifurcated in appearance. Basal thinning is a conspicuous attribute. Individual thinning scars may be widely spaced, leaving untrimmed portions of the original ground edge prior to thinning. The resulting basal edge has a ragged or weakly serrated appearance. The basal ears are usually squared but may be slightly rounded. Full haft grinding is common, although specimens lacking grinding are not atypical. Examples such as these were formerly classified as Big Sandy II (Cambron and Hulse 1960a:17; 1969).

Recent discussion of the range of traits exhibited on Big Sandy forms (DeJarnette and Knight 1976:43–44) recognizes overall similarities between types such as Dalton, St. Albans (variety B), and Big Sandy. Also noteworthy are the basic haft and basal ear similarities between the latter and Kessell (see Broyles 1971:61).

Additional variants of the Big Sandy type are described by Cambron and Hulse (1975: 15–17). These are Big Sandy broad base, contracted base, and auriculate. The descriptions of these variants do not adequately address the differences or similarities between these and the original definition of Big Sandy. The Big Sandy auriculate variant has been analyzed and discussed by Gustafson and Pigott (1981).

Age and Cultural Affiliation

Big Sandy projectile points are diagnostic of the Early Archaic period and represent one of the earliest types in the Side Notched tradition. It was the most common type recovered from the lowest zone (D) of the Stanfield–Worley Bluff in Alabama dated from about 8000–6000 B.C. (DeJarnette et al. 1962:82–84; Goodyear 1982:385). Similar material was also reported from the lowest level (26–27 feet below surface) of the Modoc Rock Shelter in Illinois also dated at ca. 8000 B.C. (Fowler 1959a:19). The Eva site in Tennessee produced these forms in deep levels at the site (Lewis and Lewis 1961). Two additional stratified sites in Alabama, Russell Cave (Griffin 1974) and LaGrange (DeJarnette and Knight 1976), have also produced Big Sandy forms in early context.

Goodyear's (1982) discussion of the Dalton horizon emphasizes the mixed nature of the lower Zone D of the Stanfield–Worley Bluff Shelter, which originally led to the assumption of the contemporaneity of such lanceolate forms as Dalton, Greenbrier, Stanfield Triangular, Beaver Lake, Hardaway Side Notched, and Big Sandy. Based on present data, Big Sandy is less solidly associated with the above types. A review of the chronology of Dalton, especially the early dates derived from Dalton hearths at the Rodgers Shelter in Missouri (Ahler 1976:124), indicates that the Dalton horizon dates from about 8500–7900 B.C. (Goodyear 1982:389–392). Big Sandy overlaps the age of Dalton cluster lanceolate types but continues to about 6000 B.C.

Distribution

Big Sandy projectile points occur in highest frequency along the Tennessee River Valley in northern Alabama and Tennessee (Kneberg 1956; Cambron and Hulse 1960a, 1975; DeJarnette et al. 1962) and peripheral areas (Jolley 1979:40, Fig. 4; Faulkner and McCollough 1973:140, 304, Plate 73). The type appears to be well represented in Kentucky (Weinland and Fenwick 1978:53). In Indiana, Big Sandy points occur in low frequency at least as far north as Rush and Morgan counties in the south-central part of the state. The presence of the type in west-central Illinois has been confirmed (see Conrad 1981:52–53). The type has also been reported in southwestern Ohio (Vickery 1976:128) and probably occurs elsewhere in that state. Big Sandy points (i.e., Bolen subtypes 1, 2, & 5) are also known across the southeastern states into Florida (Bullen 1975:50–51; Purdy and Beach 1980:118, Fig. 9).

Beyond the distribution cited above there is a dearth of information. This could be due to the preferential use of the term Otter Creek (Ritchie 1961:40–41) for side notched

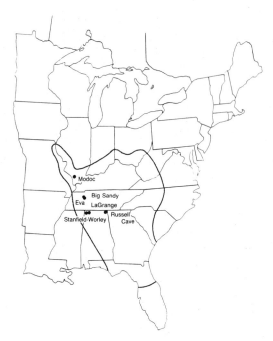

Map 23: Big Sandy—Distribution and Important Sites

GRAHAM CAVE
SIDE NOTCHED

Graham Cave Side Notched points (Scully 1951:8) are deeply concave-based and finely-flaked forms (Figure 13). Logan (1952:30) provides a thorough description of three recognized variations of the type found in the lower levels of Graham Cave in Missouri. Each of these is differentiated primarily on the basis of subtle basal ear configuration and reworking attributes of the blade. "Subtype A" is long, with small and precise side notches. The base is markedly concave with the basal ears exhibiting a barbed appearance. Pressure flaking is carefully executed. The blade may be slightly serrated and the blade contour may be recurvate due to resharpening. The cross section is often thick and biconvex and in some cases nearly diamond-shaped. "Subtype B" exhibits an ex-

Figure 13: Large Side Notched Cluster
a. Big Sandy. Muldraugh/Fort Payne chert? GBL 14/927. Rush Co., Indiana.
b. Big Sandy. Unidentified chert. GBL 13/891. Provenience unknown.
c. Big Sandy. Snapped tip. Muldraugh/Fort Payne chert? Eva site, Tennessee. Specimen ST2D–504/6Bn12, Frank H. McClung Museum, University of Tennessee. Pictured in Plate 3, c.
d. Graham Cave Side Notched. Unidentified chert. GBL 21/419. Southwestern Indiana.
e. Graham Cave Side Notched. Burlington chert. GBL 13/891. Provenience unknown.
f. Kessel Side Notched. Unidentified chert. GBL 14/206. Rush Co., Indiana. Pictured in Plate 3, g.
g. Kessell Side Notched. Paoli chert. GBL 1448/101. Southwestern Indiana. Pictured in Plate 3, b.
h. Godar. Unidentified chert. GBL 31/100. Fulton Co., Indiana.
i. Raddatz Side Notched. Unidentified chert. GBL 31/100. Fulton Co., Indiana.
j. Raddatz Side Notched. Unidentified chert. GBL 463/23. Hamilton Co., Indiana.
k. Raddatz Side Notched. Unidentified chert. GBL collections. Provenience unknown.
l–m. Osceola/Hemphill. J. A. Eichenberger casts. Originals, Burlington chert. Hoffelmeyer Hill, site 23 AN 46. Andrew Co., Missouri. From a cache of four points. Specimens 76.1.174B and 76.1.175B St. Joseph Museum. St. Joseph, Missouri.

material in the northeastern states (Tuck 1974; Brennan 1977:419). However, Mayer-Oakes (1955) and Dragoo (1959) do not illustrate Big Sandy points from sites along the upper Ohio Valley. In addition, recent attempts to clarify the Early and Middle Archaic sequences in the Northeast have not observed the presence of the Big Sandy type (Trubowitz 1979:55), although Funk (1977a:24) suggests a southeastern derivation for Otter Creek. Big Sandy forms may extend into Missouri and other areas to the west. Once again, however, published information would indicate an absence of Big Sandy forms beyond the middle Mississippi Valley. In Missouri (C. Chapman 1975:242) side notched materials are primarily morphological variations of the Graham Cave Side Notched and Raddatz types rather than Big Sandy. The former also appears at an early date at the beginning of the Side Notched tradition (see Klippel 1971).

Morphological Correlates
Big Sandy I (Cambron 1959:74); Bolen Plain/Beveled subtypes (1, 2, & 5) (Bullen 1975: 51–52; Purdy and Beach 1980:Fig. 9); Taylor (Michie 1966:123; Perino 1985:374).

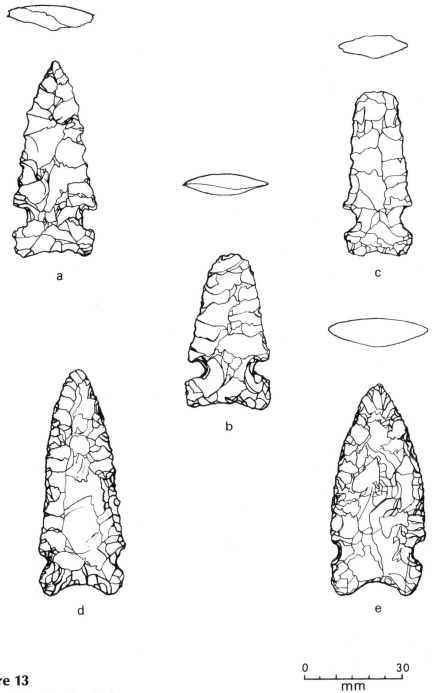

Figure 13
Large Side Notched Cluster

0   30
mm

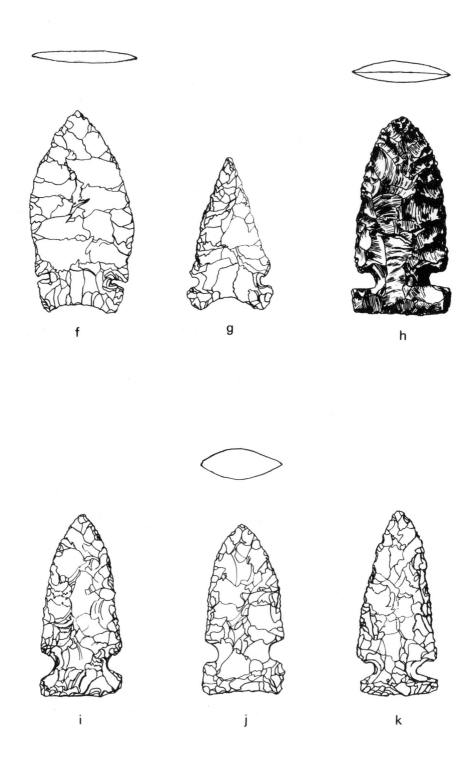

f   g   h

i   j   k

Figure 13

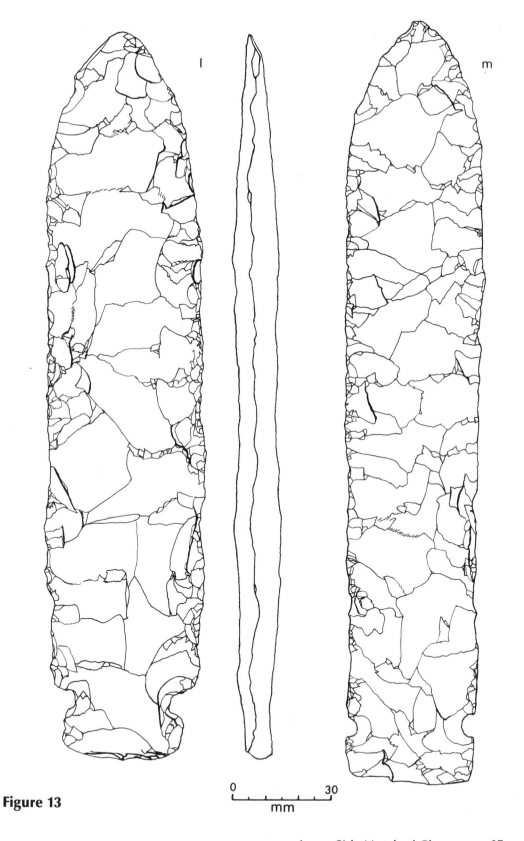

Figure 13

l   m

0   30
mm

curvate blade and has a thin cross section relative to width. "Subtype C" exhibits an excurvate blade shape and has rounded basal ears. In sum, the variation of this type involves lateral blade resharpening and basal configuration, varying from examples with a distinct basal concavity and ears to less robust examples. The type is readily distinguishable from the other side notched forms grouped in this cluster (see also Klippel 1971; C. Chapman 1975).

Age and Cultural Affiliation
Graham Cave Side Notched projectile points are diagnostic of the Early Archaic period and continue into the Middle Archaic period. An age ranging from 8000–5500 B.C. covers the duration of the type based on the occurrence of these points in the early levels at Graham Cave, Arnold Research Cave, Rice Shelter, and Rodgers Shelter in Missouri (C. Chapman 1975). Fowler (1959b:262) suggests a range of 8000–6000 B.C. for the presence of the type in Zone I at Modoc Rock Shelter in Illinois. More recently, Graham Cave Side Notched points have been recovered and dated to about 6450 B.C. in

Horizon 11 at Koster site in Illinois (Cook n.d.:9, Table 3; Anonymous 1976, in Conrad 1981:96).

Distribution
The distribution of Graham Cave Side Notched points appears to be restricted largely to the Midwest. The type occurs at a number of stratified sites in Missouri (Logan 1952; Klippel 1971; Ahler 1971) and Illinois (Fowler 1959a; Conrad 1981:96–99). It has also been identified in southern Indiana (Cook 1980:385, Plate 17.3). The type also occurs in low frequency in southern Iowa (Morrow 1984). Benedict and Olson (1978:166) recognize somewhat similar forms in the western United States, but the Billy Ross site located on the Arkansas River in eastern Oklahoma is near the limit of distribution for Graham Cave Side Notched (Galm and Hofman 1984).

Morphological Correlate
White River Serrated (Bray 1956:128–129, Fig. 25, row 4).

Map 24: Graham Cave Side Notched—Distribution and Important Sites

KESSELL SIDE NOTCHED

Kessell projectile points (Broyles 1966:18) represent a distinct type within the Large Side Notched cluster. These projectile points often exhibit a pentagonal form with the blade or blade/haft juncture forming an obvious angle. Kessell points exhibit a distinct and wide concave base. The ears are squared and often expand slightly due to base and notch indentations. Notches are typically very narrow and minute compared to other early side notched points. These are also characteristically shallow and narrow and the notch width is often greater toward the interior of the notch. The cross section of these points is flat and quite thin. Drastic blade reworking of these points has not been observed and serration is lacking (Figure 13). Overall, these projectile points exhibit a specialized flaking technique which served both to thin and shape the preform. This technique may have combined pressure and indirect percussion in the flaking process which also may have been used for resharpening.

Age and Cultural Affiliation
Kessell Side Notched points are diagnostic of the Early Archaic period. A radiocarbon date from a hearth with an associated Kessell point yielded a date of 7900 B.C. ±500 at the St. Albans site in West Virginia (Broyles 1966: 19). A single Kessell point was recovered from Early Archaic levels at the Longworth-Gick site in northern Kentucky (Collins 1979:560).

Distribution
The distribution of Kessell Side Notched is little known even in the greater portion of West Virginia, where the type was defined (Broyles 1966, 1971), yet it was present in both river valley and mountain top physiographies. Outside West Virginia, the literature indicates a low frequency distribution over a much larger area. Collections from southern Indiana and Ohio (Broyles 1971: 61) indicate the presence of the type in low numbers which is also the case for Kentucky as noted above. In addition, the type has

Map 25: Kessell Side Notched Distribution and Important Sites

been identified in western New York (Trubowitz 1979:55), which suggests a low density representation in the Northeast.

RADDATZ SIDE NOTCHED

Raddatz Side Notched points (Wittry 1959a: 44–46; 1959b:178; Perino 1971a:76) are distinctive U-shaped notched forms with squared ears (Figure 13). Raddatz points were manufactured from trianguloid preforms using percussion with pressure flaked margins. The blade shape varies considerably due to breakage and resharpening during the use-life of these tools. Pristine Raddatz blades vary from excurvate to nearly straightsided. The cross section is typically biconvex. The blade edges often converge markedly near the tip, forming a wide angle. Bifacial blade resharpening using pressure flaking is common; however, lateral edge beveling is a resharpening trait that is largely absent from Raddatz blades, although fine serration occurs in low frequency. Exhausted Raddatz forms occur in which the blade and shoulders have been totally reduced, leaving only the haft element, the neck of which may exhibit a distal bevel (i.e., hafted scraper).

The notches are typically placed perpendicular to the main axis of the blade and are nearly equal in all dimensions. Wittry's (1959a:46) sample measured 4 to 5 mm. in notch depth and width. The haft element exhibits a rectangular shape with squared ears and straight basal edge. Variation in the haft element includes slightly concave or convex edges and somewhat rounded basal ears. Raddatz points may exhibit flattened grinding facets on the basal edges and ears and also grinding in the notches. On some specimens, haft grinding may be minimal or absent.

The Raddatz type, based on definition and general usage, subsumes several named projectile point types that have appeared in the literature of the Midwest. These include Godar, Black Sand Notched, Faulkner Side Notched, and Brannon Side Notched. Each of these types exhibits a range of variation in side notching style, method manufacture, and dimensions that is comparable to Raddatz Side Notched. Other named side notched types have incorporated Raddatz forms in definition and general typological usage. For example, the Newton Falls Side Notched type describes large alternate beveled Thebes type points (Prufer and Sofsky 1965:24, Fig. 3d), but the definition also includes Raddatz type forms. In addition, the Big Sandy type name (Kneberg 1956:25) has been variously applied to Raddatz forms and side notched points generally within the Ohio Valley and elsewhere (see Lewis and Lewis 1961:38, Plate 7h, k-1; Broyles 1964:29, Fig. 15); however, the primary use of this term is reserved for Large Side Notched cluster forms which possess a range of haft and resharpening characteristics unlike those typical of Raddatz projectile points (see description of Big Sandy).

Age and Cultural Affiliation

Raddatz points are diagnostic of the Middle Archaic period. The major occupation at the stratified Raddatz Rock Shelter in Wisconsin is thought to date to about 4500 B.C. (level 12) (Wittry 1959a:60–61). Based on excavations at the Modoc Rock Shelter in Illinois (Fowler 1959) and Graham Cave in Missouri

(Logan 1952; Klippel 1971:29, Fig. 14c-d), Raddatz points are thought to have an age range from about 6000 to 3000 B.C. (Munson and Harn 1966: 150). In addition, pre–3000 B.C. placement was suggested by Fowler (1957b:7) for the heaviest concentrations of side notched Raddatz and earlier forms in a study of eight stratified multi-component archaeological sites, including the Parrish Village (Webb 1951) and Read Shell Midden (Webb 1950b) in Kentucky. Raddatz-like forms were more recently reported from stratified context at the Cherokee Sewer site in northwestern Iowa. These forms occurred in Horizons I and II at the site and were dated from ca. 6000 to 4000 B.C. (Anderson 1980:210, Anderson et al. 1980:262–263).

These forms have been recovered from mortuary context as funerary offerings. Perino (1963:96, Fig. 49) reported a cache of these points from the Godar site which possessed close continuity of manufacture and form and were oversized with wide blades, robust side notches, and fine serration (i.e., Godar points). This cache was used in the original description of the Godar type which is here considered within the range of variation of Raddatz Side Notched.

Distribution

Raddatz points are known to occur over the Midwest and a larger area including the Middle South (see Cook 1976:86). These forms are distributed in the East across southern Wisconsin (Wittry 1959a,b) and Michigan (Fitting 1970:70, Fig. 22,2), and occur throughout Indiana (Miller 1941; Dragoo 1959; Tomak et al. 1980:36–37, Plate 1; Munson 1976:42), Illinois (Winters 1963:25, Fig. 3k-p; Munson and Harn 1966; Conrad 1981:133, 146), Iowa (Anderson 1980), Missouri (Klippel 1971:27–29, Fig. 14c-d), and Ohio (Converse 1973:18; Prufer and Sofsky 1965:23–25, Fig. 3e-i). Raddatz points also occur in Kentucky (Webb 1950b:388, Fig. 7; 1951:428, 430, Figs. 5,6), Tennessee (Lewis and Lewis 1961: Plate 7), and West Virginia (Broyles 1964:Fig. 15). The type may extend further to the south and east. However, the distribution overlaps with side notched types such as Big Sandy (Kneberg 1956:25) and

Map 26: Raddatz Side Notched—Distribution and Important Sites

Otter Creek (Ritchie 1961:40, 97, Pláte 21,2). This basic projectile point form also occurs over much of the western Plains (Benedict and Olson 1978:165) represented by a host of named side notched variations.

Morphological Correlates
Big Sandy II (Kneberg 1956:8; Cook 1980: 360–364, 369, Plate 17.1); Black Sand Side Notched (Scully 1951; Montet-White 1968:99–100; Cook 1976:145); Brannon Side Notched (Cook 1976:171, Fig. 43); Faulkner Side Notched (Winters n.d., 1963:20–21; May 1982:1360, Plate 162); Four Mile (Tomak 1980b:4, Fig. 9); Godar Side Notched (Perino 1963:95, 1971a:38; Cook 1976:145, 168, Fig. 40; May 1982:1359–1360, Plate 162); Hickory Ridge (Morse 1981:11; Perino 1985: 181); Little Sioux (Morrow 1984); Robinson (Perino 1985:327); Savage Cave (Cambron 1974:210); Tama (Morrow 1984).

OSCEOLA

The Osceola type projectile point (Ritzenthaler 1946:63; Bell 1958:68) is typified by extreme blade length compared to other types in the Large Side Notched cluster (Fig-

ure 13). These forms exhibit large random percussion flake scars across the blade followed by finer marginal retouch. The blade shape varies from parallel-sided to trianguloid with the blade edges converging abruptly at the tip. Cross sections vary from flattened to biconvex. Side notches are deep and placed horizontal to the main axis of the blade. The form of the notch is similar to Raddatz and Godar forms, varying from U-shaped to squared. The basal edge varies from slightly concave to straight. The former basal attribute appears to be more characteristic, although it is weak in comparison to the Graham Cave Side Notched style. The basal ears are distinct.

The Hemphill type (Scully 1951:7; Perino 1971a:50) is a form with essentially the same attributes as those described for Osceola. These points are large. The blade margins are parallel over much of the length up from the shoulder. The blade edges then converge abruptly at the tip, forming an obtuse angle. Cross sections are biconvex. The Hemphill blade form sometimes exhibits a broadening toward the distal end beyond the shoulders, accentuating the obtuse angle formed at the tip.

Age and Cultural Affiliation

Osceola and Hemphill points are diagnostic of the Late Archaic and transitional Early Woodland periods dating from 2000 to 500 B.C. (Montet-White 1968:11; Reid 1984:77). The Osceola type is associated with the Old Copper culture of the Great Lakes area (Ritzenthaler 1946:62–65) and both forms have been aligned with the Red Ocher complex (Cole and Deuel 1937:58) and Titterington phase of the Illinois and lower Missouri Valleys (Titterington 1950; Perino 1954; Montet-White 1968:97–108; Reid 1984:80).

Bell (1958:68) cites radiocarbon dates ranging from 5000 to 3000 B.C. (Libby 1954:740), obtained from the Oconto site in Wisconsin, in his discussion of the Osceola type. However, these dates are too early for Osceola points. In fact, Ritzenthaler and Wittry (1952:210–211) observe that the few points found at the site are not characteristic Osceola points. These are short-bladed and generally small side notched forms, and one exhibits a reworked blade. Overall, the Oconto projectile points exhibit attributes more typical of Raddatz type points. The earliest accepted radiocarbon date for Osceola/Hemphill is 1500 B.C. ±250 (Reid 1984: Table 14).

Interestingly, the Hemphill site produced one Hemphill point, and possibly another (side-notched Ogival blade), associated with an unusual array of copper celts and a 24-pound nodule of raw copper among other articles (Montet-White 1968:100; Griffin 1941:200–206). A number of Osceola/Hemphill points have been reported from hilltop caches and mortuary sites in the Nebo Hill region of Missouri (see Reid 1984).

Distribution

The Osceola and Hemphill occur in a core distribution area that includes Wisconsin (Ritzenthaler 1946; 1967), the lower Illinois Valley in Illinois (Titterington 1950:19–30; Perino 1971a:50), and portions of Iowa (Anderson 1981:19), Missouri, Arkansas, Kansas, and adjacent areas bordering the Lower Missouri River Valley (Reid 1984:80–81). These forms are also present in low frequency in Indiana and possibly in other areas. The name Osceola has been used to the south in Alabama (Cambron 1959; Cambron and Hulse 1975), but typological and morphological considerations suggest that these Alabama specimens are simply pristine examples of the Big Sandy type rather than Osceola (see discussion of Big Sandy).

Map 27: Osceola—Distribution and Important Sites

Morphological Correlate
Hemphill (Scully 1951; Perino 1971a).

Morphological Correlates of the
Large Side Notched Cluster
Accokeek (Van Buren 1974:121); Archaic Side Notched (Converse 1973:18); Cache River (Cloud 1969:119; Perino 1971a:14); Cairo Side Notched (Winters n.d.); Faulkner Side Notched (MacNeish 1948:236– 237, Fig. 47; Winters 1963:19, Fig. 3; Fowler 1959a: 36–37; Denny 1972:140, Fig. 21); Madison Side Notched (Baerreis 1953); Ritzenthaler 1967:26); Newton Falls Side Notched (Prufer and Sofsky 1965:23–25, Fig. 3e–j only); Wolf Creek (Morrow 1984). Additional type: Otter Creek (Ritchie 1961:40–41, 1971, 1979; Funk 1977a:21, 24).

Kirk Corner Notched Cluster

KIRK CORNER NOTCHED

The Kirk Corner Notched type (Coe 1964: 69–70) exhibits a large triangular blade with a straight or slightly rounded base and bi-facially serrated blade edges (Figure 14). The blade edges are occasionally beveled, but basal grinding is absent. Broyles (1971) differentiates between a large and small variety of Kirk Corner Notched. The general description provided by Coe (1964) for Kirk Corner Notched is the same as the large variety Kirk described by Broyles (1971:65). In addition, Broyles observes that the faces of the blades are covered with random, wide, thinning flake scars resulting in a flattened cross section that lacks a median ridge. The shoulders are wide and definite, and most examples exhibit barbs projecting downward toward the base. The Kirk Corner Notched type lacks the degree of blade variation from resharpening characteristic of such forms as the Charleston, Pine Tree, and Palmer types, but blades become shorter from this process.

The general use of the term Cypress Creek (Lewis and Kneberg 1960:49) has implied a gross morphological similarity to the Kirk Corner Notched type. Lewis and Lewis (1961) subdivided Cypress Creek into two types (I & II). Cypress Creek I occurred early in the deposits at the Eva Site and has been correlated with Lost Lake in the Thebes cluster (Schock and Langford 1979b:7). However, Cypress Creek II correlates with Kirk Corner Notched as defined.

Age and Cultural Affiliation
The Kirk Corner Notched projectile point type is diagnostic of the Early Archaic Kirk horizon (Tuck 1974:76). The Kirk Corner Notched cluster is dated within a range from 7500 to 6900 B.C. (J. Chapman 1976:9; 1977: 166). The Palmer type was demonstrated to be ancestral to Kirk Corner Notched at the Hardaway site in North Carolina (Coe 1964: 70). Subsequent excavations at the St. Albans site in West Virginia (Broyles 1964, 1971:65) and Ice House Bottom in Tennessee (J. Chapman 1977:162) have also shown this to be true. Two dates from the lower deposits at St. Albans of 6900 B.C. ±320 and 6850 B.C. ±320 relate to the large variety of Kirk Corner Notched (Broyles 1971:65).

Dates ranging from 5570 to 5100 B.C. from Sheep Rock Shelter (Michels and Smith 1967), Harry's Farm (Kraft 1975), and a few other sites in the Northeast have been obtained for Kirk Corner Notched and Stemmed forms. General consensus suggests there is no large time gap between the appearance of Kirk type points in the Southeast and Northeast and that these latter dates are probably too recent (Funk 1977a:23).

A unique Kirk mortuary site was recently investigated in Kentucky. The Lawrence site located in the Tennessee-Cumberland River Valley area produced Kirk Corner Notched and Stemmed projectile points, along with a variety of other Kirk Corner Notched cluster types and other forms, in clear mortuary contexts (Mocas 1977). Unfortunately, the radiocarbon dates from the site fall within the latter range of dates for the Kirk Corner Notched discussed above (Mocas 1977:129; Driskell et al. 1979:21). Analysis of data from the site is providing insights into the little known Early Archaic mortuary ceremonialism (Mocas and Smith n.d.).

Distribution

Kirk Corner Notched projectile points, including the large and small (Palmer) varieties, occur over most of the eastern United States and are recognized in almost every region (Tuck 1974:77). These types occur well into the Northeast from New York (Ritchie and Funk 1971; Funk 1977a:21–23) to Maine (Tuck 1974:76) and Pennsylvania (Michels and Smith 1967:18). They are common occurrences across Indiana (Tomak 1970; Reidhead and Limp 1974:10), Ohio (Smith 1960:97; Converse 1973:40), and much of Illinois (Fowler 1957a:11, Fig. 5; Conrad 1981:113; Springer et al. 1978:292). Kirk Corner Notched forms also occur in southern Ontario (Roberts 1980:32, Plates 3 and 4) and are reported in Michigan (Fitting et al. n.d.); however, their presence in Wisconsin may be limited, as there seems to be a paucity of this material in the western Great Lakes. In most areas west of the Mississippi River, Kirk Corner Notched cluster projectile points are rare, although these points are apparently present in the Table Rock Reservoir of Missouri (Bray 1956:82, Fig. 21–row 3), and they occur in east Texas and Oklahoma (c.f. Webb et al. 1971:Fig. 5; Perino 1985:286).

Kirk Corner Notched cluster projectile points are ubiquitous across the southeastern United States to the tidewater region of the coast (Phelps and Widner 1981). Besides those areas already mentioned with the outlined stratigraphy of Kirk Corner Notched, these types are well represented in Kentucky (Weinland and Fenwick 1978:201; Boisvert et al. 1979:148), Alabama (Griffin 1974), Georgia (Coe 1964:67; Tuck 1974:77), South Carolina (Lee and Parker 1972:110), northern Florida (Bullen 1968), and Virginia (Holland 1970).

Morphological Correlates

Cypress Creek II (Lewis and Lewis 1961:41, Plate 9j–k, only); Kirk Corner Notched (large variety) (Broyles 1966:21, 1971:65).

STILWELL

Stilwell projectile points were named and described by Perino (1970:119–121). These points are similar to Kirk Corner Notched. Perino's (1970) description for Stilwell emphasizes a concave base with the relative exclusion of any other basal configuration (Figure 14). However, Stilwell differs from Kirk clearly in terms of haft morphology.

Figure 14: Kirk Corner Notched Cluster
a. Kirk Corner Notched. Wyandotte chert. GBL 14/836. Blackford Co., Indiana.
b. Kirk Corner Notched. Wyandotte chert. GBL 5/248. Warrick Co., Indiana.
c. Kirk Corner Notched. Wyandotte chert. Provenience unknown.
d. Kirk Corner Notched. Holland chert. GBL 21/393. Indiana.
e. Kirk Corner Notched. Wyandotte chert. GBL 1448/411. Southwestern Indiana.
f. Kirk Corner Notched. Wyandotte chert. GBL 119/891. Provenience unknown.
g. Stilwell. Burlington chert. GBL 14/823. Indiana. Pictured in Plate 4, l.
h. Stilwell. Wyandotte chert. GBL 421/185. Morgan Co., Indiana.
i–j. Palmer Corner Notched. Unidentified cherts. GBL 422/99. Dearborn Co., Indiana.
k. Pine Tree Corner Notched. Wyandotte chert. GBL 119/891. Provenience unknown. Pictured in Plate 4, k.
l. Pine Tree Corner Notched. Unidentified chert. GBL 482/257. Indiana.
m. Charleston Corner Notched. Wyandotte chert. GBL 119/891–2. Provenience unknown. Pictured in Plate 4, c.
n. Charleston Corner Notched. Unidentified chert. GBL 421/256. Henry Co., Indiana.
o. Decatur. Fractured (burinated) base. Wyandotte chert. GBL 1448/396. Southwestern Indiana.
p. Decatur. Fractured (burinated) base. Indian Creek chert. GBL 3921/1. Site 12 Mo 702. Monroe Co., Indiana. Pictured in Plate 4, n.
q. Decatur. Bevel resharpening. Attica chert. GBL 809/8. Site 12 Vi 48. Vigo Co., Indiana.
r. Decatur. Fractured (burinated) base. Wyandotte chert. GBL 21/393. Indiana.

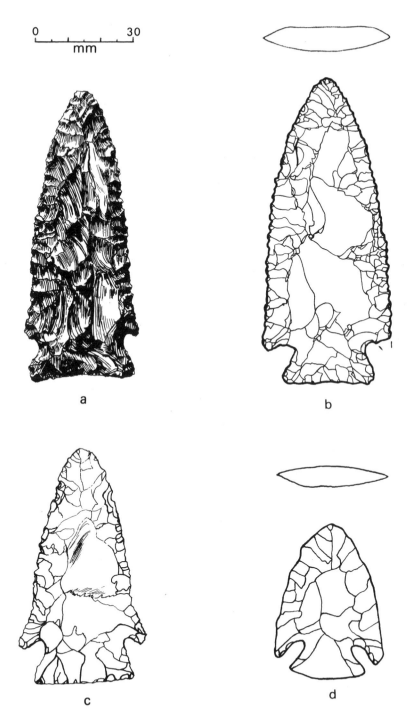

0   30
mm

a

b

c

d

Figure 14
Kirk Corner Notched Cluster

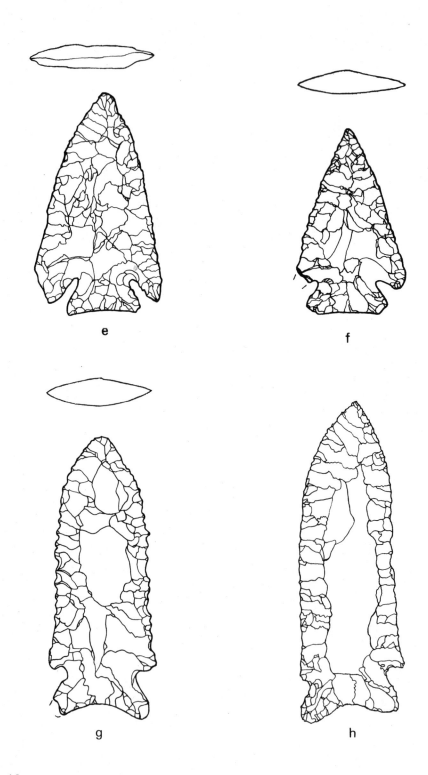

e

f

g

h

Figure 14

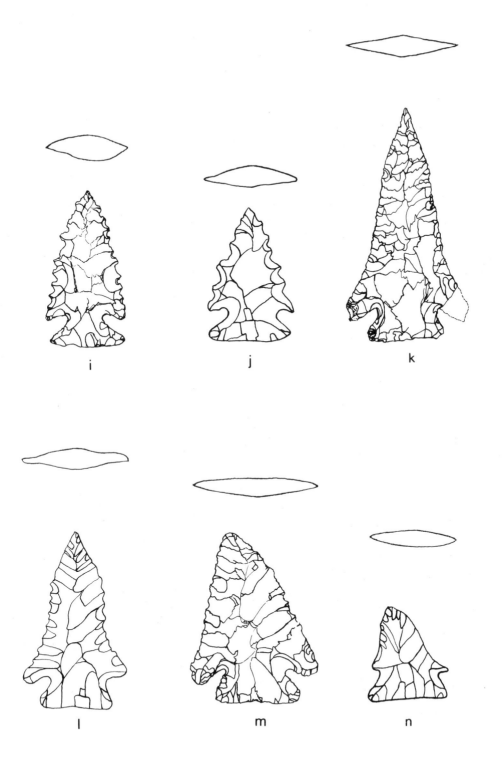

Figure 14

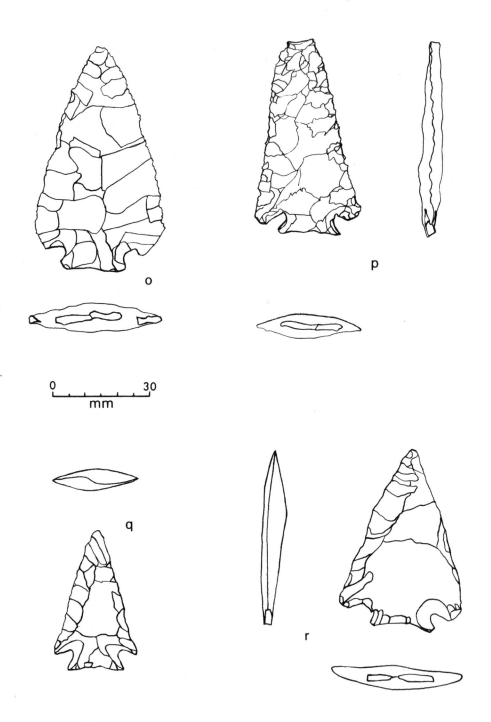

o

p

q

r

0 [|||] 30
mm

Figure 14

Map 28: Kirk Corner Notched—Distribution and Important Sites

This type exhibits a deep concave base. In addition, Stilwell blades tend to be elongated and parallel-sided, which differs from the trianguloid and convergent-sided morphology of Kirk Corner Notched. Stilwell blades are also slightly incurving near the shoulder, resulting in expansion of the barbs. Large, random, thinning flake scars are present on the blade face, producing a lenticular cross section. Basal thinning scars often terminate at the shoulder/haft juncture with light basal grinding and rounding of the basal ears.

Age and Cultural Affiliation

These projectile points are not accompanied by specific radiocarbon dates, although they are clearly Early Archaic and related to Kirk Corner Notched. The Kirk Corner Notched cluster is dated from 7500 to 6900 B.C. (J. Chapman 1976:9).

Distribution

Perino (1971a:94) indicates that these points occur in low frequency in central Illinois, Missouri, and Indiana. In a few cases this type is also represented in collections in Kentucky and Ohio. Stilwell points are represented along with Kirk Corner Notched and

Map 29: Stilwell—Distribution and Important Sites

related materials at the Butterfield shell heap in McLean County, Kentucky (Webb and Haag 1947:35, Fig. 10a), and comparable specimens are known to occur in Ohio (Converse 1973:40).

PALMER CORNER NOTCHED

The Palmer Corner Notched projectile point (Coe 1959, 1964:67) is a small corner notched form with a straight, ground base and pronounced serrations (Figure 14). The cross section is biconvex and the shoulders are barbed. Palmer Corner Notched points typically exhibit bifacial pressure flaking across the blade that relates both to manufacturing and resharpening processes. Shoulder width varies from being greater to less than basal width, and the blade edges tend to be straight but may vary slightly from incurvate to excurvate. Most examples are serrated. The basal edge may be slightly concave or convex and is thinned and heavily ground.

The Palmer Corner Notched type is also known in the literature as Kirk Corner Notched (small variety). Broyles's (1966:19, 1971:63) and J. Chapman's (1977:43–49) descriptions contain the essential characteristics described for Palmer, including the range of variability in blade form, resharpening characteristics, and haft variability. The only observed morphological difference is the heavy basal grinding typical of Palmer.

J. Chapman (1977:53) has shown that this basal treatment varies between each of the types in the Kirk Corner Notched cluster and this alone is not a significant criterion for recognizing them.

Age and Cultural Affiliation

This projectile point style is diagnostic of the Early Archaic Kirk horizon dating from about 7500 to 6900 B.C. (J. Chapman 1977; Tuck 1974). Palmer Corner Notched and the larger Kirk Corner Notched varieties occur early in the Kirk horizon preceding Kirk Stemmed. A date of 7410 B.C. ±120 for three Palmer points derived from a hearth at the Richmond Hill site in New York (Ritchie and Funk 1973:39) suggests a wide distribution within a relatively short time span. The Kirk Corner Notched (small variety) occurs prior to the large variety Kirk Corner Notched at the St. Albans site in West Virginia (Broyles 1971:63), at Ice House Bottom in Tennessee (J. Chapman 1977:162), and at the Hardaway site (Palmer) in North Carolina (Coe 1964:70). Both St. Albans and Ice House Bottom indicate that all of the named Kirk types, including Palmer, occur in the Kirk sequence later than Charleston Corner Notched

Map 30: Palmer—Distribution and Important Sites

(Broyles 1971:56–57; J. Chapman 1977:51–53). Lost Lake and Plevna are two types in the Thebes cluster which also occur earlier than Palmer and other Kirk Corner Notched types at Ice House Bottom.

Distribution
See Kirk Corner Notched.

Morphological Correlates
Cypress Creek II (Lewis and Lewis 1961:37, 40–41, Plate 9g–h, 1, only); Kirk Corner Notched (small variety) (Broyles 1966:19, 1971:63, J. Chapman 1977:43–49).

CHARLESTON CORNER NOTCHED

These corner notched points (Broyles 1971: 56) are recognized primarily by the lopsided appearance of the blade (Figure 14), which is probably due to extensive blade resharpening. Both oblique and random pressure flaking are exhibited. The base of Charleston Corner Notched points are thinned with several small flakes, and the notches are formed by removal of sizeable flakes leaving circular scars or hertzian cones of force on the terminus of each notch. Corner notch dimensions on ten specimens studied by Broyles (1971) range from 5 to 8 mm. wide and 4 to 8 mm. deep. Grinding occurs only across the basal edge. Ears are slightly rounded and the base varies from flat to convex.

Broyles (1971:57) observes differences between the Charleston Corner Notched and the related and morphologically similar Pine Tree Corner Notched type. She notes that the former is generally wider and exhibits a shorter blade, but that in terms of thickness, they are about the same. Charleston Corner Notched points were originally classified with Pine Tree (see Cambron 1957).

Age and Cultural Affiliation
These points are diagnostic of the Early Archaic period. A date of 7900 B.C. ± 500 years was obtained from a hearth in zone 36 at the St. Albans site. Two Charleston Corner

Map 31: Charleston Corner Notched
Distribution and Important Sites

Notched points were situated on top of this dated hearth (Broyles 1966:18, 1971:56). This type also occurred in the lowest levels at Ice House Bottom in Tennessee, where the type predates Kirk Corner Notched as it does at St. Albans (J. Chapman 1977:51).

Distribution
Kanawha and Boone counties in West Virginia present an area of concentration of these points (Broyles 1971:57). The Charleston Corner Notched also occurs in a much broader area, as they appear on sites in the Tennessee River Valley in Tennessee (J. Chapman 1977) and Alabama (Cambron and Hulse 1969), and within the Ohio Valley. These points occur over much of southern Indiana, at least as far north as the Patoka River Valley (Tomak 1980b:2; Cook 1980:377).

PINE TREE CORNER NOTCHED

The Pine Tree Corner Notched projectile point type is essentially a resharpening vari-

ant of Kirk Corner Notched. The name origi-
nates from the Pine Tree site in Alabama
(Cambron 1956, 1957). The following discussion includes the Pine Tree and Pine Tree
Corner Notched types described by Cambron and Hulse (1969:95–96; 1975:104–
105). These simply reflect degrees of blade
resharpening.

Pine Tree Corner Notched points generally
resemble the Kirk Corner Notched style in
the haft region. However, the thin cross section and highly refined and variable blade
morphology are distinctive (Figure 14).
Many reworked Kirk blades tend toward
shortening of the overall length, but Pine
Tree points exhibit blade length maintenance and greater width reduction. The cutting edge is commonly serrated and was
produced using a pressure flaking technique.
The resulting flake scars are long, regularly
spaced, and join at the midpoint to form collateral and horizontal transverse flaking patterns. Near the tip of these points may be an
angle along the blade, above which it forms
a straight edge and converges to the tip.
Overall, blade edges are incurvate, especially
just above the shoulder. Certain heavily resharpened specimens nearly lack a shoulder/
haft juncture (i.e., Pine Tree), in which case
the base appears to expand and broaden
down and outward beyond the shoulder. The
base on these points is always thinned, often
exhibiting thinning scars which terminate
above the notch. The basal edge is characteristically straight, although slightly convex
edges are not uncommon and basal grinding
is present.

Age and Cultural Affiliation
These points are diagnostic of the Early Archaic period. Chapman's (1977:41) Kirk Corner Notched specimens recovered from the
Ice House Bottom site include the Pine Tree
type discussed here. Radiocarbon dates from
Rose Island (J. Chapman 1975) and Ice
House Bottom for the Kirk Corner Notched
cluster type projectile points range from
about 7500 to 6900 B.C. (J. Chapman 1977:
166). The Pine Tree type may endure throughout this time period.

Map 32: Pine Tree Corner Notched
Distribution and Important Sites

Distribution
Because Pine Tree is viewed as a resharpening variant of Kirk Corner Notched (large variety) and Charleston Corner Notched, the
type has not been given great attention in the
literature. Hence the distribution of the type
is not fully understood within the wide distribution for Kirk Corner Notched. Nonetheless, the type has been recognized
within a fairly large area including Alabama
(Cambron and Hulse 1969:96; Ingmanson
and Griffin 1974:42, Fig. 28n), Tennessee
(J. Chapman 1975:117–118, 1977:41), Kentucky (Schock and Langford 1979b:35, Plate
9a–c), North Carolina (Coe 1964:71, Fig.
60a), West Virginia (Broyles 1971:57, Fig. 2),
Ohio (Converse 1973:22), and Indiana
(Cook 1980:401, Plate 17.5h–i).

Morphological Correlates
Corner Notched Serrated Points (Converse
1973:22); Pine Tree (Cambron 1956;
Cambron and Hulse 1969:95, 1975:104).

DECATUR

Decatur projectile points (Cambron 1957:17) are trianguloid, corner notched forms with the basal edge flattened by the use of a burin flaking technique to finish the base (Figure 14). The flaking and resharpening patterns on the blades of Decatur points follow those described for Kirk Corner Notched and Pine Tree Corner Notched. Alternate beveling of the blade edges and/or serration are typical resharpening attributes. The unique basal treatment of Decatur is the most characteristic trait of these points. The application of a burin technique was first accomplished by producing an indention at the center of the base to provide a stop for the subsequent burin spall detachments. The basal corners were prepared as a platform from which to detach a burin spall from each corner. Some examples exhibit burins along the edge of the haft directed toward the shoulder/haft juncture as well as along the basal edge. Basal grinding may also be seen on certain specimens. Sometimes this grinding nearly obliterates the burin facets. A number of authors have discussed this basal finishing technique (Cambron and Hulse 1969:87; Converse 1971:9; Winsch 1971:30; J. Chapman 1977:49).

Age and Cultural Affiliation
Decatur projectile points are diagnostic of the Early Archaic period. Cambron and Waters (1959:83) recovered two such points stratigraphically above the Quad level at the Flint Creek Rock Shelter in Alabama. The type has also been recovered in early contexts at other sites such as Ice House Bottom in Tennessee. Here, Decatur points were found within stratum 21, and an age of 7500 to 7000 B.C. was secured for the type (J. Chapman 1973, 1977:49).

Distribution
Decatur type projectile points are distributed primarily in the Southeast and Midwest regions. These forms have been recovered from a number of sites in the Tennessee Valley in northern Alabama (Cambron 1957:17; Cambron and Waters 1959:83), and Tennessee. The type occurs in low frequency in Kentucky (Boisvert et al. 1979:218) and occurs across much of Indiana (Tomak 1970:62) and Ohio (Geistweit 1970:113). The type is recognized north into Michigan (Fitting et al. n.d.:5) and Illinois. In west-central Illinois, Conrad (1981:62; pers. comm.) has recognized a form named Neuberger which represents a variation of the Decatur and Kirk Corner Notched types.

Morphological Correlates
Fractured Base Points (Converse 1973:20).

Morphological Correlates of the Kirk Corner Notched Cluster
Abbott (McNett 1985:106–107); Amos Corner Notched (Broyles 1971:55); Autauga (Cambron and Hulse 1969:7; J. Chapman 1977:44); Barbee Corner Notched (Winters n.d., 1963:Fig. 3; May 1982:1357); Broadhead Side Notched (McNett 1985:103–105); Bynum (Tomak (1980b:4, Fig. 8); Church Hill (Sanders 1980:64–66. This type definition

Map 33: Decatur—Distribution and Important Sites

overlaps with the Kirk Stemmed type); Harpeth River (Cambron 1970:15–18); Harpeth River Rockport variety (Adair and Sims 1970: 23–29. Certain specimens of this class may overlap with the Thebes cluster [e.g., Lost Lake]; Little River (Schock et al. 1977:29–30, Plate 1); Neuberger (Conrad 1981:62, 71, 114, 117; pers. comm.); Pulaski (Winters n.d., pers. comm.; Holland 1970:91; Conrad 1981: 73, 81–82. This designation overlaps with the Thebes cluster); Rice Lobed (Bray 1956:Fig. 21, row 3 only); San Patrice Keithville variety (Webb, Shiner, and Roberts 1971:15–17, 49; Perino 1985:339).

Kirk Stemmed Cluster

KIRK STEMMED

The Kirk Stemmed type (Coe 1964:70) is a broad stemmed form with a long blade which may exhibit deep serrations (Figure 15). The blade form is long, narrow, and may be thick. A combination of serration and recurvature on the blade edges is indicative of heavy resharpening. Blade edge beveling is also sometimes present. The basal edge varies from straight or slightly convex to concave. The haft element on Kirk Stemmed was produced using a corner notching technique which formed a broad notch opening and slight expanding stem. The notching technique also sometimes left shoulders which project downward in barb-like fashion.

Coe (1964) considered the overall technique of manufacture to be the same as that described for Kirk Corner Notched, but stylistically Kirk Stemmed was thought to be intermediate between Kirk Corner Notched and Kirk Serrated. Broyles's (1966:21, 1971:67) description of Kirk Stemmed does not distinguish between the Kirk Stemmed and Serrated types. This combination of the two type definitions is typical. However, the recognition of a technological tie of Kirk Stemmed to Kirk Corner Notched is an important observation and should be taken into account. The Church Hill type defined by Sanders and Maynard (1979) exhibits this variation from Kirk Corner Notched to Kirk Stemmed.

KIRK SERRATED

Kirk Serrated points (Coe 1964:70; Cambron and Hulse 1969:63) are similar to the Kirk Stemmed, although the haft element is generally straight sided or slightly contracting (Figure 15). The base varies from straight and blunt to thin and concave. The type exhibits a plano-convex and/or biconvex cross section and the shoulders are usually horizontal and may appear slightly barbed due to deep serration on the lower portion of the blade. The robust serration common to these points often distorts the symmetry of the blade contour in the reworking process. The basal edge is thinned and may be straight or concave.

Age and Cultural Affiliation
Both types of projectile points are considered to be diagnostic of the Early Archaic pe-

Figure 15: Kirk Stemmed Cluster
a. Kirk Stemmed. Muldraugh chert. GBL 119/ 890. Provenience unknown.
b. Kirk Stemmed. Unidentified chert. GBL 1448/453. Provenience unknown.
c. Kirk Serrated. Muldraugh chert. GBL 119/ 891. Provenience unknown.
d. Kirk Serrated. Wyandotte chert. GBL 5/239. Warrick Co., Indiana.
e. Kirk Serrated. Muldraugh chert. GBL 285/ 22–1. Clark Co., Indiana. Pictured in Plate 4, e.
f. Kirk Stemmed. Wyandotte chert. GBL 285/ 22. Clark Co., Indiana.

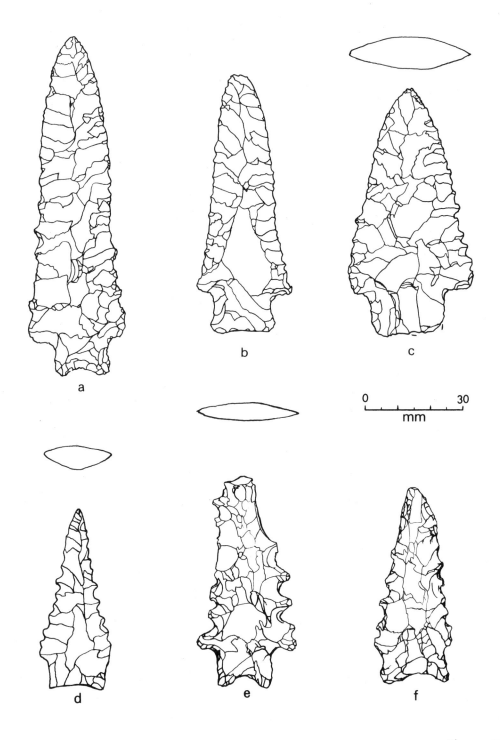

Figure 15
Kirk Stemmed Cluster

riod and date within a range of ca. 6900 to 6000 B.C. Based on the cultural sequence at the Hardaway site, Coe (1964) observed that Kirk Serrated may occur somewhat later than Kirk Stemmed. An age of 6800 B.C. was assigned to these forms at the St. Albans site in West Virginia (Broyles 1971:67), although few specimens were recovered. These were dispersed in the deposits, some in the Kirk zones and others with later Stanly forms. Additional information on the longevity of this stemmed group is derived from Ice House Bottom and the other sites in the Little Tennessee River Valley. At these sites, Kirk Serrated appears to postdate the LeCroy type which is dated to 6300 B.C. (J. Chapman 1975, 1977:166–167) and is dated somewhat earlier than Stanly Stemmed. A similar situation occurred at Russell Cave in Alabama (Griffin 1974:96) and elsewhere (Faulkner and Graham 1966:68–69). Hidden Valley Stemmed, a separate but related type, occurred in early levels (zone 1) at Modoc Rock Shelter in Illinois (Fowler 1959a:Fig. 9e). The later age estimate for zone 1 at the site is 6000 B.C. (Fowler 1959b:258).

Further work at additional stratified sites should better secure the chronological placement of these projectile points. Especially needed is a thorough technological analysis which may discriminate variations of this stemmed group and link certain materials to a wider range of variation of LeCroy and Stanly Stemmed and possibly other types.

Distribution

The Kirk Stemmed and Serrated types are represented over a large territory covering most of the eastern United States (Tuck 1974). The Kirk Serrated type appears to occur more frequently, but the term is often used to refer to both defined types. These types occur in northern Florida (Purdy 1981b), Georgia (Tuck 1974:77), Alabama (Ingmanson and Griffin 1974:43, Fig. 29), Virginia (Gardner ed. 1974), West Virginia (Broyles 1971:67), North Carolina (Coe 1964), Tennessee (Lewis and Lewis 1961:40; Faulkner 1968), Kentucky (Broyles 1969:33;

Map 34: Kirk Stemmed and Kirk Serrated Distribution and Important Sites

Weinland 1980:74, Fig. 31), Ohio (Smith 1960; Prufer 1975b: Fig. 2), Indiana (Tomak 1980b:2; Seeman 1975), and Illinois (Fowler 1957a:11, Fig. 5; 1959b:263, Fig. 2e; May 1983). These forms occur infrequently in the Northeast (Turnbaugh 1980:65, Fig. 4; Dincauze 1976:35, Plate 8,a; Funk 1977b:327, Fig. 9). They also occur in Michigan (Fitting el al. n.d.:7). These types are not well represented west of the Mississippi River.

In Missouri, Kirk Stemmed and Serrated points appear to be classified within the Jakie Stemmed type (McMillan 1965; Jolly and Roberts 1974:72, Fig. 40j; C. Chapman 1975: 174, Fig. 7–14a). Hidden Valley Stemmed, Searcy or Rice Lanceolate, and certain forms classified as Rice Contracting Stemmed are additional projectile point styles that also occur in the Early to Middle Archaic sequence in Missouri and Arkansas. These appear to be related in certain respects to a manufacturing and use trajectory similar to that recognized for Kirk Stemmed and Serrated (Perino 1968a:84; Carl H. Chapman, pers. comm.). These are thought to represent regional variants of a spacially broad early stemmed technology which includes Kirk Stemmed forms. Searcy or Rice Lanceolate, on the other hand, commonly exhibit excurvate blades and an overall lanceolate shape. These points may exhibit minimal or no shoulders, which is somewhat suggestive of Plains lanceolate types (cf. Ahler and McMillan 1976:168–169, Figs. 10.1–2; Jolly 1974: 176–177, Figs. 102–103), while incorporating beveling and/or serration as resharpening traits. Since the manufacturing and resharpening sequences of these types have not been elucidated, further research in Missouri and Arkansas should address the technological relationships of these projectile point types and the variations of Kirk Stemmed and Serrated.

Morphological Correlate
Heavy Duty Serrated Points (Converse 1973:20).

Morphological Correlates of the Kirk Stemmed Cluster
Church Hill (Sanders and Maynard 1979; Sanders 1980:64–66. This type definition overlaps with the Kirk Corner Notched type); Jakie Stemmed (Jolly and Roberts 1974:72, Fig. 40j only); C. Chapman (1975:174, Fig. 7–14a only); Jessup (Tomak 1980b:2, Figs. 4–5). Additional types: Hidden Valley Stemmed (Scully 1951:5; Fowler 1959a:Fig. 9e; C. Chapman 1975:250); Rice Lanceolate (Bray 1956:81, Fig. 20 row 1); Chapman (1975:253); Searcy (Dickson 1968:5–7; Perino 1968a:84).

Rice Lobed Cluster

RICE LOBED

Rice Lobed projectile points (Bray 1956:128; Perino 1968a:76; C. Chapman 1975:254) exhibit a concave base or wide basal notch (bifurcation) in conjunction with distinct and rounded basal ears. The haft element is produced using a wide corner notching technique which, in combination with the basal indentation, gives the typical lobed appearance. The shoulders of Rice Lobed are always prominent and often end in barbs. All angles on these forms are rounded except for the tips of the barbs. The blade edges are typically resharpened with beveling and serration and vary from excurvate to incurvate. The flaking pattern on the blade exhibits large percussion flake scars across the face. The above description relates essentially to the description provided by Broyles (1971: 71) for MacCorkle Stemmed projectile

points. However, Rice Lobed points are thick-bladed and typically beveled (Figure 16).

Bray's original description of Rice Lobed (1956:82 Fig. 21 row 3) includes corner notched forms with weakly concave bases which are recognized elsewhere in the manual as Kirk Corner Notched (large variety) projectile points.

Age and Cultural Affiliation
These forms are diagnostic of the Early Archaic period dating from about 7500 to 6500 B.C. Rice Lobed projectile points were recovered from the earliest levels at the Rice site, where they appeared within the Dalton horizon along with Kirk Corner Notched type points (Bray 1956; C. Chapman 1975). The Rodgers Shelter also produced these points in the lowest levels (Wood and McMillan 1967; Ahler 1971). The manufacturing characteristics of Rice Lobed, in addition to

Map 35: Rice Lobed—Distribution and Important Sites

the bevel resharpening trait, suggest some relationship with Thebes cluster types, especially the Thebes type (Perino 1985:322), which may well have given rise to Rice Lobed.

Distribution
While bifurcated base projectile points occur over a large area of the East, Rice Lobed is more restricted in space. The vast majority of these forms occur in Missouri (Adams 1950; C. Chapman 1956, 1975), Arkansas (Perino 1968a), and the Ozark Highlands of Oklahoma (Baerreis 1951). This type's distribution overlaps that of MacCorkle stemmed, as it occurs east in low frequency into Indiana.

Morphological Correlates
Rice Lobed (category CN8) (Bray 1956:87, 128, Fig. 21, row 4); Rice Points (Perino 1968a:76); Schoonover (Schoonover 1960).

MACCORKLE STEMMED

MacCorkle Stemmed points (Broyles 1966: 23; 1971:71) are large basal notched or bifurcated base forms. The basal ears are large and rounded, which gives the type a lobed appearance (Figure 16). The bifurcation is typically edge-retouched on one face and bears a large hertzian cone flake scar on the opposite face. Basal grinding is heavy across the haft region on MacCorkle points.

The pristine blade form of these points ex-

Figure 16: Rice Lobed Cluster
a. MacCorkle Stemmed. Wyandotte chert. GBL 14/823. Indiana.
b. MacCorkle Stemmed. Wyandotte chert. GBL 1448/174. Southwestern Indiana.
c. MacCorkle Stemmed. Wyandotte chert. GBL 281/264. Franklin Co., Indiana.
d. MacCorkle Stemmed. Unidentified chert. GBL 1448/192. Southwestern Indiana.
e. Rice Lobed. Wyandotte chert. GBL 14/859. Delaware Co., Indiana.
f. St. Albans Side Notched. Unidentified chert. GBL 14/828. Central Indiana.
g. St. Albans Side Notched. Wyandotte chert. GBL 119/891. Provenience unknown.
h. St. Albans Side Notched. Upper Mercer chert. GBL 3117/17. Allen Co., Indiana.
i. St. Albans Side Notched. Liston Creek chert. GBL 31/100. Fulton Co., Indiana.
j. St. Albans Side Notched. Exhibits impact fracture at tip. Upper Mercer chert. GBL 3117/11. Allen Co., Indiana.
k. St. Albans Side Notched. Wyandotte chert. GBL 119/891. Provenience unknown.

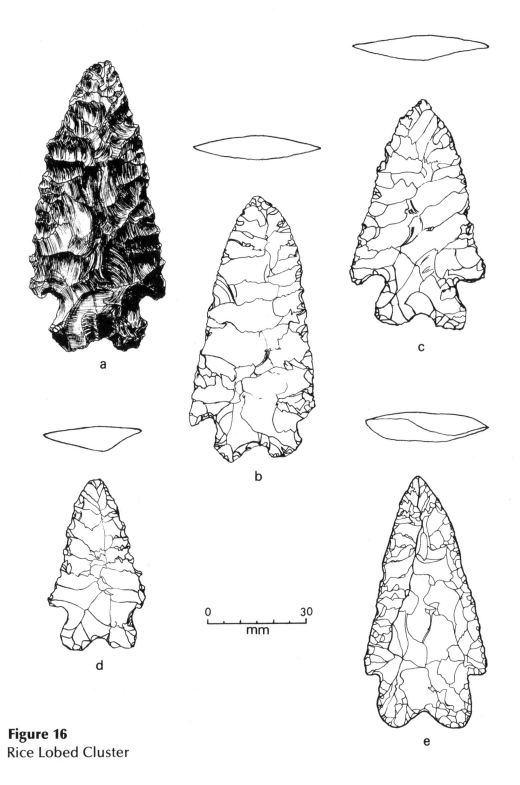

Figure 16
Rice Lobed Cluster

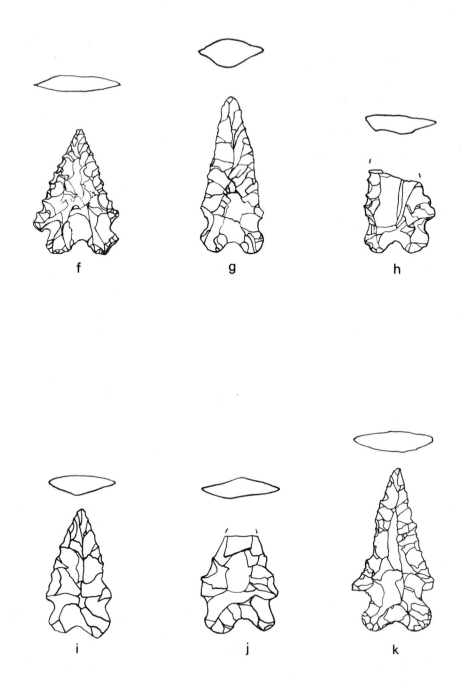

Figure 16

hibits a flattened cross section with large random flake scars. After reworking, the blade shape varies from excurvate to triangular to recurvate. These forms appear to combine controlled percussion for preform thinning and blade edge rejuvenation, judging from characteristics observed on many resharpened specimens. Heavily reworked specimens commonly exhibit serration and long narrow flake scars which erase a portion or all of the original flake scars on the blade.

Age and Cultural Affiliation
MacCorkle Stemmed projectile points are diagnostic of the Early Archaic period MacCorkle phase (J. Chapman 1976:6) dating from ca. 7000 to 6500 B.C. Broyles (1971:71) recovered MacCorkle points within Zone 14 at the St. Albans site. This position is stratigraphically transitional between the later St. Albans Side Notched and the older Kirk Corner Notched type. MacCorkle points are thought to be ancestral to St. Albans. Dates for St. Albans at the Rose Island site in Tennessee averaged 6770 B.C. (J. Chapman 1975, 1977:166).

The Jerger site located in southwestern Indiana features MacCorkle (Jerger) projectile points in an Early Archaic mortuary context. Cremation burials and artifacts were associated with use of red ocher and marine shell (Tomak 1979). This is apparently the first of its kind to be reported for the MacCorkle phase.

Distribution
MacCorkle Stemmed forms are widespread in the eastern United States. This projectile point style is recorded in Alabama (Cambron and Hulse 1965, 1969), West Virginia (Broyles 1971), Virginia (McCary 1955; Holland 1970), Tennessee (J. Chapman 1975) and Kentucky (Schock and Langford 1979b). These forms are well represented in the Midwest in Indiana (Guendling and Crouch 1977), Ohio (Prufer 1975b; Geistweit 1970; Converse 1973), Illinois (Conrad 1981:108), and southern Michigan (Fitting 1964, 1970). They also occur well into the northeastern United States (Turnbaugh 1980:64, Fig. 3; Bolian 1980).

Morphological Correlates
Cossatot River (Perino 1976:127; 1985:88); Drake Indented Base (McKenzie 1967:38–39, Fig. 3c, only. This designation overlaps with Kirk Corner Notched large variety);

Map 36: MacCorkle Stemmed—Distribution and Important Sites

Jerger (Tomak 1979:2–3); Large Bifurcates (Prufer and McKenzie 1975; Converse 1973:34).

ST. ALBANS SIDE NOTCHED

The basic characteristic of St. Albans Side Notched is the presence of slight side notching with a deep basal notch or bifurcation (Figure 16). Two varieties of this type have been defined (Broyles 1966:23; 1971:72–75).

Both varieties exhibit triangular blades with straight or excurvate sides thinned by large flakes. Secondary flaking is rare. Sides are serrated on the majority of specimens and the tips are sharp and sometimes off-center. Bases are deeply notched and ground to the shoulder. Shoulders are well defined; some are straight, but most slope toward the tip. The blade shape and tip configuration are the same as that described for variety A. Variety B lacks basal grinding and the dimensions of basal width are the same as that for the shoulder width of these points. Side

notches are shallow, and the shoulders slope toward the tip but are poorly defined.

Generally, the only distinctions for visual sorting of the varieties lie in the degree of blade reworking or blade morphology. Variety A bears an overall trianguloid blade which is short relative to shoulder width. Variety B tends toward increased lateral blade reworking which maintains the length of the blade while decreasing blade and shoulder width. The result of this blade treatment is the exhausting of the well-defined shoulder exhibited in variety A. Overall, the difference between the two varieties is primarily in blade configuration and to a lesser extent in the treatment of basal flaking or grinding. While Broyles (1971:75) considers a lack of serration as an additional characteristic of variety B, overall blade and shoulder configuration seems to be more distinctive of these points.

Age and Cultural Affiliation
These points are diagnostic of the Early Archaic period, St. Albans phase dating from about 6900 to 6500 B.C. (J. Chapman 1985: Table 7–1). Variety A was found in Zone 12

Map 37: St. Albans Side Notched—Distribution and Important Sites

at the St. Albans site in West Virginia and dated to 6880 B.C. ±700 years. Variety B was found in Zone 11 which dated to 6870 B.C. ±500 years. Three dates for St. Albans Side Notched from the Rose Island site in Tennessee averaged 6770 B.C. (J. Chapman 1977:166).

Distribution
These forms have been found over much of the eastern U.S. (see Fitting 1964). St. Albans Side Notched points occur from western Illinois (Conrad 1981:109), to Michigan (Fitting 1964), southern Ontario (Wright 1978), at Russell Cave in Alabama (Ingmanson and Griffin 1974:37, Fig. 27m−n), and as far east as West Virginia (Broyles 1966) and Virginia (McCary 1955). They have also been found at sites in Massachusetts and Rhode Island (Fowler 1968; Turnbaugh 1980:64, Fig. 3), and Maine (Spiess et al. 1983:232, Fig. 3).

St. Albans and the other bifurcate base types appear to be limited to regions east of the Plains. However, similar projectile points occur across the western U.S. and should not be overlooked. There also appears to be a sequence from larger to smaller bifurcate base forms which in some ways is similar to that recorded for the East. Material similar to St. Albans is known in the West as Pinto Basin, which in some of its variations is nearly identical (cf. Campbell and Campbell 1935:47, Plate 13 p). One age estimate for Pinto Basin of 7000 to 6000 B.C. correlates well with the known age of St. Albans Side Notched (see Wormington 1957:48; Willey 1966:57−58, 76). Others argue for a post−4000 B.C. assignment, but the styles of the "Pinto" series vary considerably without consistent typological control, and there is no continuous distribution linking eastern bifurcate base forms with similar material in the West.

LeCroy Cluster

LECROY BIFURCATED STEM

LeCroy points (Lewis and Kneberg 1955; Kneberg 1956:27−28; Broyles 1966:27) are bifurcated but exhibit pointed rather than rounded basal ears (Figure 17). Edges on most specimens are straight, but a few are excurvate or incurvate. Resharpening of the blade is characteristic. Blades are typically serrated (i.e., several sharp barbs on each blade edge) and triangular, ranging from an equilateral triangle to a short nubbin in exhausted specimens. Bases are deeply notched; this was accomplished by the removal of one or more large flakes and several smaller ones by pressure flaking. Stems vary from straight to slightly flared. On many specimens the stem is almost as wide as the resharpened blade. There is no evidence of grinding. These points are broad and usually deeply bifurcated. Basal grinding is exhibited occasionally. A small percentage of LeCroy points exhibit burin facets as a haft finishing technique.

Age and Cultural Affiliation
LeCroy projectile points are diagnostic of the Early Archaic LeCroy phase (J. Chapman 1985) which dates within a range of ca. 6500 to 5800 B.C. A date of 6300 B.C. ±100 relates to this type in association with a dated hearth at the St. Albans site in West Virginia (Broyles 1966:26−27, 1971:69). Zone three at the Longworth-Gick site in the Ohio Valley of northern Kentucky produced LeCroy points dated to 6470 B.C. ±110 (Collins 1979:579). This age was also assigned to these forms at Rose Island in Tennessee (J. Chapman 1976: 6). A stylistic differentiation of this type is thought to have resulted in the Lake Erie Bifurcated Base type.

Map 38: LeCroy Bifurcated Stem
Distribution and Important Sites

Distribution

LeCroy points appear to be widespread in the eastern United States (Broyles 1969:34). This type is recorded in Georgia (DePratter 1975:6), Virginia (McCary 1955), Kentucky (Schock and Langford 1979b:9), Tennessee (Jolley 1979:40), Indiana (Bellis 1975), Illinois (Conrad 1981:109), Ohio (Brose and White 1979), Michigan (Fitting 1964), and Pennsylvania (Broyles 1969:34). These forms also occur across the Northeast to the Atlantic coast (Ritchie 1961:115, Plate 34, 6; Wyatt 1977:400; Funk 1977b:327, Fig. 9). The westernmost distribution of LeCroy occurs in Missouri at the Rodgers Shelter site (Ahler and McMillan 1976:169; Fig. 10.2d).

LAKE ERIE BIFURCATED BASE

The Lake Erie Bifurcated Base type (Prufer and Sofsky 1965:31–32) is a small thin form similar to the LeCroy type (Figure 17). While the stem varies from straight to slightly expanding, it is relatively long and narrow and exhibits a shallow bifurcation. The blade is basically triangular in form. The blade edges are typically straight, although variation from excurvate to incurvate occurs within the finishing and resharpening processes. These projectile points have shoulders that vary from straight to asymmetrical. Serrated blades occur in high frequency with pressure flaking being the dominant technique utilized. The hafting area, as noted above, differs from LeCroy in basic proportions and lacks grinding. The lateral margin of the stem, shoulder, and basal notch sometimes exhibits burin facets (Prufer and Sofsky 1965:31; Converse 1973:30).

There has been an evolution in the application of bifurcate base type definitions which should be mentioned. The LeCroy type (Kneberg 1956) once included forms which Broyles (1966) later named St. Albans Side Notched and MacCorkle (cf. Bell 1960:

Figure 17: LeCroy Cluster

a. LeCroy. Unidentified chert. GBL 30/162. Jefferson Co., Indiana.
b. LeCroy. Unidentified chert. GBL 10/91. Crawford Co., Pennsylvania.
c. LeCroy. Exhibits drastic blade resharpening. Unidentified chert. GBL 14/828. Central Indiana.
d. Lake Erie Bifurcated Base. Liston Creek chert. GBL 3104/14. Site 12 Al 98. Allen Co., Indiana.
e. Lake Erie Bifurcated Base. Unidentified chert. GBL 2629/3. Site 12 O 72. Ohio Co., Indiana.
f. Lake Erie Bifurcated Base. Exhibits drastic blade resharpening. Unidentified chert. GBL 2691/30. Site 12 Al 68. Allen Co., Indiana.
g. Kanawha Stemmed. Wyandotte chert. GBL 14/823. Indiana.
h. Kanawha Stemmed. Unidentified chert. GBL 119/891. Provenience unknown.
i. Kanawha Stemmed. Knox Black chert. Ice House Bottom site, Tennessee. Specimen 1479/40Mr23, Frank H. McClung Museum, University of Tennessee. Pictured in Plate 5, c.
j. Kanawha Stemmed. Knox Black chert. Ice House Bottom site, Tennessee. Specimen 947/40Mr23, Frank H. McClung Museum, University of Tennessee.
k. Fox Valley Truncated Barb. Attica chert. GBL 31/100. Fulton Co., Indiana.
l. Fox Valley Truncated Barb. Attica chert. GBL 21/391. Central Indiana.
m. Fox Valley Truncated Barb. Unidentified chert. GBL 3304/185. Provenience unknown.

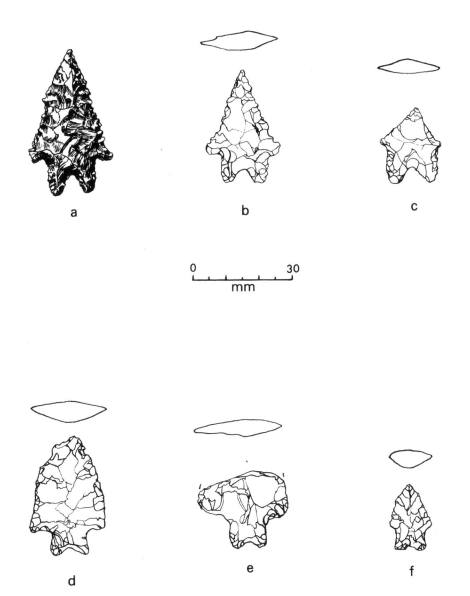

a

b

c

0   30
mm

d

e

f

Figure 17
LeCroy Cluster

Figure 17

64). In addition, Prufer and Sofsky's illustrations of Lake Erie (1965:26, Fig. 4) also include examples of both LeCroy and St. Albans. Only two of the illustrated specimens (1965:Fig. 4w–x) belong to the Lake Erie Bifurcated type as described.

Age and Cultural Affiliation

Lake Erie points are diagnostic of the Early Archaic period. The age of these points is bracketed between ca. 6300 B.C. and 5800 B.C. which covers the temporal span between LeCroy and the later Stanly Stemmed. These types bracket opposite ends of the morphological range of variation described for the Lake Erie type, based on evidence recovered at the Ice House Bottom site in Tennessee (cf. J. Chapman 1977:36, Fig. 16a). A radiocarbon date of 3352 B.C. ±90 from the Rohr Rock Shelter reported by Dragoo (1959) was originally thought to relate to Lake Erie and other bifurcate base types (cf. St. Albans, LeCroy). This association has since been shown to be erroneous, with radiocarbon dates from a number of sites in the East consistently averaging about 3,000 years earlier

Map 39: Lake Erie Bifurcated Base
Distribution and Important Sites

(see Broyles 1971; Tuck 1974; J. Chapman 1975, 1976, 1977).

Distribution

Lake Erie Bifurcate Base points occur throughout much of Ohio (Prufer 1975b; Brose and White 1979), Indiana, Illinois, Wisconsin (Munson and Downs 1966:201), and Michigan (Fitting 1964:93). The type also appears to extend in lower frequency south into the Tennessee River Valley (J. Chapman 1977).

Morphological Correlate

Fredrick (Tomak 1980b:3, Fig. 7, bottom row, c).

KANAWHA STEMMED

Kanawha Stemmed points (Broyles 1966:27) are characterized by a small triangular blade with a short, rounded and shallow bifurcated base (Figure 17). The blade edges vary from straight to incurvate with a projection at the shoulder. Many specimens were resharpened using serration. Bases are notched or bifurcated on the majority of specimens. Basal thinning scars are present on both faces. These result from the basal notching process. There is no evidence of basal grinding. The stem is small and expanding, with rounded corners, and is usually about one half the width of the blade.

Age and Cultural Affiliation

A date of 6210 B.C. ±100 was obtained for Kanawha Stemmed points from a Zone 4 hearth at the St. Albans site (Broyles 1971:59). These forms are diagnostic of the Early Archaic period Kanawha phase (J. Chapman 1976) which existed from about 6200 to 5800 B.C. The type was found in Zones 2 and 4 at St. Albans (Broyles 1966:27). These points were recovered stratigraphically above LeCroy points at the Rose Island site in Tennessee (J. Chapman 1975:125–126). Kanawha points are thought to be ancestral to the larger Stanly Stemmed type (Coe 1964:35, 54).

Map 40: Kanawha Stemmed
Distribution and Important Sites

Distribution

Kanawha points have been found on numerous sites across West Virginia (Broyles 1971). A large sample of these was obtained from the LeCroy site and other sites in Tennessee (Lewis and Kneberg 1955; Jolley 1979:40). In general, Kanawha points are found over a wide area of the eastern United States from Staten Island, New York (Ritchie and Funk 1973; Calkin and Miller 1977:309, Fig. 4b–d), and occur well into the South (Broyles 1971:59). These projectile points have been recorded in Georgia (DePratter 1975:6, Fig. 2), Kentucky (Schock and Langford 1979b:8), Ohio (Converse 1973:36), Pennsylvania (Broyles 1969:35), Indiana (Seeman 1975; Tomak 1980b), and Illinois (Conrad 1981:110), and as far north as central Michigan and southern Ontario (Wright 1978).

Morphological Correlates

Fredrick (Tomak 1980b:3, Fig. 7, bottom row, a–b only); Stanley. This designation (DeJarnette et al. 1962; Cambron and Hulse 1975) has been used for material morphologically identical to Kanawha Stemmed (Bettye J. Broyles, pers. comm.).

FOX VALLEY TRUNCATED BARB

Fox Valley Truncated Barb projectile points (Ritzenthaler 1961a,b, 1967:32) are wide-bladed and thin, with bifurcated bases. These points were made by using a combination of percussion and pressure flaking, and they often exhibit an asymmetrical blade (Figure 17). The larger shoulder has a "truncated barb" appearance in that the shoulder is squared and lacks barbs. Typically, the edge in this area is bifacially flaked, which suggests that these forms may have been made from pentagonal preforms. Some examples of the type exhibit a truncated shoulder, on one or both sides, caused by a single fracture without bifacial retouch, which is sometimes a result of use breakage. Highly symmetrical blades occur when similar finish is exhibited on both shoulders, which curve upward gracefully. The blade edges are typically incurvate, converge to a sharp tip, and are often serrated. The haft region on these forms is narrow relative to shoulder width and varies from straight to expanding. Short basal ears project downward or flare slightly. The basal edge is concave and thinned on one or both sides. This treatment is essentially the same as that found on the Lake Erie Bifurcated Base type (Fitting 1964:92–94; Munson and Downs 1966:205) and is also within the range of Kanawha Stemmed (Broyles 1971:27, Fig. 3).

Fox Valley is superficially similar to Catahoula type arrowheads, although the Catahoula type bears haft and flaking attributes more similar to Bonham and related styles than to Fox Valley. Catahoula occurs in late prehistoric context (Ford and Webb 1956: 68–69).

Age and Cultural Affiliation

There are no radiocarbon dates available for Fox Valley Truncated Barb points from sites in the Midwest. However, they belong to the latter part of the Bifurcate Base tradition which is securely dated in other areas to the Early Archaic period with a range of ca. 6200 to 5800 B.C. These forms predate the Stanly type, which represents the final phase of this tradition. The strong morphological similarity of Fox Valley to Kanawha Stemmed (Broyles 1966, 1971) suggests that these types should date to about the same period. Kanawha Stemmed has been dated to about 6210 B.C. at the St. Albans site in West Virginia (Broyles 1971:59). These forms are considered transitional between LeCroy and Stanly Stemmed (J. Chapman 1977:35).

Distribution
Truncated Barb points are common in southeastern Wisconsin and northeastern Illinois, especially in the southern Fox River Valley (Ritzenthaler 1967:32). These forms occur south into central Illinois and Indiana (Munson and Downs 1966; Guendling and Crouch 1977; Tomak 1980b). The distribution of Fox Valley appears to be less extensive than that of Lake Erie Bifurcated Base.

Map 41: Fox Valley Truncated Barb Distribution

Morphological Correlates
Clipped Wing Points (DeCamp 1967:109); Fox Valley Points (Palmer and Palmer 1962: 9–12); Fredrick (Tomak 1980b:3, Fig. 7, upper row).

Stanly Stemmed Cluster

STANLY STEMMED

Stanly Stemmed points (Coe 1964:35–36) possess broad, triangular blades and narrow, squared stems with shallow basal notches or bifurcation (Figure 18). The blade edges range from excurvate to incurvate, and serration is typical. These projectile points were manufactured using percussion thinning followed by a combination of percussion and pressure flaking of the edges. Beveling of the blade edges occurs on some specimens, but a biconvex cross section is typical. Basal thin-

ning scars are usually present and are related to the bifurcation process. Edge grinding of the haft is not a significant trait and was lacking in Coe's sample (1964:35).

Age and Cultural Affiliation
Stanly Stemmed points relate to the Middle Archaic Stanly complex and are thought to date from about 6000 B.C. (Broyles 1969:35) to no later than 5000 B.C. (Coe 1964:35–36). A range of 5800 to 5500 B.C. is suggested by J. Chapman (1985:Table 7–1) based on radiocarbon dates obtained at sites such as

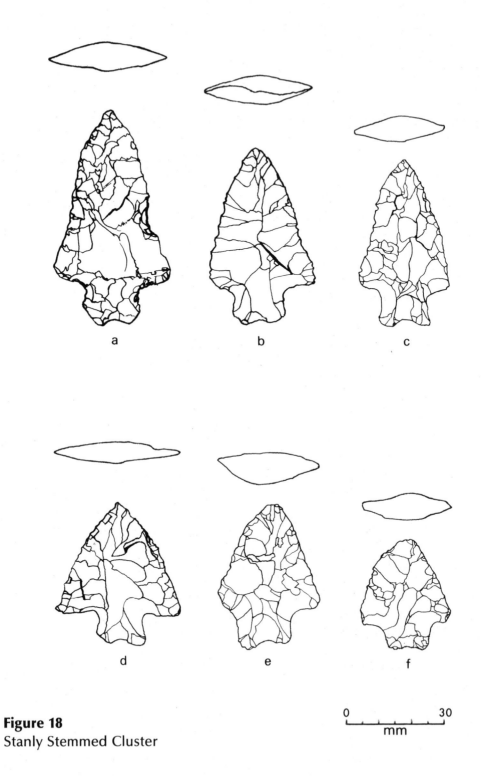

Figure 18
Stanly Stemmed Cluster

a

b

c

d

e

f

0   30
mm

Ice House Bottom. Dincauze (1976:26–29) obtained dates ranging from ca. 5800 to 5000 B.C. at the Neville site in New Hampshire, which produced projectile points within the range of variation of Stanly Stemmed (Neville Stemmed). The semilunar atlatl weight type is associated with the Stanly complex (Coe 1964:80–81).

Distribution

Stanly Stemmed projectile points are distributed over much of the eastern United States. They have been found in many areas of the Northeast (Starbuck 1980; Turnbaugh 1980:65; Dincauze 1976:29) and across the Southeast from West Virginia (Broyles 1971) and North Carolina (Coe 1964:35) to Alabama (Ingmanson and Griffin 1974:42, Fig. 28). These forms are recognized in the Tennessee Valley (J. Chapman 1977) and elsewhere in Tennessee (Jolley 1979:40, Fig. 4), Kentucky (Schock and Langford 1979b), Ohio (Shane and Murphy 1975), and southern Indiana (Tomak 1970:82). However, Stanly projectile points are largely unreported in adjacent areas. Note that projectile points identified as "Stanley" (DeJarnette et al. 1962; Cambron and Hulse 1975) belong

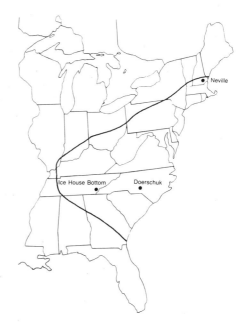

Map 42: Stanly Stemmed—Distribution and Important Sites

to the Kanawha Stemmed type (Broyles 1971) and are not Stanly points as defined above (Bettye J. Broyles, pers. comm.).

Morphological Correlate

Neville Stemmed (Dincauze 1976:26–29).

Figure 18: Stanly Stemmed Cluster
a. Stanly Stemmed. Unidentified chert. GBL 13/891. South-central Michigan.
b. Stanly Stemmed. Unidentified chert. GBL 1448/90. Southwestern Indiana.
c. Stanly Stemmed. Knox Mottled chert. Ice House Bottom site, Tennessee. Specimen 740/40Mr23, Frank H. McClung Museum, University of Tennessee.
d. Stanly Stemmed. Bryantsville Breccia chert. GBL 21/357. Indiana.
e. Stanly Stemmed. Translucent Quartz. Ice House Bottom site, Tennessee. Specimen 689/40Mr23, Frank H. McClung Museum, University of Tennessee. Pictured in Plate 5, a.
f. Stanly Stemmed. Knox Black chert. Ice House Bottom site, Tennessee. Specimen 954/40Mr23, Frank H. McClung Museum, University of Tennessee.

Eva Cluster

EVA I

Eva I projectile points (Lewis and Lewis 1961:40) are large, basally notched forms produced from a percussion flaked trianguloid preform with a relatively straight basal edge (Figure 19). Barbs vary from squared, reflecting the corners of the original preform, to pointed, and may be longer than the stem. The notches on Eva points generally exhibit circular hertzian cone flake scars at the notch terminus. This is then followed by minimal retouch on the notch periphery. Stem morphology is diminutive relative to overall blade dimensions. All edges of the stem are basically straight and the basal edge is typically thinned.

Eva I points exhibit angular, recurved blade edges in resharpened state. A combination of percussion and pressure flaking was used for blade thinning, form shaping, and edge resharpening. This left the blade thin, uniform, and quite sharp. Eva drills were produced with final blade width reduction using pressure without removing the barbs, which indicates their derivation from pristine Eva forms with sizeable blades.

Age and Cultural Affiliation
Eva I style projectile points are diagnostic of the Middle Archaic Eva phase (Lewis and Kneberg 1959:164) and are estimated to date from about 6000 to 4000 B.C. Eva I projectile points were most numerous in Stratum IV top at the Eva site. A radiocarbon date of 5200 B.C. ±500 was obtained from the bottom of Stratum IV (Lewis and Lewis 1961: 173). Kirk Corner Notched (large variety) points and Kirk Serrated points were the next most common types associated with the Eva component at the site, indicating admixture. A few earlier and later projectile points styles were also found in the Eva component.

Smith Basal Notched points (Baerreis and Freeman 1960; C. Chapman 1975) and other basal notched types similar to Eva I occur in Middle to Late Archaic contexts, but their relationship to Eva cannot be discerned with present data. Most basal notched types of the Late Archaic period exhibit shortened barbs and triangular form in resharpened state, and overlap with types in the Terminal Archaic Barbed cluster.

Distribution
Eva style projectile points appear to have a distribution confined primarily to the middle South, mainly in the Tennessee Valley (Broyles 1969:35). Kneberg (1956:24) observed few Eva projectile points outside of western Tennessee. Several excavated sites in Alabama, such as Little Bear Creek (Webb and DeJarnette 1948b), Flint Creek Rockshelter (Cambron and Waters 1957), and Stanfield-Worley Bluff Shelter (DeJarnette et al. 1962:55), have produced Eva style points in later Archaic contexts.

A few instances of the occurrence of these forms outside the above region can be cited. A single Eva I projectile point was recovered out of context at the Lawrence site in Kentucky (Mocas 1977:178, Fig.11). The

Figure 19: Eva Cluster
a. Eva I. Impact fracture at tip. Fort Payne chert. Eva site, Tennessee. Specimen ST2.B–1627/6Bn12, Frank H. McClung Museum, University of Tennessee. Pictured in Plate 5, f.
b. Eva I. Fort Payne chert. Eva site, Tennessee. Specimen F.10–1/6Bn12, Frank H. McClung Museum, University of Tennessee.
c. Eva I. Fort Payne chert. Eva site, Tennessee. Specimen ST4T–1527/6Bn12, Frank H. McClung Museum, University of Tennessee.
d. Eva II. Fort Payne chert. Eva site, Tennessee. Specimen ST2T–618/6Bn12, Frank H. McClung Museum, University of Tennessee.
e. Eva II. Unidentified chert, heat treated? Eva site, Tennessee. Specimen B15–1/6Bn12, Frank H. McClung Museum, University of Tennessee. Pictured in Plate 5, o.
f. Eva II. Fort Payne chert. Eva site, Tennessee. Specimen ST3–635/6Bn12, Frank H. McClung Museum, University of Tennessee.
g. Eva II. Drill. Fort Payne chert? Eva site, Tennessee. Specimen 6T4T–746/6Bn12, Frank H. McClung Museum, University of Tennessee.

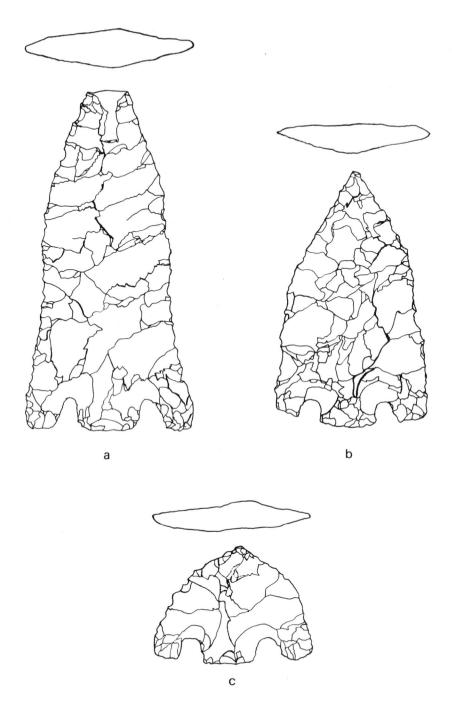

a

b

c

Figure 19
Eva Cluster

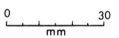

0   30
mm

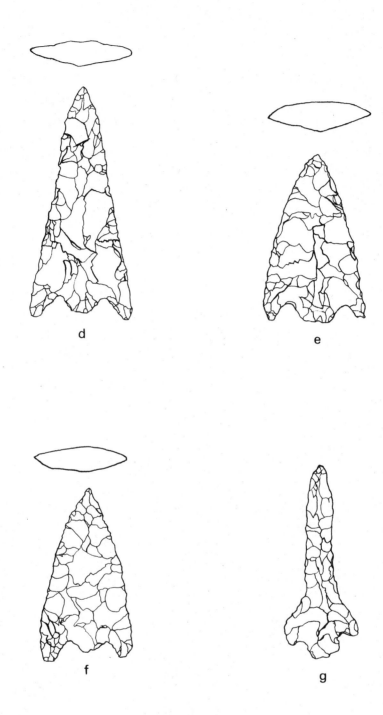

d

e

f

g

Figure 19

Map 43: Eva I—Distribution and Important Sites

be the Ouachita type discussed by Perino (1980, 1985).

EVA II

Eva II type projectile points (Lewis and Lewis 1961:40) are smaller than Eva I and have straight or slightly excurvate blades which lack the recurved or angular blade shape frequently present on Eva I (Figure 19). In addition, the barbs are typically pointed and often longer than the stem. The notching technique of Eva II is essentially the same as Eva I, exhibiting circular hertzian cone flake scars that form the basal notches. Percussion and pressure techniques were used in manufacture and resharpening.

Age and Cultural Affiliation

Eva II projectile point forms are apparently a later Archaic development of Eva I at the Eva site in Tennessee. These were present in the Three Mile component at the site, which represents the later portion of the Eva phase defined at the site, dating from roughly 4000 to 2000 B.C. (Lewis and Lewis 1961:173). A plethora of projectile point types, such as Little Bear Creek, Big Sandy (Raddatz), and Cypress Creek II (Kirk Corner Notched), were present in this component, which suggests that the deposit was mixed. Nonetheless, this component shows an emphasis on fishing and mussel collecting and other new cultural traits, suggesting a significant change in economy during the Late Archaic period.

Distribution

As was noted for the distribution of Eva I, these points are poorly represented outside of western Tennessee (Kneberg 1956:24) and northern Alabama (Cambron and Hulse 1969:78). Eva points are present in small numbers in southern Illinois (MacNeish 1948), Ohio (Converse 1981:36), and southern Indiana. In addition, Eva II type points were recovered at the Lawrence site in Trigg County, Kentucky (Mocas 1977:161, Fig. 96).

Information regarding the distribution of

Faulkner site in southern Illinois produced three Eva basal notched points in preceramic levels (MacNeish 1948:236, Fig. 47, 17–18). The Smith Basal Notched type (Baerreis and Freeman 1959) occurs in Oklahoma, Arkansas, and Missouri and appears to strongly grade into the morphology of Eva I. The implication is that the Missouri area represents the maximum western extent of the Eva I style (cf. C. Chapman 1975:Figs. 7–14c, 8–14b).

North of the Ohio Valley in Ohio and Indiana, Eva I projectile points are present in low frequency and appear to be uncommon (Converse 1973:28, 1981:36). Beyond the occurrence of a single Eva I point recorded in Shelby County in the upper reaches of the White River, there is meager evidence for the presence of this style in southern Indiana.

In another case, Griffin et al. (1970:89, Plate 91) describe a cache of seven basally notched projectile points, somewhat similar to Eva I, recovered from the premound humus line under Mound 14 of the Knight group. However, these appear to represent Middle Woodland Hopewellian manufacture (cf. Braun et al. 1982:Fig. 91a). These may

Map 44: Eva II—Distribution and Important Sites

Eva style points in the upper Ohio Valley appears to be lacking (Mayer-Oakes 1955). Within the Delaware River Valley far into the Northeast, basally notched points named Eshback (Kinsey 1972:417–418) occur in

low frequency. The relationship of this late Archaic type to Eva I and II is not known. However, there are obvious formal similarities, and the types date to about the same period.

Comments

Long and Josselyn (1965:143) have suggested a morphological evolution from Eva I and II into the Morrow Mountain I and II series described by Coe (1964). Successive blade reworking of an Eva II point could reduce the length and shape of the distinctive barbs and lead to confusion between it and Morrow Mountain. However, the consideration of ancestry of Eva and Morrow Mountain is complex and probably involves other types such as White Springs.

Morphological Correlates
of the Eva Cluster
Smith Basal Notched (Baerreis and Freeman 1959; Perino 1968a:90; C. Chapman 1975:256, Fig. 8–14). This type also includes material that overlaps the Etley cluster.

Morrow Mountain Cluster

MORROW MOUNTAIN I

The Morrow Mountain I type (Coe 1964: 37–43) is a small point with a broad triangular blade and a short, pointed, contracting stem (Figure 20). Excurvate blades are typical, although straight and incurvate blade edges also occur. Serration is sometimes exhibited on the blade edges. Maximum width occurs at the shoulder. The stem of Morrow Mountain I is short and tapers inward from a wide and sloping shoulder. Larger specimens were manufactured using a percussion technique, whereas the smaller examples were finely flaked using pressure. Grinding may occur on the shoulder and stem of

some specimens, but it is never pronounced and occurs infrequently.

Morphological Correlates
Morrow Mountain Rounded Base (DeJarnette et al. 1962; Cambron and Hulse 1969:81); Morrow Mountain Round Base variant (DeJarnette et al. 1962; Walthall 1980:59); Florida Morrow Mountain (Bullen 1968:32, 1975:34).

MORROW MOUNTAIN II

Morrow Mountain II projectile points (Coe 1964:37) are related to the Morrow Mountain I type. Essential characteristics, such as the contracting stem and sloping shoulder/haft juncture are present. Cross sections on these points are biconvex as in Morrow Mountain I. However, the distinguishing characteristic of this type is the elongated stem, which differs markedly from Morrow Mountain I (Figure 20).

The blade of Morrow Mountain II is long and narrow with straight or slightly rounded sides. Some specimens tend to flare or curve outward at the shoulder. Shortened blades are a result of blade reworking. Stems on these points are long and tapered with a more definite break at the shoulder/haft juncture than is described for Morrow Mountain I. Methods of manufacture were essentially the same for both Morrow Mountain types in Coe's (1964) sample, although haft grinding was lacking for Morrow Mountain II.

Morphological Correlates
Morrow Mountain Straight Base (DeJarnette et al. 1962; Cambron and Hulse 1960b, 1969:38); Straight Stemmed Gypsum Cave (Cambron 1958a); Stark Stemmed (Dincauze 1976:29–38, Plate 4).

Age and Cultural Affiliation
The Morrow Mountain complex is a Middle Archaic phenomenon which dates to about 4500 B.C. (Coe 1964:123), with a longevity apparently confined to a few centuries earlier and later. Several dates have been reported in Alabama that cluster around Coe's original estimate (Walthall 1980:42). For example, dates ranging from 4030 B.C. ±200 to 4360 B.C. ±140 were obtained at Russell Cave for this complex (Miller 1957; Griffin 1974:12–15). A date of 4500 B.C. ±120 derived from a Morrow Mountain occupation at the Stucks Bluff Rock Shelter is noteworthy (DeJarnette et al. 1975:116). Another radiocarbon date of 5045 B.C. ±245 obtained at the Ice House Bottom site in Tennessee is the earliest accepted date for Morrow Mountain, suggesting that the type was in use as early as 5000 B.C. (J. Chapman 1977:30, 167).

The stratigraphic position of Morrow Mountain has been established at several sites. Excavations at the Eva site demonstrated that Morrow Mountain postdates the Eva II type. Morrow Mountain is also shown to postdate the earlier Stanly type at several stratified sites such as the Doerschuk site (Coe 1964:123), Ice House Bottom (J. Chapman 1977), and the Neville site in New Hampshire (Dincauze 1976). The Morrow Mountain style apparently became obsolete prior to the appearance of the Savannah River style. A Morrow Mountain occupation occurred immediately below Guilford and Savannah River levels at the Doerschuk site (Coe 1964:24–25), and three feet below Savannah River at the Lake Spring site in Georgia (Miller 1949; Caldwell 1954:38–39).

The typological relationship between Morrow Mountain and Eva II has been discussed by Long and Josselyn (1965), suggesting that stylistic change within Eva II technology resulted in the Morrow Mountain style. A possible stylistic trend from earlier stemmed types has also been suggested (J. Chapman 1977:34). The later development of the Morrow Mountain style is more difficult to assess, as it occupies a temporal position which may or may not be responsible for a portion of the Late Archaic development of multiple contracting and straight stemmed styles that appear over much of the East, within regionally restricted technological traditions. There is some suggestion that Morrow Mountain II continued later in time than Morrow Mountain I (Coe 1964:43), although data on the latter are too limited to address the problem of stylistic differentiation at or immediately following the time span of Morrow Mountain II.

The Morrow Mountain occupation of the Tennessee River Valley is fairly well documented. The locally named Sanderson Cove phase is fully described in many of its dimensions including the mortuary complex. Walthall (1980:58–67) provides a good summary of a variety of the relevant assemblages, as well as the development of Middle Archaic economy. Of special interest are burials from Stanfield-Worley attributed to the Morrow Mountain complex. These produced associations of cache blades (Morrow Mountain

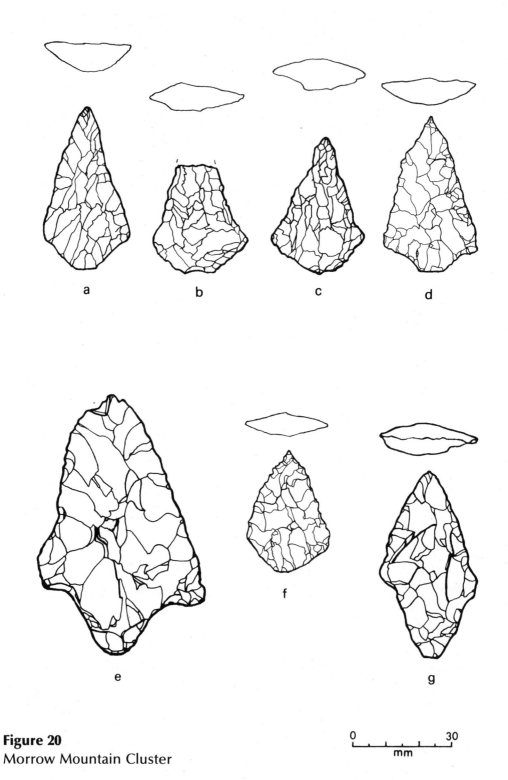

Figure 20
Morrow Mountain Cluster

0 ⊢——————⊣ 30
mm

Round Base variant), preforms, and several named types included in the Morrow Mountain cluster with White Springs, Crawford Creek (i.e., a named type similar to White Springs), and the use of the atlatl with tubular type weights (Webb and DeJarnette 1942, 1948 a,b; DeJarnette et al. 1962).

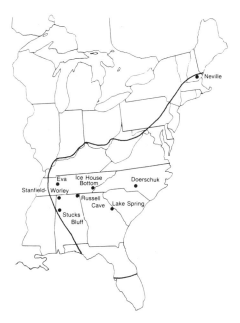

Map 45: Morrow Mountain I and II Distribution and Important Sites

Distribution

When projectile points of this kind were first recognized in the East, they were compared to material from Gypsum and Manzano Caves in the Far West (Coe 1959, Cambron 1958a), leading to the conclusion that the basic form has a wide distribution over much of North America (Coe 1964:37). To the contrary, the Morrow Mountain type is fairly restricted to the southeastern United States. The Morrow Mountain I type is well known in Alabama (DeJarnette et al. 1962), Georgia (Caldwell 1954), Florida (Bullen 1968:32), South Carolina (Stoltman 1974: 118, 171), Tennessee (Lewis and Lewis 1961: 37), North Carolina (Coe 1964), West Virginia (Jensen 1970), and Virginia (Holland 1955: 170, 1970). It may also occur north of the Ohio Valley but in very limited numbers (Cook 1980:420). Morrow Mountain II forms have a greater concentration in the Middle Atlantic Coastal Plain area and Tidewater region (Broyles 1969:35; Phelps 1981), although they are represented across much of the area defined above for Morrow Mountain I. In addition, Morrow Mountain II extends into the Northeast, at least as far as New Jersey (Cross 1941), Massachusetts (Robbins 1980), and New Hampshire. In these areas the term Starke Stemmed has been applied to the forms (Dincauze 1976; Starbuck and Bolian 1980).

Figure 20: Morrow Mountain Cluster
a. Morrow Mountain I. Quartz. GBL 22/70. Virginia.
b. Morrow Mountain I. Quartz. GBL 3088/1. North Carolina.
c. Morrow Mountain I. Quartz. GBL 3088/1. North Carolina.
d. Morrow Mountain I. Knox Black chert. Ice House Bottom site, Tennessee. Specimen 1025/40Mr23, Frank H. McClung Museum, University of Tennessee. Pictured in Plate 5, i.
e. Morrow Mountain II. Unidentified chert. GBL 5465/1. North Carolina.
f. Morrow Mountain I. Knox Black chert. Ice House Bottom site, Tennessee. Specimen 1523/40Mr23, Frank H. McClung Museum, University of Tennessee.
g. Morrow Mountain II. Quartzite. GBL 242/2. North Carolina.

White Springs Cluster

SYKES

Sykes projectile points (Lewis and Lewis 1961:40–41) are broad, short-stemmed forms with the haft element produced from the removal of the corners of a trianguloid preform (Figure 21). The resulting finished Sykes type exhibits shallow indentations forming the stem and shoulders, which are largely a result of notch formation. Notch flake scars often cover the lateral margins of the stem and shoulders, leaving little available space for stem edge retouch. The shoulders are squared and lack barbs, but may slope downward slightly. Basal morphology of Sykes points is distinctive in that the edge is relatively straight, bifacially flaked at a steep angle, and quite thick (Faulkner and Graham 1966:71–72; Faulkner 1968:182).

Little is known of changes in blade morphology caused by resharpening processes. The Sykes type blade shape varies from excurvate to straight, possibly without the occurrence of more exhausted forms with incurvate or recurvate blade edges due to resharpening. Drills, hafted scrapers, and other forms exhibiting a Sykes type haft element were apparently lacking at Eva, the type site; nor were they part of the tool inventory at other sites (Faulkner 1968).

Age and Cultural Affiliation
Sykes points are diagnostic of the Middle to Late Archaic transitional period. At the Eva site in Tennessee, White Springs cluster projectile points were present in the Eva component, the earliest of three components recognized and concentrated within Big Sandy, the latest component at the site. This suggests that Sykes style projectile points appeared sometime after 6000 B.C. and were most popular before 2000 B.C. (Lewis and Lewis 1961:31, 173). White Springs cluster points occurring prior to the Big Sandy component at Eva have been reclassified as the White Springs type (Faulkner 1968:70–72), which is related morphologically to Sykes.

Zone D (7–8 foot levels) at the Westmoreland-Barber site in Tennessee produced Sykes points, along with one Morrow Mountain point. This association led Faulkner and Graham (1966:121) to consider Sykes as part of the Three Mile phase of 3500 B.C. in the western Tennessee Valley (Lewis and Kneberg 1959:164) and the Morrow Mountain complex. The latter, defined at the Stanfield-Worley Bluff Shelter in Alabama, had Morrow Mountain and White Springs cluster material in the lower levels of Zone A (DeJarnette, Kurjack, and Cambron 1962:80–82).

WHITE SPRINGS

White Springs projectile points (DeJarnette, Kurjack, and Cambron 1962:70) are clearly related to Sykes points morphologically, and are the prototype for the latter. All of the essential attributes of Sykes are present, but White Springs is more refined (Figure 21). The type is usually thin, flattened, rarely biconvex, and trianguloid in shape. The stem is short and wide, and the basal edge is straight or slightly concave. The shoulders of the type are squared and relatively narrow, as in Sykes. Cambron and Hulse (1969:116) note that White Springs points rarely exhibit incurvate blade edges due to resharpening,

Figure 21: White Springs Cluster
a. Sykes. Fort Payne chert? heat fractured. Eva site, Tennessee. Specimen ST5–477/6Bn12, Frank H. McClung Museum, University of Tennessee. Pictured in Plate 5, m.
b. Sykes. Fort Payne chert. Eva site, Tennessee. Specimen ST1–509/6Bn12, Frank H. McClung Museum, University of Tennessee.
c. White Springs. Wyandotte chert. GBL 1448/227. Southwestern Indiana.
d. White Springs. Wyandotte chert. GBL 281/264. Franklin Co., Indiana. Pictured in Plate 5, l.
e. White Springs. Fort Payne chert. Eva site, Tennessee. Specimen B1/6Bn12, Frank H. McClung Museum, University of Tennessee. Pictured in Plate 5, n.

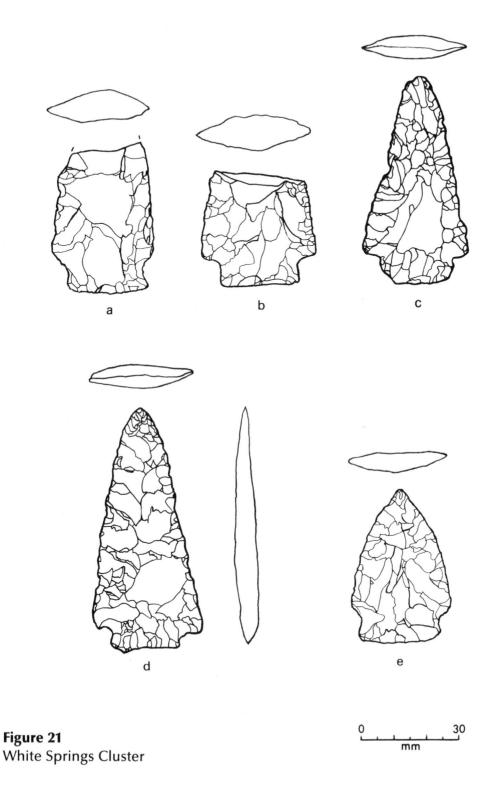

Figure 21
White Springs Cluster

and possess thinned bases. Faulkner's (1968: 182) distinction between White Springs and Sykes lies in basal attributes alone: the stem is shorter in White Springs, and basal thinning is characteristic of White Springs alone. Sykes projectile points typically exhibit a thick and steeply flaked base. Technologically, White Springs exhibits flaking attributes of Early Archaic forms such as those exhibited in the Kirk Corner Notched cluster.

Age and Cultural Affiliation
White Springs projectile points are considered to be diagnostic of the Middle Archaic period (Walthall 1980:58–61). They are estimated to date between 5000 and 4000 B.C. (Cambron and Hulse 1969:116). Burials related to the Morrow Mountain complex at Stanfield-Worley produced a range of named Morrow Mountain projectile point forms. However, Burial 8 at the shelter produced a single White Springs and also a Crawford Creek type point with Morrow Mountain (Round Base variant) points and a variety of other burial goods (DeJarnette et al. 1962: 14). Elsewhere, Morrow Mountain I and II projectile points have been dated to about 4500 to 5000 B.C. (Coe 1964:123; J. Chapman 1977:125). White Springs projectile points occurred with Morrow Mountain and Kirk Stemmed cluster forms in upper layer G at Russell Cave in Alabama (Ingmanson and Griffin 1974:Table 8), which again could indicate that White Springs appears in the record earlier than 5000 B.C., but additional data are required to confirm an earlier placement for White Springs.

Distribution
The Sykes and White Springs types have been identified primarily in the Tennessee

Map 46: Sykes and White Springs Distribution and Important Sites

River Valley. They are reported in Mississippi (Thorne, Broyles, and Johnson 1981:191–193), and in Tennessee (Lewis and Lewis 1961; Faulkner and Graham 1966; Faulkner 1968:182; Jolley 1979:40). They also occur in Kentucky (Weinland 1980:74, Fig. 31) and are present in low frequency in Ohio (Converse 1973:41) and southern Indiana. These types appear to be limited to a region encompassing the Tennessee and lower Ohio River Valleys in distribution.

Morphological Correlates of the White Springs Cluster
Additional type: Crawford Creek (DeJarnette, Kurjack, and Cambron 1962:53); Cambron and Hulse 1969:29, 1975:35); Ingmanson and Griffin 1974:43–45).

Benton Cluster

BENTON STEMMED

This is a large projectile point type named by Kneberg (1956:25–26; Lewis and Lewis 1961:34). It is easily recognized by the presence of oblique parallel flaking that often occurs on the blade (Figure 22). Edge beveling of the base and notch, and sometimes of the blade, is also a distinctive feature of these points. The edge bevel is bifacially flaked so that the cross section of the haft exhibits a flattened hexagon shape. This contrasts with the rhomboidal blade shapes characteristic of certain Early Archaic projectile points. The shoulders of Benton Stemmed points are never barbed. One or both sides of the blade exhibit oblique parallel flaking, accomplished by either percussion or pressure techniques. Examples with this characteristic on a single face often exhibit large percussion thinning scars on the opposite face and have a plano-convex cross section.

Age and Cultural Affiliation

These points are diagnostic of the Middle to Late Archaic periods dating from about 3500 to 2000 B.C. A radiocarbon date of 3055 B.C. ±260 was obtained from the Benton zone at the Spring Creek site in Tennessee (Peterson 1973:44). These forms predate Cotaco Creek and Mulberry Creek points and other Late Archaic types at Spring Creek, a site with good stratigraphic separation.

At the Eva site in Tennessee, Benton Stemmed points are associated with the early Big Sandy component (Lewis and Lewis 1961:34). The type was also well represented in later Archaic contest at the Stanfield-Worley Bluff Shelter (DeJarnette et al. 1962).

Distribution

Benton Stemmed points appear to have a limited distribution, as they occur primarily in northern Alabama (Ingmanson and Griffin 1974:45, Fig. 30), Mississippi (Thorne et al. 1981:231–234), Tennessee (Lewis and Lewis 1961; Faulkner 1968), and Kentucky (Wein-

Map 47: Benton Stemmed
Distribution and Important Sites

land and Fenwick 1978:55). These forms are mentioned in the recent literature for southern Illinois (May 1982:1374). These points also occur in low frequency north of the Ohio Valley into central Indiana (Black 1933:345, Plate 33; Edler 1970:70–71).

Morphological Correlate

Benton Broad Stemmed (Cambron and Hulse 1969:12).

ELK RIVER STEMMED

This is a medium-to-large, straight stemmed type that is plano-convex in cross section (DeJarnette, Kurjack, and Cambron 1962). Shoulders are often tapered, sometimes expanding. The stem is typically straight sided but is sometimes expanding or contracting, with a straight or, rarely, excurvate base (Figure 22). Of the original series (DeJarnette et al. 1962), about one-fourth had lightly ground bases. Oblique flaking on one or (usually) both faces is typical. It carries from the blade edges almost to the center of the blade, and sometimes forms a wide medial ridge. As a result of the flaking technique, marginal retouch is minimized (Cambron and Hulse 1964:82). The overall flaking pattern of the blade is essentially the same as that of the Benton Stemmed type.

Age and Cultural Affiliation

Elk River occurs during a period from 3500 to 2000 B.C., based on a date of 3055 B.C. ±260 from the Benton zone at the Spring Creek site in Tennessee (Peterson 1973:43).

The type was recovered from Levels 8 and 9 Zone A, at the Stanfield-Worley Bluff Shelter (DeJarnette et al. 1962). A Middle to Late Archaic position was also secured at Russell Cave (Ingmanson and Griffin 1974), Flint River Mound (Webb and DeJarnette 1948a), and other sites.

Distribution

These points are distributed across northern Alabama and southern Tennessee (Cambron and Hulse 1969:83; Griffin 1974). They also occur at sites in Kentucky, such as Parrish (Webb 1951:428, Fig. 5a) and Indian Knoll (Webb 1946:265, Fig. 36). The type appears dispersed in low frequency throughout the lower Ohio River Valley. Elk River projectile points have been identified in Harrison County, Indiana (Seeman 1975), as well as Rockhouse Hollow Shelter in Perry County. A

Map 48: Elk River Stemmed Distribution and Important Sites

cache of six Elk River and related points was found in a mortuary context at the Shaffer site in Greene County, Indiana (Black 1933: 275, 334, Plate 12).

Morphological Correlates of the Benton Cluster

Buzzard Roost Creek (Cambron 1958a; DeJarnette et al. 1962; Cambron and Hulse 1975:21; Webb and DeJarnette 1948b:70, Fig. 34).

Figure 22: Benton Cluster

a. Benton Stemmed. Dover/Fort Payne chert. GBL 21/367. Boone Co., Indiana. Pictured in Plate 5, h.

b. Benton Stemmed. Fort Payne chert. Florence, Alabama. Marshall L. Fallwell collection.

c. Benton Stemmed. Holland chert. GBL 31/106. Indiana.

d. Elk River Stemmed. Wyandotte chert. GBL 1817/2. Site 12 Cr 109. Shaffer Cemetery. Greene Co., Indiana.

e. Elk River Stemmed. Cobden chert. GBL 4204/2. Site 12 Po 188. Posey Co., Indiana. Pictured in Plate 5, g.

f. Elk River Stemmed. Wyandotte chert. GBL 3645/249. Provenience unknown.

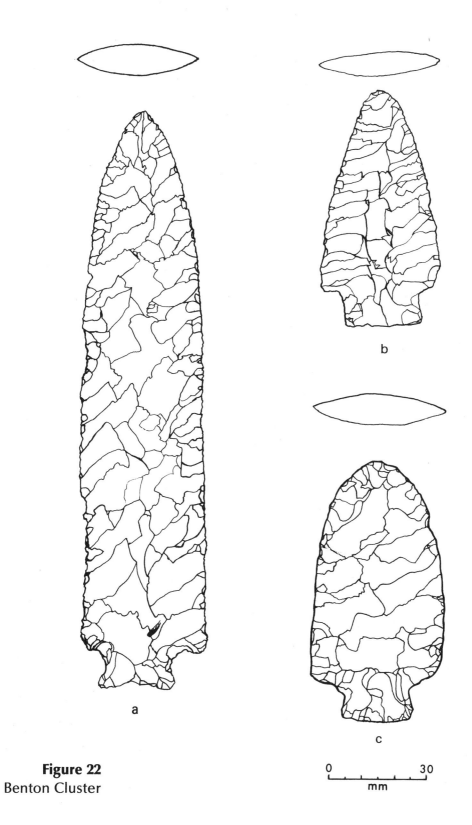

Figure 22
Benton Cluster

0 _____ 30
mm

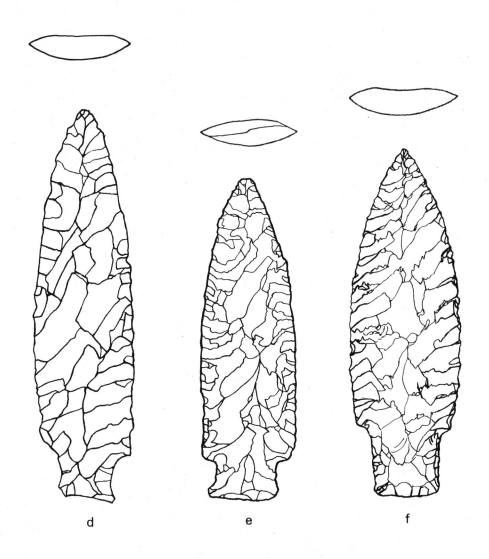

d   e   f

Figure 22

Brewerton Corner Notched Cluster

BREWERTON CORNER NOTCHED

Brewerton Corner Notched projectile points (Ritchie 1961:16) are broad-bladed and relatively thick forms. The definitive characteristic of this type is the very wide shoulders that extend beyond the basal ears (Figure 23). The blade is trianguloid in outline and biconvex in cross section. The blade edges are usually excurvate, less often straight, and rarely incurvate. Basal edges on these points are typically straight or slightly convex, and basal grinding is common. Serration and patterned pressure flaking are seldom present.

BREWERTON SIDE NOTCHED

Brewerton Side Notched points (Ritchie 1961:19) are thick, broad, trianguloid-bladed forms which are resharpening variants of the Corner Notched type (Figure 23). The blade edges vary from straight to excurvate, with incurvate edges sometimes exhibited. The base of these points varies from straight to convex. Concave bases occur in low frequency. Certain specimens sometimes bear faint blade serration and, in some cases, dual notching of the haft element. The majority of Brewerton Side Notched points exhibit basal grinding.

Brewerton Side Notched points exhibit notches at an angle and low on the preform, leaving rather sharp basal ears (Ritchie 1961: Plate 7, bottom 2 rows). Manufacturing characteristics are similar to Brewerton Corner Notched type. Blade characteristics of these two types differ in that the corner notched form exhibits prominent downward projecting shoulder barbs and a more pronounced excurvate blade. These differences indicate that blade resharpening is the primary cause for some of the overlap between these two forms. The range of variation included in Ritchie's plate 7 (upper 2 rows) incorporates

side notched forms with squared ears (Otter Creek) and weak side notched forms (Brewerton Eared) that are not relevant to this discussion of the Brewerton Side Notched type.

Age and Cultural Affiliation

Brewerton Corner Notched and Side Notched projectile points are characteristic of the Late Archaic Laurentian tradition Brewerton phase in New York and the surrounding region. These side notched forms were represented in high frequency at the Robinson and Oblander type sites (Ritchie 1969a:91–92). The Brewerton phase dates between 2980 and 1723 B.C. (Ritchie 1969a: 91; Michels 1968:310). Both Brewerton Side Notched and Corner Notched types were recovered from comparable strata at the Sheep Rock Shelter in Pennsylvania (Bebrich 1968: 310, 326).

Distribution

Brewerton Corner Notched and Side Notched projectile points occur across south-

Map 49: Brewerton Corner Notched and Side Notched Distribution and Important Sites

ern New England generally (Ritchie 1961: 16, 19). The type is recorded for New York, Pennsylvania, and southern Ontario. It is also present in most states bordering the upper Ohio Valley (Mayer-Oakes 1955; Dragoo 1959:192–193). Brewerton Side Notched points have been found in Michigan and referred to as Feeheley points (Taggart n.d.; Brunett 1966; Harrison 1966:60). The type has also been identified in Indiana, Ohio (Smith 1960; Prufer and Sofsky 1965:26; Shane and Murphy 1975; Shane 1975a:136; Vickery 1976), and as far west as Starved Rock in northern Illinois (see Mayer-Oakes 1951).

VOSBURG CORNER NOTCHED

The distinctive attributes of Vosburg (Ritchie 1961:55) are the small and narrow corner notches placed low and at the corners of a straight edged trianguloid preform (Figure 23). These notches are narrow to the interior and form weak barbs. Cross sections vary from slightly biconvex to nearly flat. The blade edges vary from straight to slightly convex. Other variant blade configurations are rare or indistinct. Weak serration occurs, although beveling or other distinct resharpening attributes are absent. The haft element is short resulting from the placement of the notches. The basal edge varies from straight to slightly concave with a high frequency of basal grinding. This type grades into the morphological range of the Brewerton Corner Notched type (Ritchie 1961:16).

Age and Cultural Affiliation

The Vosburg type is diagnostic of the Vosburg phase and appears early in the Late Archaic Laurentian tradition of New York (Ritchie 1969a:84). A date of 2780 B.C. ±80 (Funk 1965:146) was obtained for the Vosburg phase at the Sylvan Lake Rock Shelter in New York. An age range of about 3200 B.C. to 2500 B.C. is suggested (Funk 1965:139). Beekman Triangle points have also been attributed to the Vosburg phase (Funk 1965). These forms often exhibit basal grinding and other basic traits of Vosburg, although a pos-

sible manufacturing relationship with Vosburg points has not yet been investigated. Vosburg points were associated with Brewerton Eared forms, and all three occurred directly above the lowest levels of Sylvan Lake containing side notched Otter Creek points of the Vergennes phase (1965:145–146). In addition, the Vosburg type was recovered

Map 50: Vosburg Corner Notched Distribution and Important Sites

Figure 23: Brewerton Corner Notched Cluster
a. Brewerton Corner Notched. Bayport chert. GBL 13/891. South-central Michigan. Pictured in Plate 6, a.
b. Brewerton Corner Notched. Jeffersonville chert. GBL 31/100. Fulton Co., Indiana.
c. Brewerton Corner Notched. Jeffersonville chert. GBL 3117/58. Allen Co., Indiana.
d. Brewerton Side Notched. Liston Creek chert. GBL 2687/95. Site 12 Al 64. Allen Co., Indiana.
e. Brewerton Side Notched. Unidentified chert. GBL 10/60. Erie Co., Pennsylvania.
f. Brewerton Side Notched. Unidentified chert. GBL 2687/101. Site 12 Al 64. Allen Co., Indiana.
g. Vosburg. Chert. GBL 10/86. Erie Co., Pennsylvania.
h. Vosburg. Unidentified chert. New York. Redrawn from Ritchie (1971a:55).
i. Vosburg. Bayport chert. GBL 13/891. South-central Michigan.

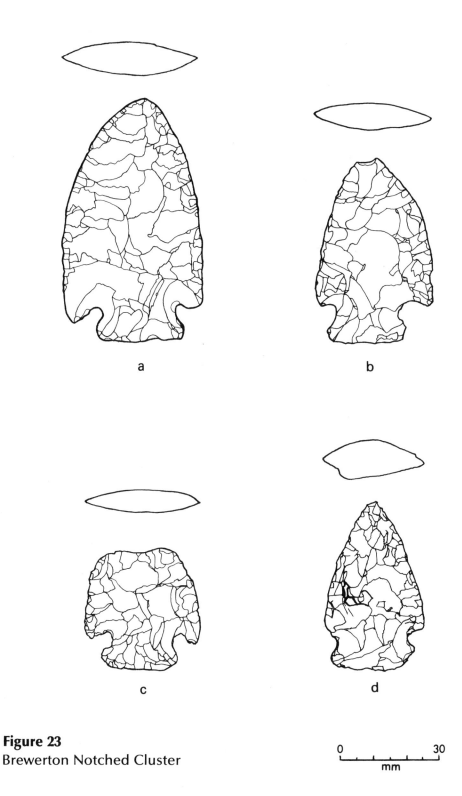

Figure 23
Brewerton Notched Cluster

0   30
mm

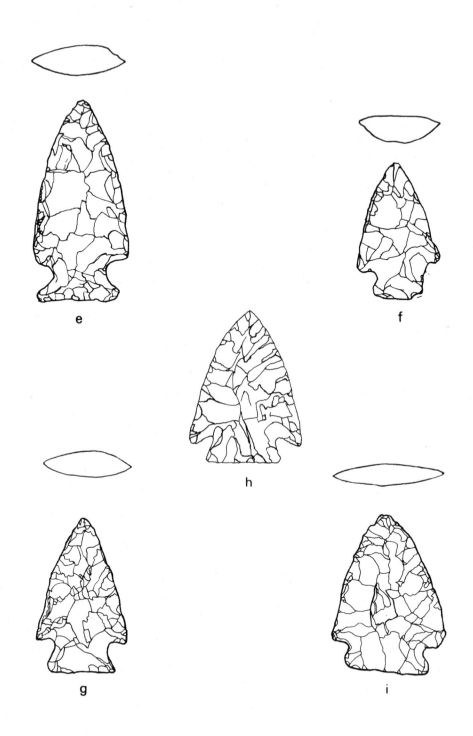

e

f

h

g

i

Figure 23

from deposits above those containing Neville points at the Neville site in New Hampshire (Dincauze 1976:36). Neville stemmed points correlate with the Stanly type defined by Coe (1964).

Distribution

Vosburg projectile points occur primarily in eastern New York in the major river valleys (Ritchie 1961:55). The type is also reported in the upper Delaware and Hudson Valleys and is present across much of the Northeast to the coast (Kinsey 1972; Rose 1965:36; Starbuck 1980; Bourn 1977). Vosburg points also occur east into Ohio, where they have been recognized at a number of Archaic sites (Prufer and Sofsky 1965:32–33; Vickery 1976: 141). The type appears to occur in very low frequency in Indiana.

Morphological Correlates of the Brewerton Corner Notched Cluster

Feeheley Points (Taggart n.d., 1967:154–156, Harrison 1966:60; Roosa 1966:29; Fitting 1970:74–75, Fig. 27, Fitting et al. n.d.:6–7). Additional type: Sylvan Side Notched (Funk 1965; Ritchie 1971a:129).

Matanzas Cluster

MATANZAS SIDE NOTCHED

The Matanzas Side Notched type (Munson and Harn 1966:153–154) is a small, shallow, side notched form with notches placed low on the preform (Figure 24). Straight basal edges are most typical, although concave and convex bases occur in low frequency.

Matanzas points from Horizon 6 at Koster site have been thoroughly studied by Cook (1976:140–144), who subdivided the Matanzas Side Notched sample from Koster into five classes based on varying notch dimensions (i.e., Modal, Flared Stem, Faint Side Notched, Deep Side Notched, and Straight Stem). The Modal Matanzas is the classic morphological type named by Munson and Harn (1966). The others (see Cook 1976: 164–167, Figs. 36–39), with the exception of the straight stemmed form, cover the range of variation of Matanzas Side Notched. Cook indicates that the Straight Stem Matanzas is very different from the others (1976:144), and it is not included here.

The remaining description of Matanzas Side Notched is based on Cook's (1976) discussion of Modal Matanzas. The blades of these points are highly symmetrical, bi-convex in cross section, and tend toward a diamond shape in reworked specimens. Long and narrow pressure flake scars typically cover the blade. The shallow side notches mentioned above are placed so low on the preform that the basal ear margins do not exhibit a continuation of the blade contour, as in the Raddatz Side Notched and Godar types. A very high percentage of Matanzas points exhibit grinding on the base and within the notch. Only a few examples lack grinding.

Age and Cultural Affiliation

Matanzas points are diagnostic of the Late Archaic period (Munson and Harn 1966; Munson 1976). These projectile points are representative of two known phases, the Helton phase defined for the lower Illinois River Valley (Cook 1976), and the French Lick phase defined for southern Indiana (Munson and Cook 1980). Matanzas points were recovered within Horizon 6 (middle) at the Koster site, which is dated from about 3700 to 3000 B.C. (Cook 1976:Tables 16–17). A number of Late Archaic midden sites in southern Indiana and adjacent areas have produced dates which overlap this period and extend to about 2000 B.C. (see Janzen

1977; Munson and Cook 1980:Table 19.2). However, specific radiocarbon dates from prehistoric sites with campfires or pits containing Matanzas points exclusively are largely unknown.

The Uebelhack site, a multicomponent site located in Posey County, Indiana, is significant from a chronological standpoint. A date of 2260 B.C. ±85 was derived from a level directly above a level containing two Matanzas points. This suggests that the terminal date for Matanzas Side Notched points was prior to 2000 B.C. Raddatz and Kirk Corner Notched projectile point styles occurred below the Matanzas level. Late Archaic and Early Woodland materials such as Saratoga and Motley were recovered from the upper levels of the site.

Distribution

Matanzas points are common across much of central and southern Indiana and Illinois (Munson and Harn 1966; Munson 1976; Cook 1976, 1980; Conrad 1981). They occur in high frequency along the central Mississippi River Valley and lower Missouri and Illinois River Valleys (Perino 1968a:54). These forms are also common in the Ohio River Valley of southern Indiana and Kentucky (Guernsey 1942; Bellis 1968). The eastern extent of distribution for these forms may be within the state of Ohio where these forms were named "Fishspear points" (Converse 1973; Oplinger 1981:26, Fig. 7e). The distributions of Brewerton Eared forms and Matanzas overlap in the Ohio Valley (Vickery 1976:128; Shane and Murphy 1975). Both occupy the same temporal unit, suggesting a possible technological interface or a chronological difference which is not presently demonstrated within the Midwest.

Morphological Correlates

Helton (Houart 1971:36, Fig. 11c–f); Modal Matanzas; Flared Stem Matanzas; Faint Side Notched Matanzas; Deep Side Notched Matanzas (Cook 1976:140–146, Figs. 163–167); Fishspear Points (Converse 1973:46); Brunswick (Tomak 1980b:4, Fig. 9).

Map 51: Matanzas Side Notched Distribution and Important Sites

Figure 24: Matanzas Cluster
a. Matanzas Side Notched. Wyandotte chert. GBL 1448/62. Southwestern Indiana.
b. Matanzas Side Notched. Holland chert. GBL 421/275. Greene Co., Indiana.
c. Matanzas Side Notched. Jeffersonville chert. GBL 102/40. Decatur Co., Indiana.
d. Matanzas Side Notched. Attica chert. GBL 3243/1. Knox Co., Indiana.
e. Matanzas Side Notched. Unidentified chert. GBL 1448/81. Southwestern Indiana.
f. Matanzas Side Notched. Unidentified chert. GBL 5/239. Warrick Co., Indiana.
g. Brewerton Eared-Notched. Indian Creek chert. GBL 2090/15. Site 12 Hr 150. Harrison Co., Indiana.
h. Brewerton Eared-Notched. Unidentified chert. New York. Redrawn from Ritchie (1971a:17).
i. Brewerton Eared-Notched. Jeffersonville chert. GBL 817/92. McCain site, 12 Du 14. Dubois Co., Indiana. Pictured in Plate 6, e.
j. Brewerton Eared-Triangle. Unidentified chert. GBL 281/265. Vermont.
k. Brewerton Eared-Triangle. Unidentified chert. New York. Redrawn from Ritchie (1971a:18).
l. Brewerton Eared-Triangle. Unidentified fossiliferous chert. GBL 817/90. McCain site, 12 Du 14. Dubois Co., Indiana. Pictured in Plate 6, j.

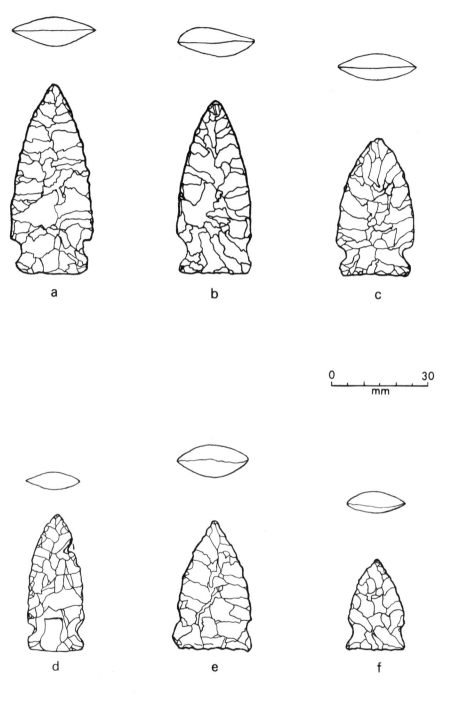

a

b

c

0   30
mm

d

e

f

FIGURE 24

Figure 24
Matanzas Cluster

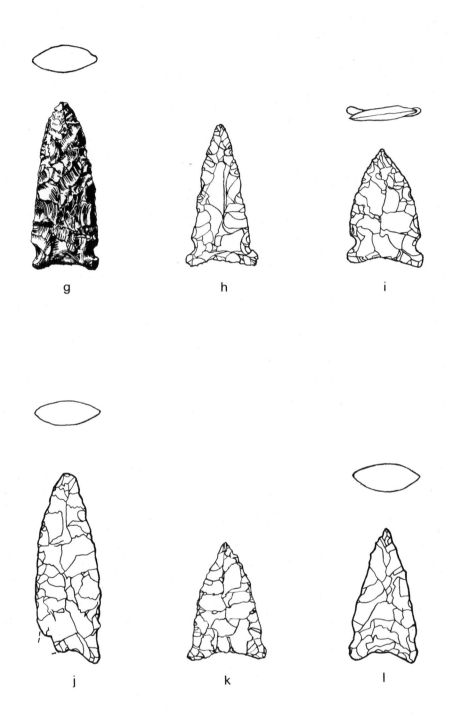

Figure 24

BREWERTON
EARED-NOTCHED

Brewerton Eared-Notched points (Ritchie 1961:17) are thick, weakly side notched points with concave bases, and ears which project beyond the blade edges (Figure 24). The blade shape of Brewerton Eared-Notched is trianguloid, with straightened or slightly excurvate edges. The cross section of the blade is biconvex. The ears and base are finely retouched with unground or slightly ground edges.

The Brewerton Eared-Triangle type (Ritchie 1961:18) is considered here as a variation of the Eared-Notched type. This is a slightly wider variant exhibiting a thinner blade (relative to blade width) than the Brewerton Eared-Notched type. This type also exhibits occasional grinding on the ears. All essential characteristics of these two named types are the same. The ranges of variation overlap and they exhibit few attributes which would separate them. Blade characteristics of both types suggest a highly reworked state and possibly degrees of resharpening of a single basic form.

Age and Cultural Affiliation

Both Brewerton Eared projectile point forms are diagnostic of the Late Archaic period in the northeastern United States. In New York, these named types are a small percentage of the projectile point inventory of the Brewerton phase sites such as Robinson and Oblander No. 1. Brewerton phase dates range between 2980 and 1723 B.C. (Ritchie 1969a: 89–91). Bebrich (1968:327) dates these types derived from the Sheep Rock Shelter in Pennsylvania toward the middle of the range of dates for New York (2350 B.C.). Recently, at the Miler A site in southern Indiana (Cook 1980:373), a date of 2535 B.C. ±70 was obtained for these points, which also fits well within the dates for New York.

Brewerton Eared type points were recovered from burials covered with Red Ocher at the Bliss Yard site in Connecticut. These were funerary offerings associated with atlatl weights, axes, scrapers, metallic nuggets,

quartz crystal, sheet mica, animal bone, nuts, and seeds. The Bliss Burial complex is dated from 2825 ±120 B.C. to 2585 ±95 B.C. which complements the above age estimates (Pfeifer 1984:74–75).

Distribution

Brewerton Eared projectile points are known over much of the Northeast and within the Ohio River Valley and tributaries. These points are well documented in the northeastern states, especially New York and Massachusetts (Ritchie 1961:17). Shell middens on Martha's Vineyard situated along the southern New England coast also produced these points (Ritchie 1969b:39). They have also been recovered from sites in Pennsylvania (Kinsey 1972; Michels and Dutt 1968) and extend across southern Ohio, where they occur at sites such as Maple Creek (Vickery 1976).

Brewerton Eared points occur in buried shell middens and other sites at the Falls of the Ohio in Indiana and Kentucky (Guernsey 1939; Jansen 1971; Boisvert et al. 1979). They are also represented in the collections from the McCain (Miller 1941), Breeden (Bellis 1982), and other sites in southern Indiana.

Map 52: Brewerton Eared-Notched and Eared-Triangle
Distribution and Important Sites

Brewerton Eared points extend down the lower Ohio Valley into southern Illinois in declining frequency (Butler et al. 1979:94).

Morphological Correlates of the Matanzas Cluster
Kittatinny (Kraft 1975:23–28; McNett 1985: 107–108, 111); Stubby Shallow Side Notched

(Duffield 1966:60–61; Boisvert et al. 1979: 225); Salt River Side Notched (Janzen 1971, 1977; Munson and Cook 1980:723, Table 19.2).

Table Rock Cluster

TABLE ROCK STEMMED

Projectile points exhibiting refined and symmetrical blades and ground stems were first noted at the Rice site in the Table Rock Reservoir in Missouri (Bray 1956:127). Table Rock points exhibit a slightly expanding stem with a basal edge which varies from straight to slightly concave. Full haft grinding occurs across the base and lateral margins to the shoulder. Those specimens which appear better finished normally exhibit the heaviest haft grinding. Shoulders on these points are gently rounded. The blade edge is straight to slightly convex with a biconvex cross section. These points were manufactured using a combination of refined percussion and pressure flaking (Figure 25).

As a rule, Table Rock points are larger, more thickly biconvex or plano convex than the closely similar Bottleneck type. Table Rock Stemmed points exhibit wider haft dimensions relative to shoulder width than Bottleneck. In addition, Bottleneck points are finished using a delicate pressure flaking technique which commonly covers the blade with numerous minute and lengthy flake scars.

Age and Cultural Affiliation
The Table Rock Stemmed point type is diagnostic of the Late Archaic period. Its age is estimated to be from 3000 to 1000 B.C. (C. Chapman 1975:258).

Distribution
Table Rock Stemmed points occur in Missouri, northern Arkansas, eastern Kansas, and northeastern Oklahoma (Perino 1968a:96; C. Chapman 1975:258). Table Rock points occur in southern Indiana, Kentucky (Schock and Langford 1979b:39, Plate 11, g–i), southern Illinois (May 1982:1374), and probably in adjacent areas, but apparently in much lower frequency than Bottleneck. The vast majority of Table Rock cluster projectile points identified in Ohio, Indiana, and Illinois belong to the Bottleneck type, not Table Rock.

BOTTLENECK STEMMED

The Bottleneck Stemmed type (Kramer 1947) characteristically exhibits superb pressure flaking over much of the blade surface (Figure 25). Large round notches which constrict the stem are well executed with per-

Figure 25: Table Rock Cluster
a. Table Rock Stemmed. Unidentified chert. GBL 13/890. South-central Michigan.
b. Table Rock Stemmed. Leiber chert. GBL 31/ 100. Fulton Co., Indiana.
c. Bottleneck Stemmed. Holland chert. GBL 1069/5. Site 12 Mr 114. Marshall Co., Indiana.
d. Bottleneck Stemmed. Liston Creek chert. GBL 2670/4. Site 12 Al 45. Allen Co., Indiana.
e. Bottleneck Stemmed. Burlington chert. GBL 22/59. Missouri.

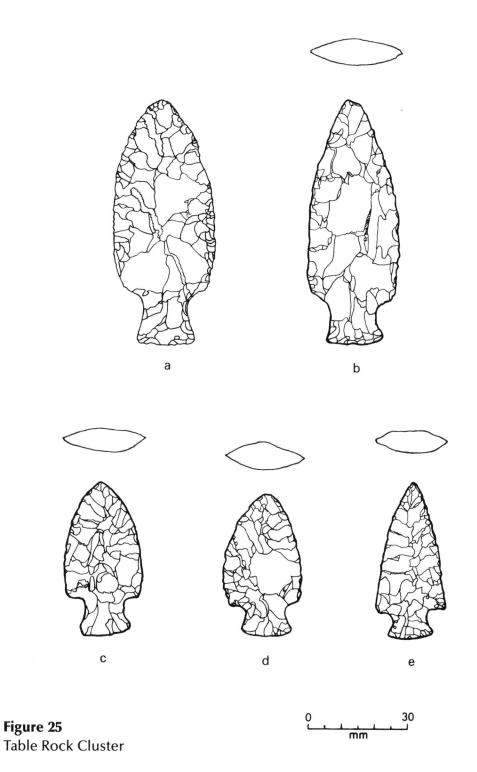

Figure 25
Table Rock Cluster

0   30
mm

Map 53: Table Rock Stemmed—Distribution and Important Sites

cussion. The stem expands below rounded shoulders, producing a bottleneck-shaped base that is graceful in form. Heavy grinding is present on both the interior of the notch and the stem basal edge. The basal edge can appear straightened, although commonly the base is convex. In the former case the ears often curve upward prior to joining the lower edge of the notch. Cross sections are always very regular plano convex or biconvex. Blade edges are consistently excurvate throughout resharpening using pressure flaking, which simply reduces the size of the blade (Converse 1973:43; Shane 1975a: 164–165).

Table Rock is similar to Bottleneck Stemmed, although less refined, and with maximum length and width dimensions greater than Bottleneck Stemmed.

Age and Cultural Affiliation
Bottleneck Stemmed points are diagnostic of the Late Archaic period. Little exists in the way of sound radiocarbon determinations and solid associations for these forms. The Bottleneck Stemmed type was recovered from Horizon 6 at Koster site in Illinois which is dated from ca. 3770 to ca. 3000 B.C. This type was reported within a class referred to as Apple Blossom Stemmed at the site (Cook 1976:147–148, Fig. 42; Conrad 1981:131). Bottleneck Stemmed is probably derived from Matanzas Side Notched.

Distribution
Bottleneck Stemmed points are distributed in low frequency in the Midwest. The type is present across much of Ohio (Kramer 1947; Converse 1973; Shane 1975a) and Indiana (Guendling and Crouch 1977:100, Fig. 2a), although few have been recorded at Archaic sites in the Ohio River Valley. Conrad (1981: 131–132) identified several Bottleneck points in west-central Illinois, which suggests that the type may be more widespread in the state as a whole. Bottleneck Stemmed points occur in the Missouri area overlapping the distribution of Table Rock Stemmed (C. Chapman 1975:196, Fig. 8–9a). Their distribution may be across a somewhat larger undefined area such as the Great Lakes region where somewhat similar Lamoka cluster forms predominate.

Map 54: Bottleneck Stemmed—Distribution and Important Sites

Morphological Correlate
Apple Blossom Stemmed (Cook 1976:147–148, Fig. 42, lower right; pers. comm.).

*Morphological Correlates of
the Table Rock Cluster*
Additional type: Flint Creek (Cambron 1958b; DeJarnette et al. 1962; Cambron and Hulse 1975; Oakley and Futato 1975).

Lamoka Cluster

LAMOKA

Lamoka projectile points (Ritchie 1932; 1961: 29–30) are small, narrow, and thick forms with hafting elements that vary from expanding to straight stemmed with sloping shoulders (Figure 26). The blade shape is trianguloid in outline with a biconvex to diamond-shaped cross section. The blade edges vary from excurvate to straight. The haft region is as thick as the blade with the basal edge varying from straight to oblique to convex. An unmodified portion of the original flake, block, or pebble often remains intact on the base. This unflaked surface is a prime diagnostic feature of Lamoka points.

Two other named projectile points should be mentioned, as they are considered to be regional names of the Lamoka point. The Dustin point (Binford and Papworth 1963: 105) of Michigan and the Durst Stemmed point (Wittry 1959a,b) of Wisconsin exhibit attributes similar to those of Lamoka, making them visually inseparable (Binford and Papworth 1963:105). Wittry (1959b:179) described the low frequency occurrence of the unworked base and thick cross section of Durst. Harrison (1966:57) reported that

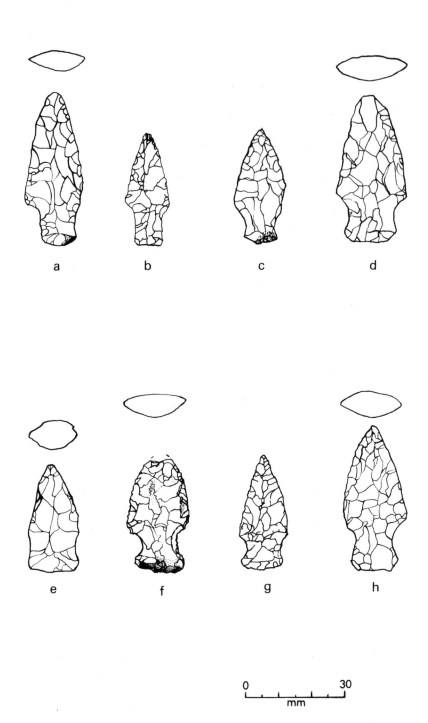

a   b   c   d

e   f   g   h

0   30
mm

nearly one-half of the sample of Dustin points from the Schmidt site in Michigan exhibited unfinished bases and a predominance of thick biconvex to diamond-shaped cross sections. All three of these named point types share similar blade form, variable haft attributes, and reworking processes. Note that points from the Lamoka Lake site in New York were products of a pebble industry, accounting in part for the intact original surfaces. Finished bases and basal grinding also occur in the range of forms discussed here (Harrison 1966:57; Wittry 1959a:48).

Age and Cultural Affiliation

Lamoka points signify a Late Archaic association in the Northeast and elsewhere. They have been dated to within a range of 3500 to 2500 B.C. for the New York Archaic Lamoka phase (Ritchie 1961:29–30, 1969a:31–32). An age of 2570 to 1800 B.C. has been obtained in the upper Susquehanna Valley for a Lamoka occupation suggesting a later continuation of this phase (see Funk and Rippeteau 1977:30).

Within eastern and southern New York, points of the Lamoka type are associated with other narrow stemmed point variations such as Bare Island and Wading River (Ritchie 1971a:132, 1971b:5). These and other types occur on the Atlantic coast at a number of localities such as the Fastener site in Connecticut (Lavin and Salwen 1983), on Martha's Vineyard (Ritchie 1969b), and at Twombly

Figure 26: Lamoka Cluster

a. Lamoka. Liston Creek chert. GBL 2682/8. Site 12 Al 59. Allen Co., Indiana.
b. Lamoka. Unidentified chert. New York. Redrawn from Ritchie (1971a:29).
c. Lamoka. Unidentified chert. GBL 2681/62. Whiting site, 12 AL 58. Allen Co., Indiana.
d. Lamoka. Bayport chert. GBL 13/891. South-central Michigan.
e. Lamoka. Unidentified chert. GBL 10/53. Erie Co., Pennsylvania.
f. Lamoka. Upper Mercer chert. GBL 3117/46. Allen Co., Indiana.
g. Lamoka. Unidentified chert. New York. Redrawn from Ritchie (1971a:29).
h. Lamoka. Unidentified chert. GBL 13/891. South-central Michigan. Pictured in Plate 6.

Landing (Brennan 1967). These small, narrow stemmed type projectile points appear related technologically and make up what has been referred to as the Taconic tradition, which is best known from shell midden sites (Brennan 1967).

Distribution

The Lamoka phase of the Laurentian Archaic is confined to the northeastern states (Ritchie 1932, 1961, 1969a: Leslie 1963). Yet Lamoka cluster points (i.e., Dustin and Durst Stemmed) essentially the same forms as Lamoka are distributed throughout the Great Lakes region and occur in low frequency in the Ohio Valley. Eastern Iowa (Anderson 1981:19) probably represents the maximum western extent of these projectile points. Lamoka points appear to have a maximum southern distribution within the states of Virginia (Holland 1970) and Kentucky (Schock et al. 1977:29; Schock and Langford 1979b: 90). These types are represented in low frequency over much of Ohio (McKenzie 1967: 37–39; Shane 1975a:138; Vickery 1976:128) and central Indiana (Guendling and Crouch 1977:103).

Map 55: Lamoka—Distribution and Important Sites

Morphological Correlates
Durst Stemmed (Wittry 1959a,b); Dustin
(Binford and Papworth 1963; Wright and
Morlan 1964; Shane 1975a:139).

Morphological Correlates of
the Lamoka Cluster
Bare Island, Wading River (Ritchie 1971a,b);
MacPherson (Kinsey 1972:411–412, Fig.
117a). Additional type: Normanskill (Ritchie
1971a:37; Kinsey 1972; 414–415; Walsh 1977:
34, Plate 3).

Merom Cluster

MEROM EXPANDING STEMMED

Merom Expanding Stemmed points (Winters
1969) are small, side-notched to expanding-
stemmed points with a trianguloid blade and
unbarbed shoulders (Figure 27). The cross
section varies from flattened to biconvex.
Light serration of the blade occurred nearly
45 percent of the time in Winters's (1969)
sample. Basal beveling occurs to a lesser extent with a low incidence of very light basal
and lateral grinding. Stems range from markedly flaring to slightly flaring with convex
basal edges. Length to width ratio averages
1.9 for the major group of Merom points.
Blade to length of stem ratio was 3.9 in the
sample from the Riverton site. These points
were manufactured using variable percussion and pressure flaking techniques.

TRIMBLE SIDE NOTCHED

Trimble Side Notched points (Winters 1969)
are small trianguloid-shaped points that are
related to Merom Expanding Stemmed (Figure 27). These points have notches close to
the base and generally perpendicular to the
long axis of the point. The notching characteristics overlap with those of the Merom
Expanding Stemmed type. Trimble Side
Notched points exhibit little or no basal beveling, and serration is not common. These
points show greater frequency of lenticular
cross sections, and straight sided blade edges

are more common. The blades of Trimble
points tend to be longer and narrower than
Merom points. These projectile points often
exhibit refined pressure flaking across the
blade and haft element.

Age and Cultural Affiliation
Trimble Side Notched and Merom Expanding Stemmed projectile points are diagnostic
of the Late Archaic Riverton culture which
dates from about 1600 B.C. to 1000 B.C. (Winters 1969). Recently a date of 810 B.C. ±95
was reported from the Cooke site in Parke
County, Indiana (Pace and Coffing 1978:81),
which is the latest radiocarbon date yet derived for this manifestation.

Dealing only with the projectile points,
Winters (1969:108–109, 152, 154) suggested
that these forms may have appeared prior

Figure 27: Merom Cluster
a–b. Merom Expanding Stemmed. Attica
chert. GBL 1448/344. Southwestern Indiana.
c. Merom Expanding Stemmed. Attica chert.
GBL 1448/342. Southwestern Indiana.
d. Merom Expanding Stemmed. Wyandotte
chert. GBL 1130/172. Site 12 Sp 44. Spencer
Co., Indiana.
e. Trimble Side Notched. Unidentified chert.
GBL 1961/19. Site 12 Sw 19. Switzerland Co.,
Indiana.
f. Trimble Side Notched. Unidentified chert.
GBL 113/5. Site 12 D 26. Dearborn Co., Indiana.
g. Trimble Side Notched. Unidentified chert.
GBL 3716/1. Site 12 B 187. Bartholomew Co.,
Indiana.
h. Trimble Side Notched. Unidentified chert.
GBL 962/8. Raaf Mound, 12 Sp 1. Spencer Co.,
Indiana. Pictured in Plate 6, m.

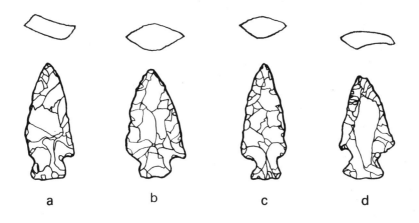

a   b   c   d

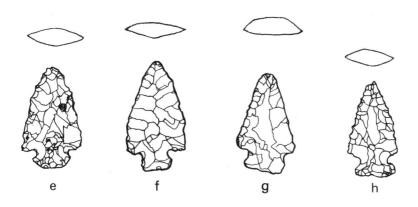

e   f   g   h

Figure 27
Merom Cluster

to 2000 B.C. Additionally, the Trimble Side Notched type was found in higher frequency in the lower strata at the Swan Island and Riverton sites in the Wabash Valley. Its popularity declined rapidly after 1500 B.C. Winters (1969:154) suggested that these points may represent a later manifestation of the Side Notched tradition. The closest possible ancestor from a morphological point of view is the Matanzas Side Notched type defined by Munson and Harn (1966:153–154). In the original illustrations of Trimble type variations, one can find a few examples which are either well within the range of Matanzas cluster forms or good examples of the Matanzas type itself (see Winters 1969:Plate 14, L). Matanzas points occur in the Late Archaic period just prior to the appearance of Trimble Side Notched. The overall suggestion is that the lithic technology of the Helton (Cook 1976), French Lick (Munson and Cook 1980), or another undefined Late Archaic phase with diagnostic Matanzas cluster points was responsible for the appearance of the lithic technology of the Riverton culture.

Distribution

The distribution of Merom Expanding Stemmed and Trimble Side Notched projectile points was originally defined in the central Wabash Valley from a sample of approximately thirty Riverton culture sites identified in Indiana and Illinois (Winters 1969:110). These forms are now known to occur across a much larger area covering nearly all of southern Indiana including the East and West Forks of the White River (Tomak 1982, 1980b:4). The Wint site in Bartholomew County is a Riverton base camp near the eastern boundary (Wolfal, McClure, and Pace 1978:81). These forms are also present in the Ohio River Valley of southern Indiana (Seeman 1975), Ohio (Vickery 1976: 141), Kentucky (Boisvert et al. 1979:159–165), and Illinois (Butler, Harrell, and Hamilton 1979:35; May 1982:1374). They are also

Map 56: Merom Cluster—
Distribution and Important Sites

reported in western Illinois including the Illinois River Valley (see Conrad 1981:174).

It is important to note that the distribution of small point assemblages in general does not correlate with the distribution of Riverton culture sites. In most areas that were formerly glaciated, such as southern Michigan and northern Indiana, where chert resources are not abundant, projectile points representing all periods in prehistory tend to be small when manufactured from chert pebbles found in local glacial gravel. The same holds true for chipped stone tools made from chert pebbles selected out of gravel bars in rivers south of glaciated areas. Winters (pers. comm.) warns that the identification of Riverton culture manifestations requires the analysis of whole assemblages.

Morphological Correlates of the Merom Cluster

Robeson Constricted Stem (Winters n.d., 1963, 1969:37; pers. comm.); Birdpoint (Converse 1973:72).

Late Archaic Stemmed Cluster

KARNAK UNSTEMMED

The Karnak Unstemmed projectile point (Cook 1980:390) is a thick lanceolate form (Figure 28). Based on the three measures of length, width, and thickness, Cook (1980: Table 17.15) found little difference between this and the Karnak Stemmed type discussed in this cluster. However, Karnak Unstemmed lacks shoulders and straight stemmed margins, nor does it possess slight basal ears typical of the Karnak Stemmed type. All essential morphological characteristics of the unstemmed form are shared with Karnak Stemmed with the exception of an obvious haft element. Percussion flaking is the typical reduction technique followed by pressure flaking of the edges for resharpening. Overall, Karnak Unstemmed projectile points apparently served both as a viable finished tool and as preforms for Karnak Stemmed Points.

Age and Cultural Affiliation
These projectile points are diagnostic of the Late Archaic Helton and French Lick phases and date from 3700 to 3000 B.C. (Cook 1976: Tables 16–17; Munson and Cook 1980).

Distribution
In their core area in the Midwest, Karnak Unstemmed points seldom occur without the Karnak Stemmed form. In central and southern Illinois, Cook (1976, 1980) and Winters (1963) report the presence of this morphological duality (see also May 1982). In central Indiana (Little 1970; Munson 1976; Cook 1980), especially in the Karst area of Monroe and surrounding counties, manufacturing debris representing Karnak forms occurs in large quantities on a series of sizeable recorded Late Archaic base camps, such as Oliver's Vineyard and the Sisson site. Karnak Unstemmed projectile points occur in greatly reduced numbers in northern Kentucky (Webb 1950a:308) and southern Ohio (Vickery 1972). Beyond the core area defined

Map 57: Karnak Unstemmed Distribution and Important Sites

above, little information exists on locations of camps of comparable magnitude. Karnak Stemmed forms appear to have a slightly wider distribution into south-central Kentucky (Schock and Langford 1979b).

The Guilford complex (Coe 1964) of North Carolina, outside the core area for Karnak material, is typified by the Guilford Lanceolate and Guilford Rounded Base projectile point types. These appear to share some basic attributes and dimensions of Karnak Unstemmed. However, any traditional link between Karnak and Guilford is doubtful. Geographically, Guilford complex material ranges from the Tennessee River Valley of northern Alabama northeast into the central Appalachian region. Guilford complex material does not appear to be as concentrated at identified sites as Karnak material on Late Archaic French Lick phase sites.

It is more appropriate to compare and contrast the assemblages of Late Archaic sites in Missouri which contain material similar to Karnak Unstemmed, such as the Booth Site (cf. Klippel 1969:9–13, Figs. 3–5). The Sedalia and Nebo Hill reduction strategies at this site resulted in miniature lanceolate points that compare rather well with Karnak. It is also noteworthy that the distributions of these types overlap with Karnak. Each of these requires studies of its manufacturing trajectories in order to adequately demonstrate differences and/or commonalities. In additional geographic areas, there are yet other lanceolate stemmed forms that are percussion flaked in a manner like Karnak. In Michigan and southern Ontario, similar materials occur within Late Archaic Satchel complex assemblages (see Kenyon 1980b:28, Fig. 3). But factors of frequency and raw material usage within these assemblages should reflect differences in the manufacturing trajectory that do not compare with Karnak and there is also no distributional overlap.

Morphological Correlate
Modesto (Tomak 1980a:106, Fig. 1).

KARNAK STEMMED

The Karnak Stemmed type (Winters n.d., 1963, 1967:19; Cook 1976:138–139) is a thick and narrow, crudely made, square-stemmed projectile point with an elongated blade (Figure 28). The stem is usually straight-edged and trapezoid in shape with the broader edge of the stem at the shoulder/haft juncture. Occasionally there are slight ears at the corner of the stem. The base varies from concave to convex, but seldom deviates over 2 mm. from a straight edge. Light to moderate basal and lateral grinding occur, although these are not requisite attributes of the type. Cook notes that the blades of these points are generally laurel-leaf in shape with maximum width occurring above the shoulder. Upon resharpening, the blade assumes a straightened edge and hexagonal cross section with a shortening of the blade length. Those points exhibiting distinct shoulders sometimes possess biconvex cross sections. Incurving blade edges in conjunc-

tion with distinct shoulders are also typical of resharpened blades (see Denny 1972: 152–153; May 1982:1367–1369).

Age and Cultural Affiliation
Karnak Stemmed points occur during the Late Archaic period and date from approximately 3700 to 3000 B.C. (Cook 1976:Tables 16–17). The Karnak point is a diagnostic artifact of the Helton phase defined for the lower Illinois River Valley (Koster site, Horizon 6) and is a typical diagnostic of the French Lick phase of interior southern Indiana (Cook 1976; Munson and Cook 1980).

Figure 28: Late Archaic Stemmed Cluster
a–c. Karnak Unstemmed. Basal fragments. Unidentified chert. GBL 3976. Sisson site, 12 Mo 133. Monroe Co., Indiana.
d. Karnak Unstemmed. Unidentified Fossiliferous chert. GBL 3207/117. Olivers Vineyard, 12 Mo 141. Monroe Co., Indiana.
e. Karnak Unstemmed. Unidentified chert. GBL 5/213. Warrick Co., Indiana.
f. Karnak Stemmed. Exhibits resharpened blade. Wyandotte chert. GBL 623/27. Site 12 Gi 13. Gibson Co., Indiana.
g. Karnak Stemmed. Hafted scraper. Wyandotte chert. GBL 817/83. McCain site, 12 Du 14. Dubois Co., Indiana.
h. Karnak Stemmed. Exhibits resharpened blade. Wyandotte chert. GBL 625/32. Site 12 Gi 30. Gibson Co., Indiana.
i. Karnak Stemmed. Haney chert. GBL 817/95. McCain site, 12 Du 14. Dubois Co., Indiana.
j. Karnak Stemmed. Unidentified Fossiliferous chert. GBL 3976/32. Sisson site, 12 Mo 133. Monroe Co., Indiana.
k. Karnak Stemmed. Wyandotte chert. GBL 5241/1. Site 12 Cr 25. Crawford Co., Indiana.
l. McWhinney Heavy Stemmed. Muldraugh chert. GBL 112/28. Brown Co., Indiana.
m. McWhinney Heavy Stemmed. Unidentified chert. GBL 1448/81. Southwestern Indiana.
n. McWhinney Heavy Stemmed. Unidentified chert. GBL 219/5. Elrod site. 12 Cl 1. Clark Co., Indiana.
o. McWhinney Heavy Stemmed. Unidentified chert. GBL 14/927. Rush Co., Indiana.
p. McWhinney Heavy Stemmed. Jeffersonville chert. GBL 1978/23. Site 12 Sw 36. Switzerland Co., Indiana.
q. McWhinney Heavy Stemmed. Muldraugh chert. GBL 219/4. Elrod site. 12 Cl 1. Clark Co., Indiana. Pictured in Plate 6, n.
r. McWhinney Heavy Stemmed. Muldraugh chert. GBL 285/10. Clark Co., Indiana.

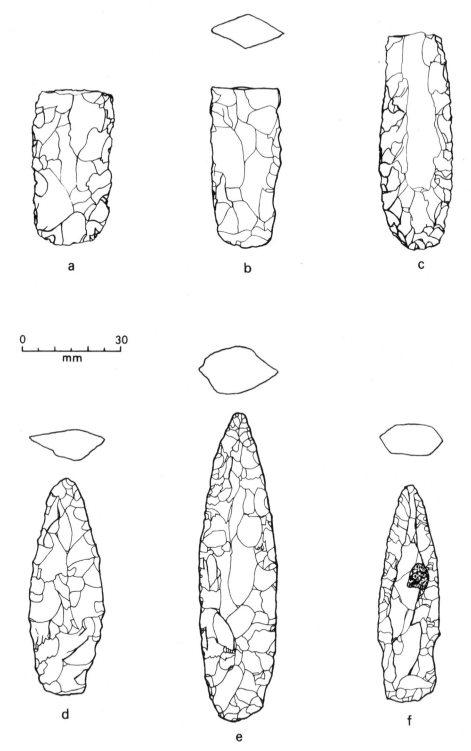

a

b

c

0 —————— 30
mm

d

e

f

Figure 28
Late Archaic Stemmed Cluster

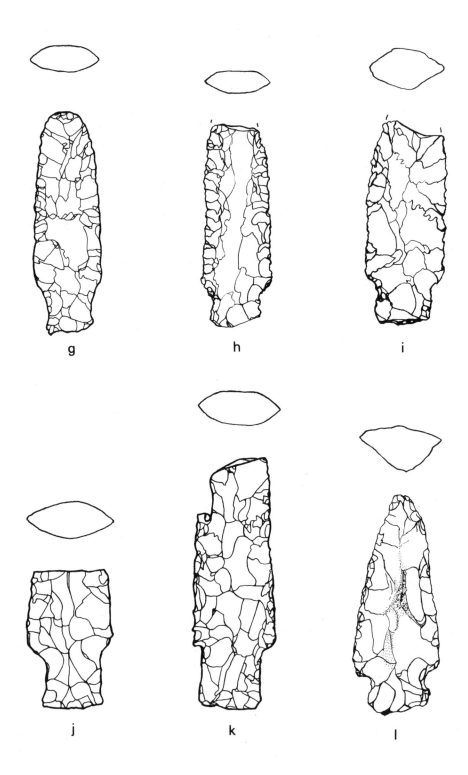

g   h   i

j   k   l

Figure 28

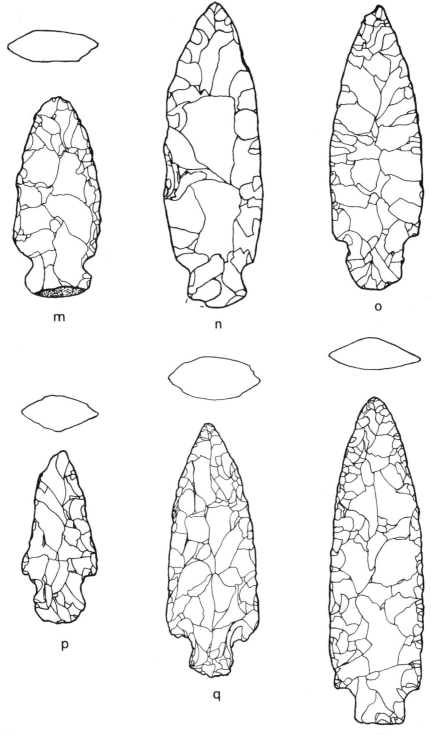

Figure 28

m

n

o

p

q

r

Distribution

Karnak points occur throughout the region surrounding the confluence of the Illinois and Mississippi River Valleys (Cook 1976). Its presence has been observed in central and southern Illinois (Perino 1962:46; May 1982) and in low frequency in Iowa (Morrow 1984). Winters (1963) also found this type in low frequency in the lower Wabash Valley of Illinois and it is present in Kentucky (Mocas 1976; Schock and Langford 1979b).

Map 58: Karnak Stemmed
Distribution and Important Sites

In southern Indiana, Karnak points are widespread. These points were recovered from within shell middens at Clark's Point (Guernsey 1939) and other sites in the Falls of the Ohio region (Janzen 1977). The well-known McCain site in Dubois County, Indiana, produced these points (Miller 1941). Numerous Karnak forms were also present at the Sisson site and on large midden sites in the Monroe Reservoir area (Munson 1976: 115) and were represented at sites in the Patoka Reservoir (Cook 1980:391). The northern limit of Karnak points is apparently in central Indiana near the southern limit of the

Tipton Till Plain, although this material may occur further north within the Wabash River Valley.

Morphological Correlate
Poag Stemmed (Munson 1971:5, Table 2, Fig. 4e, g).

MCWHINNEY HEAVY STEMMED

McWhinney projectile points (Geistweit 1970:149–150; Vickery 1972) are relatively thick-stemmed forms that often retain cortex from waterworn pebbles and residual blocks from which they were manufactured (Figure 28). Special features of the type include a medial ridge on one face, lack of basal grinding, and, usually, cortex at the base of the stem.

The haft element of this type exhibits the most variation of any portion of the point (Vickery 1972). McWhinney Heavy Stemmed points have short stems relative to blade length and width. The haft element is produced by a side notching technique. The resulting variation in the hafting element changes from a narrow side notch to a wide side notched flake scar morphology which appears as an expanding or nearly straight stem. The resulting haft variation is due to the uncontrolled variable size of the hertzian cone flake scars produced during the side notching process. The basal edge varies from straight or convex to slightly concave. The latter portion of this variation is due to basal modification, such as the thinning of certain thick edged specimens, and is technological in nature. Adding to this, Vickery (1972:3) includes basal fracturing. He suggests that this was a method periodically used to remove cortex. Striking platform remnants also occur at the basal end of certain points.

Age and Cultural Affiliation
McWhinney Heavy Stemmed points are among the various projectile point styles common in the Late Archaic period of the Ohio Valley. These points are thought to date

from about 4000 to 1000 B.C. based on radiocarbon dates from the Maple Creek site in Ohio (Vickery 1972:5). E. Y. Guernsey's (1934–35) excavations at Clark's Point near the Falls of the Ohio in Indiana produced this point style within a stratified shell midden. McWhinney style points were associated with prismoidal atlatl weights and carved bone atlatl hooks within burials at the site.

Distribution
McWhinney points have been recovered from many sites in southwestern Ohio

Map 59: McWhinney Heavy Stemmed Distribution and Important Sites

(Moffett 1949; Long 1962:60; Vickery 1976:128) and in Kentucky (Mocas 1976:46–50, Fig. 7). They are common across southern Indiana and are found as far north as Monroe, Marion, and adjacent counties in the central portion of the state. Upland camps have produced these and Karnak points numbering into the hundreds (Little 1970; Munson 1976; Tomak 1980a,b).

Morphological Correlates
Stubby Broad Base (Weinland 1980:80); Thick Stemmed (Converse 1973:32); Friendship (Brennan 1975:56).

Morphological Correlates of the Late Archaic Stemmed Cluster
Mocas (1976:45–50) discerned several varieties of a type named Rowlett by Duffield (1966:66–69). These follow the range of variation proposed for the Late Archaic Stemmed cluster. This morphological range overlaps with the McWhinney Heavy Stemmed, Karnak Stemmed, and Karnak Unstemmed types. A suggested morphological correlation is provided below:

Rowlett varieties (Mocas 1976:46–50, Fig. 7): variations a–c, e–f compare with Karnak Stemmed; variations d and g compare with McWhinney Heavy Stemmed; Rowlett preforms compare with Karnak Unstemmed. Archaic Stemmed (Converse 1973:31; Cook 1980:391); Scherschel (Tomak 1980a:105–106, Fig. 1, 1980b:4, Fig. 10).

Nebo Hill Cluster

NEBO HILL LANCEOLATE

The Nebo Hill type projectile point (Shippee 1948:29–32, 1957:42–46) is a thick lanceolate form with a narrow blade (Figure 29). These forms are primarily percussion flaked over much of the blade, although pressure

flaking occurs at varying locations. Maximum width normally occurs above the midline. Blade shape varies from an excurvate nearly bi-pointed form to examples exhibiting a constriction in the haft region with a straight basal edge. This latter variant may exhibit a weak shoulder-like division between the haft

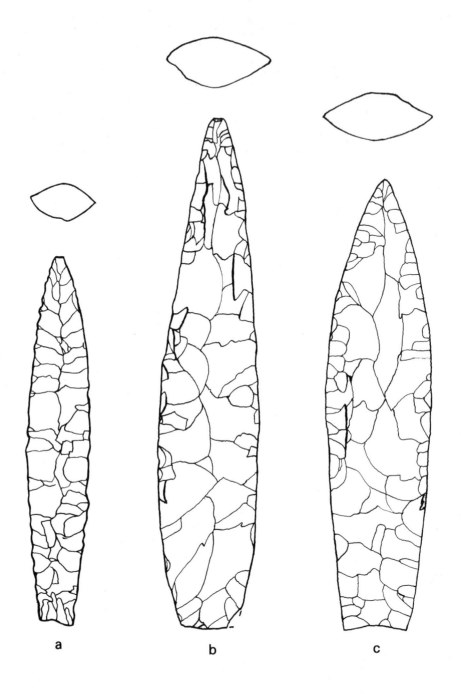

Figure 29
Nebo Hill Cluster

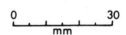

0   30
mm

Map 60: Nebo Hill—Distribution and Important Sites

and blade about 25 mm. from the base. Chapman (1975:251) observed that the basal edge also varies from slightly convex to concave. Basal thinning is nonexistent, and there is no basal or lateral grinding on the haft of Nebo Hill points. In addition, the cross section of these points ranges from biconvex to nearly diamond-shaped (see also Perino 1968a:60).

Age and Cultural Affiliation

The Nebo Hill complex is closely allied to the Sedalia complex which dates to the Late Archaic period. Two radiocarbon dates have been obtained from Nebo Hill sites in Missouri of 1605 B.C. ±65 and 1020 B.C. ±490, which indicate a Late Archaic association (Reeder 1981:30). Typical cultural materials associated with Nebo Hill camps include

Figure 29: Nebo Hill Cluster

a. Nebo Hill Lanceolate. J. A. Eichenberger cast. Clay Co., Missouri. J. M. Shippee collection.
b. Sedalia Lanceolate. Unidentified chert. GBL 482/253. Marion Co., Missouri.
c. Sedalia Lanceolate. Burlington chert. GBL 3304/11. Missouri.

light and heavy-duty bifaces, ground stone manos and slabs, and three-quarter grooved axes. Chert digging tools and gouges characteristic of the Sedalia complex are also present in low frequency (Brown and Ziegler 1981:43).

Distribution

Nebo Hill projectile points are distributed primarily within the prairie regions of northern Missouri (C. Chapman 1975:251). The settlement pattern of the Nebo Hill complex includes camps located on bluff tops and river terraces (see Reeder 1981; Brown and Ziegler 1981). The distribution of this type extends east into central Illinois (Roper 1978).

These forms have been compared somewhat favorably to the lanceolate points of the Guilford complex defined for the Carolina Piedmont area (Coe 1952, 1964:43–44, Figs. 35–36; Wormington 1957:147). However, the Guilford complex dates to ca. 4000 B.C., and the distributions of the Guilford Lanceolate and Nebo Hill are restricted to widely separated areas. Guilford is limited to the Appalachian area including Piedmont Georgia, north into West Virginia (Broyles 1969:35).

SEDALIA LANCEOLATE

Sedalia points (Seelan 1961:307; C. Chapman 1975:255–256) are large excurvate-bladed lanceolate forms. The typical Sedalia point is irregularly percussion flaked and exhibits a straight base, although these points can vary from convex to mildly concave at the base. Maximum width often occurs toward the tip. The width is nearly one-third to one-fifth the length, and the blade is extremely long in proportion to width and tapers toward the base. While a majority of Sedalia points exhibit excurvate blades, some points possess slight recurvate blade edges near the base. Cross sections of these projectile points are relatively thin and lenticular. Lateral grinding occurs on certain specimens although this trait is not typical and could relate to generous edge abrasion that was simply not removed in the finishing stages of manufacture.

Age and Cultural Affiliation
Based on the occurrence of the type at Koster site, these projectile points are diagnostic of the Late Archaic Titterington phase (Titterington 1950; Griffin 1952; C. Chapman 1975:256; Cook 1976:40). An age range of 2000 to 1000 B.C. relates to Sedalia (Reid 1984:Table 14). Sedalia points have been recovered along with Wadlow and Etley forms at a number of sites in Illinois (Cook 1976; Roper 1978) and northern Missouri (Klippel 1969). Sedalia points have also been included as part of a larger Nebo Hill cultural system (Reid 1984).

Distribution
Perino (1968a:86) and Cook (1976:42) observe a distribution of these points in the Missouri River Valley from Kansas City to the confluence of the Mississippi. They also occur along the Mississippi River north above Quincy, Illinois, and in counties along the Illinois River northeast to near Peoria. These also extend east in the Sangamon Valley to the Airport site in central Illinois (Roper 1978). Chapman (1975:256) notes that the distribution of Sedalia points is probably more extensive, including much of the northern Missouri prairie regions and probably the Prairie Peninsula that extends across central Illinois into Ohio. The collections from Indiana include a few Sedalia points, yet evidence for a definite occupation of Sedalia point makers east of central Illinois is negligible.

Map 61: Sedalia—Distribution and Important Sites

Wadlow Cluster

WADLOW

The Wadlow type (Perino 1968a) is a large unnotched lanceolate form (Figure 30). Wadlow specimens generally have straight bases and parallel sides. Lateral margins are sometimes recurved or convex. Some points having convex bases may also have rounded basal corners. Those specimens which do not possess parallel sides are widest two-thirds to three-fourths of the distance from the base to the tip. Blades that have recurved sides may also have needle-like tips. These points are entirely percussion flaked and the basal edges are never ground. It has also been suggested that the basic Wadlow form was used for the manufacture of Etley points (Perino 1968a; Cook 1976:42) as well as the Osceola/Hemphill type.

Age and Cultural Affiliation
These points are diagnostic of the Late Archaic Titterington phase. This type has been associated with Etley, Sedalia, Osceola/Hemphill, and other projectile point forms which are dated from 2000 to 1000 B.C. (C. Chapman 1975:256). Burial caches of Wadlow points have been recovered from the Etley site in Illinois (Perino 1968a:98) and from a number of other sites west into the middle Missouri River valley (see Reid 1984:73–81). Wadlow, Sedalia, and Etley points were recovered in association at Booth, Koster, and a number of other camp sites, indicating a temporal and technological relationship.

Distribution
The distribution of Wadlow points is similar to that of Etley and Sedalia forms (Cook 1976:42). Perino (1968a:98) notes that Wadlow specifically has been found in caches along the Missouri River from Jefferson City to the Mississippi River, within the Mississippi Valley from St. Louis to Quincy, Illinois, and east into central Illinois (i.e., Airport site). These forms are discontinuously distributed in Missouri and occur in northwest Arkansas and northeastern Oklahoma.

Map 62: Wadlow—Distribution and Important Sites

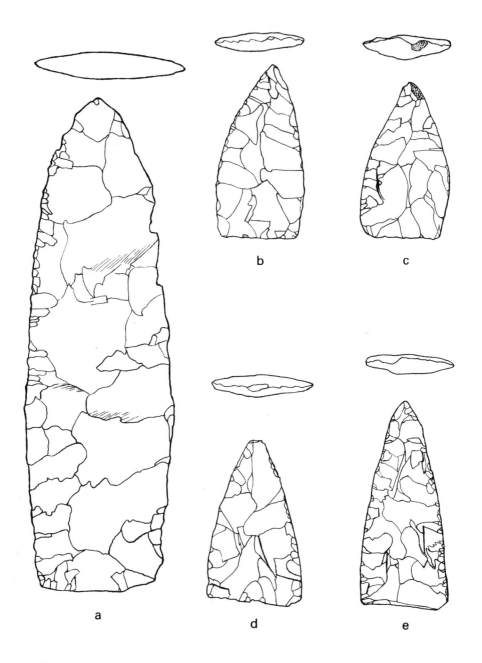

Figure 30
Wadlow Cluster

a

b

c

d

e

0   30
mm

Morphological Correlates
Red Ochre Lanceolate (C. Chapman 1975: 251); Ogival blades (Montet-White 1968: Fig. 44).

POMRANKY

Pomranky points (Binford 1963a; Binford and Papworth 1963) are basically wide, trianguloid forms with excurvate blade edges. A distinctive defining characteristic of the Pomranky point is the oblique basal orientation (Figure 30). These points were manufactured primarily using percussion followed by minimal edge retouch with an irregular pressure technique. The manufacturing strategy often resulted in non-aligned blade edges or a slight twisted blade. The blade form varies from triangular to trianguloid with straight to excurvate blade edges. Certain specimens exhibit a break in edge contour near the base to form a straight, parallel-sided configuration to join with the basal edge. At the Pomranky site, Binford (1963a) recognized three varieties of the Pomranky type (Midland, Swan Creek, and Saginaw). All of these share the basic characteristics noted above.

There are close similarities between Pomranky and the Meadowood mortuary blades noted by Ritchie (1955:42). The relationship of both of these cache blade forms to the Hodges (Binford 1963b:130–131) and Meadowood (Ritchie 1955; 1961:35–36) projectile point types has been recognized wherein the Pomranky and Meadowood cache blade types serve both as mortuary offerings and as preforms in the manufacturing trajectory for the latter types (Binford and Papworth 1963:114–115; Granger 1981).

Age and Cultural Affiliation
Pomranky points are diagnostic of the Late Archaic Red Ochre complex and date from

Figure 30: Wadlow Cluster
a. **Wadlow.** Burlington chert. GBL 14/867. Grant Co., Indiana?
b–e. **Pomranky.** Liston Creek chert. Lorbet cache. Site 12 Js 18. Jasper Co., Indiana. Courtesy of Avery Lewis and George L. Johnson.

about 1300 to 500 B.C. (Binford and Papworth 1963:121; Binford 1963a,b). Sites attributable to the Red Ochre complex occur across a broad area encompassing the Great Lakes and the Illinois River Valley. It is one of the first recognized burial complexes known from the Late Archaic/Early Woodland periods in the eastern U.S.

Binford (1963a:191) feels that comparison of the Pomranky material with other similarly dated manifestations would place the Pomranky site burial and associated artifacts at about 800 B.C. The Hodges site Pomranky materials in Michigan were compared with closely related material (Meadowood cache blades) from the Oblander II Station and the Morrow site in New York (Guthe 1958:11). All three of these sites produced trianguloid cache blades with side notched points (Hodges/Meadowood) in the same contexts. Another site in New York with this association (Fortin II) has been radiocarbon dated to 1230 B.C. ±95 (Funk, Rippeteau, and Houck 1973:16).

The mortuary feature at the Pomranky site in Midland County, Michigan, exhibited the use of red ocher with cremation burials in association with two basic forms of bifacial cache blades. In addition to a small cache of fourteen Fulton Turkey-tail points, a large number of Pomranky points (516) were found in the feature. The Peterson site in Pulaski County, Indiana, produced Pomranky points in association with the Hebron Turkey-tail type. Pomranky points were also found as a large cache at a site in Marshall County, Indiana (Faulkner 1960b:42, Fig. 2). Pomranky point burial caches have also been found at sites in northern Indiana associated with very large lanceolate points (Red Ocher blades) made from chert from western Illinois or northern Missouri.

Distribution
Pomranky points (Meadowood cache blades) are known across much of the Great Lakes region from Michigan (Binford 1963c; McPherron 1967:154–155, Plate 34; Fitting 1970), and southern Ontario (Williamson 1980:3–5), southern Quebec, and Pennsylvania, to New York and other parts of the

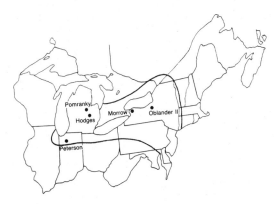

Map 63: Pomranky—Distribution and Important Sites

Northeast (Ritchie 1955; Granger 1981:Table 1). The type is also known from caches in northern Indiana (Ritzenthaler and Quimby 1962:245).

Morphological Correlates
Meadowood cache blades (Ritchie 1955:42–45; Granger 1981:63–102).

Morphological Correlates of the Wadlow Cluster
Additional types: Red Ocher (Cole and Deuel 1937:53–55, Fig. 14; Scully 1951:9; Perino 1968a:72); Morton Lanceolate (Montet-White 1968:31–38, Fig. 11).

Etley Cluster

ETLEY

Etley points (Scully 1951:2; Perino 1968a:98; C. Chapman 1975:246) are large with elongated blades relative to a short variable haft which ranges from straight stemmed to corner notched (Figure 31). These points exhibit distinct barbed shoulders accentuated by an incurving blade edge just above the shoulder region. Maximum shoulder width occurs at the tip of the barbs. Barb lengths on pristine specimens measure from 7–10 mm. Flake scars on the blade are flat, expanding, and massive. Blade contours vary from parallel-sided to triangular. Changes in blade morphology due to reworking also affect the barbs, which vary from expanded to absent. The Booth site in northeastern Missouri has produced the full range of variation in the manufacture and use-life recognized for Etley points (see Klippel 1969).

Age and Cultural Affiliation
Etley points are diagnostic of the Late Archaic Titterington phase in the lower Illinois Valley. The Titterington phase is estimated to date between 3000 and 1000 B.C. (Cook 1976:65). Several radiocarbon dates from

the Go-Kart North site clustered at 2100 B.C. (Fortier 1984:182–183). Go-Kart North produced caches of Etley and Wadlow points as well as a full range of variation of these forms and the Stone Square Stemmed type. At the Booth site in Missouri and the Airport site in Illinois, Etley points were associated with Wadlow preforms and Stone Square Stemmed points, in addition to narrow lanceolate forms similar to Nebo Hill and Sedalia (Klippel 1969; Roper 1978).

Distribution
Scully (1951:2) and Bell (1960:36) note that Etley points are found chiefly in the St. Louis,

Figure 31: Etley Cluster
a. Etley. Contracting stemmed variant. Burlington chert. GBL 22/52. Missouri.
b. Etley. Burlington chert. GBL 14/952. Warren Co., Missouri. Pictured in Plate 6, c.
c. Etley. Burlington chert. GBL 637/25. Provenience unknown.
d. Etley. Drill form. Burlington chert. GBL 42/241. Macoupin Co., Illinois.
e. Etley. Expanded stemmed variant. Burlington chert. GBL 22/52. Missouri.
f. Etley. Corner notched variant. Burlington chert. GBL 3304/215. Saline Co., Missouri.

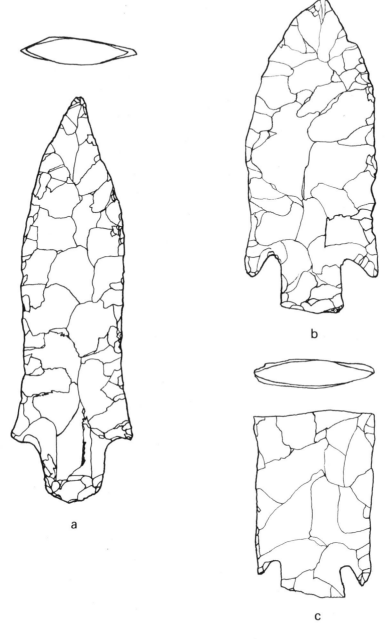

Figure 31
Etley Cluster

a

b

c

0 _____ 30
mm

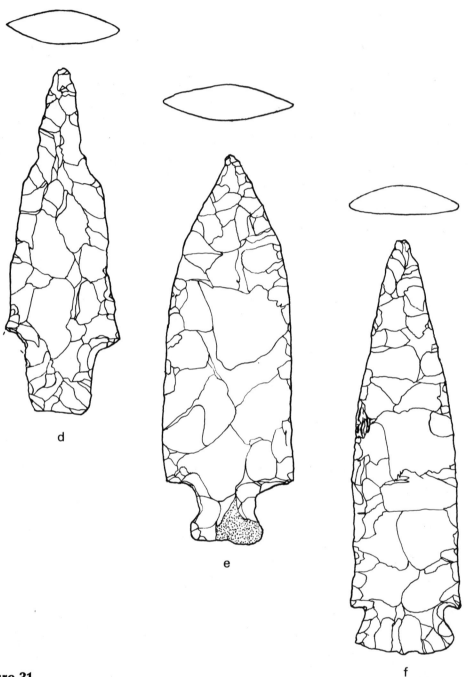

Figure 31

Map 64: Etley—Distribution and Important Sites

Missouri area including central Illinois and east-central Missouri. Etley points also occur in southern Illinois (May 1982:1374) and could extend in low frequency further east in the lower Ohio Valley (Stemle 1981:116). A single Etley point made of Burlington chert was recovered from a burial at the Crib Mound site in Spencer County, Indiana (Nick Nye, pers. comm.).

Morphological Correlates of the Etley Cluster

Etley Barbed (Scully 1951:2); Etley Stemmed (C. Chapman 1975:246). Additional types: Stone Square Stemmed (Klippel 1969:11, Fig. 4e–f; C. Chapman 1975:257, Figs. 8–9c; 8–13b, 8–18a); Smith Basal Notched (Baerreis and Freeman 1959; Perino 1968a:90; C. Chapman 1975:256, Fig. 8–14). This type includes material that overlaps the Eva cluster.

Ledbetter Cluster

LEDBETTER STEMMED

The Ledbetter Stemmed type (Kneberg 1956:26; Bell 1960:66; Cambron and Hulse 1969:65) is a contracting stemmed form with an asymmetrical blade (Figure 32). The sides of the blade are usually recurvate, but the recurvature is reversed on the two sides of the blade. This feature is combined with unequal barb-like shoulders. The unequal shoulders often exhibit a barb on one side while the other is straight or slanting, possibly due to resharpening of the blade. The basal edge of the stem is typically straight, and grinding is lacking across the haft element. Overall, the stem is relatively short in comparison to the large and narrow blade and varies from contracting to slightly expanding. The cross section of these points is biconvex and the flaking pattern on the blade and haft exhibits broad, random, flake scars. These forms

were made primarily using a percussion technique followed by short pressure flaking along the edges for resharpening.

Ledbetter projectile points share many attributes with the Mulberry Creek and Pickwick types defined by DeJarnette et al. (1962). The only discriminating characteristics are expressed in the contour of the blade and relate to edge sharpening and rejuvenation. Pickwick points exhibit recurvate blade edges that produce a more symmetrical form and are distinguishable from Ledbetter (see description). The Mulberry Creek type, however, falls primarily within the early resharpening range of Ledbetter points and is very difficult to distinguish. In fact, Kneberg's (1956) original description of Ledbetter includes the Mulberry Creek form which exhibits an incurvate blade just above the shoulder and maximum width that can occur high on the blade. All three forms pos-

sess contracting stems which may be slightly
expanded at the base (see Thorne, Broyles,
and Johnson 1981:219–225).

Age and Cultural Affiliation

Ledbetter projectile points are diagnostic of
the Late Archaic period Ledbetter phase and
date from 2500 to 1000 B.C. In the upper
Duck River Valley in Tennessee, this type,
along with Pickwick style points, is associated on sites with a full complement of cultural features, including the remains of
house structures (Bowen 1979:142). The
Spring Creek site produced these forms
along with Cotaco Creek, Mulberry Creek,
and Little Bear Creek points in the Perry
zone, which is thought to date from 2500 to
1400 B.C. (Peterson 1973:44). This zone lies
stratigraphically above a zone containing
Benton points. Ledbetter and Pickwick style
points were also recovered from Late Archaic
levels at Russell Cave in Alabama (Ingmanson and Griffin (1974:45, Fig. 30) and the
Eva site in Tennessee (Lewis and Lewis 1961).

Distribution

Ledbetter projectile points are common
throughout the Tennessee River Valley (Bell
1960:66). These points are known from Alabama (Griffin 1974), Georgia (Schock et al.
1977:29), Mississippi (Thorne et al. 1981),
Tennessee (Sims 1971:68–69; Peterson
1973:36), Kentucky (Schock and Langford
1979a,b), and Missouri within the Mississippi
River Valley (Griffin and Spaulding 1951:
Fig. 1). The type occurs in southern Illinois
(Cremin 1975c) and may extend as far north
as central Indiana, since it is present in the
White and Wabash River Valleys.

Projectile points of this basic style have
been recovered at various sites in the Southeast, but these have not been separated from
better known Late Archaic types such as Savannah River and material representing the
Broadpoint horizon discussed by Turnbaugh
(1975). Holland (1970:88) recognized the
type in Virginia, but similar material in Virginia has also been referred to as Savannah
River variants (Reinhart 1975:145–147,
Fig. 6: see also Claflin 1931). Ledbetter-like

Map 65: Ledbetter Stemmed—Distribution and
Important Sites

points are recorded in North Carolina (Purrington 1983:Fig. 3.5) and the type is represented among a series of Late Archaic types
at the Senator Edwards lithic workshop in
northern Florida (Purdy 1975:Fig. 6).

Figure 32: Ledbetter Cluster

a. Ledbetter Stemmed. Fort Payne chert.
Florence, Alabama. Marshall L. Fallwell
collection.
b. Ledbetter Stemmed. Wyandotte chert. GBL
1241/18. Site 12 Sp 221. Spencer Co., Indiana.
c. Ledbetter Stemmed. Unidentified chert.
GBL 119/891. Provenience unknown. Pictured
in Plate 6, b.
d. Ledbetter Stemmed. Heavy blade resharpening. Wyandotte chert. GBL 1448/277. Southwestern Indiana.
e. Pickwick. Fort Payne chert. Florence, Alabama. Marshall L. Fallwell collection. Pictured
in Plate 6, h.
f. Pickwick. Heavy blade resharpening. Fort
Payne chert. Florence, Alabama. Marshall L.
Fallwell collection.
g–i. Pickwick. Fort Payne chert. Florence,
Alabama. Marshall L. Fallwell collection.
j. Pickwick. Drill form. Unidentified chert.
Florence, Alabama. Marshall L. Fallwell
collection.

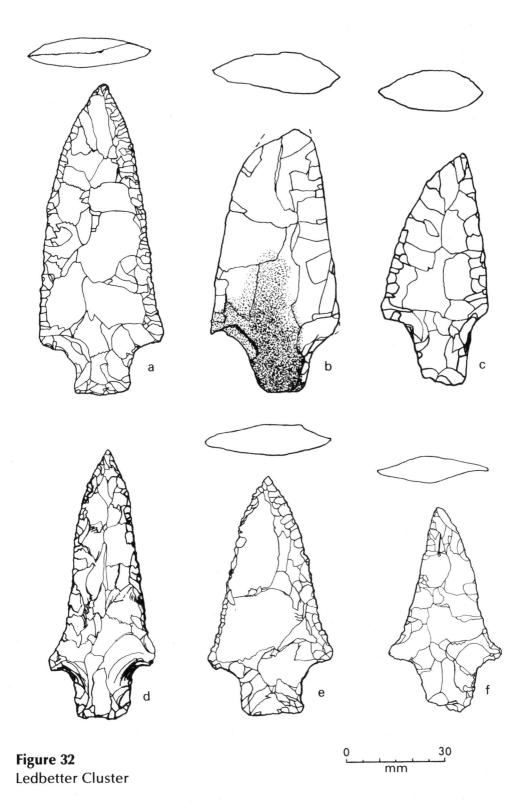

Figure 32
Ledbetter Cluster

0 _____ 30
mm

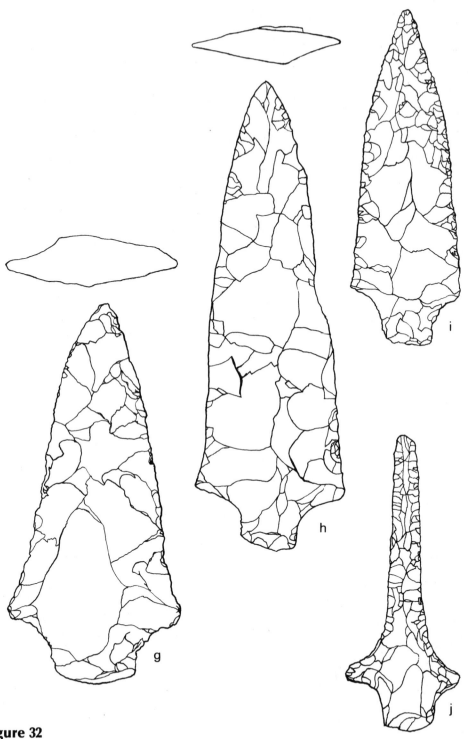

Figure 32

Morphological Correlates

Maples Broad Stemmed (DeJarnette et al. 1962:62; Thorne, Broyles, and Johnson 1981); Wetaug Stemmed (Winters n.d., pers. comm.; Denny 1972).

PICKWICK

The Pickwick type (DeJarnette et al. 1962:66; Cambron and Hulse 1975:103) is related to Ledbetter but is distinguished by the presence of a recurvate blade in conjunction with expanded shoulder barbs (Figure 32). These points exhibit primarily contracting stems with a wide and sloping shoulder/haft juncture. The dimensions of the shoulder barbs tend to be equal. The usual blade form is recurvate and tends to be symmetrical, although variations in overall symmetry are common. The basal edge varies from straight to convex. Cross sections vary from flattened to biconvex. The manufacturing strategy of Pickwick involved broad percussion thinning, which often resulted in forms with slightly twisted blades. A median ridge on one or both faces is often present due to consistent step or hinge fracturing of thinning scars from one side at the center of the blade. The blade edge is typically pressure flaked. A careful and regular strategy was used to remove consistently short and steep flakes from both faces to produce both relatively even and finely serrated edges.

Thorne, Broyles, and Johnson (1981) have reported on a large sample of Pickwick points. Many larger examples of the type exhibit wide blades with a tendency toward more excurvate edges with slight recurvature. Resharpening strategies of this type apparently employed both percussion thinning or shaping of the edge and pressure retouch with final blade reduction to drill forms while maintaining much of the original width at the shoulder.

Age and Cultural Affiliation

Pickwick type projectile points are diagnostic of the Late Archaic period. They appear in the archaeological record at about the same time as Ledbetter, dating from about 2500 to 1000 B.C. Pickwick occurs in the same sequence with Ledbetter at Russell Cave (Ingmanson and Griffin 1974) and the Eva (Lewis and Lewis 1961) and Spring Creek sites (Peterson 1973). Pickwick type points are included in the Ledbetter phase defined in the upper Duck River Valley of Tennessee (Bowen 1979). Pickwick points and drills made from these points are common in shell middens and open sites in the Tennessee River drainage.

Distribution

Pickwick projectile points are distributed across basically the same area as the Ledbetter type. However, Pickwick is less common overall. Pickwick is present in highest frequency in the Tennessee River Valley and tributaries in northern Mississippi, northern Alabama, and Tennessee (Thorne et al. 1981; Ingmanson and Griffin 1974; Bowen 1979). These points occur north into the Ohio Valley of southern Illinois and Indiana, but do not appear to be as common as the Ledbetter type.

Map 66: Pickwick—Distribution and Important Sites

Hale (Ford and Webb 1956:64–66); Mulberry Creek (DeJarnette et al. 1962; Cambron and Hulse 1969:34); Thonotossasa (Bullen 1975:40). Additional types: Elora (Cambron and Hulse 1960b; DeJarnette, Kurjack, and Cambron 1962:54; Cambron and Hulse 1969:40); Mountain End Lake (Manley 1967:94–98). This type designation was offered for Ledbetter cluster material from Georgia that is not to be confused with "Late Prehistoric" Randolph type points defined by Coe (1964:50).

Saratoga Cluster

SARATOGA
BROAD BLADED

The Saratoga Broad Bladed type (Winters n.d., 1963, 1967:19, 25, 1969:42; May 1982:1364) is a large, straight to slightly expanding, stemmed form with a wide haft and narrow shoulders (Figure 33). These projectile points are characteristically wide and thick with a biconvex to flattened cross section. Blade shapes range from elongated and excurvate-sided to triangular and short with straight sides. The shoulders are rounded, vary from straight to sloping, and join a wide stem. A combination of percussion thinning and pressure flaking was used in manufacture. The basal edge is straight with treatments varying from the common snapped or beveled characteristics noted for the Saratoga Parallel Stemmed type to examples that are bifacially thinned. The latter Saratoga type is very similar to Saratoga Broad Blade in highly resharpened condition.

The Oak Grove I (a + b) type projectile points (Schock et al. 1977:47–51; Schock and Langford 1979b:10) are medium to large straight stemmed forms which conform in all essential aspects to the Saratoga Broad Bladed type described above. However, the definition of Oak Grove is derived from a unique single component manufacturing station in Kentucky. The type exhibits pristine long-bladed forms as well as resharpened examples. Its blade edge is straight to slightly excurvate in outline and may be asymmetrical. The cross section is generally plano convex, but can vary to almost biconvex in

shape. The blade configuration is due to the manufacturing strategy which includes partial flaking (e.g., ventral surface of original flake intact) to total bifacial flaking of the blade. The basal edge varies from straight to

Figure 33: Saratoga Cluster
a. Saratoga Broad Bladed. Wyandotte chert. GBL 21/337. Clark Co., Indiana.
b. Saratoga Broad Bladed. Cobden chert. Sugar Camp Hill site, southern Illinois. Specimen 52.6/44, Center for Archaeological Investigations, Southern Illinois University at Carbondale, Illinois.
c. Saratoga Parallel Stemmed. Unidentified chert. Cache River Valley, southern Illinois. Specimen 53.17/8, Center for Archaeological Investigations, Southern Illinois University at Carbondale, Illinois.
d–e. Saratoga Parallel Stemmed. Wyandotte chert. GBL 1527/227. Rockhouse Hollow Shelter, site 12 Pe 100. Perry Co., Indiana.
f. Saratoga Parallel Stemmed. Wyandotte chert. GBL 3988/112. Uebelhack site, 12 Po 51. Posey Co., Indiana.
g. Saratoga Expanding Stem. Unidentified Fossiliferous chert. GBL 21/245. Washington Co., Indiana.
h. Saratoga Expanding Stem. Cobden chert. GBL 4133/2. Site 12 Po 607. Posey Co., Indiana.
i. Saratoga Expanding Stem. Cobden chert. GBL 1448/411. Southwestern Indiana.
j. Saratoga Expanding Stem. Cobden chert. GBL 4133/3. Site 12 Po 607. Posey Co., Indiana.
k. Saratoga Expanding Stem. Wyandotte chert. GBL 4013/2. Site 12 Po 512. Posey Co., Indiana.
l. Saratoga Expanding Stem. Cobden chert. Carrier Mills, southern Illinois. Specimen 79.7.331, Center for Archaeological Investigations, Southern Illinois University at Carbondale, Illinois.

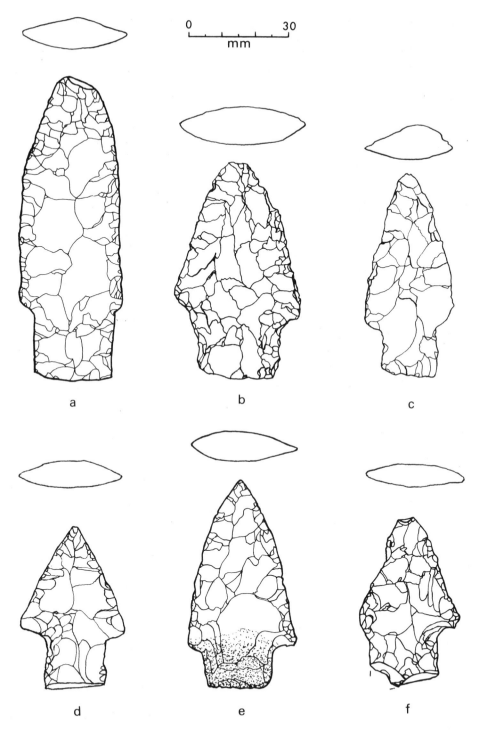

a

b

c

d

e

f

Figure 33
Saratoga Cluster

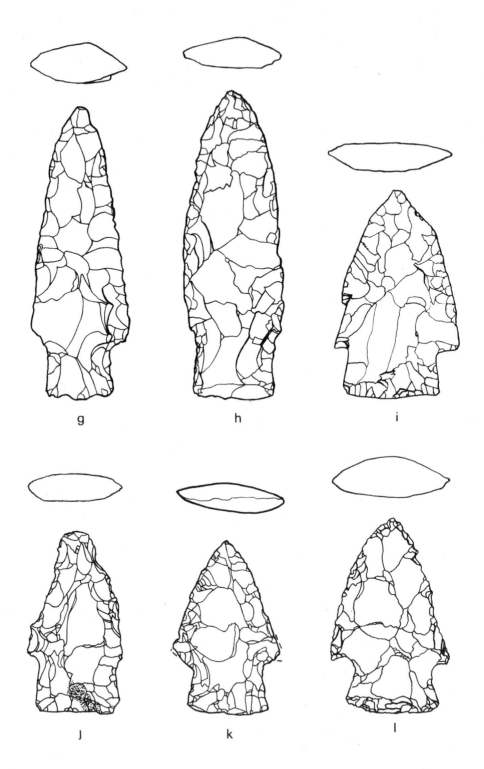

g h i

J k l

Figure 33

slightly excurvate. The basal edge morphology includes bifacially thinned or beveled forms and unflaked or snapped bases. Limestone cortex is also sometimes exhibited on the base. These forms are manufactured using percussion thinning followed by a combination of percussion and irregular pressure edge retouch. Preform bifaces exhibit large flake scars on both sides of the blade and are lanceolate in shape. The range of resharpened and rejuvenated Oak Grove points includes narrow, trianguloid-bladed drill forms and hafted scrapers with unifacially beveled distal ends. A similar, if not identical, manufacturing and resharpening sequence is exhibited within original assemblages which characterize the Saratoga cluster (see Maxwell 1951: Plates 6–12).

Morphological Correlates
Oak Grove I a, b (Schock et al. 1977: 47–52; Schock and Langford 1979b: 10); Kays Stemmed (Kneberg 1956: 26; Cambron and Hulse 1969: 59, 1975: 72; Webb 1946: Fig. 32a).

SARATOGA PARALLEL STEMMED

The Saratoga Parallel or Straight Stemmed type was one of three Saratoga types originally proposed and utilized by Winters (n.d., 1963: 22, 1967: 19, 25, 1969: 42; Denny 1972: 91). These forms are basically straight stemmed and possess triangular blades which vary from larger examples with excurvate sides, to those which are short with straight blade edges converging rapidly from the shoulders to the tip (Figure 33). The latter examples represent nearly exhausted forms in the resharpening process. The shoulders vary from upward slanting to squared; examples with sloping shoulders rarely occur. Cross sections of these points are relatively thick and vary from plano convex to biconvex. The basal edge is primarily straight with two forms of basal treatment recognized. The basal edge can be truncated, having an unfinished (e.g., striking platform or original flake remnant) or intentionally

snapped appearance. The other form of basal treatment exhibits a steeply flaked, primarily unifacial bevel produced by a pressure flaking technique (May 1982: 1363). This form grades strongly into the Saratoga Broad Bladed type.

SARATOGA EXPANDING STEM

The Saratoga Expanding Stem type (Winters n.d., 1963, 1967: 19, 25, 1969: 42; Denny 1972: 144; May 1982: 1364) is very similar to the other two Saratoga types in blade and stem length and in basic flaking characteristics, and it is most similar to Saratoga Broad Bladed in these respects (Figure 33). The basic distinguishing attribute is the presence of a slight expanding stem (Howard D. Winters, pers. comm.). The blades of these points are lanceolate in shape and were manufactured using percussion thinning, followed by pressure flaking. Cross sections vary from thin and flat to biconvex. Shoulders are upward slanting and exhibit a wide shoulder/haft juncture. The lateral stem edges are primarily straight sided and lack the notch curvature characteristic of corner notched and expanding stemmed types. Basal edge configurations include straight to convex shapes. Examples with unflaked cortex as well as those with bifacially flaked or unifacially beveled basal edges occur. The Oak Grove II (a, b) type (Schock et al. 1977: 49–51) relates to the variation described for Saratoga Expanding Stem.

The overall manufacture of Saratoga Expanding Stem and Saratoga Broad Bladed, while lacking the wide blade and corner notches, foreshadows the flaking technology characteristic of Snyders. The specific origin of the Snyders's manufacturing technology is not so easily resolved, as Motley cluster materials bear certain formal ratios as well as a wide corner notching trait similar to Snyders. Both the Saratoga and Motley type clusters occupy a time segment preceding the appearance of classic Snyders type projectile points.

Morphological Correlates

Barbeau Stemmed (Fowler 1959a:67–78, Fig. 9b, right; Fig. 20. This type designation incorporates all expanded, stemmed points from the Modoc Rock Shelter. An unspecific group of Saratoga Expanding Stem points were originally lumped in this class. The remaining materials do not belong to the Saratoga cluster); Cave Run (Rolingson and Rodeffer 1968:20, Fig. 8b); Forman Broad Base (Winters n.d., pers. comm.; Denny 1972:150–152, Fig. 24); Oak Grove II varieties a & b (Schock et al. 1977:49–51; Schock and Langford 1979b:10); Straight Stemmed Matanzas (Cook 1976:144, Fig. 38; 1980:404, 415, Plate 17.7 a,d).

Age and Cultural Affiliation

Saratoga cluster projectile points are diagnostic of the Late Archaic to Early Woodland periods. Saratoga projectile points occurred in the upper levels of Modoc Rock Shelter in Illinois and were most frequent in deposits thought to date after 2000 B.C. (see Fowler 1959a:37, Figs. 9c, 14; Denny 1972:143–144). There is good evidence that Saratoga points persist into the Early Woodland period, where they commonly occur within early Crab Orchard contexts in southern Indiana and Illinois. The earliest suggested date for the Crab Orchard tradition is about 650 B.C. (McNerney 1975:405–408). These points are represented at the Sugar Camp Hill (Maxwell 1951) and were recovered from Crab Orchard features at the Throgmorton Dam site (Cremin 1975c:223) in southern Illinois. The Uebelhack site (12 Po 51) in Posey County, Indiana, produced Saratoga points in Early Crab Orchard context, but acceptable radiocarbon dates for the Crab Orchard component are not available. These occupation levels were nevertheless placed stratigraphically well above and separated from a level containing Matanzas points dated to about 2260 B.C. ±85.

The occurrences of Saratoga or Oak Grove projectile points at sites relating to the Green River Archaic in Kentucky (Webb 1946; Rolingson 1967; Schock et al. 1977:56) apparently represent the earlier end of the Late Archaic temporal span for Saratoga cluster material. Although specific radiocarbon dates are not available, the contexts relate primarily to preceramic occupations.

Distribution

Saratoga cluster type points are common across southern Illinois (Denny 1972; May 1982), southern Indiana, and much of northern Kentucky. Rolingson's (1967) reanalysis of the Green River Archaic noted the presence of Saratoga/Oak Grove points (e.g., Rolingson's cluster 5), as well as a host of other types (cf. Schock et al. 1977:51). Examples of each of the Saratoga types occur at a number of well-known shell midden sites such as the Parrish Village (Webb 1951:Fig. 5a, row 2, left) and Indian Knoll (Webb 1946: Fig. 32a). Saratoga cluster material occurs in eastern Kentucky, where it has been referred to as Cave Run (Rolingson and Rodeffer 1968:17), and similar material is found in Tennessee and northern Alabama under the name of Kays Stemmed (Kneberg 1956; Faulkner and McCollough 1973:121). The points apparently occur as far east as eastern Tennessee (Rolingson and Rodeffer 1968:8) and into southwestern Virginia (Holland

Map 67: Saratoga Cluster—Distribution and Important Sites

1970:91), but not up the Ohio River Valley into the Northeast (cf. Mayer-Oakes 1955; Ritchie 1961). Projectile points of the Saratoga type cluster probably occur as far west as the Mississippi River Valley.

Morphological Correlates of the Saratoga Cluster
Type 4 (Maxwell 1951:115–116; Plate VI upper row, 2–6; Plate IX second row, 5–6);

Hiller Stemmed (Fowler 1959a:67, Figs. 14, 20). This type designation includes all straight stemmed points from the Modoc Rock Shelter. The only material relevant to this placement is the presence of an unspecified group of Saratoga Parallel Stemmed and Saratoga Broad Bladed points included in the Hiller Stemmed class, which also includes material that is morphologically outside the range of the Saratoga cluster.

Genesee Cluster

GENESEE

The Genesee type (Ritchie 1945, 1961:24–25) is a large, thick, straight stemmed point of medium breadth (Figure 34). The blade is trianguloid in outline and biconvex in cross section. The stem is rectangular and straight or parallel sided. The shoulders are weak and have a horizontal orientation without the presence of barbs. The basal edge is straight. Light edge grinding of the haft element occurred on 40 percent of the specimens studied by Ritchie (1961:24).

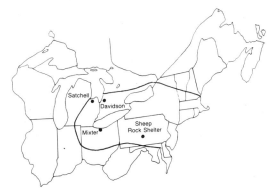

Map 68: Genesee—Distribution and Important Sites

Age and Cultural Affiliation
Genesee points are diagnostic of the Terminal Archaic period in the Northeast (Ritchie 1971b:8). These forms, part of the Frontenac and Laurentian manifestations, have been radiocarbon dated from 2980 B.C. ±260 (Arnold and Libby 1951:114) to 1723 B.C. ±250 (Ritchie 1961:24, 1969a:108). The type is also diagnostic of the tentatively defined Batten Kill complex (Ritchie 1971b:8; Ritchie and Funk 1973:47). In addition, Genesee points are diagnostic of the Satchell complex of southern Ontario and Michigan (Peske 1963; Roosa 1966). The Satchell complex Davidson site in southwest Ontario is dated to 1830 B.C. ±85 (Kenyon 1980a:20).

Distribution
Ritchie (1961:24) observed the presence of these projectile points across much of the

Northeast, with a concentration of Genesee points in central and western New York. The type also occurs in southern Ontario (Kenyon 1980a:12, 25), Vermont (Perkins 1970), and the Great Lakes area (Fitting 1963c:136; Shane 1975a:137). It is recognized across much of Pennsylvania (Bebrich 1968:334), Ohio (Prufer and Sofsky 1965:28–29), and eastern Indiana. Genesee does not appear to extend further west or into the southeastern United States.

SNOOK KILL

The Snook Kill type defined by Ritchie (1958:93, 1971a:47–48) is a broad, triangular-bladed projectile point with straight to contracting stems (Figure 34). The blade edges vary from excurvate to slightly incurvate and may be asymmetrical. The shoulders are pronounced, typically project on a horizontal plane, and lack barbs. The shoulder/haft juncture is variable, ranging from wide and sloping to angular. Cross sections on these forms are normally biconvex or plano convex. The basal edge is typically straight, and basal grinding occurs only infrequently. Snook Kill points exhibit large and random percussion flake scars across the blade followed by a minimum of pressure flaking. Much of the variation in blade size and shape is due to edge resharpening, which was accomplished basically with the same techniques utilized in manufacture.

The Lehigh Broad spearpoint defined by Witthoft (1953) and the Koens-Crispin type described by Cross (1941) and Kraft (1970) represent strong morphological overlaps with Snook Kill. Each of these types includes comparable variation from pristine to resharpened examples (Snow 1980:236; Perino 1985:223). Narrow-bladed examples of Snook Kill also intergrade with the Genesee type (Ritchie and Funk 1973:47).

Age and Cultural Affiliation
The Snook Kill type is diagnostic of the Late Archaic Snook Kill phase which is dated from about 1800 to around 1600 B.C. A date of 1470 B.C. ± 100 was obtained from a cooking pit at the type site (Ritchie 1969a:135). Additional radiocarbon dates fall a few centuries earlier, such as 1670 B.C. ± 130 from the Kuhr No. 1 site in the Upper Susquehanna drainage (Funk and Rippeteau 1977: 30). Most dates average around 1700 B.C. (Snow 1980:236). Also noteworthy is the Davidson site in southern Ontario which produced a date of 1830 B.C. ± 85 for a series of stemmed broadpoints. Projectile points recovered include those analogous to Genesee, Snook Kill, Koens-Crispin, and Lehigh Broad (Kenyon 1980a,b). Davidson is a Satchell complex site originally defined for a number of cultural expressions in eastern Michigan which utilized rough, grainy, raw material such as argillite and Greywacke (Peske 1963; Kenyon 1980a,b). The Satchell complex represents basically the western periphery of the Broadpoint horizon. The Snook Kill phase precedes the adoption of ceramic technology. Snook Kill and the other types mentioned above have been compared on a technological level to Savannah River points of the Eastern Coastal Plain (Ritchie 1969a:142, Turnbaugh 1975).

A Snook Kill workshop, the Dead Sheep site, has been investigated (Weinman and Weinman 1969). Preforms and numerous Snook Kill type points were recovered along with quantities of flake debris. Other tool types present included end and side scrapers, drills, hammerstones, and stone anvils.

Distribution
The Snook Kill type occurs throughout much of the Northeast, including New York, New Jersey, Connecticut, Massachusetts, and Ver-

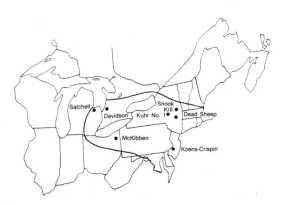

Map 69: Snook Kill—Distribution and Important Sites

Figure 34: Genesee Cluster
a. Genesee. Metasiltstone/Sandstone. GBL 13/892. South-central Michigan.
b. Genesee. Unidentified chert. New York. Redrawn from Ritchie (1971a:24).
c. Genesee. Unidentified chert. GBL 13/892. South-central Michigan.
d. Genesee. Exhibits resharpened blade. Unidentified chert. GBL 31/106. Fulton Co., Indiana.
e. Genesee. Quartzite. GBL 281/266. Chester Co., Pennsylvania.
f. Snook Kill. Bayport chert. GBL 13/892. South-central Michigan.
g–h. Snook Kill. Silicified Tuff, Rhyolite. GBL 281/258. Northwestern Vermont.
i–j. Snook Kill. Bayport chert. GBL 13/891. South-central Michigan. I, pictured in Plate 7, f.

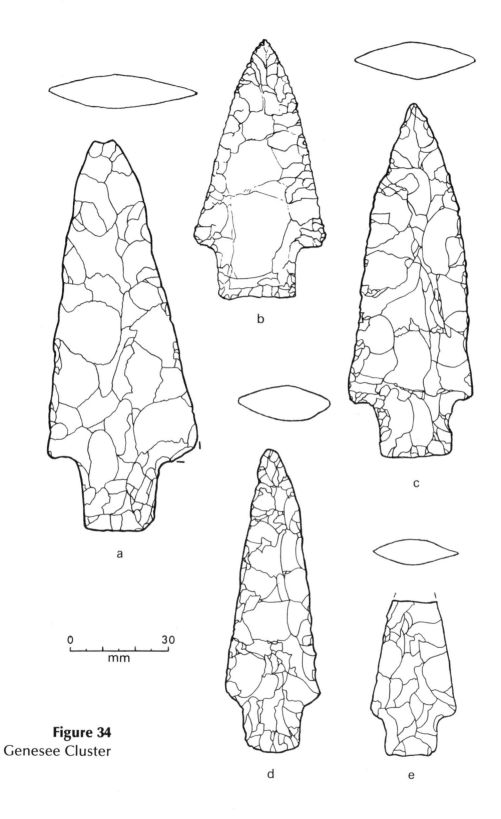

0   30
mm

Figure 34
Genesee Cluster

a

b

c

d

e

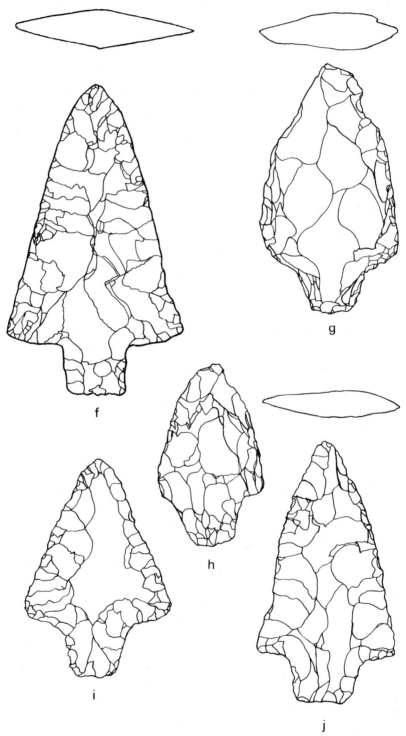

f

g

h

i

j

Figure 34

mont (Ritchie 1961:48; 1969a:134). The type is well represented in eastern Pennsylvania (Witthoft 1953) and occurs across southern Ontario (Kenyon 1980a,b) into eastern Michigan (Peske 1963; Fitting 1970). It also occurs in minor frequency in northern Ohio (cf. Prufer and Sofsky 1965:29, Fig. 5a–c) and may extend into southeast Wisconsin, where it has been compared to the Fox River Valley Stemmed type (Ritzenthaler 1967:21).

Morphological Correlates of the Genesee Cluster
Additional types: Bare Island (Ritchie 1961: 14–15; Stephenson and Ferguson 1963:141–142, 182, Plate 23; Roosa 1966:32–33); Koens-Crispin (Kraft 1970:58–59; Kinsey 1972:423–426); Lackawaxen Straight Stem (Leslie 1967:111–114; Kinsey 1972:408–411; see also Perino 1968a:46); Lehigh Broad (Witthoft 1953:21–22; Ritchie 1961:47; Roosa 1966:32; Shane 1975a:142).

Savannah River Cluster

SAVANNAH RIVER STEMMED

The Savannah River type projectile point is a large trianguloid-bladed form with a broad stem (Claflin 1931:33–39; Coe 1964:44–45; Cambron and Hulse 1969:104; Oliver 1981). The blade is often fairly long relative to stem length and exhibits straight to excurvate edges and wide, thinning flake scars. The shoulders tend to be angular, placed at a right angle to the stem, and are never barbed (Figure 35). Variations include specimens that exhibit a wide arc at the shoulder/haft juncture, which produces an indefinite division between the stem and blade. Progressive resharpening of the blade edges is not readily observed, since the usual characteristics, such as incurvate edges, serration, or beveling coupled with a change in flaking patterns and technique, are often lacking; but drills and hafted scrapers made from these points are typical. A straight sided stem is typical, although stem characteristics vary from slightly expanding to mildly contracting. The basal edge is typically concave, although straight to slightly rounded basal edges also occur. The cross sections of Savannah River points vary from thick biconvex forms to relatively thin and flat ones.

Savannah River Stemmed points were manufactured from square-based lanceolate bifaces using percussion techniques followed by light retouch along the margins to align and sharpen the edges. The stem was apparently produced using a combination of techniques. The flake scars are somewhat difficult to observe, since these forms were often manufactured from raw materials such as quartzite, quartz, argillite, rhyolite, and andesite, which are available in the Appalachian area. Stoltman (1972:46) mentions a size difference between Savannah River points made from chert and quartz at coastal sites and those from igneous rocks in the Carolina Piedmont, the latter being larger.

Age and Cultural Affiliation
Savannah River projectile points are diagnostic of the Late Archaic period and are part of the material culture of the Savannah River phase defined for the Southeast (Fairbanks 1942; Caldwell 1952; Coe 1952). These projectile points are relatively common within a period from just before 3000 B.C. to 1000 B.C. postdating the Guilford, Halifax, and Morrow Mountain complexes in the Carolina Piedmont area (Coe 1964:123). A date of 1944 B.C. ±350 was obtained from a Savannah River hearth at the Doerschuk site (Coe 1964:55). The earliest accepted date for the Savannah River phase is 3560 B.C. from the Warren Wilson site in North Carolina (Oliver 1981:159). This type occupies the early seg-

ment of what has been termed the Broad-point horizon of the Eastern Coastal Plain. The Broadpoint horizon incorporates a large group of projectile point types relating to a variety of local hunting and gathering traditions linked on the basis of a seasonal maritime economy (Turnbaugh 1975).

Savannah River points appear within pre-ceramic levels of shell middens in the coastal areas along with carved steatite (i.e., soapstone) cooking vessels, chipped cruciform drills and end scrapers derived from the projectile points, incised bone pins, winged (butterfly) atlatl weights, antler atlatl hooks, and other articles (see Claffin 1931; Fairbanks 1942; Miller 1949; Williams 1968).

At about 2500 B.C. and later, fiber tempered ceramics appear in many of these same Stallings and related middens (Stoltman 1974:11–15, 232). Bullen and Stoltman (1972) recently discussed these associations, including the origin of fiber tempered pottery, which appears to be ultimately from northern South America. This pottery pre-dates all presently known indigenous Early Woodland ceramic complexes. Apparently, the additon of this pottery had little impact on local lithic industries, which continued to use the Savannah River style projectile point until a few centuries prior to 1000 B.C. (Stoltman 1974:235).

Distribution

This type is one of the first widely recognized projectile point styles of the southeastern United States. Its distribution covers most of the Appalachian mountain system but it is also widespread outside the mountainous regions, including the Coastal Plain and Tidewater regions (Phelps 1981). The type is particularly common in an area from Georgia (Claflin 1931; Miller 1949; Caldwell 1954) through much of Florida (Bullen 1975: 35), South Carolina (Stoltman 1972, 1974), North Carolina (Coe 1964), and Virginia (McCary 1976; Reinhart 1979). Savannah River projectile points also occur further north along the Atlantic coast into New Jersey and elsewhere (Manson 1948:223–227; see also Turnbaugh 1975:55, Fig. 1). In New York,

Map 70: Savannah River—Distribution and Important Sites

the type apparently overlaps with the morphology recognized for the Snook Kill type (Ritchie 1961:47). Its distribution also extends southwest into Alabama (Cambron and Hulse 1969:104) and Tennessee. The Appalachian Stemmed type defined by Lewis and Kneberg (1957) at the Camp Creek site

Figure 35: Savannah River Cluster
a. Savannah River Stemmed. Quartzite. GBL 3087/2. North Carolina.
b. Savannah River Stemmed. Quartzite. GBL 1448/92. Southwestern Indiana.
c. Savannah River Stemmed. Basal fragment. Quartz. GBL 3087/3. North Carolina.
d. Savannah River Stemmed. Silicified Tuff. GBL 3087/1. North Carolina.
e. Savannah River Stemmed. Unidentified chert. Muskogee Co., Georgia. Courtesy of Benjamin H. and Jack W. Justice.
f. Savannah River Stemmed. Quartzite. GBL 21/ 378. Provenience unknown.
g. Savannah River Stemmed. Quartzite. GBL 242/3. South Carolina. Pictured in Plate 6, q.
h. Savannah River Stemmed. Basal fragment. Unidentified fossiliferous chert. Muskogee Co., Georgia. Courtesy of Benjamin H. and Jack W. Justice.
i. Savannah River Stemmed. Quartz. GBL 422/79. Georgia.

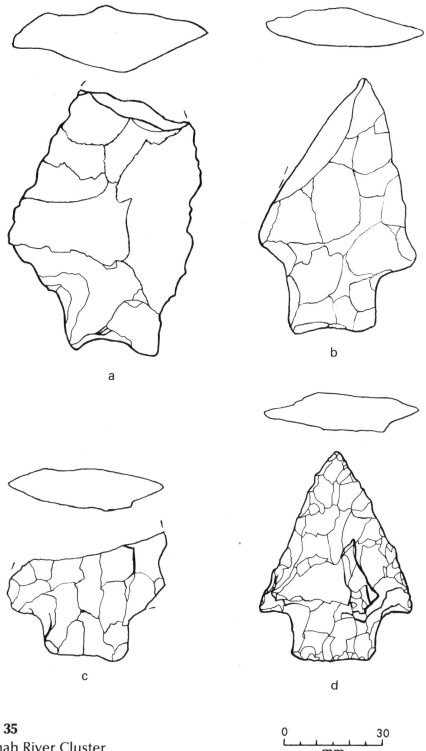

Figure 35
Savannah River Cluster

0   30
mm

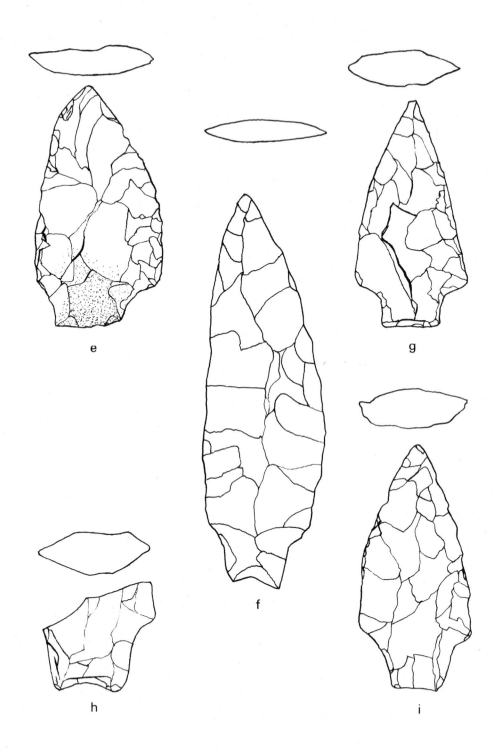

e

f

g

h

i

Figure 35

in Tennessee is essentially the same form as the Savannah River type. Other named types have formerly been linked with Savannah River, namely, Benton Stemmed, Kays Stemmed (Coe 1964:45), and a variety of other Late Archaic forms of the Middle South and Middle Atlantic area. However, all of these stand as separate named types distinguishable from Savannah River.

Morphological Correlates
Appalachian Stemmed (Kneberg 1956:25–26, 1957:66; Lewis and Kneberg 1957:21,

Fig. 16); Small Savannah River Stemmed (South 1959:153–157; Oliver 1981).

Morphological Correlates of the Savannah River Cluster
Broad River (Michie 1970a:7; Perino 1985:49); Gypsy Stemmed (Keel 1976; Oliver 1981); Hamilton (Bullen 1975:38); Oatlands (Van Buren 1974:179); Otarre Stemmed (Keel 1976:194–196; Oliver 1981:164; Purrington 1983:130). Additional type: Swannanoa Stemmed (Keel 1976:196–198; Oliver 1981).

Susquehanna Cluster

SUSQUEHANNA BROAD

This is a broad-bladed projectile point type (Witthoft 1953:7–8) with an expanded stem (Figure 36). The blade is triangular with slightly recurvate edges. Frequently the blade is asymmetrical and the cross section biconvex. Pristine Susquehanna points exhibit blade edges finished by retouch, usually from a single face. The shoulders are finely retouched, angular, and sharp. The haft element was produced by detaching large flakes initially from the corners with marginal retouch from opposite faces of the stem. Thus, the notch itself is alternately beveled and has a wide V-shape. The base is narrower than the shoulders, and the basal ears are generally acute and prominent. The basal edge is usually slightly concave. Full haft grinding is typical.

Some additional information regarding this type deserves mention. Dincauze (1968) discussed the relationship of two named types (i.e., Mansion Inn and Wayland Notched) which were coined in a study of cremation cemeteries in eastern Massachusetts. Both of these types comprise portions of the formal variation, including manufacturing trajectory, recognized for the Susquehanna Broad type. The Mansion Inn preform/cache blade type

(Dincauze 1968:18–22) is composed of one lanceolate and two contracting stemmed varieties. This has been shown to be technically related to the Wayland Notched type in the same manufacturing tradition (1968:23–26). The latter type conforms largely to the type description of Susquehanna Broad. The Dudley and Coburn varieties of Wayland Notched may be found to be intermediate between Susquehanna and Orient Fishtail (1968:26). Orient Fishtail (Ritchie 1961) is an additional type within the Susquehanna cluster.

Prufer and Sofsky (1965:33–34) noted that the Ashtabula type defined by Mayer-Oakes (1955:62) for the upper Ohio Valley is essentially the same form falling into the morphological range of Susquehanna Broad. Ashtabula is regarded as a morphological correlate of Susquehanna Broad. Those materials illustrated by Mayer-Oakes and also Converse (1973:48) exhibit long stems and crude appearance compared to illustrations of Susquehanna Broad and could constitute a variety of this basic style.

Age and Cultural Affiliation
Susquehanna Broad points relate to the Late Archaic/Early Woodland transitional period in the Northeast. An age of ca. 1700 to 700 B.C. is

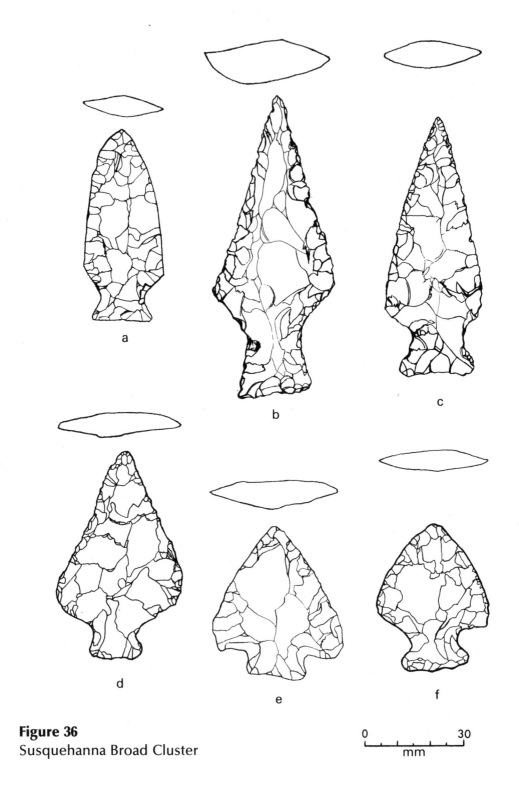

Figure 36
Susquehanna Broad Cluster

0   30
mm

suggested. These forms have been radio-carbon dated from 1670 B.C. ±110 to 1520 B.C. ±125 in eastern Massachusetts (Dincauze 1968:72–77; Kinsey 1972:429). Susquehanna Broad points are diagnostic of the Frost Island phase. In the Susquehanna Valley, vessels and beads of steatite (soapstone) plus steatite tempered Marcey Creek Plain ceramics are associated with Susquehanna Broad points. The latter pottery is modeled after the shape of carved stone bowls (steatite) and appears later in the sequence. The Wilson site in Pennsylvania produced this manifestation stratigraphically below levels containing Early Woodland Vinette I pottery (McCann 1962:55).

Distribution

Susquehanna Broad points are distributed throughout much of the Northeast to the coast (Kinsey 1972; Bourn 1977). The center of this manifestation, however, lies within the Juniata River Valley (Fred W. Kinsey III, pers. comm.) and to a lesser extent the Susquehanna River Valley of Pennsylvania (Ritchie 1969a:150–151). The type is reported in West Virginia (Jensen 1970) and occurs in low frequency in Michigan (Roosa 1966:32–33). It is relatively common in eastern Ohio (Prufer and Sofsky 1965:33; Shane 1975a:140), and has been identified in eastern Indiana.

Morphological Correlates

Ashtabula (Mayer-Oakes 1955:62, Plate 16; Prufer and Sofsky 1965:33–34; Converse 1973:48); Forest Notched (Mayer-Oakes

Figure 36: Susquehanna Cluster
a. Susquehanna Broad. Onondaga chert. GBL 10/83. Erie Co., Pennsylvania.
b. Susquehanna Broad (Ashtabula). Coshocton chert. GBL 14/859. Delaware Co., Indiana.
c. Susquehanna Broad. Unidentified chert. GBL 281/265. Northwestern Vermont.
d. Perkiomen Broad. Onondaga chert. GBL 13/891. South-central Michigan. Pictured in Plate 7, g.
e. Perkiomen Broad. Onondaga chert. GBL 10/85. Erie Co., Pennsylvania.
f. Perkiomen Broad. Onondaga chert. GBL 10/82. Erie Co., Pennsylvania.

Map 71: Susquehanna Broad—Distribution and Important Sites

1955:60–61, Plate 15); Wayland Notched; Watertown, Dudley, Coburn varieties (Dincauze 1968:29, 23–26).

PERKIOMEN BROAD

Perkiomen Broad points (Witthoft 1953:16–17; Ritchie 1961:42–43) are large triangular-bladed forms with a small expanding stem (Figure 36). The blade generally approximates an equilateral triangle with asymmetrical recurvate edges. The blade has a flattened cross section with large percussion flake scars on each face rarely producing a median ridge on either face. The shoulders are wide and robust and described as barbed, although they seldom exhibit bilateral symmetry. One shoulder may be elongated and project downward slightly while the other may be horizontal and short. Other specimens exhibit a V-shaped notch in which the shoulder may project upward slightly, which is similar to Susquehanna Broad. The shoulder edges are thin and sharp and flaked similar to Susquehanna. The haft element exhibits a constricted neck and flared stem with a straight to convex base. Full haft grinding occurs up to the shoulder/haft juncture. Bifacial resharpening of the blade includes reduction, which results in rejuvenated cutting edges, scrapers, drills, and other forms (see Kraft 1970:6). One study has shown that these points were used as knives and cleaving tools (see Dunn 1984).

Age and Cultural Affiliation
This is a Late Archaic/Early Woodland transitional form in the Northeast and is considered to date within the time range of Susquehanna Broad (Ritchie 1961:43; Prufer and Sofsky 1965:33). Radiocarbon dates range from 1720 b.c. ± 120 to 1500 b.c. ± 120 (Kinsey 1972:427). Caches of these forms, covered with red ocher, have been found in funerary contexts in New York. The association in the Northeast of Perkiomen points with steatite vessels and Early Woodland Vinette I ceramics is noteworthy, indicating that Perkiomen points extend into the Early Woodland period (Ritchie 1969a:153–156).

Distribution
Perkiomen Broad points are known best from eastern New York (Ritchie 1969a:153) and the surrounding region. Outside New York, the distribution of these forms extends into Virginia (Holland 1970; McCary 1972), Pennsylvania (Leslie 1963; Bebrich 1968:329), and Ohio (Prufer and Sofsky 1965; Shane 1975a:141–142). These forms also occur in low frequency in eastern Indiana.

Early Woodland Cotaco Creek type projectile points occur in the middle South (i.e., Tennessee, Alabama) and share some basic characteristics, such as a broad triangular

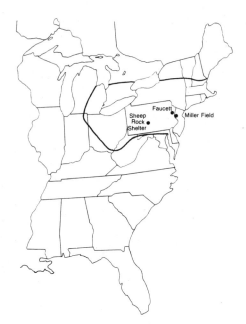

Map 72: Perkiomen Broad—Distribution and Important Sites

blade, with the Perkiomen type (Walthall 1980:89–90). However, the Perkiomen type appears limited to the Northeast in distribution.

Morphological Correlates of the Susquehanna Cluster
Clagett (Stephenson and Ferguson 1963: 142–143, 177, Plate 24); Egypt Mills (Kinsey 1972:413, Fig. 116D; cf. Witthoft 1953, Plates 2–3). Additional types: Abbey (Cambron and Hulse 1969:1); Dry Brook (Kinsey 1972:430–432; Fig. 119b); Orient Fishtail (Ritchie 1971a:39, 54; 1969a:154; Kraft 1970:8–9; Walsh 1977:35, Plate 4).

Meadowood Cluster

MEADOWOOD

Meadowood projectile points (Ritchie 1961: 35) are thin and delicate trianguloid forms with wide side notches (Figure 37). These

projectile points range from somewhat small and crude to large and refined. The latter are made from refined preforms or cache blades (Pomranky/Meadowood) described in the Wadlow cluster and represent the "classic"

Meadowood type. The other forms represent the variation in form in the use-life of these tools. Meadowood points exhibit a trianguloid shape with straight to excurvate blade edges. Cross sections are thin and flat resulting from a refined bifacial thinning technique utilized in preform manufacture. These forms are side notched low on the preform. Certain specimens are double notched on one or both sides. Notch openings are narrow, and the notch depth is shallow. The basal edge is typically convex, although variation of the basal morphology includes those with a straightened edge. Sometimes Meadowood points exhibit serration and beveling. The latter trait is undoubtedly related to the bifacial thinning technique functioning as platform preparation for controlled flake detachments. Basal grinding is characteristic of the type.

Map 73: Meadowood—Distribution and Important Sites

Age and Cultural Affiliation

This projectile point style is diagnostic of the Early Woodland Meadowood phase in the Northeast. Meadowood manifestations have been dated within a range of 1300 B.C. to 500 B.C. (Ritchie and Funk 1973:116; Granger 1981:63). Relevant radiocarbon dates are 1230 B.C. ±95 from the Fortin 2 site (Funk, Rippeteau, and Houck 1973:16) and 750 B.C. ±100 from the Faucett site (Kinsey 1972: 191). Other diagnostic materials of the Meadowood phase include Meadowood cache blades or Quaternary Blanks (Ritchie 1952; Granger 1981:93) and Vinette I ceramics. Adena points are also sometimes associated with Meadowood (Ritchie and Funk 1973:115–116, 347).

Distribution

Meadowood points are known from a variety of sites in New York, Connecticut, Vermont, and other areas in the Northeast (Perkins 1970; Thompson 1973; Ritchie 1969a; Kinsey 1972; Ritchie and Funk 1973). The type occurs west into Pennsylvania (Bebrich 1968:

Plate 2), Ohio (Shane 1975a:163), and elsewhere. In Indiana, the type is present in low frequency and is largely undocumented in the literature for the state. Meadowood projectile points occur in the Great Lakes area, especially in Michigan. Hodges points defined by Binford (1963b:130–131) from the Hodges site in Michigan are essentially the same as those described here, which were manufactured from Pomranky type cache blades or blanks. A single Meadowood-like point was recovered from a burial at the Reigh site in Wisconsin (Baerreis et al. 1957: 249, Fig. 1, h; Converse n.d.:106).

Morphological Correlate

Hodges (Binford 1963b:129–131).

Morphological Correlates of the Meadowood Cluster

Davis (Binford and Papworth 1963:100–102; Binford 1963b:130, 133–134, Fig.2); Hunt (Binford 1963b:132–134, Fig. 2).

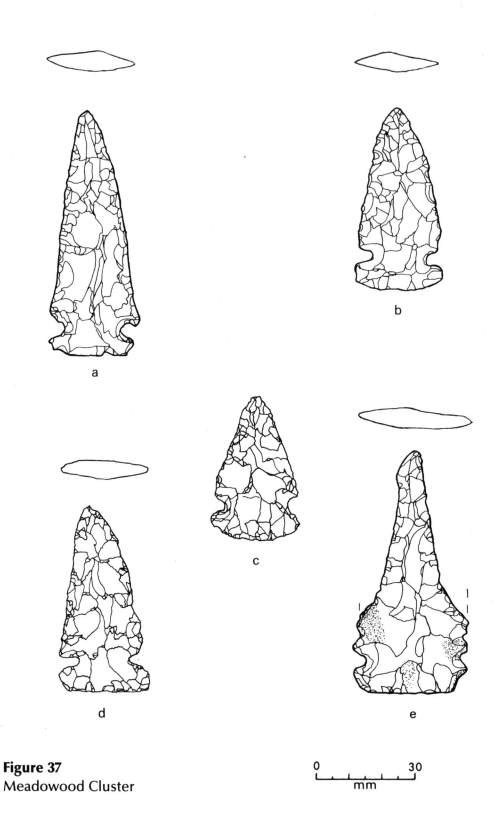

Figure 37
Meadowood Cluster

0   30
mm

Turkey-tail Cluster

The Turkey-tail type (Scully 1951:11; Ritzenthaler and Niehoff 1958:117; Bell 1960:90) as originally described is now known in three subtypes (Harrison, Fulton, Hebron) and several varieties (Binford 1963d). Didier (1967) later used these varieties (a total of ten) in a distributional study of the Turkey-tail type (primarily exotic caches) over a large area of the Northeast. The variety distinctions in some cases make "hair-line" divisions of shape that cannot be standardized for consistent identification. Actually, some of the varieties, especially those of the Fulton type, are very difficult to distinguish. Attempts to define specific manufacturing trajectories are in progress (Justice 1981b). Note below that the original ten varieties can be recombined into six categories based on overall characteristics (Figure 38). This regrouping provides tighter morphological units. Nonetheless, four of the original varieties were sufficiently distinctive to remain as they are.

Subtype	Variety	Revised for Discussion
Harrison	marshall	
		Harrison (mm)
Harrison	mitchell	
Hebron		
Fulton	dickson	
Fulton	kimmel	
Fulton	fulton	
Fulton	knox	
Fulton	ross	Fulton (fkrs)
Fulton	spoon	
Fulton	stemmed	

Figure 37: Meadowood Cluster
a. Meadowood (Hodges). Eastport chert. GBL 13/397. Eaton Co., Michigan.
b–d. Meadowood. Onondaga chert. GBL 10/75–77. Erie Co., Pennsylvania.
e. Meadowood. Drill form. Onondaga chert. GBL 10/49. Erie Co., Pennsylvania. Pictured in Plate 7, c.

The important result of presenting clearer morphological distinctions of the general Turkey-tail class lies in the similarity of a given-named type or variety to a potential ancestral or later form(s), a relationship which may not be the same for the other forms in the class. Thus, the Turkey-tail cluster is presented much like the other clusters of types in this manual. Turkey-tail caches and utilitarian forms of the same type are classified with the same nomenclature. Turkey-tail cache blades are among a special class of artifacts which tend to possess over-sized blade proportions, and are very thin and delicate in comparison to smaller and cruder utilitarian forms or manufacturing discards that exhibit the characteristic haft element. At both ends of the range of variation of the Turkey-tail type, overlaps with other clusters occur. Only after further study of funerary, camp, and manufacturing loci of Turkey-tails (see Myers 1981; Justice 1981b) from a series of sites can temporal and cultural relationships be ascertained within the time period in which they occur. Considering overall size and proportions of Turkey-tail cache blades, interesting comparisons can be made between these and the tanged and socketed copper spears and knives diagnostic of the Old Copper culture of the Great Lakes (see Wittry 1951:11; Fogel 1963:Fig. 4).

HARRISON (MM)

The Harrison (mm) combines the mitchell and marshall varieties. Both varieties have narrow width to length proportions and a triangular shaped stem larger than those exhibited on other Turkey-tails. The notches and stems on these specimens also tend to be wider than on other Turkey-tail types. The resulting form has a sturdier haft in comparison to the others (Perino 1971a:46).

HEBRON

Hebron Turkey-tails in outer form appear more related stylistically to the large group of Late Archaic tanged, straight stemmed, and shoulder barbed points that exist. Hebron types exhibit a straight stem with a rounded basal edge. Maximum blade width is at the shoulder.

FULTON/DICKSON

The Fulton/dickson variety Turkey-tail exhibits an expanding stem with a straight to convex basal edge. This variety of Turkey-tail lacks obvious shoulders. The excurvate contour of the blade edge expands from the tip to an approximate midpoint on the blade, then constricts to join the stem without interference from shoulders. The resulting form is lenticular and nearly elliptoid, with the small short stem protuding beyond this basic shape.

FULTON/KIMMEL

This variety of Fulton Turkey-tail exhibits comparable blade configuration with that of the Fulton/dickson. However, maximum blade width is shifted from the center of the blade closer to the basal area. Like the Fulton/dickson, the kimmel variety lacks obvious shoulders. The blade edges constrict to join with the stem. Stem characteristics are similar to the Hebron Turkey-tail, sharing a straight sided stem with a rounded basal edge. These points compare in outline to socketed and tanged copper points of the Old Copper culture of the western Great Lakes (Ritzenthaler and Wittry 1952).

FULTON (FKRS)

The Fulton (fkrs) combines four varieties of the Fulton subtype: fulton, knox, ross, and spoon. These four share qualities of form rather than unique characteristics (such as degree of blade recurvature) which might be used to subdivide them. The four varieties share comparable wide excurvate blades made from bipointed preforms. The stem of this group is set apart from the blade only by side notching. In other words, the edges of the stem are in line with the blade edge at the shoulder. Thus, the Fulton (fkrs) is a bi-pointed form with side notches. All other Turkey-tail styles exhibit stems which tend to break the symmetry of the overall form. There is little question that the Fulton (fkrs) is the most common kind of Turkey-tail known.

FULTON STEMMED

The Fulton stemmed haft morphology is divided into two parts. This variety exhibits the basal form of the Fulton type below a straight stemmed extension. Blade characteristics are basically similar to other Turkey-tails except that well defined shoulders are exhibited. These can either be weak and sloping or robust and squared. A subvariety of this haft characteristic is a segmented form which

Figure 38: Turkey-tail Cluster
a. Harrison Turkey-tail. Wyandotte chert. GBL 13/866. South-central Michigan.
b. Harrison Turkey-tail. Wyandotte chert. GBL 1448/447. Southwestern Indiana.
c. Hebron Turkey-tail. Wyandotte chert. GBL 21/410. Monroe Co., Indiana.
d. Fulton dickson Turkey-tail. Wyandotte chert. GBL 14/823. Indiana.
e. Fulton kimmel Turkey-tail. Wyandotte chert. GBL 14/872. Greene Co., Indiana.
f. Fulton (fkrs) Turkey-tail. Wyandotte chert. GBL 5455/3. Site 12 Or 73. Orange Co., Indiana.
g. Fulton (fkrs) Turkey-tail. Wyandotte chert. GBL 5455/5. Site 12 Or 73. Orange Co., Indiana.
h. Fulton (fkrs) Turkey-tail. Wyandotte chert. GBL 5455/2. Site 12 Or 73. Orange Co., Indiana.
i. Fulton (fkrs) Turkey-tail. Wyandotte chert. GBL 1448/154. Southwestern Indiana.
j. Fulton stemmed Turkey-tail. Wyandotte chert. GBL 1448/145. Southwestern Indiana.
k. Fulton stemmed Turkey-tail. Wyandotte chert. GBL 14/823. Indiana. Pictured in Plate 6, o.

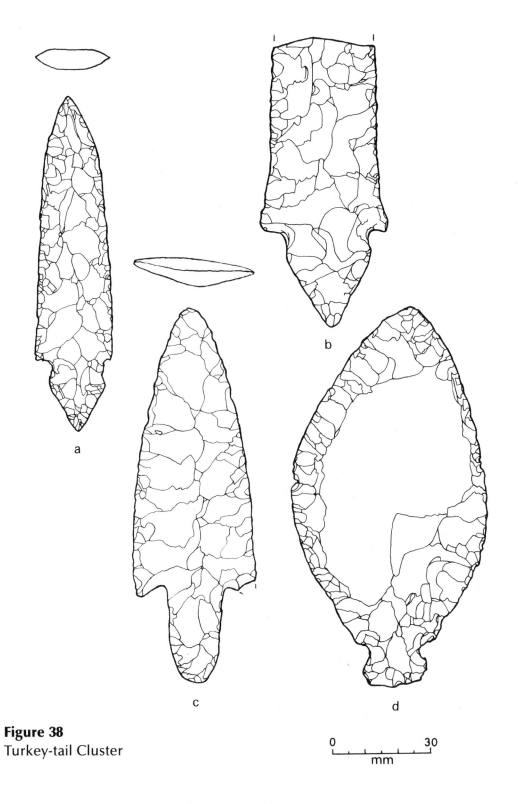

Figure 38
Turkey-tail Cluster

0   30
mm

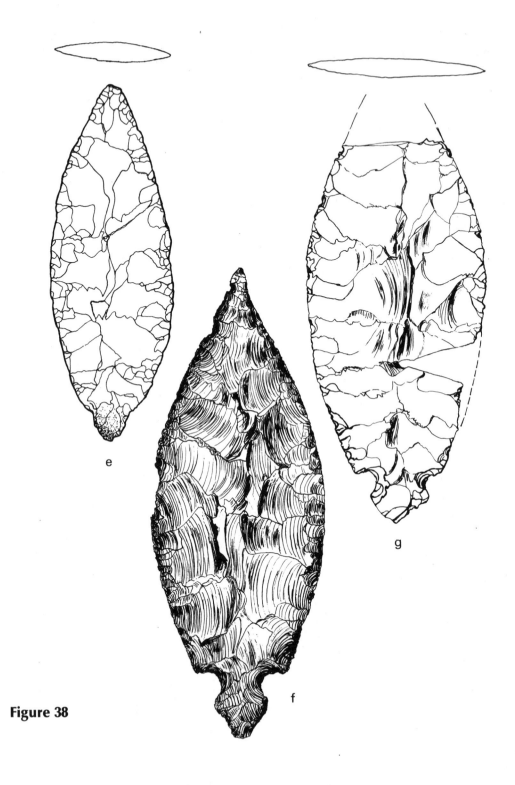

e

f

g

Figure 38

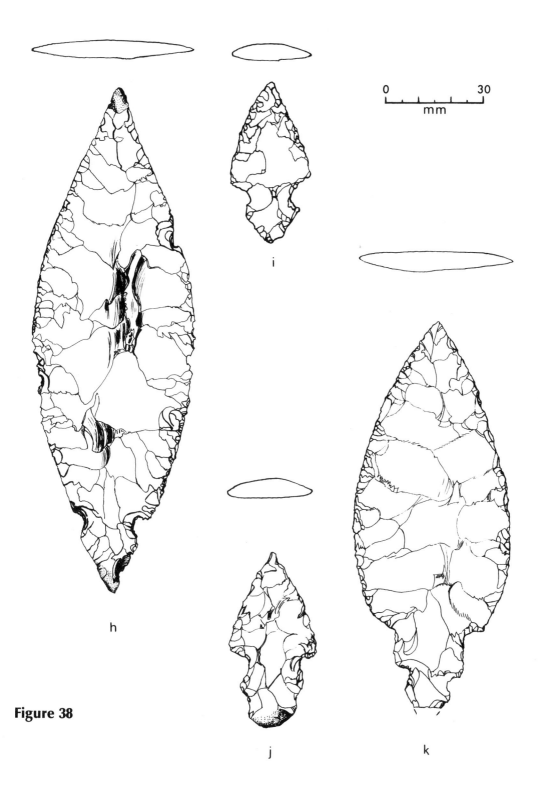

Figure 38

h

i

j

k

exhibits a full straight sided dual segment with a straight or slightly convex base.

Age and Cultural Affiliation

Turkey-tails are diagnostic of the Late Archaic/Early Woodland transitional period. Culturally, Turkey-tails relate to what has been named the Red Ocher complex (Cole and Deuel 1937), known primarily from funerary contexts in the Illinois Valley and Midwest generally. These have also been found in Meadowood phase contexts in New York (Ritchie 1969a:181–183). Associated materials include Pomranky (Faulkner 1960b) and Red Ocher type points (Scully 1951:9; Perino 1968a:72), copper, marine shell, and other artifacts (Ritzenthaler and Quimby 1962; Binford 1963a). In addition, Conrad (1981:185, Plate 35b) has named another associated form, the Merkle Side Barbed. Turkey-tail points have also been associated with Adena points and Early Woodland ceramics (Schock and Dowell 1981). Didier (1967:10) places Turkey-tails within a time period beginning about 1500 B.C. and lasting until about 500 B.C., where they overlap morphologically with the Adena Ovate-base style (Adena Stemmed). Some dated sites with reported Turkey-tail associations are provided below. Those with dates later than 500 B.C. are associated with material which overlaps the Adena Ovate-base style.

Map 74: Turkey-tail Cluster
Distribution and Important Sites

Michigan	
Andrews	1220 B.C. ±300 (Crane and Griffin 1960:34; Fitting 1970:84).
New York	
Oblander II	998 B.C. ±170 (Libby 1952:77).
Kentucky	
15 Wa 981	160 B.C. ±105 (Schock and Dowell 1981:1).
15 Si 7	495 B.C. ±90; 535 B.C. ±70 (Schock and Langford 1981:46).

Distribution

Turkey-tail distribution covers much of the Great Lakes and Midwest regions on into New York state, southern Ontario, and Connecticut (Lavin 1984). Refer to Didier (1967) for a detailed attempt to construct regional distributions of the various types. Turkey-tails occur in low frequency as far south as Tennessee (Smith and Hodges 1968:109). A biface type somewhat similar to the Turkey-tail is present at the Spiro site (Caddoan Mississippian) in Oklahoma. Nonetheless, any connection has been discredited (Brown 1976:131), and the western extent is probably confined to eastern Missouri, Iowa, and Wisconsin in the Mississippi Valley.

The vast majority of Turkey-tails were manufactured in the localized raw material source areas of southern Indiana (primarily Harrison County), southern Illinois, and northern Kentucky (Stemle 1981:115–116). The Harrison County chert source has recently been studied in Harrison and Crawford Counties, Indiana (Bassett 1981; Justice 1981a; Munson and Munson 1981). The bedrock units have been identified in the Fredonia Member of the St. Genevieve Limestone (Bassett 1981). The chert occurs as a unit named the Wyandotte chert zone containing oolitic and non-oolitic nodular (i.e., the primary raw material used to make Tur-key-tails) and lense cherts of varying quality and thickness (Justice 1981a). Probably no other prehistoric chipped stone artifact in North America was traded as extensively as the Turkey-tail or had such a high degree of continuity in raw material utilized in its production.

Terminal Archaic Barbed Cluster

DELHI

Delhi points (Ford and Webb 1956:58–60; Perino 1971a:22) are straight stemmed forms with barbed shoulders (Figure 39). The blades of these points are generally long and tri-anguloid in shape. The edges vary in contour from straight to excurvate. Typical specimens possess the latter attribute. Shoulders are barbed and project downward. Characteristic features of the haft element are the straight (parallel-sided) stems with straight basal edges. The corners of the stem are often squared, exhibiting a 90° angle. The basal edges are occasionally slightly convex and, more rarely, concave. The stem and barbs of Delhi points are formed by the use of a cor-ner notching technique. Circular hertzian cone flake scars surround the notch termi-nus extending onto the barbs. These flake scars cover a portion of the stem but are erased by subsequent retouch, forming the straight stem. Stems vary slightly from ex-panding to contracting due to the degree of stem edge retouch following the notching process. Cross sections on Delhi points tend to be biconvex, having been formed by con-trolled percussion flaking. Blade beveling and serration occur in low frequency and are not typical of the type.

Age and Cultural Affiliation
This projectile point style is diagnostic of the Late Archaic and Early Woodland periods. The type is dated from 1300 to 200 B.C. with other types at the Poverty Point site (Ford and Webb 1956:117). There are no specific dates from the site which relate solely to De-

lhi points. This type of projectile point was recovered from a mortuary context at the Pete Klunk site (crematory C, Klunk mound 7) located near Kampsville, Illinois, and a date of 920 B.C. ±75 is reported (Crane and Griffin 1963:233). Here it was referred to as the Kampsville Barbed type, which is de-scribed by Perino (1968b:80, Fig. 37) and re-lated to the Kampsville phase for the lower Illinois River Valley. Along with "Kampsville Barbed" points were found limestone slab covered, flexed and bundled burials, crema-tion burials, copper and shell ornaments, plummets (teardrop-shaped weights), galena (natural lead), red ocher, and other materi-

Map 75: Delhi—Distribution and Important Sites

als. Two Delhi points were also found in transitional context at the Throgmorton Dam site in southern Illinois (Cremin 1975c: 222).

Distribution
Delhi points occur from the lower Mississippi Valley to the Gulf Coast in Louisiana (Ford and Webb 1956; Webb 1977) and Mississippi (Ford, Phillips, and Haag 1955) and also northern Alabama and southeast Arkansas (Perino 1971a: 22). The type is present north into Kentucky (Weinland 1980: 69–70, Fig. 29), southern Indiana, and much of southern Illinois (Perino 1968b, 1971a; Cremin 1975b: 80).

Morphological Correlate
Kampsville Barbed (Perino 1968b: 80; 1971: 22).

WADE

Wade projectile points (Cambron and Hulse 1960b, 1969: 110) are basically straight-stemmed forms with wide barbs. These were fashioned from trianguloid bifaces by producing deep and narrowing basal notches (Figure 39). The resulting projectile point style exhibits long barbs or elongated shoulders expanding away from a narrow, straight to slightly expanding stem. In certain specimens, the barbs extend just short of being in the same plane as the basal edge of the point. Cross sections range from biconvex to flattened. Blade edges may be excurvate or straight. Random flaking is exhibited across the preform, with short and deep flake scars occurring on the outer margins of the blade and stem edges.

Age and Cultural Affiliation
The Wade projectile point type appears to overlap the Late Archaic and Early Woodland transition dating from 1000 B.C. to 500 B.C. in the Tennessee River Valley and elsewhere (see Faulkner and McCollough 1973: 149; Ison 1982b: 5–6). These points have been found both in preceramic contexts in Shell Middens (Cambron and Hulse 1969: 110)

and in Early Woodland contexts associated with pottery (Webb and DeJarnette 1948a). At the Stanfield-Worley Bluff Shelter in Alabama (DeJarnette, Kurjack, and Cambron 1962), Wade points were more numerous in the Late Archaic levels than in Early Woodland. Yet a Wade type point was recovered at the Banks III site in Tennessee associated with a steatite vessel fragment and dated to 1010 B.C. (Faulkner and McCollough 1974: 294). Similar points were common in the Early Woodland levels at the Westmoreland-Barber site in Tennessee dating from 755 B.C. ±155 to 340 B.C. ±150 years (Faulkner and Graham 1966).

Distribution
Wade points occur in highest frequency in a core area which centers along the Tennessee River Valley drainage in northern Alabama and Tennessee (Cambron and Hulse 1969). The type is recognized across much of Tennessee (Faulkner and McCollough 1973; Faulkner 1968) and Kentucky (Schock and Langford 1979b: 13). The maximum extent of distribution is not known. A few specimens of the type have been found north of the Ohio River Valley in southern Indiana.

Figure 39: Terminal Archaic Barbed Cluster
a. Delhi. Fort Payne chert. Florence, Alabama. Marshall L. Fallwell collection.
b. Delhi. Unidentified chert. GBL 14/884. Jennings Co., Indiana.
c. Delhi. Unidentified chert. GBL 637/38. DeSoto Co., Mississippi.
d. Wade. Unidentified chert. GBL 637/6. DeSoto Co., Mississippi.
e. Wade. Fort Payne chert. Florence, Alabama. Marshall L. Fallwell collection.
f. Wade. Unidentified chert. GBL 1448/232. Southwestern Indiana.
g. Buck Creek Barbed. Wyandotte chert. GBL 304/637. Provenience unknown. Pictured in Plate 6, i.
h. Buck Creek Barbed. Muldraugh chert. GBL 285/13. Clark Co., Indiana.
i. Buck Creek Barbed. Cobden chert. GBL 304/635. Provenience unknown.
j. Buck Creek Barbed. Holland chert. GBL 5/239. Warrick Co., Indiana.

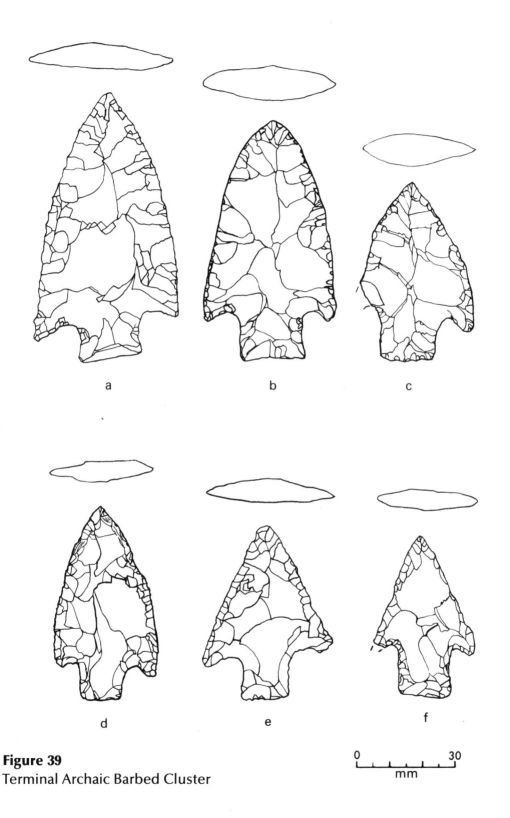

Figure 39
Terminal Archaic Barbed Cluster

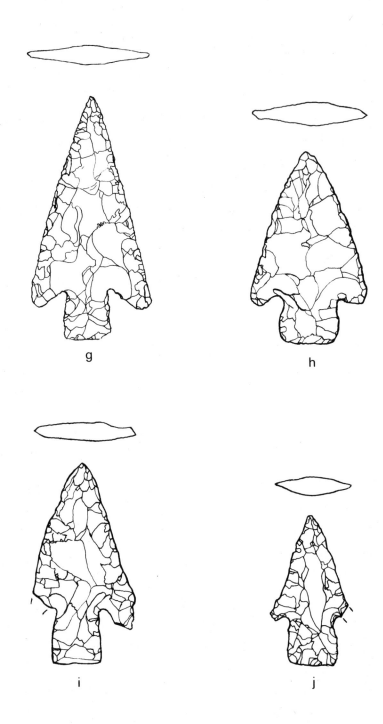

g

h

i

j

Figure 39

Map 76: Wade—Distribution and Important Sites

BUCK CREEK BARBED

The Buck Creek Barbed projectile point style (Seeman 1975:107) is typically medium-sized, stemmed, and exhibits strongly barbed shoulders (Figure 39). The blade is triangular in shape with a straight blade edge. Cross sections are lenticular or plano convex. The barbs and upper portion of the stem are produced by a corner notching technique. The lateral edges of the lower stem and the base are carefully chipped on both faces to produce a beveled edge. The stem is usually thinned from the base, one-third to one-half of the way up the length of the stem. Typical stems are long in relation to the total length of the point, expand slightly toward a straight base, and are often indented at the shoulder/haft juncture. The base is never ground. The Buck Creek Barbed style also attains cache blade quality, in that certain specimens are larger and thinner than average with patterned thinning flake scars as well as large hertzian cones at the notch terminus. In these cases, most are triangular and have distinct barbs and straight stems, although some lack the edge bevel on the stem.

Age and Cultural Affiliation

This point style appears in the Late Archaic period and extends into the Early Woodland period (Seeman 1975) and dates from about 1500 to 600 B.C. Radiocarbon dates for similar types such as Dyroff and Springly points range as late as 900 to 600 B.C. (Emerson 1984:312). More specific dates for Buck Creek Barbed have not been obtained. In addition, a single Buck Creek Barbed-like point was associated with Turkey-tails and other material at a rock shelter in Kentucky (Guthe 1964:82; Seeman 1975).

Distribution

These points are found primarily in southern Indiana along the Ohio River and adjacent drainages. They are more common in southeastern Indiana and extend into southern Ohio and northern Kentucky. This and similar types extend as far north as central Indiana (Guendling and Crouch 1977:102, Fig. 3). The Cypress Stemmed type (Winters n.d.) incorporates a portion of the range of variation of Buck Creek (cf. Denny 1972:Fig. 22d–f). This type is present across much of southern Illinois (Winters 1967:50; Denny 1972:146).

Map 77: Buck Creek Barbed
Distribution and Important Sites

Morphological Correlate
Crooked Creek (Tomak 1980b:5, Fig. 20).

Morphological Correlates of the Terminal Archaic Barbed Cluster
Apple Creek (Perino 1975:50–51, Fig. 38); Cypress Stemmed (varieties 2–4) (Winters n.d., 1963, 1967:50; Denny 1972:145–146, Fig. 22); Dyroff (Emerson 1984:258–266); Glacial Kame Stemmed (Potter 1968:21; Seeman 1975:106); Lone Tree (Tomak 1980b); Mo-Pac (McElrath and Fortier 1983: 119–120); Smithsonia (Cambron and Hulse (1975:115); Springly (Munson 1971: 89, Fig. 26a–c; Emerson 1984:266–268). Additional types: Bulverde (Kelley 1947; Suhm, Krieger, and Jelks 1954:404; Bell 1960:12); Carrolton (Suhm, Krieger, and Jelks 1954:406; Bell 1958:12).

Early Woodland Stemmed Cluster

KRAMER

Munson (1966a; 1971:6–7, 49, Fig. 4) defined the Kramer point as a lanceolate-bladed form exhibiting a distinctive long, straight stem with heavy lateral stem grinding (Figure 40). The Kramer projectile point type exhibits a basic trianguloid blade shape with straight to excurvate sides. The total blade length is quite variable due to reworking. The stem edges are essentially straight but may vary to slightly excurvate. Nearly all of the specimens examined by Munson exhibited a proximal shoulder edge that sloped in a wide arc at the shoulder/haft juncture. Rarely are the shoulders squared, and shoulder barbs are not an attribute of the type.

Age and Cultural Affiliation
Kramer points have been associated with Early Woodland Marion Thick ceramics and are diagnostic of the Marion phase. The Marion phase appeared in the latter portion of the Red Ocher complex (Munson 1966a, 1971:6, 1982:1). Kramer points were the predominant point style at the Late Archaic/Early Woodland Sheets site in Illinois which also produced Marion Thick pottery. Dates for Marion phase sites average slightly earlier than 500 B.C. (see Munson 1966b:117; 1982:3). Comparable dating of Kramer points (Fitting 1972a:195) at the Schultz site in Michigan is significant (Fitting 1972b:268; Kenyon 1980a:21).

Distribution
Munson (1966b:112, Fig. 1; 1982:10, Fig. 1) reported that the distribution of Kramer points covers primarily northwestern Indiana, much of Illinois, southwestern Michi-

Figure 40: Early Woodland Stemmed Cluster
a. Cresap Stemmed. Drawn from photograph. Original, unidentified chert. Cresap Mound, West Virginia. Courtesy of the Carnegie Museum of Natural History, Division of Anthropology, specimen accession (3112–a). Not to scale, oversized.
b. Cresap Stemmed. Upper Mercer chert. GBL 14/885. Jennings Co., Indiana.
c. Cresap Stemmed. Jeffersonville chert. GBL 4627/17. Marysville, Ohio.
d. Kramer. Unidentified chert. GBL 134/134. Nowlin Mound, site 12 D 7. Dearborn Co., Indiana.
e. Kramer. Attica chert. GBL 4307/13. Site 12 T 10. Tippecanoe Co., Indiana.
f. Kramer. Unidentified chert. GBL 260/1. Hamilton Co., Indiana.
g. Robbins. Flint Ridge chert. GBL 134.69. Nowlin Mound, site 12 D 7. Dearborn Co., Indiana.
h. Robbins. Flint Ridge chert. GBL 134/55. Nowlin Mound, site 12 D 7. Dearborn Co., Indiana. Pictured in Plate 8, s.
i. Robbins. Flint Ridge chert. GBL 14/922. Shelby Co., Indiana.

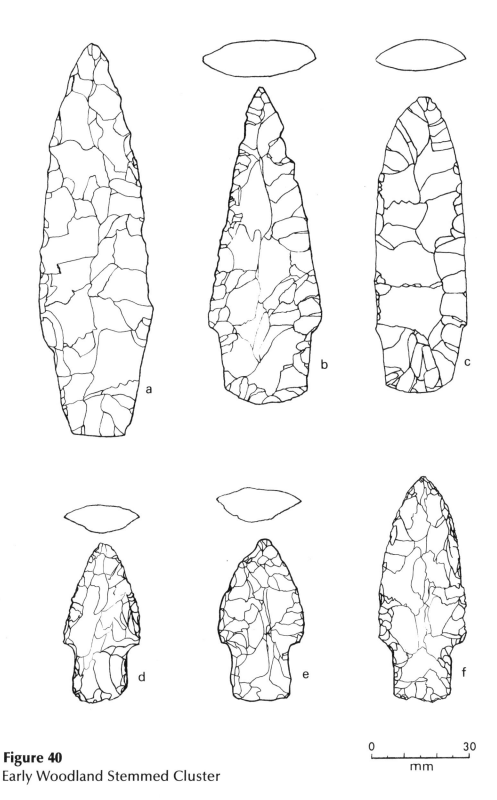

Figure 40
Early Woodland Stemmed Cluster

0 30
mm

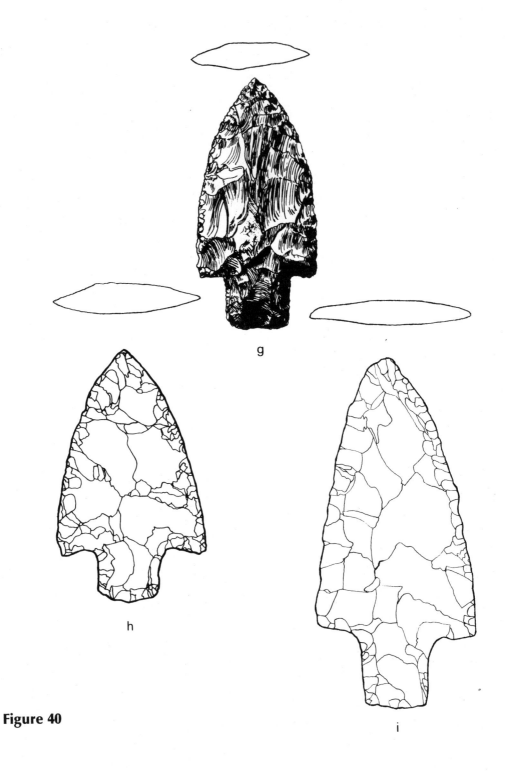

g

h

i

Figure 40

Map 78: **Kramer**—Distribution and Important Sites

Map 79: Cresap Stemmed
Distribution and Important Sites

gan, southern Wisconsin, and the extreme northeast portion of Missouri and eastern Iowa.

CRESAP STEMMED

Cresap points (Dragoo 1963:109–110, 178; Converse 1973:55) are categorized as flat-based, tapered-stemmed blades with weak shoulders (Figure 40). The tapered stem equates with a mild form of contracting stemmed points not to be confused with the wide-shouldered and distinct contracting stemmed forms characteristic of the Dickson cluster. The Cresap stem usually tapers from the shoulder with a small shoulder/haft juncture. These points are long and slender with a fine flaking quality produced by a combination of percussion and pressure flaking techniques. The blade edges are excurvate and the basal edge is thin and flat. A lenticular cross section is typical.

Age and Cultural Affiliation
Cresap points are diagnostic of the early Adena culture of the Early Woodland period. This projectile point type was found at the

floor of the Cresap Mound in West Virginia and within pits below the base of the mound. The Cresap type is the earliest recognized Adena diagnostic preceding the Adena Stemmed type which is typical of the middle phases of Adena. An age of 1000 B.C. to before 500 B.C. is thought to relate to Cresap points and the lower zones of the Cresap Mound (Dragoo 1963:290–291, 1976b:1).

Distribution
Cresap points occur generally within the middle Ohio Valley. Dragoo (1963:109) observed that this form is not a common Adena diagnostic within the Adena homeland. The type is known from Indiana, Ohio (Converse 1973:55; Shane 1975a:163), and West Virginia (Dragoo 1963:109). It apparently extends in low frequency into the Northeast, since material similar to Cresap points has been identified at Rosenkrans, an Adena-related mortuary site in New Jersey (see Kraft 1976:15, Fig. 2).

ROBBINS

Robbins points (Dragoo 1963:113–114; Perino 1971a:82) are broad-bladed, straight stemmed forms (Figure 40). The blade edges are typically excurvate with maximum blade width occurring at or slightly above the shoulder. Both biconvex and plano convex cross sections are typical. Random percussion flake scars produce an even surface morphology, and fine marginal retouch results in straight blade edges. Shoulders are pronounced and well defined. Morphology of the shoulders varies from straight and horizontal to the main axis of the blade, to sloping downward and forming wide barbs. Early variations of the haft element include slightly excurvate or ovate stem margins with weak indentations below the shoulders similar to the earlier Adena Stemmed type. Robbins points exhibiting the sloping shoulder trait in conjunction with straight or slightly expanded stems represent the latest trend in evolution and share certain similarities with the Snyders type in this respect. The haft region of Robbins is typified by straight stems with slightly excurvate basal edges. Full haft grinding is characteristic of Robbins points.

Robbins preforms range from basic ovate and trianguloid to lanceolate shapes. Robbins leaf-shaped blades (Dragoo 1963:180, Fig. 10e) and Morton Lanceolate (Montet-White 1968:31–38) are named cache blade styles, the basic shape of which served as preforms for Robbins points.

Age and Cultural Affiliation
Robbins points are diagnostic of the late Adena Robbins complex of the Early Woodland period (Dragoo 1963:289–291). Dragoo (1967b:2) placed the middle and late phases of Adena from about 500 B.C. to A.D. 200. The Robbins complex dates roughly to the latter half of this range. Robbins points occurred as mortuary offerings in the east tomb of the Nowlin Mound in Dearborn County, Indiana (Black 1936:282, 341, Plate 66). The transition from the middle to late phases of Adena is considered abrupt and incorporates Hopewellian elements (see Dragoo 1963:277) with regard to the majority of diagnostic traits. The changes, viewed from Adena Stemmed to Robbins points, appear to indicate a gradual trend in the lithic technology from narrow ovate-based forms

to wide-bladed straight stemmed forms. However, later in the Robbins complex, certain traits typical of Snyders are also reflected.

Early and Middle Adena ceramics are the typical Early Woodland interior and exterior cord marked, grit-tempered pottery referred to as Marion Thick, Fayette Thick, Vinette I, etc. However, thinner vessel walls and smoothed surfaces are typical of late Adena. Two named ceramic types of the Robbins complex are Paintsville Simple Stamped and Montgomery Incised (see Haag 1942:341–349; Dragoo 1963:275). The sherds recovered from the Nowlin Mound in Indiana are limestone tempered with smooth exteriors and are referred to as Adena Plain (Webb 1940:79).

Distribution
Robbins type projectile points, unlike Adena Stemmed, appear to have a distribution confined primarily to the known area of the Adena culture. Robbins points are known to occur from the Northeast (Ritchie and Dragoo 1960:43, Plate 8; Ritchie 1961:114, Plate 33) to Ohio (Converse 1973:52; Prufer 1975b:323, Fig. 4; Shane 1975a:163), West Virginia (Dragoo 1963, Cresap Mound), Ken-

Map 80: Robbins—Distribution and Important Sites

tucky (Webb and Elliott 1942:438–439, Figs. 29–30, Robbins Mounds), and Indiana (Black 1936:313, 341, Plates 13 and 66; Swartz 1973: 20–47). Apparently the western extent is confined to eastern Illinois. A similar type occurs within the Illinois Valley and elsewhere in Illinois and has been referred to as Liverpool Stemmed (Montet-White 1968). Although these projectile points are straight stemmed, the manufacturing characteris-

tics are not the same as those outlined for Robbins.

Morphological Correlates of the Early Woodland Stemmed Cluster
Additional type: Liverpool Stemmed (Montet-White 1968:66, Fig. 26, no. 10; Morse and Morse 1964:95, No. 10; Conrad 1981:184, Plate 34).

Dickson Cluster

GARY CONTRACTING STEMMED

Gary Stemmed points (Newell and Krieger 1949:164–165) are trianguloid-bladed, contracting stemmed forms (Figure 41). These have been described by several authors (Suhm, Krieger, and Jelks 1954:430; Ford and Webb 1956; Bell 1958:28; C. Chapman 1980:308) since the original description was prepared. The definition no longer includes straight stemmed forms. The blade edges of Gary points are typically straight to slightly excurvate. Some specimens exhibit incurvate to recurvate blade edges in resharpened form, and the shoulders typically flare outward widely, almost at a right angle to the main axis of the blade. The shoulder/haft juncture varies from a short right-angled arc joining a straight or slightly sloping shoulder to a wide arc joining a slightly upward-projecting shoulder. Stems contract strongly to either a narrow pointed or somewhat rounded base. These haft configurations normally exhibit straightened as opposed to excurvate edges. It appears that an irregular flaking pattern is typical of the type, although the degree of refinement in finished examples varies from crude to refined.

Age and Cultural Affiliation
Gary Contracting Stemmed points have been reported from contexts which suggest their appearance from the latter part of the Late Archaic period into the Middle Woodland period (Suhm, Krieger, and Jelks 1954:430; Cambron and Hulse 1969:47). Although these forms have frequently appeared in mixed contexts such as at the Stanfield-Worley Bluff Shelter in Alabama (DeJarnette et al. 1962:77) and the Williams Shelter in Missouri (Jolly and Roberts 1974:69, 74, Fig. 41), their age range is from about 1500 B.C. to about A.D. 100.

Of special note in this regard is the Zilpo site in Kentucky which was occupied from the Late Archaic to Early Woodland periods. Gary points, referred to as Cogswell Contracting Stemmed, were associated with a small number of Early Woodland ceramics and a single Adena Stemmed point in the upper levels of the site (Rolingson and Rodeffer 1968:38). This material occurred above deposits containing Saratoga points (i.e., Cave Run).

The longevity of the Gary variants into an Early Woodland time frame is known from Fourche Maline culture sites in southwest Arkansas (see Schambach 1982:133, 138). In addition, other Gary variants (e.g., Mabin) dominate Middle Woodland Marksville and Tchefuncte sites on the Gulf Coast (Phillips 1970:614; Toth 1979; Greenwell 1984: 140–143).

Map 81: Gary Contracting Stemmed—Distribution and Important Sites

Distribution

Bell (1958:28) observed that Gary points are a well known contracting stemmed style in an area from Texas (Newell and Krieger 1949) to Alabama (Ford and Webb 1956), Arkansas (Hoffman 1977:38, Fig. 1.15), and Missouri (Jolly and Roberts 1974:69; C. Chapman 1980:308). These points also occur at coastal sites such as Avery Island (Gagliano 1967). Gary points are also known from Tennessee (Faulkner and McCollough 1973:113, Plate 44), Kentucky (Rolingson and Rodeffer 1968:16–17), Illinois (Montet-White 1968:65), and southern Indiana (Cook 1980). The distribution of these forms in the East is not clear. Many contracting stemmed types of similar morphology are named in the literature. Further investigation into the temporal, spatial, and cultural significance of these forms is needed.

Morphological Correlates of Gary Contracting Stemmed

Belknap (Parmalee et al. 1972:4, Table 2); Burkett (Baerreis et al. 1958; Bell 1958; Montet-White 1968:65, Fig. 25; C. Chapman 1980:306); Cogswell Contracting Stemmed (Rolingson and Rodeffer 1968:16–17, Fig. 8a); Gary varieties: gary, leflore, camden (Schambach 1982:174–177); Gary varieties: gary, maybon (Williams and Brain 1983:230–233); Mabin (Toth 1979; Greenwell 1984).

DICKSON CONTRACTING STEMMED

The Dickson Broad Bladed type recognized by Winters (n.d.; 1963:Fig. 5b–d) is described later as Dickson Contracting Stemmed. Both Montet-White (1968:64–65) and Perino (1968a:18) provide descriptions of this type, which exhibits distinct, wide trianguloid blades as a primary characteristic (Figure 41). The blade edges are typically straight, although they may vary slightly from excurvate to incurvate. Maximum width occurs at the shoulders. Shoulders are predominantly squared but frequently exhibit a gentle curve at the shoulder/haft juncture. The haft element is contracting stemmed with rounded to square (truncated) basal edges. Basal edges vary from straight to concave on specimens with squared bases. The bases are thinned, and these forms seldom exhibit obvious edge grinding across the haft.

The Dickson style is similar to the Gary Contracting Stemmed type. Dickson points tend to be longer, generally wider, and exhibit more detailed formal refinement of the haft element than Gary points.

Age and Cultural Affiliation

Dickson Contracting Stemmed points are diagnostic of the Early Woodland period. Overall, Dickson Contracting Stemmed points are thought to range in time from approximately 500 B.C. to no later than 100 B.C. in the Midwest. The Peisker site in Illinois (Perino 1966b) produced Dickson Contracting Stemmed points dating from 500–300 B.C. Cord marked ceramics from the site include Pinched and Fingernail Impressed designs similar to that described for the Florence phase (Emerson 1983:177). Radiocarbon dates from the Florence Street site almost duplicate the Peisker dates. Adena Stemmed/Waubesa (Mason) points typify the Florence Street lithic assemblage, but there is a strong stylistic gradation in contracting stemmed points between these and other sites in western Illinois during this period.

Distribution

Perino (1968a:18) noted a heavy concentration of Dickson Contracting Stemmed points along the Illinois and Kaskaskia River Valleys in Illinois. These forms occur in a fairly wide area including most of Illinois (Fowler 1957: 11, Fig. 5; Winters 1963; Montet-White 1968). The distribution of Dickson points extends into portions of Iowa (Anderson 1981:29), northern Kentucky (Weinland and Fenwick 1978:59, 119, Fig. 41; Ottesen 1981:381, Plate 2 c–f), and Indiana (Seeman 1975: Guendling and Crouch 1977:102, Fig. 3). Perino (1968a:18) also observed the distribution of these points in Wisconsin, Missouri, and northeast Oklahoma.

Morphological Correlates

Dickson Broad Bladed (Winters n.d., 1963, Fig. 5 b–d); Dickson Knives (Winters and Hammerslough 1970:139; Cantwell 1980:49).

Map 82: Dickson Contracting Stemmed Distribution and Important Sites

ADENA STEMMED

Ovate-base, tapered-stemmed blades (Dragoo 1963:111–113, 178; Kneberg 1956:26; Bell 1958:4; Montet-White 1968:61–64) are commonly known as Adena Stemmed points. The form has also been referred to as "Beavertail" for the characteristic ovate haft element (Figure 41). The stems of Adena points are well formed and often exhibit weak side notches or indentations below the shoulder which gives the stem an overall rounded appearance. The basic shape of Adena is lanceolate with even excurvate margins. Fine percussion and pressure flaking are exhibited across the surface of the type, producing fine symmetry in all dimensions. Cross sections vary from lenticular to biconvex. Maximum width may occur at the shoulders to about the middle of the blade. Shoulders are weak, typically horizontal, and lack exaggerated barbs. The flaking quality of the haft is essentially the same as that noted for the blade, with excurvate margins and smooth surface. The full haft region is often ground, including the weak side notches. The Waubesa type defined by Ritzenthaler

(1967) conforms in essential attributes to Adena Stemmed but lacks the weak indentations at the shoulder/haft juncture.

Recognized Early Woodland cache blade types such as Adena Leaf-shaped blades (Dragoo 1963:107–109, 180, Fig. 10) and Morton Lanceolate blades (Montet-White 1968:31–35, 64, Fig. 24) are often associated at sites with Adena style points. This basic leaf shape served as the preform for Adena points. The range of variation of the cache blade forms includes specimens which are essentially finished Adena points which lack only a haft element. This similarity includes the method of manufacture and flaking pattern.

Age and Cultural Affiliation

Adena points are diagnostic of the Early Woodland period Adena culture which is a well-known mortuary and ceremonial phenomena. Radiocarbon dates from a series of Adena mounds suggest an age ranging from about 800 to 300 B.C. (cf. Hemmings 1978:5, 38). Adena lithic technology appeared in the Late Archaic period and the projectile point style evolved during the Early Woodland temporal span. The Adena ovate-base, tapered-stemmed blade, or Adena Stemmed point represented the most common and long-lived projectile style present within the lower and middle zones of the Cresap Mound in West Virginia. This type was found in an area between Cresap points recovered from subfloor pits and Robbins points associated with the final building stage of the mound (Dragoo 1963:110–114). Adena points occur as ceremonial grave offerings as well as wasted tools on habitation sites. Other Adena artifacts include groundstone celts, cones, gorgets, and other articles.

These points (i.e., long-stemmed Adena points) were associated with limestone tempered ceramics (i.e., fabric impressed and check stamped) in the Spring Branch zone of the stratified Spring Creek site in Tennessee. This zone is dated between 800 and 200 B.C. (Peterson 1973:40). As expected, Adena points at the site predate Copena cluster forms, which date into the Middle Woodland period (Walthall 1972:144).

Adena (i.e., Waubesa) points have recently been recovered in good context at the Florence Street site in the American Bottoms of western Illinois. The Florence phase dates from 500–300 B.C. based on three radiocarbon assays from features at the site (Emerson 1983:176–178). Grog tempered, cord marked ceramics typify this phase. Decoration includes fingernail pinching and impression as well as stab and drag impression and patterned cord marking (1983:133).

Adena-like points associated with Early Woodland Vinette I pottery and Meadowood

Figure 41: Dickson Cluster

a. Gary Contracting Stemmed. Unidentified chert. GBL 3304/280. Provenience unknown.
b. Gary Contracting Stemmed. Novaculite. GBL 670/2. Little Italy site. Jefferson Co., Arkansas.
c. Gary Contracting Stemmed. Unidentified chert. GBL 22/58. Arkansas.
d. Dickson Contracting Stemmed. Burlington chert. GBL 14/823. Indiana. Pictured in Plate 7, e.
e. Dickson Contracting Stemmed. Burlington chert. GBL 13/866. South-central Michigan.
f. Adena Stemmed. Wyandotte chert. GBL 5/238. Warrick Co., Indiana.
g. Adena Stemmed (Waubesa). Wyandotte chert. GBL 421/181. Ripley Co., Indiana.
h. Adena Stemmed. Wyandotte chert. GBL 14/823. Indiana.
i. Adena Stemmed. Wyandotte chert. GBL 304/144. Spencer Co., Indiana.
j. Adena Stemmed. Wyandotte chert. GBL 1448/145. Southwestern Indiana.
k. Little Bear Creek. Fort Payne chert. Eva site, Tennessee. Specimen ST1–157/6Bn12, Frank H. McClung Museum, University of Tennessee.
l. Little Bear Creek. Fort Payne chert. Florence, Alabama. Marshall L. Fallwell collection.
m. Little Bear Creek. Dover/Fort Payne chert. Florence, Alabama. Marshall L. Fallwell collection.
n. Little Bear Creek. Holland chert. GBL 5/239. Warrick Co., Indiana.
o. Cypress Stemmed. Unidentified chert. GBL 1448/145. Southwestern Indiana.
p. Cypress Stemmed. Cobden chert. Sugar Camp Hill, southern Illinois. Specimen 24B4–1, A–4023/1, Center for Archaeological Investigations, Southern Illinois University at Carbondale, Illinois.
q. Cypress Stemmed. Wyandotte chert. GBL 1448/145. Southwestern Indiana.

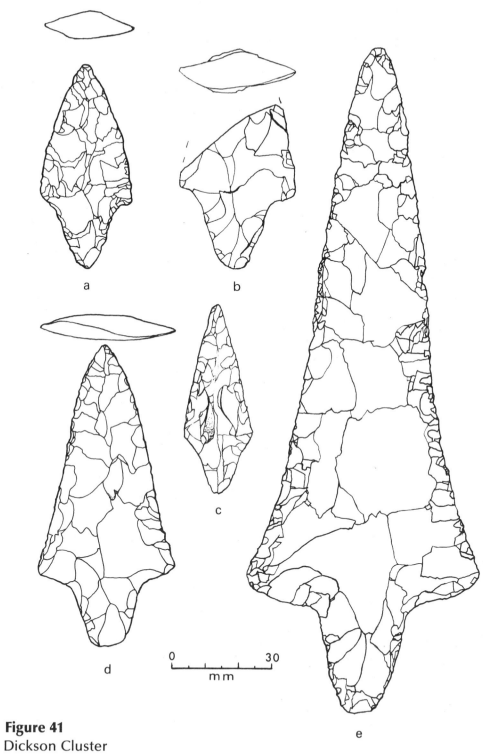

Figure 41
Dickson Cluster

a

b

c

d

e

0   30
m m

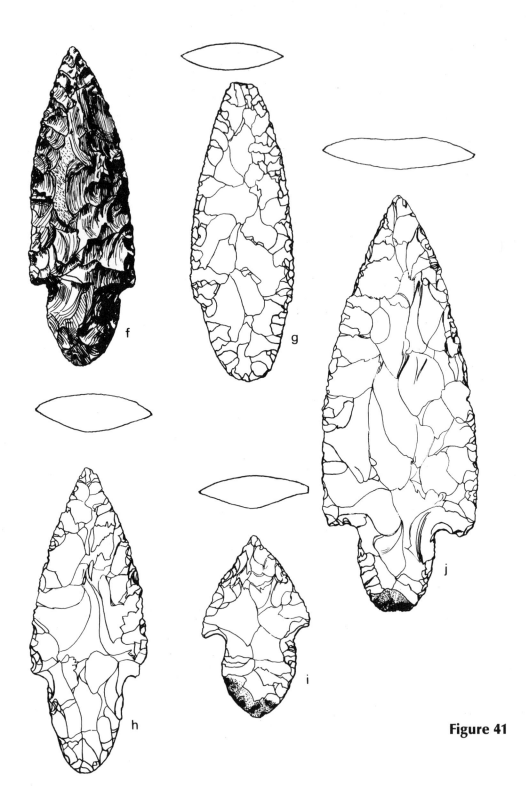

f

g

h

i

j

Figure 41

194 • Stone Age Spear and Arrow Points

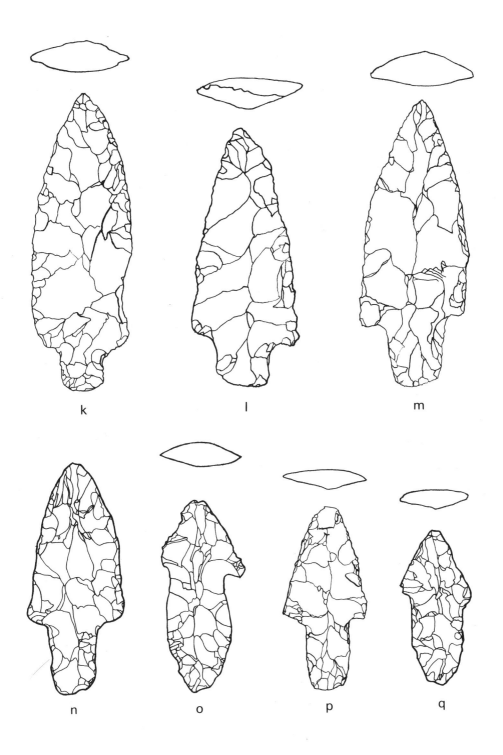

k   l   m

n   o   p   q

Figure 41

points have been recovered from sites in the Northeast (Ritchie and Dragoo 1960).

Distribution

Adena points occur over a wide territory encompassing much of eastern North America, although the Adena culture area lies within the central Ohio Valley and major tributaries (Webb and Baby 1957; Dragoo 1976b:1). These forms are recognized in low frequency from Alabama (Cambron and Hulse 1969:2–3) to Florida (Bullen 1975:22), north into Wisconsin (Ritzenthaler 1967:27) and the upper Great Lakes region (Cleland and Peske 1968:24–26, Fig. 7), and east into the New York area (Ritchie 1961). Ritchie (1971a:123) considers the Lagoon type of southern New England to be morphologically similar to Adena points. However, the core area for the Adena culture is within the Ohio Valley drainage system (see Webb and Snow 1945; Dragoo 1963). Adena points are present in highest frequency within this core area which includes southwestern Pennsylvania (Mayer-Oakes 1955; Dragoo 1963), the northwest portion of West Virginia (Dragoo 1963), Ohio (Converse 1973; Prufer 1975b:

Map 83: Adena Stemmed
Distribution and Important Sites

323, Fig. 4), Kentucky (Schock and Langford 1979b:4–5) and Indiana (Tomak 1970:86, Fig. 14; Kellar 1973; Reidhead and Limp 1974:10, Fig. 4; Seeman 1975; Tomak and O'Conner 1978). Appreciable numbers of Adena style projectile point forms also occur over most of Illinois including the Illinois River Valley (Winters 1963:27, Fig. 5; Montet-White 1968:61; Butler, Harrell, and Hamilton 1979:35; Ahler et al. 1980). Furthermore, Adena points are also present in areas of Tennessee, especially the Tennessee River Valley (Faulkner 1968:81, Plate 2; Peterson 1973:28, Plate 5).

Morphological Correlates

Adena Narrow Stemmed (Cambron and Hulse 1969:3); Florida Adena (Bullen 1975:22); Mason Contracting Stemmed (Montet-White 1968:61–62); Waubesa (Ritzenthaler 1967:27).

LITTLE BEAR CREEK

Little Bear Creek projectile points (DeJarnette et al. 1962:61; Webb and DeJarnette 1948b:50) are medium to large with slightly excurvate blade edges and long stem (Figure 41). The cross section of the blade is biconvex. The haft element varies from straight to contracting stemmed with grinding on the lateral margins of the stem. The basal edge form varies from straight to convex and may be thick and unmodified or unfinished on contracting stemmed specimens. The shoulders of these points may be horizontal or tapered (Cambron and Hulse 1969:67).

Age and Cultural Affiliation

Little Bear Creek points are diagnostic of the Late Archaic/Early Woodland transitional period. The suggested age of these projectile points is from about 1500 to 500 B.C.

The Spring Creek site in Tennessee (Peterson 1973) contains a well-documented and stratified sequence which sheds light on the chronology of Little Bear Creek points. These points appeared within the upper levels of the Perry zone and were most frequently encountered within the following

Kirby zone at the site. The radiocarbon date derived from the Kirby zone is 1370 B.C. ±160. Kirby zone cultural materials also included Motley projectile points, the remains of a semisubterranean house, and a few fiber tempered ceramics. The Kirby zone is thought to date no later than 800 B.C. Peterson (1973) suggested that the morphology of pentagonal and long-stemmed Adena points present in the later Spring Branch zone at the site indicates a continuity of form related to Little Bear Creek projectile points as an ancestral population (1973: 28–35). Another date of 1650 B.C. ±180 was derived from a pit containing Little Bear Creek points at a site in Alabama (see Oakley and Futato 1975).

Distribution

Little Bear Creek projectile points are well known in an area centering in and around the Tennessee River Valley in northern Alabama and Tennessee. This core area is probably the result of the use of the Little Bear Creek type name in a restricted area rather than a fact of geography in prehistory. More objective consideration of the morphological attributes of Little Bear Creek and related forms will undoubtedly enlarge the

Map 84: Little Bear Creek
Distribution and Important Sites

area of distribution of the type. For example, straight stemmed points similar to Little Bear Creek occur in southern Indiana and are probably present in other areas of the lower Ohio Valley.

CYPRESS STEMMED

The Cypress Constricting Stem and Straight Stemmed types defined by May (1982:1366–1367) overlap with narrow stemmed examples of the ovate-based haft morphology (Figure 41). Cypress points as a whole are typified by short, commonly resharpened, trianguloid blades and narrow, elongated, contracting stems. The apparent resharpened condition of the vast majority of Cypress points with variable degrees of shoulder degeneration can easily lead to confusion with other types, including some outside the Dickson cluster. For instance, the haft regions of some examples of Cypress Straight Stemmed (c.f. May 1982:Plate 165) are similar to those of utilitarian examples of Hebron Turkey-tails. The remaining specimens illustrated by May (1982) are clearly related to Adena Stemmed projectile points.

The original description of the Cypress Stemmed type (Winters n.d.) provided by Denny (1972) is composed of five unnamed varieties. While including material which corresponds to the definition offered by May (1982), Denny's discussion is more inclusive, closely following Winter's original work. All of the variations have short trianguloid blades, but only variety five (Denny 1972: Fig. 229) is correlated with the Dickson cluster and may include resharpened variants of Adena Stemmed and Little Bear Creek. The first variety corresponds to Saratoga Parallel Stem described by May (1982) and discussed in the Saratoga cluster in this manual. On the other hand, Cypress varieties two through four (Denny 1972:146–147, Fig. 22) are morphological correlates of the Terminal Archaic Barbed cluster. These Cypress variations appear to include forms representing nearly every defined type in that cluster. The Cypress type is therefore necessarily split into the respective projectile point clusters to which each variety belongs based on its correlation with typologies in current usage. The Cypress Constricting and Straight Stemmed types described above are included here based on their morphological similarity to types within the Dickson cluster (see also Pauketat 1984).

Age and Cultural Affiliation

Cypress Stemmed projectile points date from about 1000 to 300 B.C. based on their occurrence at a number of excavated sites in southern Illinois. This type is strongly related to other types in the Dickson cluster, especially Adena Stemmed. Cypress points have been found within deposits related to the Terminal Archaic on through early Crab Orchard contexts (Denny 1972; Cremin 1975a; May 1982; Pauketat 1984). Thus, Cypress Stemmed is essentially an Early Woodland projectile point type.

Map 85: Cypress Stemmed
Distribution

Distribution

Cypress Stemmed projectile points are known from a rather small geographic area including southwestern Indiana, northwestern Kentucky, and southern Illinois. These points are virtually nonexistent in other areas.

Morphological Correlates of the Dickson Cluster

Goose Lake Knives (Emerson 1983:70, Fig. 24e–g); Morgan (Tomak 1980b:5, Fig. 18).

Additional types: Lackawaxen Tapered Stem (Leslie 1967:111–114; Kinsey 1972:410–411); Lagoon (Ritchie 1969a, 1971a:123; Kinsey 1972:436–437); Langtry (Suhm, Krieger, and Jelks 1954:438, Plate 98; Bell 1958:38, Plate 19; Jolly and Roberts 1974:66, Figure 35); Poplar Island (Kinsey 1959; Ritchie 1961, 1971a:44–45; Roosa 1966:32); Rossville (Ritchie 1961, 1971a:46; Stephenson and Ferguson 1963:145, 184–185; Kinsey 1972:435–436).

Motley Cluster

MOTLEY

Motley projectile points (Ford, Phillips, and Haag 1955:129–130; Ford and Webb 1956:57) are large forms with deep corner notches and straight to slightly convex blade edges (Figure 42). The notching is typically wide and rounded, leaving a narrow neck width and wide shoulders. Thus, features such as

downward projecting shoulder barbs and expanded stems are characteristic of the type. The basal edge on these forms varies from straight to convex. Overall blade form is basically trianguloid and widest at the shoulders. The flaking quality is refined with large bifacial thinning flakes producing a biconvex to flattened cross section. Short, marginal edge retouch serves to straighten and sharpen the blade edges. Cambron and Hulse (1969:39) observed basal grinding on Motley points, although the trait occurs in low frequency. Motley and another type named Epps by Ford and Webb (1956:58–59) possess nearly identical haft regions, the latter of which represents resharpening activity.

Motley projectile points are generally similar to the Snyders type, but Motley points have very narrow neck widths in contrast to the overall wide neck width characteristic of Snyders. In addition, Snyders points were manufactured from wide, ovate preforms and exhibit marked excurvature of the blade edge and a different flaking pattern.

Age and Cultural Affiliation

Motley points appear in the Late Archaic period and survive into the Early Woodland period. The type was placed within an age range of 800 B.C. to 600 B.C. based on its occurrence in the Poverty Point levels at the Jaketown and Poverty Point sites in the Deep South which were radiocarbon dated to about 1300 B.C. (Ford and Webb 1956:116, 123). These points may signify social differentiation at the Poverty Point site in Louisiana (Webb 1970). The majority of these points

were made from chert sources in Tennessee, Oklahoma, and the Ohio Valley area of Indiana, Illinois, and Kentucky (Neuman 1984).

More recently, Motley points have been recovered in ceramic contexts at the stratified Spring Creek site in Tennessee (Peterson 1973). These forms were found within the Kirby zone at the site associated with the first appearance of straight stemmed Little Bear Creek points, a few pieces of fiber-tempered pottery, and the remains of a semisubterranean house. A date of 1370 B.C. ±160 was obtained from the zone, which is thought to have been deposited between 1400 and 800 B.C. Stratigraphically, Motley points postdate Ledbetter cluster forms and occur prior to the appearance of Adena Stemmed points and the earliest occurrence of fabric marked and check stamped, limestone tempered ceramics (1973:31, 35–36).

Motley points may be a prototype for wide corner notched Snyders points common in the Middle Woodland period (see Ford and Webb 1956:57). Winters (1967:90) observed that Motley points are a dominant lithic type of the Early Woodland Sugar Camp Hill culture. The Sugar Camp Hill in southern Illinois produced a wide range of projectile point types including Saratoga cluster points

Map 86: Motley—Distribution and Important Sites

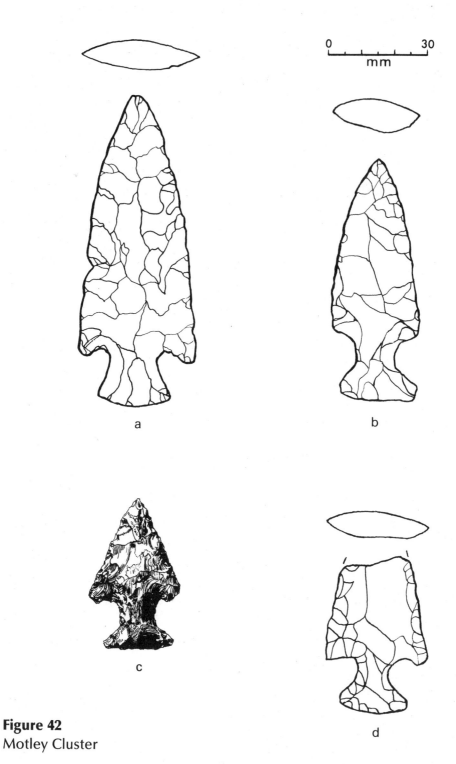

Figure 42
Motley Cluster

a

b

c

d

Figure 42: Motley Cluster
a. Motley. Unidentified chert. GBL 53/2. Site 12 Gr 18. Greene Co., Indiana.
b. Motley. Unidentified fossiliferous chert. GBL 5/239. Warrick Co., Indiana.
c. Motley. Unidentified chert. GBL 285/13. Clark Co., Indiana.
d. Motley. Wyandotte chert. GBL 1197/1. Site 12 Sp 144. Spencer Co., Indiana.

which also foreshadow the bifacial reduction technology of Snyders but lack the ovate preform shape and corner notches typical of Snyders. Motley points were also recovered from the Weber Mound at the Twenhafel site in southern Illinois (Winters: pers. comm.; Denny 1972; Hofman 1980).

Distribution
Motley points are recognized over a large area from the Deep South to the Midwest. The type has been found at sites in Mississippi (Ford et al. 1955:129), northern Louisiana (Ford and Webb 1956), and Alabama (Cambron and Hulse 1969:39). The type is

known across much of Tennessee (Faulkner 1968; Jolley 1979:44, Fig. 7), and Kentucky (Webb 1946, 1950a:308; Schock and Langford 1979a, b). Motley points also occur north of the Ohio River Valley in Ohio (Griffin 1952; Vickery 1976:128), Indiana (Seeman 1975), and Illinois (Winters 1963: 109). The northern extent of these forms is not known, although the type has been identified in central Indiana (Guendling and Crouch 1977:81) and Illinois (Munson and Harn 1966:153, Fig. 2).

Morphological Correlates
Epps (Ford and Webb 1956:58–59, Fig. 20; Perino 1971a:32); Expanding Stem Points (Converse 1973:30).

Morphological Correlates of
the Motley Cluster
Tipton (Morrow 1984). Additional types: Crater Flared Base (Winters n.d., 1963:109–113); Weber (Winters n.d., pers. comm.; See also White 1965:357–359).

Snyders Cluster

SNYDERS

Snyders points (Scully 1951:12; Bell 1958: 88) are broad bladed, corner notched points (Figure 43). The corner notches were produced by an indirect percussion technique, leaving broad hertzian cone flake scars on alternate sides, followed by pressure edge retouch. Maximum notch width sometimes occurs toward the interior of the notch rather than at the margins. Thus, the notch may expand slightly and is often large, resulting in bold shoulder barbs in classic examples of the type. A smaller counterpart of Snyders was referred to as Manker Corner Notched by Montet-White (1968:71). These points are typical Snyders points, although they are not as large and refined as those from mound contexts in Illinois. However,

these points exhibit the characteristic haft morphology and manufacturing trajectory of Snyders. Manker reflects a more utilitarian function found commonly on habitation sites (Montet-White 1968:73). Snyders preforms are basically ovate in shape and were manufactured primarily with percussion. A named cache blade type, the North point (Perino 1969, 1971a:66), is manufactured essentially the same way as Snyders and served as a preform for larger examples of this type.

Age and Cultural Affiliation
Snyders projectile points are diagnostic of the early Middle Woodland period and appear with the rise of Hopewell ceremonialism. The Mund site in Illinois produced dates of 130– 120 B.C. for the Snyders com-

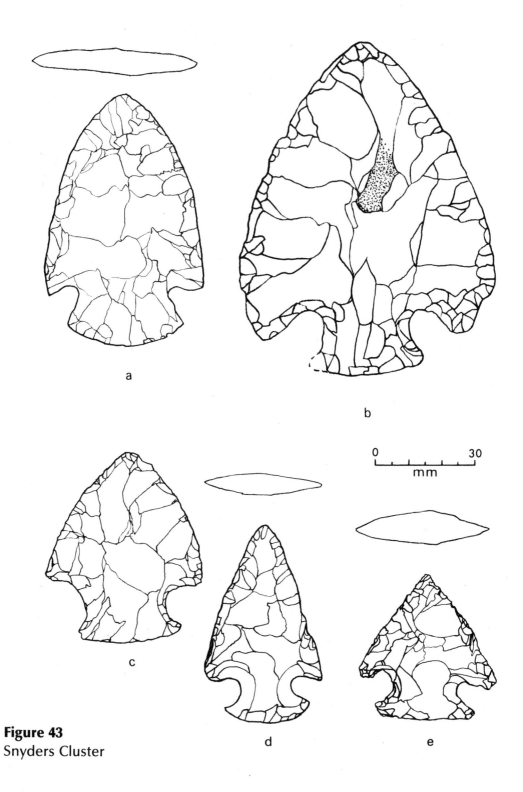

Figure 43
Snyders Cluster

Map 87: Snyders Corner Notched and Affinis Snyders
Distribution and Important Sites

ponent (Fortier et al. 1983:395). The type occurs within the Scioto, late Crab Orchard, Havana, and North Bay traditions in the Midwest and Great Lakes regions. The Middle Woodland period lasted from about 200 B.C. to about A.D. 400 (Seeman 1977). However, Snyders points were replaced by expanding stemmed forms (i.e., Steuben Expanding Stemmed) of the Lowe cluster during this period, which probably took place around A.D. 200. This judgment is based on dates obtained from terminal Middle Woodland sites in Indiana (Pace and Apfelstadt 1978:69; Kellar 1979:101), and Illinois (Fortier et al. 1983:252– 259), and also from the technology of assemblages representing the transition from terminal Middle Woodland into Late Woodland material culture. Middle

Figure 43: Snyders Cluster
a. Snyders. Flint Ridge chert. GBL 13/891. South-central Michigan.
b. Snyders. Burlington chert. GBL 31/106. Fulton Co., Indiana. Pictured in Plate 8, b.
c. Snyders. Burlington chert. GBL 14/947. Rush Co., Indiana.
d. Snyders. Wyandotte chert. GBL 14/947. Rush Co., Indiana.
e. Affinis Snyders. Wyandotte chert. GBL 623/24. Site 12 Gi 13. Gibson Co., Indiana.

Woodland lithic assemblages normally contain exotic raw materials such as obsidian, mica, galena (lead), and quartz crystal. Large numbers of prismatic blades and cores are also typical.

Distribution
Snyders points occur throughout the central Mississippi and Ohio River Valleys. These forms are distributed into the Kansas City area in Kansas, across Missouri (Johnson 1979:90–91; Jolly and Roberts 1974), and in northeast Oklahoma (Bell 1958:88). The type also occurs in low frequency at sites in the Upper Peninsula of Michigan (Cleland and Peske 1968:42–43, Fig. 15) and New York (Ritchie 1971a:49). Snyders projectile points are rare or absent in the Southeast, where Copena, Mabin, and related forms are the major diagnostic projectile points of the Middle Woodland period. However, Snyders type points extend down into the lower Mississippi Valley, where they were recovered in two caches at the Bynum Mounds (Cotter and Corbett 1951:Plate 5) and a few other sites (Williams and Griffin, in Davis [ed.] 1984:323). The core area of distribution of Snyders is primarily within Illinois (Montet-White 1968), Indiana (Black 1936:341;

Tomak 1970:280; Kellar 1973), southern Michigan (Fitting 1970), and to a lesser extent Ohio (Prufer 1965; Shane 1975a).

Morphological Correlates
Hopewell Points (Converse 1973:59); Manker Corner Notched (Montet-White 1968:71); Snyders Notched (Scully 1951:12).

AFFINIS SNYDERS

Defined by Winters (n.d., 1963, 1967), Affinis Snyders, as the name implies, are Middle Woodland corner notched points that are closely related morphologically to the large-bladed Snyders points that are well known from mortuary and habitation sites. Overall basal forms, notching characteristics, and general haft flaking pattern are attributes that fit the range of variation of Snyders.

The blade morphology of the Affinis Snyders style sets it apart from the Snyders type. The blades of the former appear drastically reduced in size relative to haft dimensions (Figure 43). Blades are often triangular with straight rather than broad excurvate edges. The shortened appearance of the blade is often complemented with a thick cross section relative to width. This occurs in conjunction with regular flake scars emanating from the blade edges on both faces. These latter attributes often suggest blade reworking or resharpening, which is common on utilitarian forms of projectile points (White 1965:359–360).

Age and Cultural Affiliation
This is a Middle Woodland form contemporary with Snyders points and ubiquitous in habitation debris.

Distribution
Winters (1963, 1967) recognized this style of projectile point within the Wabash valley drainage of southeastern Illinois. These forms are also recorded in the adjacent parts of southwestern Indiana (Tomak 1970:280; Cook 1980:426) and elsewhere. Given that this type is largely a reworked utilitarian form of the Snyders type, it is present at many Middle Woodland sites. Its distribution should therefore coincide with the distribution of Middle Woodland habitation sites which are known over a large territory. The McGraw site in Ohio produced these forms (Prufer 1965:87, Fig. 4.2L). This type occurs as far north as the Upper Peninsula of Michigan (Cleland and Peske 1968).

Morphological Correlates of the Snyders Cluster
Bay de Noc Side Notched (Cleland and Peske 1968:26–28, Fig. 8); Burnt Bluff Expanded Stemmed (Cleland and Peske 1968:22–24, Fig. 6); Dayton (Morrow 1984); Grand (Baerreis and Freeman 1959:62; Perino 1985:156); Lang Corner Notched (Cleland and Peske 1968:35–39, Figs. 12–13). Additional types: Gibson (Scully 1951:13; Montet-White 1968:75); Norton Corner Notched (Montet-White 1968:71); Ross Barbed Spears/Ross Points (Mills 1907; Kramer 1951; Griffin 1965:117; Perino 1968a:80; Seeman 1977:142).

Copena Cluster

COPENA

Copena points (Webb and DeJarnette 1942:37; Cambron and Hulse 1969:25) are symmetrical trianguloid forms with distinct recurvate blade edges (Figure 44). This recurvature approximates the flaring of the haft element of other flared base projectile points. However, the Copena point shape was often produced simultaneously during the manufacture of the entire point without a significant change in flaking technique. Thus there does not appear to be any specific trianguloid preform stage prior to finishing the recurvate blade shape on many specimens. The basal edge on these points is typically straight, although excurvate and incurvate basal preparations also occur. The base and lower blade edges often exhibit light grinding. The tip is usually acute. Broad and flat percussion flaking was employed to thin the blade. Resulting flake scar pattern is usually random but may be collateral. Cross sections vary from biconvex to flat and lenticular. A low median ridge sometimes occurs as a result of the thinning technique employed. Marginal edge retouch is fine and is produced using a pressure flaking technique. Both utilitarian and large ceremonial examples of this type occur.

Age and Cultural Affiliation

This is a Middle Woodland form. The term "Copena" signifies a burial mound complex identified in the Tennessee Valley region of northern Alabama (Webb 1939:201). Tomb construction, among other things, draws comparison with Middle Woodland mortuary practices in the Midwest. Some of the characteristic artifacts associated with Copena burials include copper reel-shaped ornaments and other articles, marine shell cups and beads, galena nodules, greenstone celts and digging implements, steatite elbow and effigy pipes, and large recurvate-bladed Copena points or cache blades (DeJarnette 1952: 278). Radiocarbon dates from Copena tombs in the Tennessee Valley suggest that a fully developed Copena mortuary complex occurs about A.D. 300–400. However, the temporal span for the Copena point is from about A.D. 150 to A.D. 500 (Griffin 1967:177; Walthall 1972:144).

Distribution

The Copena point was originally found primarily in the Tennessee River Valley in northern Alabama, Mississippi, Tennessee (Webb and DeJarnette 1942), and the Middle South in general (Faulkner 1969:53–54). Copena points have also been found in Ken-

Map 88: Copena and Copena Triangular Distribution and Important Sites

tucky (Schock and Langford 1979b; Weinland 1980) and at the Mann site in southwestern Indiana. Materials with formal characteristics similar to Copena have also been found in southern Illinois (Perino 1968b:63; Hofman 1980). Although the Ansell type from the Illinois Valley described by Montet-White (1968: 73, Fig. 32) is somewhat similar to Copena in basic outline, the flaking characteristics do not reflect a Copena manufacturing technology. The western limit of distribution of Copena lies primarily east of the Mississippi Valley.

Similar materials such as Gahagan Knives have been recorded at the George C. Davis site in Texas (Newell and Krieger 1949) as well as other Mississippian sites. Gahagan Knives date after 1100 A.D., are often very large, and are not related to the Copena type. Some Gahagan Knives have recurvate blades and may have the basic shape of Copena, but they are extremely thin and percussion flaked like the Ramey Knife, another Mississippian knife type (c.f. Durham and Davis 1975; Moore 1912).

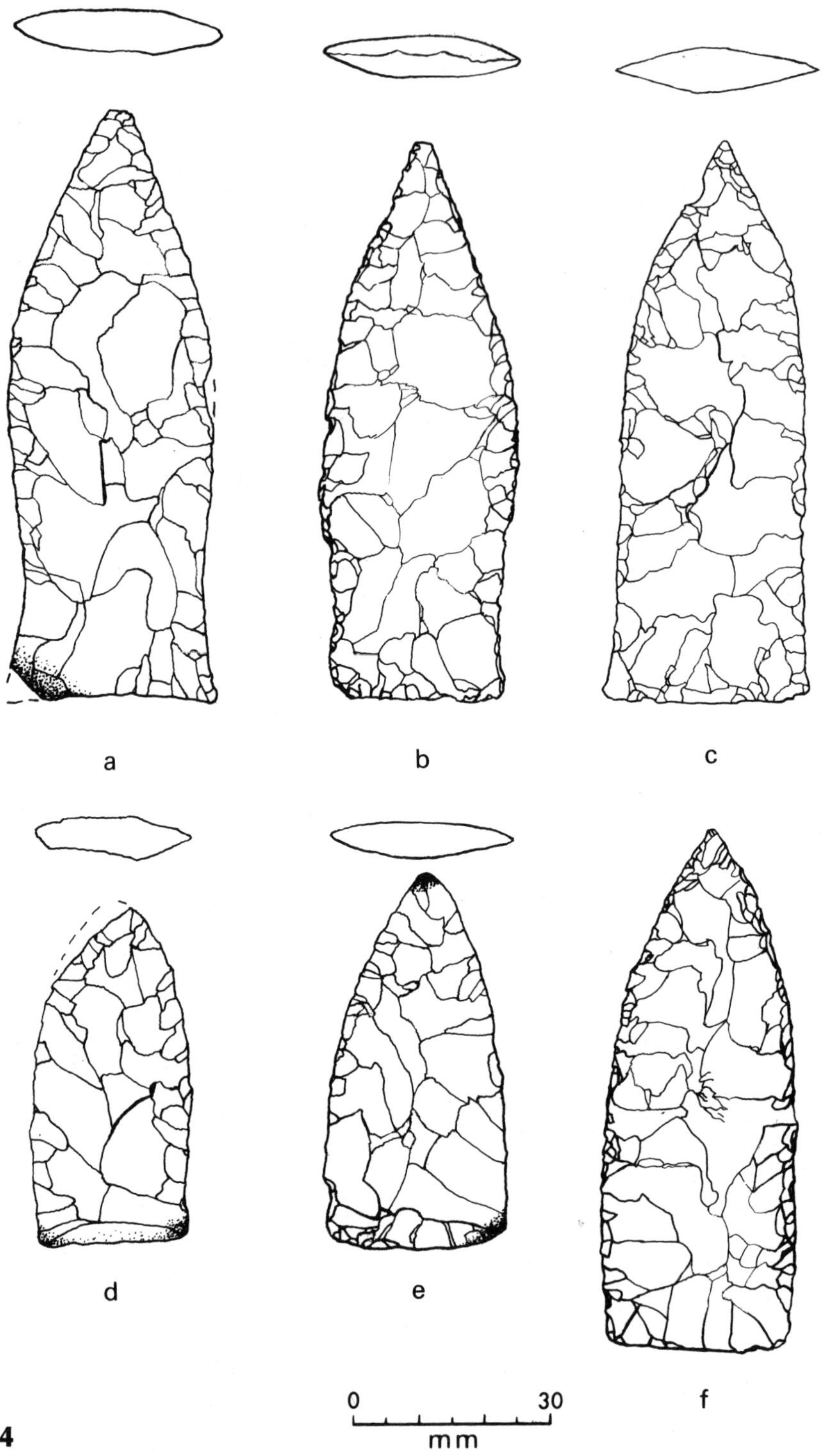

Figure 44
Copena Cluster

COPENA TRIANGULAR

The Copena Triangular type projectile point is a medium to large trianguloid form related to the "classic" Copena type (Cambron 1958b:10; Cambron and Hulse 1969; Faulkner 1969:54; Faulkner and McCollough 1973:96, 148). The trianguloid type is characterized by blade edges that vary from straight to excurvate; most exhibit the latter blade form (Figure 44). The blade shape of these points also grades into the recurvate morphology exhibited in the Copena type described above and sometimes exhibits basal ears. Similar forms have been termed "Village Copena" (Bacon n.d.). Other examples of the Copena Triangular style are pentagonal in shape. The cross section of Copena Triangular is nearly always biconvex and rarely plano convex. The basal edge varies from straight to concave and frequently exhibits light grinding. Straight-based specimens are sometimes also ground on the lateral margins of the blade near the base. A random flaking pattern is characteristic. Bases are thinned, with broad, shallow flake scars that are usually short; however, some examples possess thinning scars which extend across the proximal end of the blade. Flaking techniques include percussion used in bifacial thinning followed by light pressure retouch of the edge.

There is a technological and morphological relationship between Copena Triangular and the Baker's Creek and Lowe Flared Base types in which Copena Triangular serves as a preform. The term "Stemmed Copena" (i.e., Baker's Creek), originally applied to these forms (Cambron 1958b), has now been dropped from usage. While the Copena Triangular type serves as a preform for material in the Lowe cluster it also serves as a finished tool and thus carries a dual purpose.

Age and Cultural Affiliation

Copena Triangular points are diagnostic of the Middle Woodland Copena complex in Tennessee and the Middle South. The type is common on Copena habitation sites. The temporal span for this type is from A.D. 150 to A.D. 500 (Walthall 1972:144). Named trianguloid types such as Greenville, Candy Creek, and Nolichucky (Kneberg 1957:64–65; see also Salo 1969) are similar to and occur with Copena Triangular. This group was previously referred to as the McFarland cluster (Bacon n.d.) because of their presence at the multi-component Woodland McFarland site in the Duck River Valley (see Faulkner and McCollough 1973:148). It is quite probable that these trianguloid forms represent the beginning of a development that continued into the Late Woodland period (Ison 1982a:1). Copena Triangular points are a significant part of the lithic technology of the terminal Middle Woodland Mann complex and the Late Woodland Allison-LaMotte cultural manifestations in southern Indiana and elsewhere in the Wabash River drainage (Kellar 1973, 1979; Pace and Apfelstadt 1978:39, 80).

Distribution

In most respects, the distribution of the Copena Triangular type is similar to Copena with a concentration of these materials in the Middle South, especially Tennessee (Faulkner and McCollough 1973; Jolley 1979). These types are also fairly common in northern Alabama (Cambron and Hulse 1969; Ingmanson and Griffin 1974:47, Fig. 31), Georgia (Jefferies 1976:30–31), Kentucky (Schock and Langford 1979b:6), and Florida (Bullen 1976). The Copena Triangular type is well represented in southern Indiana and Illinois in the vicinity of the Ohio and lower Wabash River Valleys (Pace and Apfelstadt

Figure 44: Copena Cluster
a. Copena. Wyandotte chert. GBL 119/890. Provenience unknown. Pictured in Plate 8, a.
b. Copena. Wyandotte chert. GBL 21/332. Indiana.
c. Copena. Fort Payne chert. Middle South. Specimen 1275/41, Frank H. McClung Museum, University of Tennessee.
d. Copena Triangular. Wyandotte chert. GBL 1448/343. Southwestern Indiana.
e. Copena Triangular. Wyandotte chert. GBL 1448/297. Southwestern Indiana.
f. Copena Triangular. Burlington chert. GBL 303/134. Mann site, 12 Po 2. Posey Co., Indiana.

1978:80, Fig. 8), and the White River Valley (Black 1933; Tomak 1980b:6). This type is also represented in the Illinois River Valley at Middle Woodland sites (cf. Griffin et al. 1970: Plate 10b).

Morphological Correlates of the Copena Cluster
Copena (Bell 1960:20, Plate 10); Florida Copena (Bullen 1975:23). Additional types: Badin Crude Triangular (Coe 1964:45; Keel 1972:172–173); Garden Creek Triangular (Keel 1972:173–174, Fig. 3.40a; 1976:130–131, Plate 21d); Greenville, Candy Creek, Nolichucky (Kneberg 1957:64–65; Lewis and Kneberg 1957:17–19; DeJarnette et al. 1962); Cambron and Hulse 1969, 1975); Transylvania Triangular (Keel 1976:130, Plate 21c).

Lowe Cluster

STEUBEN EXPANDED STEMMED

Steuben Expanded Stemmed (Morse 1963: 57–58; Montet-White 1968:56–60; Perino 1968a:94) exhibits gracefully upward curved notches in conjunction with an excurvate blade (Figure 45). The notches were produced using a corner notching technique followed by additional retouch along the notch margins. This ultimately formed a curved edge across the lateral haft margin in finished specimens. The basal edge varies from straight to convex and basal grinding is sometimes present.

The manufacturing strategy employed in the production of Steuben Expanded Stemmed was refined percussion thinning followed by minimal light percussion or pressure retouch to align the edge. These projectile points often exhibit basal flake scars directed toward the center of the blade. The overall flaking pattern of Steuben demonstrates a clear technological link between this type and Snyders Corner Notched from which it is derived. The variations of Steuben observed by Morse (1963) at the Steuben site in Illinois reflect this evolutionary relationship. Resharpening of Steuben necessitated little change in technique from manufacture, but blades were sometimes modified significantly to include hafted scrapers and drill forms.

Age and Cultural Affiliation
Steuben Expanded Stemmed points are diagnostic of the terminal Middle Woodland to early Late Woodland periods. Dates obtained for carbon samples recovered at the Steuben village and mounds in Illinois range from

Figure 45: Lowe Cluster
a. Steuben Expanded Stemmed. Burlington chert. GBL 375/90. Mann site, 12 Po 2. Posey Co., Indiana.
b. Steuben Expanded Stemmed. Unidentified chert. GBL 1448/300. Southwestern Indiana.
c. Steuben Expanded Stemmed. Flint Ridge chert. GBL 14/859. Delaware Co., Indiana.
d–g. Bakers Creek. Fort Payne chert. Florence, Alabama. Marshall L. Fallwell collection. Specimen F, pictured in Plate 8, h.
h. Lowe Flared Base. Wyandotte chert. GBL 21/345. Washington Co., Indiana. Pictured in Plate 8, k.
i. Lowe Flared Base. Wyandotte chert. GBL 1722/47. Hamilton Co., Indiana.
j. Lowe Flared Base. Wyandotte chert. GBL 285/13. Clark Co., Indiana.
k. Lowe Flared Base. Wyandotte chert. GBL 1448/215. Southwestern Indiana.
l. Chesser Notched. Flint Ridge chert. GBL 3142/966. Mann site, 12 Po 2. Posey Co., Indiana.
m. Chesser Notched. Flint Ridge chert. GBL 911/507. Sand Ridge site. Hamilton Co., Ohio.
n. Chesser Notched. Flint Ridge chert. GBL 421/302. Indiana.
o. Chesser Notched. Haney chert. GBL 65/65. Hastings Village site, 12 Gr 126. Greene Co., Indiana.

Figure 45
Lowe Cluster

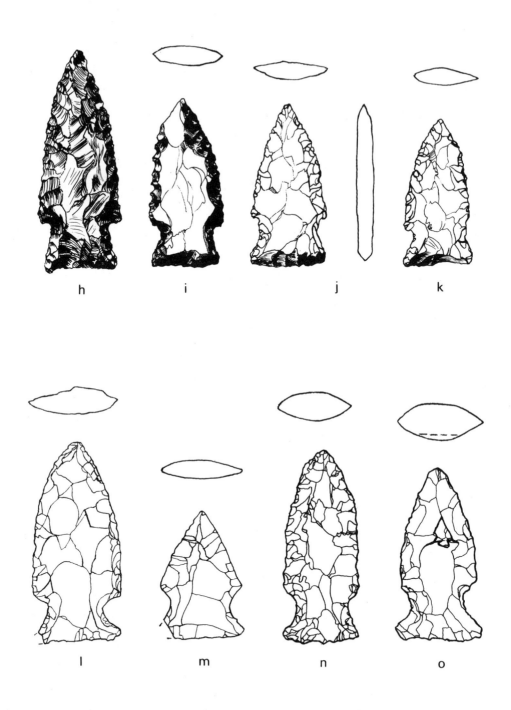

Figure 45

about A.D. 100 through A.D. 500–800 (Morse 1963:113–114). Materials at the site spanned Hopewellian through Weaver components. A date of A.D. 450 based on good context at the Scovill site is a secure Weaver phase date, correlating well with terminal Middle Woodland dates obtained elsewhere outside the Illinois Valley (Munson, Parmalee, and Yarnell 1971:411). Expanded Stemmed points are ubiquitous in Weaver components (Wray and MacNeish 1961: Fig. 15). In the late portion of the Illinois Valley sequence, the Steuben Expanded Stemmed style is modified, conforming more to that described as Lowe Flared Base and Bakers Creek.

Distribution
Steuben Expanded Stemmed forms occur in high frequency in the central Illinois Valley, west-central Illinois, and parts of Missouri and Iowa (Perino 1968a:94; C. Chapman 1980:313; Anderson 1981:29). The type also occurs across much of Wisconsin (Freeman 1969:59, Fig. 18; Mason 1966:122–123, Plate 10), in Michigan (Griffin et al. 1970:Plate 52b), Indiana (e.g., Mann site), and in limited numbers in collections in Ohio (cf. Converse

Map 89: Steuben Expanded Stemmed
Distribution and Important Sites

1973:61). Steuben Expanded Stemmed type points also occur south of the Ohio River Valley, as similar material is present in the Normandy Reservoir area of Tennessee (Faulkner and McCollough 1973:146). Steuben points are also reported from terminal Middle Woodland contexts in Arkansas (Hemmings 1982:233).

BAKERS CREEK

The Bakers Creek projectile point type (Cambron 1958b; DeJarnette et al. 1962:47; Cambron and Hulse 1969:8) is an expanding stemmed point with a triangular blade and straight or excurvate edges. The base is straight or convex, with slight grinding. The long, expanding stem is the result of notching of the basal corners, and the blade exhibits squared shoulders (Figure 45). The preform of Bakers Creek is the Copena Triangular type which was shaped by broad and random percussion flaking, followed by edge retouch, forming a flattened to biconvex cross section. The indentation of the lateral margin to form the notch leaves a maximum basal width nearly equal to the shoulder width. Bakers Creek shares many characteristics with Lowe Flared Base but lacks the characteristic hexagonal cross section typical of the latter. The Bakers Creek type was previously named Stemmed Copena, recognizing their close relationship in manufacturing trajectories and the apparent historical relationship in a single evolving lithic tradition.

Age and Cultural Affiliation
Bakers Creek projectile points are diagnostic of the middle and terminal Middle Woodland periods and appear in the Southeast around 150 A.D. based on radiocarbon dates from the McFarland site in Tennessee (Kline, Crites, and Faulkner 1982:69). Dates derived from good context at Peter's Cave indicate that these forms endure through the latter part of the Copena complex at about A.D. 400 to 600 (Hartney 1962; Faulkner and McCollough 1973:146; Walthall 1973). The McFarland and Owl Hollow phases date within this range. Bakers Creek points appear along with

Copena types in the former and show a development to narrower heavily resharpened forms in Owl Hollow. Owl Hollow is similar in many respects to Allison-LaMotte to the north, which is represented by Lowe Flared Base type points (Kline et al. 1982; Faulkner 1978).

Distribution
Bakers Creek projectile points are common at sites along the Tennessee River Valley in Tennessee and Alabama (Faulkner and McCollough 1973:146; DeJarnette et al. 1962). They are also typical at sites of the period such as Tunacunnhee and St. Catherines Island in Georgia (Jefferies 1976; Thomas et al. 1979), Mississippi (Perino 1971b:6), Louisiana (Phillips 1970:751, Fig. 380), Kentucky (Weinland 1980; Schock and Langford 1979b), and West Virginia (Graybill 1979:5; Jensen 1970). Seeman (1975:56) has identified the type in the Ohio Valley and it is known to occur sporadically throughout this region at a variety of terminal Middle Woodland sites. One major ceremonial center where these points occur is the Mann site in Posey County, Indiana.

Map 90: Bakers Creek—Distribution and Important Sites

Morphological Correlate
Stemmed Copena (Cambron 1958b:10–11).

LOWE FLARED BASE

The Lowe Flared Base projectile point type (Winters 1963, 1967:90–92; Apfelstadt 1975; Kline and Apfelstadt 1975; Pace and Apfelstadt 1978) is a distinctive expanding stemmed form that exhibits a trianguloid blade with straight to excurvate edges and a markedly flaring, straight-edged stem (Figure 45). These points were manufactured from Copena Triangular type preforms. Flattened faces of the blade and haft region are typical, resulting from controlled percussion bifacial thinning. Flake scar patterns range from those with flake scars terminating at the center of the preform to those that transgress the blade on alternate faces with the flake terminus removed by lateral edge retouch. Some specimens exhibit the ventral surface of the original flake with nothing more than lateral edge retouch.

Bifacial beveling to shape the blade and stem is a unique characteristic of Lowe Flared Base. The flake scars are short and narrow, produced from detachments on a steep angle. Most Lowe Flared Base forms exhibit hexagonal cross sections, but a few are lenticular. This marginal edge treatment is produced in roughly the same fashion on both the stem and blade, allowing for controlled shaping of the stem, which tends to have an angular shoulder/haft juncture. Finished basal edge forms range from the unmodified blunt edge of the original flake, which may exhibit a cortical surface, to a flat flake facet. Specimens exhibiting basal thinning from this unmodified basal condition show variation in treatment from unifacial to bifacial thinning, depending on the degree of angle represented on a given original flake surface. Basal and lateral haft grinding are typical.

Resharpening variations of Lowe Flared Base include serration produced with the same strategy as the bifacial edge bevel. Blades became shorter with repeated rejuvenation. Other functional classes, such as hafted scrapers and drills made from Lowe points, are not characteristic.

Age and Cultural Affiliation

Lowe Flared Base points signify a terminal Middle Woodland horizon. These points replace the large corner notched forms of the period by around A.D. 200 and are a dominant style during the Hopewellian ceremonial climax which extends to about A.D. 500. The Lowe Flared Base type is closely related to Bakers Creek of the Tennessee Valley and represents a stimulus from that region. It is diagnostic of the Mann complex in southwestern Indiana (Kellar 1973, 1979) and also of the Allison-LaMotte culture in the lower Wabash drainage in Indiana and Illinois (Beeson 1952; Helman 1952; Winters 1967; McMichael and Coffing 1970; Clouse et al. 1971). Several dates ranging from A.D. 270 ±40 to A.D. 510 ±50 have been obtained in terminal Middle Woodland contexts at Mann site (Kellar 1979:101). Dates from the Daugherty-Monroe site (Allison-LaMotte) range from A.D. 200 to A.D. 600 (Pace and Apfelstadt 1978:69). These points are also present in the terminal Middle Woodland/ early Late Woodland Weaver phase of the central Illinois Valley (Munson 1971:9; Behm and Green 1982:40).

Distribution

The distribution of Lowe projectile points is mostly limited to the lower Ohio Valley and its tributaries, which include primarily the lower Wabash and Ohio Rivers in southern Illinois, Indiana, and northern Kentucky. These points are also found in lower frequency in central Indiana within the White River Valley (Tomak 1970:114), and across southern Illinois into the Illinois River Valley (Barth 1979; Behm and Green 1982:40, Fig. 7, 11). The distribution of Lowe Flared Base projectile points spreads through Kentucky (Weinland 1980:83; Adovasio et al. 1982:592, Fig. 222f) into the Tennessee River Valley (Faulkner and McCollough 1973:146).

Morphological Correlate

Allison Expanding Stem (Stephens 1974:37, Figs. 31–32).

Map 91: Lowe Flared Base
Distribution and Important Sites

CHESSER NOTCHED

The Chesser Notched type (Prufer 1975a:21) is a side notched to expanding stemmed form with wide notch openings (Figure 45). These were manufactured using a percussion thinning technique followed by irregular pressure flaking applied to the edges. The blades are long and triangular in shape and exhibit a slight tendency toward rather crude bilateral serration of the edges. The notching exhibits an expanded U-shape. The haft element was produced within a range of notching angles from those oriented diagonally on the lower margin of the preform to those oriented at the side. The distinctiveness of the notching technique (e.g., corner notching to side notching) is not clearly defined since the resulting notches are shallow and wide, often extending in a rough arc to the basal ears. Those Chesser Notched specimens made from trianguloid preforms exhibit maximum width at the base. Additional traits include biconvex to lenticular cross sections, and straight basal edges with bifacial thinning.

Lowe Cluster • 213

Age and Cultural Affiliation

Chesser Notched projectile points appeared during the terminal Middle Woodland period at ca. 300 A.D. and attained popularity during the Late Woodland period (Prufer and Shane 1970:84). Residual Middle Woodland affinities are expressed at the Cain, Bluff Point, and other mound sites in New York (Ritchie 1969a:218–226). The relevant radiocarbon dates derived from sites producing this style, such as McGraw, Raven Rocks, and other sites in Ohio, range as late as A.D. 500 to A.D. 700 (Shane 1975b; Prufer 1981:78). It is apparent that Chesser Notched points fit chronologically between Middle Woodland Snyders cluster material and Late Woodland forms such as Jack's Reef Corner Notched. This is the same basic chronology established for Steuben, Lowe, and Bakers Creek projectile points.

Distribution

Chesser Notched points are most commonly identified within central and southern Ohio (Pi-Sunyer 1965; Converse 1966; Prufer and Shane 1970:84, Fig. 12; Prufer 1975a). This type is also reported in eastern Kentucky (Johnson 1982:613–614, Fig. 226), West Virginia (McMichael 1965:Fig. 36), and Pennsylvania (Bebrich and Morgan 1968:238), extending into eastern New York (Ritchie 1969a). Collections from the Mann site in southwestern Indiana contain appreciable numbers of Chesser Notched points. Another site that has produced similar expanding stemmed points in Middle to Late Woodland context is the Schultz site in Michigan (Fitting 1972a:199–203).

Chesser Notched points are either absent or occur in very low frequency west of the defined area. The Ansell Constricted Stem type described for the Illinois Valley appears to be similar to Chesser Notched (cf. Montet-White 1968:73, Fig. 32). However, this type is poorly defined and was in part confused

Map 92: Chesser Notched
Distribution and Important Sites

with Late Archaic Matanzas cluster materials. The technological affinities of Ansell are in general reflective of the Lowe and Copena clusters.

Morphological Correlates of the Lowe Cluster

Bradford (Bullen 1968:18); Perino 1985:44); Clear Lake (Montet-White 1968:81); Edwards (Phillips 1970:653; Greengo 1964:78, Fig. 37c, d); Manker Stemmed (Montet-White 1968:73, Fig. 29, 1–3); Marshall Barbed (Morse 1963:30, Plate 7, Fig. 2; Montet-White 1968:77, Fig. 32); Middle Woodland Points (Converse 1973:61); Mund (Fortier et al. 1983:252–259). Additional types: Columbia (Bullen 1975:19); Jackson (Bullen 1975:21); Pigeon Side Notched (Keel 1976:127–129, Plate 21b); Rice Side Notched (Bray 1956: 127, Fig. 23, row 2; C. Chapman 1980:311); Swan Lake (Cambron and Hulse 1960b:239–240; Cambron and Waters 1961); DeJarnette et al. 1962:68).

Unnotched Pentagonal Cluster

JACK'S REEF PENTAGONAL

This form is compatible in many respects with Ritchie's (1961, 1971a:27) definition of the Jack's Reef Corner Notched type, but it lacks a haft element (Figure 46). These points exhibit a pentagonal shape, usually with straight sides. The sides of the blade are variable, producing a wide obtuse angle which may then be straight and parallel-sided or contracting toward the base. The bases of these points are typically straight. Cross sections are very thin resulting from the use of a refined percussion thinning technique in manufacture followed by minimal pressure flaking along the edges. The flaking pattern is often similar to, if not the same as, Jack's Reef Corner Notched, linking this type as a blank or preform in a manufacturing continuum. However, these forms also served as viable finished tools. These unnotched forms were referred to as "pentagonal-shaped points" in Ritchie's earlier work (1940, 1944, 1946). The Raccoon Notched type also appears to be manufactured from this type.

Age and Cultural Affiliation

Jack's Reef Pentagonal points are diagnostic of the Late Woodland period and date from about A.D. 500 to 1000 in the Northeast. The Jack's Reef style occurs within Late Point Peninsula contexts and especially at sites related to the transition into early Owasco, which is a Late Woodland complex (Ritchie 1969a: 229–234). The White site near Norwich, New York produced these points in good context and was radiocarbon dated to A.D. 905 ±250 (Crane 1956:668; Ritchie 1971a:28).

Jack's Reef Pentagonal points and Jack's Reef Corner Notched points were recovered in funerary contexts in the Albee Mound in Sullivan County, Indiana (MacLean 1931:173, Plate 47). These points, in conjunction with distinctive collared globular ceramics, are diagnostic of the Late Woodland Albee phase in Indiana. The Albee phase is thought to date roughly from A.D. 800– 1200 (Winters 1967: 81; Pace and Thiel 1983).

Distribution

Jack's Reef Pentagonal points occur in highest frequency in the Northeast (Ritchie 1961:28; Perkins 1970) and west into Ohio (Mills 1922) and Indiana (MacLean 1931). In eastern Michigan similar forms have been referred to as Late Woodland cache blades (Fitting 1970:170, Fig. 97). These forms are represented in southeastern Illinois, extending over an area possibly less than the distribution of Albee phase ceramics (see Lewis 1975). The distribution of Jack's Reef Pentagonal points across the South is not well known, but similar material is recognized in Late Woodland contexts in northern Alabama (Cambron and Hulse 1969:60; Ingmanson and Griffin 1974:47, Fig. 31).

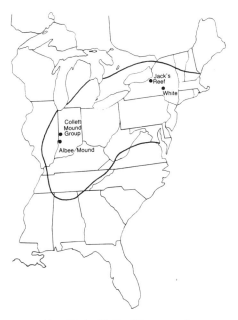

Map 93: Jack's Reef Pentagonal Distribution and Important Sites

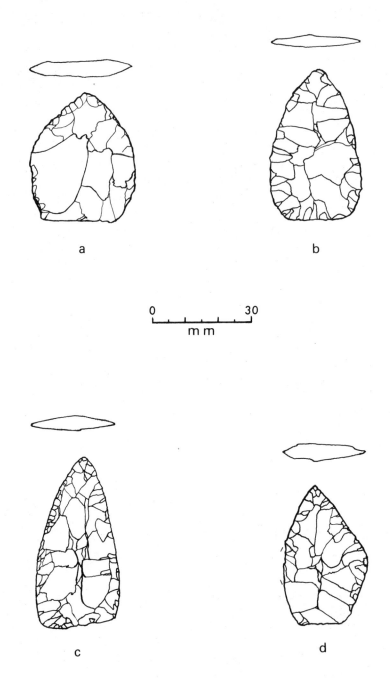

a

b

0 _____ 30
m m

c

d

Figure 46
Unnotched Pentagonal Cluster

Figure 46: Unnotched Pentagonal Cluster
a. Jack's Reef Pentagonal. Unidentified chert. GBL 672/3. Collett Mound Group, 12 Ve 2. Vermillion Co., Indiana.
b. Jack's Reef Pentagonal. Unidentified chert. GBL 39/42. Albee Mound, 12 Su 1. Sullivan Co., Indiana.
c. Jack's Reef Pentagonal. Unidentified chert. GBL 413/11. Site 12 H 15. Hamilton Co., Indiana.
d. Jack's Reef Pentagonal. Unidentified chert. GBL 3896/63. Site 12 Po 296. Posey Co., Indiana.

Morphological Correlates
Mounds Stemless Group III (Winters 1967: Fig. 5r–t).

Morphological Correlates of the Unnotched Pentagonal Cluster
Additional types: Pee Dee (Coe 1964:49; Fig. 43); South Appalachian Pentagonal (Keel 1972:179).

Jack's Reef Cluster

JACK'S REEF CORNER NOTCHED

Jack's Reef Corner Notched projectile points (Ritchie 1971a:26) are very thin and wide-bladed forms (Figure 47). The blade is tri-anguloid, with the edges varying from relatively straight to excurvate. Within this range of variation, the blades of some specimens exhibit an obtuse angle along each edge. This obtuse angle can be distinct and sharp with straight edges converging from the tip and shoulder, or it can be an indistinct joining of two excurvate edges between the tip and shoulder. The basal edge on Jack's Reef Corner Notched points is commonly straight and may occasionally exhibit light grinding. Corner notches are usually narrow and deep. The resulting basal ears and shoulder barbs are thin and delicate. These points were manufactured from Jack's Reef Pentagonal preforms and carry all essential flaking characteristics of the type. The percussion flaking technique utilized was highly refined and resulted in a cross section exceedingly flat and thin relative to width. Pressure retouch was used to sharpen and align the edges.

Age and Cultural Affiliation
Jack's Reef Corner Notched points appeared in the Northeast at ca. A.D. 500 and are diagnostic of the latter part of the Middle Woodland and Late Woodland periods. They probably represent one of the first true arrowheads in the eastern U.S. They attained popularity within the Point Peninsula culture, Kipp Island, and Hunters Home phases in New York (Ritchie 1969a:228, 1971a:26). Within the Hunters Home phase, Jack's Reef is superseded by the Levanna triangular type (Ritchie 1969a:254, 1971a). A date of A.D. 905 ±250 years was obtained for early Owasco (Crane 1956:668), which suggests a terminal date for the Jack's Reef style. This projectile point style is also diagnostic of the Late Woodland Albee phase in Indiana and Illinois, which dates from approximately A.D. 800 to 1000 or 1200 (Winters 1967:81; Pace and Thiel 1983). Jack's Reef Pentagonal and Corner Notched forms were recovered from funerary contexts at the Albee Mound in Sullivan County, Indiana and are typically found in other similar contexts in the White River Valley (Tomak 1970, 1980b:7). The distinctive Albee Cord Marked ceramics identify the Albee phase (MacLean 1931). These are also the typical chipped stone forms of the Walkerton phase of northern Indiana (Faulkner 1960a). Jack's Reef points are also diagnostic of what was termed the Intrusive Mound culture in Ohio (Mills 1922; Ritchie 1937).

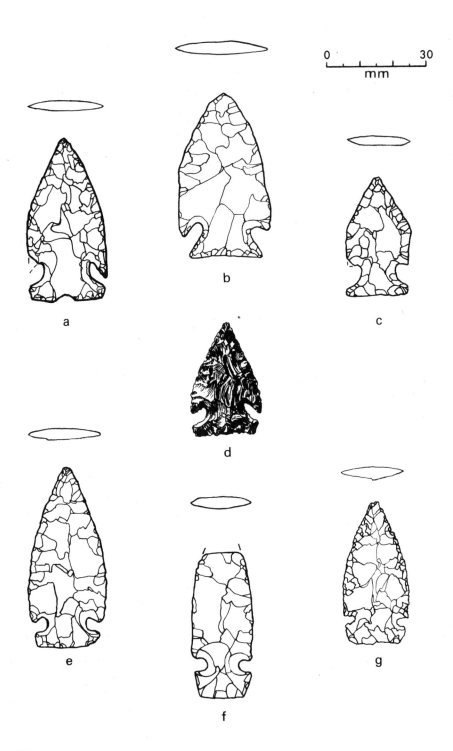

Figure 47
Jack's Reef Cluster

Distribution

Jack's Reef Corner Notched points are well represented across the Northeast and in the Great Lakes area, including southern Ontario (Ritchie 1969a; Fitting 1970; Perkins 1970). The type is commonly found in Ohio (Converse 1973:56; Tallan 1977:15), Indiana (MacLean 1931:158, Plate 25; Tomak 1970, 1980b), and Michigan (Fitting 1970:170, Fig. 97). Jack's Reef Corner Notched are also present in Illinois (Winters 1967:Fig. 16k–l). The type extends south into Tennessee (Faulkner and McCollough 1973:105–106) and northern Alabama (Cambron and Hulse 1969:69), but the western and southeastern distribution of this type remains undefined.

Morphological Correlates

Intrusive Mound Points (Converse 1973:56); Elliston (Tomak 1980b:7, Fig. 23).

RACCOON NOTCHED

The Raccoon Notched type (Mayer-Oakes 1955:87) is very similar to the Jack's Reef Corner Notched type; the only major difference is that Raccoon Notched is side notched (Figure 47). The short description offered by Mayer-Oakes noted that the notches are most often squared-sided, although one variety is corner notched. The corner notched variety relates to Jack's Reef defined later by Ritchie (1961). The Raccoon Notched type exhibits squared ears and a straight or concave basal edge that lacks grinding. Jack's Reef and Raccoon Notched share blade shape characteristics that include the pentagonal preform and thin cross section relative to width. Preform manufacture was accomplished using a refined percussion technique.

Age and Cultural Affiliation

Raccoon Notched points are diagnostic of the early Late Woodland period in the Midwest. These, along with Jack's Reef, probably are the first true arrowheads in the eastern U.S. Mayer-Oakes (1955:87) originally recognized the presence of this projectile point style in post-Hopewellian context in the upper Ohio Valley. Raccoon Notched, along with Jack's Reef Corner Notched, is linked to what was formerly recognized as the Intrusive Mound culture of Ohio (Mills 1922; Ritchie 1937), of the Late Woodland period, which reused ancient Hopewell sites for less elaborate burial ceremony.

Raccoon Notched points appear to have a chronology which correlates with Jack's Reef Corner Notched. Within the lower Wabash drainage system of Indiana and Illinois, these projectile point types, along with unnotched pentagonal preforms, are the characteristic lithic implements of the Late Woodland Albee phase. The Albee phase dates from

Map 94: Jack's Reef Corner Notched and Raccoon Distribution and Important Sites

Figure 47: Jack's Reef Cluster
a. Jack's Reef Corner Notched. Wyandotte chert. GBL 1448/102. Southwestern Indiana.
b. Jack's Reef Corner Notched. Wyandotte chert. GBL 21/ 393. Central Indiana.
c. Jack's Reef Corner Notched. Wyandotte chert. GBL 119/891. Provenience unknown.
d. Jack's Reef Corner Notched. Unidentified chert. GBL 1448/102. Southwestern Indiana.
e–f. Raccoon Notched. Leiber chert, unidentified chert. GBL 281/268. Provenience unknown.
g. Raccoon Notched. Wyandotte chert. GBL 482/258. Vigo Co., Indiana.

slightly earlier than A.D. 800 to about A.D. 1000 to 1200 (Winters 1967:81; Tomak 1980b:7; Pace and Thiel 1983). In the Northeast, Raccoon Notched and Jack's Reef projectile points appear in the late Point Peninsula, Kipp Island phase at about A.D. 500 and are later replaced by the Levanna Triangular type at about A.D. 1000 in the Hunters Home phase (Ritchie 1969a:254, 233, Plate 81).

Distribution

The Raccoon Notched point distribution conforms largely to that of Jack's Reef Corner Notched. The type is present in New York and southern Ontario (Ritchie 1969a:233) and extends across the Great Lakes area. The type occurs in Pennsylvania and the northern part of West Virginia (Mayer-Oakes 1955:86–87) into Ohio (McKenzie 1975:73; Prufer and Shane 1970:85–86), Michigan (Fitting 1965:51, Plate 26a), Indiana (MacLean 1931; Tomak 1980b), and Illinois (Winters 1967: Fig. 5v–w). Raccoon Notched also occurs on

Late Woodland sites in Kentucky (Weinland 1980:66–68, Fig. 28h) and may extend into the Deep South. In northern Alabama, a similar form has been referred to as Knight Island (Cambron and Hulse 1969:71). This latter type has not occurred at sites in significant numbers, nor has it been definitely related to a specific Late Woodland culture.

Morphological Correlates

Knight Island (Cambron and Hulse 1969:71); Logan (Tomak 1980b:7, Fig. 24); Mounds Stemless Group IV (Winters 1963:29, Fig. 5u–w); Side Notched Triangular (Converse 1963:65).

Morphological Correlates of the Jack's Reef Cluster

Long Bay, Port Maitland (Ritchie 1969a:Plates 81–82, 1971a:125). Additional types: Garver's Ferry Corner Notched, Kiski Notched, Murphy's Stemmed (George 1982:205–209).

Scallorn Cluster

SCALLORN

Scallorn projectile points (Kelley 1947:122; Miller and Jelks 1952:176; Suhm et al. 1954:506; Suhm and Jelks 1962) are small corner notched or expanding stem arrowheads with barbed shoulders (Figure 48). These forms vary from broad to slender, with straight to convex blade edges. Incurvate blade edges and/or fine serration may also be exhibited. Distinctly barbed shoulders are characteristic of the type, but this trait is lacking on some specimens. When nearly squared shoulders occur, this variation is associated with notch openings which approach maximum dimensions. Conversely, narrow corner notches correlate with specimens bearing distinct barbs on sloping angular shoulders. Because of the variable notch width, the haft element on these

points exhibits either an expanding stem or a corner notch, depending on the case. A straight basal edge is typical.

The original description of Scallorn included forms that were later segregated and

Figure 48: Scallorn Cluster
a–c. Scallorn. Unidentified chert. GBL 3304/453, 454, 475. Provenience unknown. Specimen b, pictured in Plate 8, g.
d. Scallorn. Unidentified chert. GBL 31/112. Kansas.
e. Sequoyah. Burlington chert. GBL 13/895. South-central Michigan.
f. Sequoyah. Burlington chert. GBL 119/898. Hamilton Co., Tennessee.
g. Sequoyah. Unidentified chert. GBL 21/419. Southwestern Indiana.
h–i. Sequoyah. Unidentified chert. GBL 31/110. Madison Co., Arkansas.
j. Sequoyah. Unidentified chert. GBL 3304/471. Provenience unknown. Pictured in Plate 8, q.

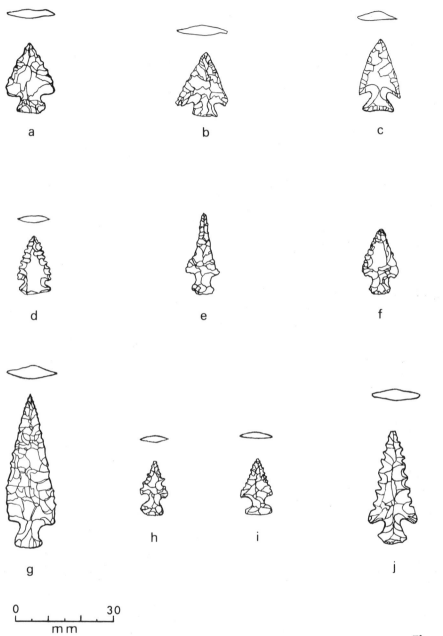

a b c d e f g h i j

Figure 48
Scallorn Cluster

defined under the name Sequoyah (Bell 1960:84; Brown 1968). However, in terms of usage these types have been confused. For example, there was a morphological gradation recognized between Scallorn and Sequoyah at the Williams Shelter in Missouri, and it was difficult to differentiate between the two types (c.f. Jolly and Roberts 1974: Figs. 31–32). The Sequoyah type is similar to Scallorn in basic shape, but Sequoyah points are often deeply serrated, often have elongated blades, and exhibit much narrower haft dimensions.

Age and Cultural Affiliation

Scallorn points date from about A.D. 700 to A.D. 1100, which places the type in the transitional period from Late Woodland to Mississippian. Scallorn and Sequoyah points are associated with the Late Woodland Meramec Spring phase occupation at the Williams Shelter in Missouri (Jolly and Roberts 1974: 65). Excavations in Mound 72 at the Cahokia site in Illinois produced Scallorn and Alba Barbed points as exotic interments among multiple burial caches of fine quality Cahokia points. Scallorn points and other foreign forms appear at the Cahokia site during the

Mississippian Fairmount phase which lasted from A.D. 900 to A.D. 1050. This is the interval when much of the ceremonial center construction began that was completed in the following Stirling phase by A.D. 1150 (Fowler and Hall 1975:3–5).

Distribution

Scallorn points occur over most of Texas and west into New Mexico (Turner and Hester 1985:189). The type occurs to the north over much of Oklahoma (Perino 1968a:84) and into bordering states. The type is well recognized in Missouri (Bray 1956; Jolly and Roberts 1974; C. Chapman 1980). The Scallorn type also occurs at coastal sites. One such site is Avery Island, Louisiana (Gagliano 1967). Scallorn points occur at large Mississippian towns such as Cahokia in Illinois (Titterington 1938:21, Fig. 13; Fowler 1969) and within the Mississippi Valley in general (Perino 1968a).

Morphological Correlates

Scallorn coryell, eddy, sattler (Jelks 1962); Brown 1968:81, Fig. 17g–s).

Map 95: Scallorn—Distribution and Important Sites

SEQUOYAH

Sequoyah points (Brown 1968, 1976:90–92; Perino 1968a:88) are relatively slender forms with coarse serrations and expanding haft elements that often are not geometrically uniform (Figure 48). Blade shapes are triangular with slightly excurvate sides. The shoulders are well defined, and about one half are distinctly barbed. The haft elements of Sequoyah points are narrow and often elongated. Notch openings are typically wide and produced from the corners of the ovate or trianguloid preform. Many specimens exhibit notch openings that are wider and deeper than neck width. In addition, the notch terminus often is rounded so that the neck is nearly parallel-sided below the shoulders before expanding toward the basal edge. A convex basal edge is characteristic of Sequoyah.

Age and Cultural Affiliation
Sequoyah points were the most common form of arrowhead at the large Caddoan Mississippian Spiro site in Oklahoma. At Spiro, Sequoyah points date from about A.D. 1000 to the end of the Spiro phase at about A.D. 1350 (Brown 1968). The type is common within the Late Woodland period but also appears in Mississippian context in Missouri such as in the Meramec Spring phase (Marshall 1966), which is transitional between these two periods. Other types often associated with Sequoyah points are other Scallorn cluster points, Cahokia cluster forms, and what is referred to as Crisp Ovate (unnotched) points (Bray 1956; C. Chapman 1980:98–100). The Crisp Ovate type (Marshall 1958:134) is thought to be a preform for Scallorn and/or Sequoyah points (C. Chapman 1980:307).

Distribution
The Spiro site situated on the Arkansas River in eastern Oklahoma lies near the western fringe of the geographic range for the Sequoyah type (Brown 1976:90). It occurs east along the Arkansas River into the Prairie/Plains area, the Ozarks, and to the north in Arkansas. In addition, the type is known throughout Missouri (Bradham 1963:Fig. 36; Jolly and Roberts 1974:62). Outside of these regions the appearance of the type in small numbers has been reported, such as at the

Map 96: Sequoyah—Distribution and Important Sites

Cahokia site in Illinois (Titterington 1938:21, Fig. 14).

While other forms of arrowheads (i.e., Alba, Hayes, etc.) present at Spiro are distributed into northeast Texas, Sequoyah points are lacking. The same situation is true for Mississippian sites east along the Ohio River. Alba points and other arrowhead forms occur at Kincaid in Illinois (Cole 1951:121, Fig. 37) and at Angel site in southern Indiana (Kellar 1967:435, Fig. 484), but Sequoyah points are not reported from either of these large Mississippian sites. These projectile point forms do, however, occur in low frequency in southwestern Indiana.

Morphological Correlates of the Scallorn Cluster
Cedar Valley (Morrow 1984); Massard (Brown 1968:68–69); Mills (Morrow 1984);
Okoboji (Morrow 1984); Rockwall (Soll-berger 1970:3; Perino 1985:328); Table Rock Corner Notched (Bray 1956:126, Fig. 18, rows 4–5); Washington (Cambron and Hulse 1969:111, 1975:123). Additional types: Collins (Williams and Brain 1983; Perino 1985:83); Klunk Side Notched (Perino 1971a: 100–101; 1973:67, Fig. 31); Koster Corner Notched (Perino 1963:99, 1973:65–66, Fig. 30; Munson 1971:12); Roxanna (Munson 1971:9–10, Fig. 18n–p; Titterington 1938: 21, Fig. 13); Schild Spike (Perino 1971a:100–101, Plate 50; 1973:106, Fig. 56; Fortier et al. 1984); Wanda (Munson 1971:10, Fig. 18q–u; Munson and Anderson 1973:40, Fig. 17b–d).

Late Woodland/Mississippian Triangular Cluster

MADISON

The Madison type (Scully 1951:14; Ritchie 1961:33; Perino 1968a:52; Cambron and Hulse 1969:53) is basically a straight sided isosceles triangular arrowhead with excurvate-bladed variants (Figure 49). Straight and slightly concave bases are both characteristic of the type. Minimal excurvature of the base is also included within the range of variation. Madison points exhibit variable cross sections that may be plano convex, biconvex, flattened, or lenticular. Flaking characteristics range from rough percussion to fine pressure flaking. Note that maximum width of Madison points is always at the base.

Age and Cultural Affiliation
Madison is a standard point style representative of a myriad of Late Woodland and Mississippian cultural phases across eastern North America. Dates range from about A.D.

Figure 49: Late Woodland/Mississippian Triangular Cluster
a. Madison. Unidentified chert. GBL 13/868. South-central Michigan.
b. Madison. Unidentified chert. GBL 1448/346. Southwestern Indiana.
c. Madison. Unidentified chert. GBL 10/93. Erie Co., Pennsylvania.
d. Fort Ancient. Paoli chert. GBL 422/98. Hamilton Co., Ohio. Pictured in Plate 8, n.
e. Fort Ancient. Wyandotte chert. GBL 285/12. Clark Co., Indiana.
f. Fort Ancient. Rockport chert. GBL 296/20. Yankeetown site, 12 W 1. Warrick Co., Indiana.
g–h. Levanna. Unidentified chert. GBL 281/265. Vermont.
i. Levanna. Liston Creek chert. GBL 2685/5. Site 12 Al 62. Allen Co., Indiana.
j. Hamilton Incurvate. Wyandotte chert. GBL 285/12. Clark Co., Indiana.
k. Hamilton Incurvate. Attica chert. GBL 103/1. Site 12 Bl 1. Blackford Co., Indiana.
l. Hamilton Incurvate. Indian Creek chert. GBL 1099/665. Bowen site. Marion Co., Indiana.

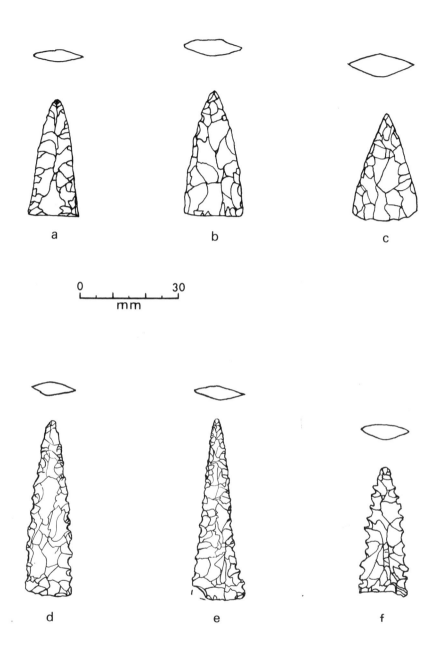

a

b

c

0 ⊢——┴——┴——┴——┴——┤ 30
mm

d

e

f

Figure 49
Late Woodland/Mississippian
Triangular Cluster

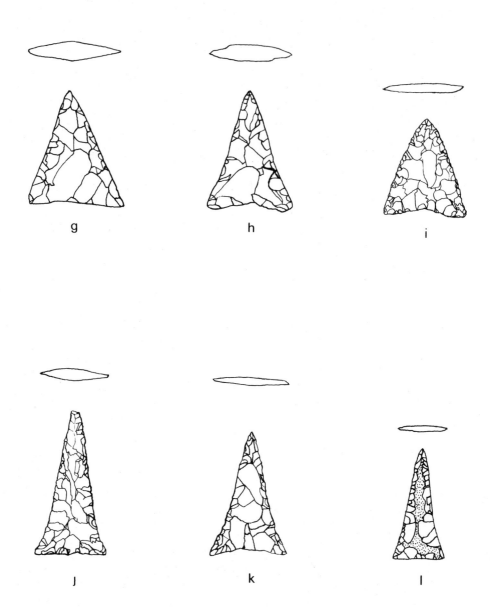

Figure 49

800 to the beginning of the Historic period. Depending on the particular area involved, these forms may appear in the record as late as A.D. 1300. In the Northeast, Madison points replace the Levanna style at about A.D. 1350 (Ritchie 1961:31).

Distribution

The type is common in all regions of the eastern United States and beyond. Fresno (Kelley 1947) is a name given to similar forms, but primarily in the western United States, especially Texas and adjacent areas.

Map 97: Madison—Distribution and Important Sites

FORT ANCIENT

Fort Ancient points (Bell 1960:40; Griffin 1943:70–71; Cambron and Hulse 1969:75) are long and slender isosceles triangular forms with straight bases and deep serrations (Figure 49). These points are narrow and exhibit an elongated tip. The blade edges are generally straight, although they may vary from slightly incurvate to convex. The convex-sided examples are rare. The basal edges may vary from straight to excurvate. Cross sections are biconvex on these points. The presence of deep serration is most char-

acteristic of the type. Unserrated forms occur, although these are sometimes difficult to identify from other triangular forms, especially the Madison type. Serrations on the Fort Ancient type are characteristically robust with deep bifacial hertzian cone flake scars covering much of the blade, resulting from the serration process.

Age and Cultural Affiliation

Fort Ancient points are diagnostic of the Late Woodland to early Mississippian periods. These projectile points were defined as the principal point type of the Feurt phase (Feurt site) of the Fort Ancient tradition in Ohio (Griffin 1943:70–91). The transition from Late Woodland to Fort Ancient occurred from about A.D. 1100 to about A.D. 1200 (McKenzie 1975:76) where Fort Ancient points predominate until ca. A.D. 1450 (Johnson 1982). The Fort Ancient tradition as presently known may have endured to as late as A.D. 1750 in some areas, with several phases recognized. The Madisonville phase may be the latest of these, occupying a region which includes portions of southeastern Indiana (see Essenpreis 1978).

Map 98: Fort Ancient—Distribution and Important Sites

Distribution

The occurrence of Fort Ancient points over a large area is not well understood. The type is recognized from Ohio (Griffin 1943) south to Alabama (Cambron and Hulse 1969:75). It is present at sites in the Ohio Valley. The distribution of the type does not appear to extend to any degree into the Northeast, the Great Lakes region, or west of Indiana. Serrated triangular forms generally occur over a larger undefined area, although the majority of these belong to the other triangular types in this cluster.

LEVANNA

Levanna points (Ritchie 1928; 1961:31) are basically equilateral, concave-based, triangular arrowheads (Figure 49). These forms are characteristically as long as they are wide. A broad isosceles form with a concave base occurs less frequently, although it is considered within the range of variation of the type. The blade edges are normally straight, but a slight deviation includes variation from incurvate to slightly excurvate. The basal concavity often exhibits a marked indentation from the basal edge reaching a termination directly below the distal end of the point. Certain specimens are nearly V-shaped at the base, with prominent barbs at the lateral margins of the base.

Age and Cultural Affiliation

The Levanna arrow point type is diagnostic of the early Late Woodland period and is prevalent in the archaeological record from between A.D. 700–900 to about 1200, when it is finally supplanted by the Madison type (Ritchie 1969a:254, 278; Fitting 1965:50; David M. Stothers, pers. comm.). Levanna points are the characteristic projectile point type of the Owasco and cultures of the Northeast that precede the Historic Iroquois (Ritchie 1961:31).

Levanna points are well represented in the early Late Woodland sequence of the Great Lakes region as a whole. These points occur in the early phases of the Western Basin tradition (Stothers and Pratt 1981), and they are

an integral part of the early Princess Point complex of southwestern Ontario (Stothers 1977:61). Certain sites, such as Cayuga Bridge in Ontario (Wilmeth 1978:120), have produced radiocarbon dates in good context as early as A.D. 600 to 800 (cf. Stothers 1972, 1975, 1977), suggesting that Levanna points appear across the Great Lakes and Northeast at about the same time without a lag in time between areas. The early dates are probably correct considering that Levanna may well be a technological derivative of the Jack's Reef Pentagonal type which temporally precedes Levanna in its area of distribution.

Distribution

Levanna points occur over much of New England and extend to coastal sites such as Hammonasset Beach (Bourn 1977). The type has been identified in West Virginia (McMichael 1965) and southwest Virginia (Holland 1970:88). To the west, the type is present in Pennsylvania (Bebrich 1968), Ohio (Shane 1975a:167), northeastern Indiana, Michigan (Fitting 1965:48), and southern Ontario. The type may extend into the Southeast, where it overlaps morphologically with the Yadkin type described for the Carolina Piedmont (Coe 1964:49; Perino 1968a:100).

Map 99: Levanna—Distribution and Important Sites

HAMILTON INCURVATE

Hamilton Incurvate arrowheads (Lewis and Kneberg 1946:110– 111; Lewis 1955; Bell 1960; Cambron and Hulse 1969:58; Holland 1970:87) are isosceles triangular forms with characteristic incurvate blades (Figure 49). Basal edges of these points include straight and excurate variations. Extreme delicacy and symmetry are characteristic of the type, resulting from refined flaking techniques. The blade edges frequently exhibit fine serrations and the tip and basal margins of these points are acute and needle-like in degree of refinement. The faces are shaped by broad, shallow flake scars resulting in a flattened cross section with fine retouch along the blade margins. The basal edge flaking characteristics differ. However, basal thinning scars are mostly restricted close to the lateral margins of the base.

Age and Cultural Affiliation
Hamilton Incurvate points are diagnostic of the Late Woodland Hamilton culture with several known phases. These date from about A.D. 500 to about A.D. 1000 (Kneberg 1956:24). The above age estimate has been substantiated by several radiocarbon dates relating to Hamilton culture occupations in Tennessee (see Faulkner and McCollough 1973:426–427; see also Schroedl 1978: 196–197). Hamilton Incurvate points occurred both as a cause of death and as funerary offerings in burial contexts at Hiwassee Island in Tennessee. Lewis and Kneberg (1946:110–111) suggested that the shape of these points is related to their function as lethal weapons in warfare.

Several types of early trianguloid points were recovered from the Camp Creek site in Tennessee, along with Hamilton points. On the whole, this site presents a succession of Middle to Late Woodland trianguloid points. The Camp Creek type, while poorly known, is considered to be the probable ancestor of the Hamilton type (Lewis and Kneberg 1957:19, 22; see also Faulkner and Graham 1966:65).

Distribution
Hamilton Incurvate points occur in relatively high frequency across most areas of Tennessee (Lewis and Kneberg 1957; Faulkner and Graham 1966:131; Faulkner 1968; Jolley 1979:46). The type occurs in northern Alabama (Cambron and Hulse 1969), Kentucky (Weinland 1980:64), southwest Virginia (Holland 1970), West Virginia (McMichael 1965), and probably in a somewhat larger area. The type occurs as far north as central Indiana (Black 1935:Plate 1; Swartz 1982:18, Fig. 21).

Map 100: Hamilton Incurvate Distribution and Important Sites

Morphological Correlates of the Late Woodland/Mississippian Triangular Cluster
Haywood Triangular (Keel 1972:177–178, Fig. 3.40d; J. Chapman 1973:83, Plate 28a); Juntunen Triangular (McPherron 1967:148– 153, Plate 33); Mounds Stemless Groups I + II (Winters 1963:Fig. 5); Ohio Triangles (Wachtel 1957); Pisgah Triangular (Keel 1972, 1976:199, Plate 40); Potomac (Stephenson and Ferguson 1963:145–146, 195, Plate 26); Roanoke Large Triangular (Coe 1964:110, Fig. 108). Additional types: Camp Creek (Kneberg 1956:23; Faulkner and Graham

1966:65); Caraway Triangular (Coe 1964: 49–50, Fig. 43); Clarksville Small Triangular (Coe 1964:112, Fig. 108a; Holland 1970:85); Connestee Triangular (Keel 1972:176–177, Fig. 3.40c); Dane Sharks Tooth (Ritzenthaler 1967:30); Fresno (Kelley 1947; Suhm et al. 1954:498; Bell 1960); Humpbacked Knife (Munson and Munson 1972:31– 36); Pinellas (Bullen 1975:8); Scarem, Speidel, Equilateral Monongahela (Mayer-Oakes 1955:221, Fig. 25); Scully (May 1982:1373); Yadkin (Coe 1964:45–49, Fig. 42; Perino 1968a:100. See also Keel 1972:293).

Nodena Cluster

NODENA ELLIPTICAL

Nodena points (C. Chapman and Anderson 1955:15; Bell 1958:64; C. Chapman 1980: 310; Perino 1966a:35) are excurvate-bladed (i.e., willow-leaf shaped), elliptical forms (Figure 50). Maximum width of the blade varies from a placement at the middle of the blade to between the midpoint and the proximal end or base. The latter appears to be most typical, while a few specimens of the type may exhibit maximum width between the midpoint and tip. Overall shape characteristics vary from elliptical bi-pointed forms to specimens exhibiting a narrow tear-drop shape with a rounded base. The haft region or proximal end is not set apart from the blade contour and is sometimes difficult to discern. Refined pressure flaking is the characteristic method of finishing and resharpening, while combinations of percussion and pressure flaking were used in manufacture. Serration of the lateral margins of these points is not uncommon.

Morphological Correlate of the Nodena Elliptical Type
White River Elliptical (Bray 1956:125–126).

NODENA BANKS VARIETY

The term Nodena Banks Variety (Perino 1966a:33–35; Morse 1973:80) is used to distinguish a formal class of essentially straight-based, excurvate-bladed Nodena cluster points from those that are basically elliptical in shape (Figure 50). Perino (1966a) recognized these two basic shapes of Nodena points at the Banks village site in Arkansas. In addition to the Nodena Elliptical form, there were narrow, long-bladed triangular variants with "parallel-convex sides" and straight bases. The basic pressure flaking pattern of these points is similar to Nodena Elliptical, and these forms also exhibit maximum width above the base. Varying degrees of serration sometimes occur on these points. The Guntersville type (Cambron and Hulse 1969:50) is an excurvate-bladed, straight-based form that varies within the range of the Banks variety Nodena. In addition, the Shetley type (Perino 1971a:92) exhibits essential attributes of the Banks variety.

Morphological Correlates
Guntersville (Cambron and Hulse 1969:50); Shetley (Perino 1971a:92).

Figure 50: Nodena Cluster
a. Nodena Elliptical. Unidentified chert. GBL 3645/231. Provenience unknown.
b. Nodena Elliptical. Unidentified chert. GBL 4023/2. Site 12 Po 522. Posey Co., Indiana.
c. Nodena Elliptical. Burlington chert. GBL 31/110. Madison Co., Arkansas. Pictured in Plate 8, j.
d–f. Nodena Banks variety. Unidentified chert. GBL 119/891. Arkansas? Specimen e, pictured in Plate 8, d.

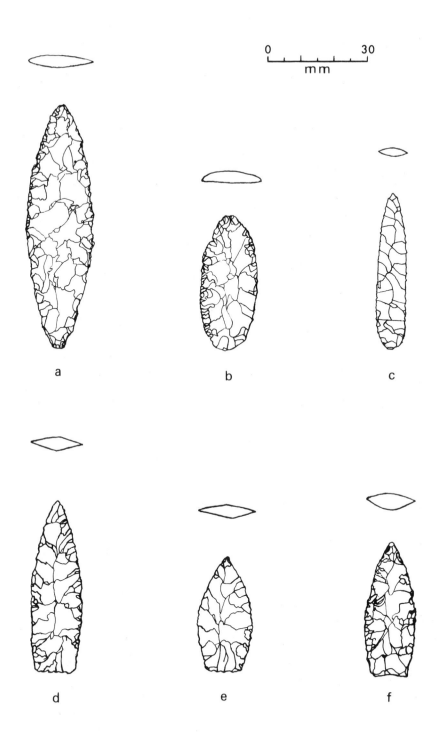

Figure 50
Nodena Cluster

Age and Cultural Affiliation

Nodena cluster projectile points are diagnostic of the late Mississippian and proto-Historic periods dating from roughly A.D. 1400 to A.D. 1700 and after. The name Nodena signifies the Late Mississippian Nodena phase of Arkansas and vicinity (Morse 1973: 80; Baker 1974:13, Fig. 10). These forms also occur in the tool kits of a number of other recognized Mississippian phases in the East (see below).

Distribution

Nodena cluster forms are distributed over a fairly large area. Proto-Historic Quapaw phase sites in Arkansas produce significantly more Nodena forms that any other arrowhead style (Ford 1961:157, Plates 25, 29; Hoffman 1977:31, 35; Hemmings 1982:227–228, Fig. 58). Nodena points are characteristic lithic forms in late Mississippian contexts of Missouri (Bray 1956:125–126; C. Chapman 1980:310), Dallas phase Mississippian sites in Tennessee (Lewis and Kneberg 1946: Plate 66d; Phillips 1970:Fig. 447), and in other late Mississippian components in Kentucky (Weinland 1980:64). The style is also present in the lithic assemblages of the Oneota Orr phase manifestations in Iowa (Anderson 1981:49; Straffin 1971:18, Plate 7c; McKusick 1973) and southern Wisconsin (McKern 1945:135, Plate 39). These forms also occur at Upper Mississippian sites in northern Indiana (Faulkner 1970:130– 131, Plate 17) and proto-Historic sites in the central Wabash Valley in Indiana. Nodena points are characteristic of the Caborn-Welborn

Map 101: Nodena Elliptical and Nodena Banks Variety—Distribution and Important Sites

phase which centers at the confluence of the Wabash and Ohio Rivers in southwestern Indiana, and adjacent parts of Illinois and Kentucky (Green and Munson 1978:303). Nodena points (Banks variety) are reported in the Deep South in Alabama (Cambron and Hulse 1969:50, 88) and Florida (Bullen 1975:9).

Morphological Correlates of the Nodena Cluster

Ichetucknee (Bullen 1975:9); Tampa (Bullen 1975:11).

Cahokia Cluster

CAHOKIA

The Cahokia projectile point type (Scully 1951:14–15; Perino 1968a:12, 1971b:126– 130) is a side notched triangular arrowhead that often exhibits distinct and well executed serration or shallow multiple notching of the blade edges (Figure 51). The basic Cahokia preform resembles the Madison type in manufacture and is isosceles in shape. A basal notch is often present which is produced in the same fashion as the side notches and is often the same depth. Additional notches are often placed at the lateral margins of the base and on the blade edges. These additional notches are more like deep serrations similar to those that sometimes occur on the blade. These are relatively shallow, unlike the side and basal notches characteristic of the haft. The stylistic variations of the type were originally described by Scully (1951) in four groups: Cahokia double, triple, and multiple notched, and Cahokia serrated.

Age and Cultural Affiliation

Cahokia arrowheads are diagnostic of the early Mississippian (emergent) period (Hall 1975:22). The type occurs in the Fairmount phase at the Cahokia site in Illinois, which Fowler and Hall (1975:3) and Hall (1975:18) place from A.D. 900 to A.D. 1050. Within Mound 72 at the site, two large caches of arrowheads (over seven hundred specimens) were found in funerary contexts. Several types of arrowheads were associated, including fine serrated Madison, Cahokia, and Alba Barbed points (Fowler 1973:21, Fig. 20). The Schild cemetery in Illinois also produced Cahokia points in early Mississippian funerary contexts, with suggested age of A.D. 1000 to A.D. 1150 (Perino 1971b:126, 136). Later in the Mississippian sequence, unnotched Madison points are thought to replace Cahokia points (1971b:130).

Distribution

Cahokia points are known in the Midwest principally from the large Mississippian Cahokia site in Illinois, where they are most numerous, and at the Aztalan site in Wisconsin. They are found at most Cahokia-affiliated sites along the Mississippi and Caddo-Mississippi routes to Spiro and other Caddoan sites (Perino 1968a:12). In addition, this basic style occurs well into the southwestern United States (see Wasley 1960:246, Fig. 3), in the Plains (i.e., Washita), and Great Basin (i.e., Desert).

Several varieties have been found at the Schild site in Illinois (Perino 1971b:126) and at the Button Cairn in Missouri (Bray 1963:41). Side notched Cahokia points with and without a basal notch have also been found on Mississippian camps in the Ohio River Valley in southwestern Indiana. Intensive survey of this portion of the Ohio Valley has produced low numbers of Cahokia style

Map 102: Cahokia—Distribution and Important Sites

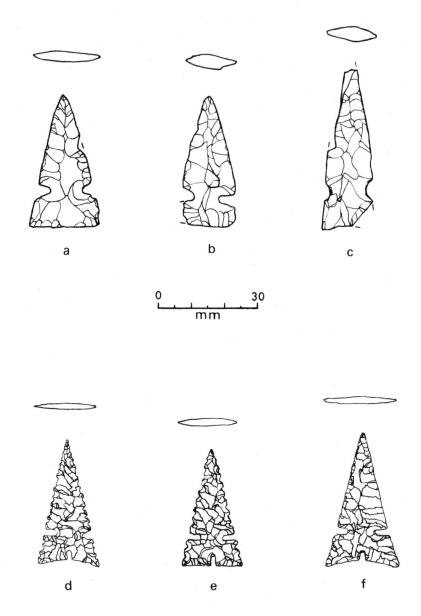

Figure 51
Cahokia Cluster

a. Cahokia. Burlington chert. GBL 3887/1. Site 12 Po 283. Posey Co., Indiana. Pictured in Plate 8, l.
b. Cahokia. Unidentified chert. GBL 21/419. Southwestern Indiana.
c. Cahokia. Impact fracture at tip. Unidentified chert. GBL W10D/312. Angel site, 12 Vg 1, Vanderburgh Co., Indiana.
d–f. Cahokia. Peter A. Bostrom casts. Originals, Burlington chert. Mound 72, Cahokia site, Illinois. Illinois State Museum Collection. Specimens M–37, 38, 40, Lithic Casting Lab., Troy, Illinois.

points from short-term camps in the floodplain and low terrace. The type also occurs at the Angel site in Vanderburgh County, Indiana (Black 1967; Kellar 1967:435, Fig. 484).

Morphological Correlates of the Cahokia Cluster
Des Moines (Morrow 1984). Additional types: Harrell (Suhm, Krieger, and Jelks 1954:50; Suhm and Jelks 1962:275); Baerreis 1954:44; C. Chapman 1980:308–309); Reed (Bell 1958:76); C. Chapman 1980:311); Schugtown (Morse 1969; Perino 1985:347); Washita (Bell 1958; Cambron and Hulse 1975:124); Washita garvin, chaffee, peno (Brown 1968: 105–109, Fig. 20).

Alba Cluster

ALBA BARBED

The Alba Barbed arrowhead type (Newell and Krieger 1949:126; Brown 1976:61) is characterized by a recurved blade and flaring barbs and somewhat variable haft morphology (Figure 52). The blade edges of these points are sometimes finely serrated. The basal edge varies from straight to slightly convex. The overall stem morphology varies from nearly straight parallel-edged to bulbous and fan-shaped. The fan-shaped variation occurs with slight expanding stems due to difference in notch depth. Wide notch openings and relatively broad straight-sided stems are more characteristic, but expanded stemmed variations can be confused with Hayes Barbed type forms. Distinctly fan-shaped or "diamond-shaped" haft elements are characteristic of Hayes and also Agee and Homan type points (see Brown 1976). Another similar form, Bonham Barbed, differs from Alba with regard to blade shape and dimensions of the haft element (Krieger 1946: 185; Bell 1960:10).

Age and Cultural Affiliation
Alba points are diagnostic of the Missis-

sippian period and date from about A.D. 900 to 1200 (Turner and Hester 1985:163). These arrowhead forms are assigned to the Harlan phase at the Spiro site in Oklahoma (Brown 1976:61). This type was recovered among a series of exotic forms found in funerary context at the Cahokia site in Illinois. Mound 72 produced caches of Cahokia, serrated Madison, and Alba, among other types (Fowler 1973:19–27, Figs. 19–20). These are assigned to the Fairmount phase at Cahokia, which dates from about A.D. 900 to A.D. 1050 (Fowler and Hall 1975:3–4).

Distribution
Alba arrowheads are chiefly distributed in the Caddoan area of northeast Texas (Newell and Krieger 1949; Stephenson 1952) and eastern Oklahoma (Brown 1968, 1976). This type occurs south to the Gulf Coast where it was found at Avery Island, Louisiana (Gagliano 1967), and in the Mississippi Valley north to at least St. Louis (Fowler 1973). It also occurs in the Ohio Valley as far east as Angel site and vicinity in southern Indiana.

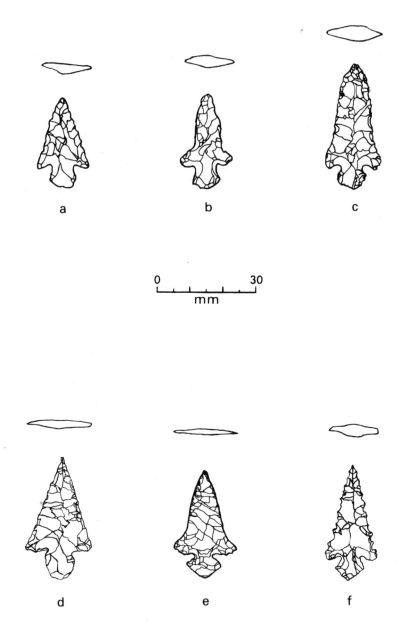

Figure 52
Alba Cluster

Map 103: Alba Barbed—Distribution and Important Sites

Three such points are reported from the site (Kellar 1967:435, Fig. 484 bottom row).

Morphological Correlates of the Alba Cluster

Bonham Barbed (Krieger 1946:185, Plate 22); Bulbar Stemmed (Corbin 1974:29; Perino 1985:52); Hayes Barbed (Newell and Krieger 1949:162; Durham and Davis 1975; Suhm and Jelks 1962:277; Brown 1976:65–67). Additional types: Agee/Homan (Wood 1963; Perino 1968a:4; Brown 1968:73–79); Catahoula (Bell 1960:16; Cambron and Hulse 1969:19); Howard (Webb 1959:187; Perino 1985:189).

Figure 52: Alba Cluster

a. Alba Barbed. Unidentified chert. GBL 21/419. Southwestern Indiana.

b. Alba Barbed. Unidentified chert. GBL W 11 A/953, Angel site, 12 Vg 1. Vanderburgh Co., Indiana.

c. Alba Barbed. Unidentified chert. GBL P159/16. Angel site, Vanderburgh Co., Indiana.

d. Alba Barbed. Peter A. Bostrom cast. Original, indurated siltstone. Provenience unknown. Specimen C–4, Lithic Casting Lab., Troy, Illinois.

e. Hayes Barbed. Unidentified chert. GBL 3304/423. Provenience unknown.

f. Hayes Barbed. Peter A. Bostrom cast. Original, Pitkin chert? Mound 72, Cahokia site, Illinois. Illinois State Museum Collection. Specimen M–43, Lithic Casting Lab., Troy, Illinois.

Morris Cluster

MORRIS

The Morris type arrowhead (Bell and Hall 1953; Bell and Dale 1953; Bell 1958:60) is set apart from other forms by the presence of a distinctive basal notch (Figure 53). Morris points exhibit side notches and basal notch sharing similar dimensions and U-shape. The blade edges are basically straight but may be slightly convex and often bear minute serrations. The presence of serrations represents a basic morphological difference between Morris and the related Sallisaw type (Brown 1968; Perino 1968a:82; Brown 1976:83). The Sallisaw variant also bears a wide basal notch and narrow corner notches, but the basal ears are long and pointed.

Age and Cultural Affiliation
Morris type arrowheads relate to the Harlan and Spiro phases of the Caddoan Mississippian occupation in eastern Oklahoma and adjacent areas (Brown 1976:97). These points are dated from A.D. 900 to 1200 at the Harlan site (Bell 1972:261). They also occur later in the Spiro phase which dates from about A.D. 1200 to 1300 at the Spiro site (Brown 1971:220).

Distribution
Morris type arrowheads have a sparse distribution outside of eastern Oklahoma. However, the type does occur along the Arkansas River into Kansas (Bell 1958:60; Brown 1976:93). The distribution of the Morris type has also been confirmed at excavations in Arkansas (Thomas and Davis 1966) and Mis-

Figure 53: Morris Cluster
a–b. Morris. Burlington chert. GBL 31/110. Madison Co., Arkansas. Specimen a, pictured in Plate 8, o.
c. Morris. Unidentified chert. GBL W11B/1454. Angel site, 12 Vg 1, Vanderburgh Co., Indiana. Pictured in Plate 8, r.
d. Morris. Peter A. Bostrom cast. Provenience unknown. Specimen C–6, Lithic Casting Lab., Troy, Illinois.
e–f. Sallisaw. Unidentified chert. Spiro site, Oklahoma. Redrawn from Perino 1985:335, bottom row, second from left, fourth from left.

Map 104: Morris—Distribution and Important Sites

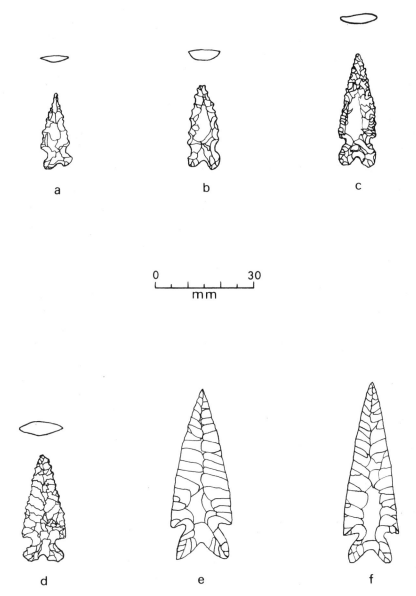

Figure 53
Morris Cluster

souri (Bray 1956:79, 131). The type is largely unknown outside of the above area except for its presence at large Mississippian towns such as Kincaid in southern Illinois (Cole 1951:121, Fig. 37) and Angel site in southwestern Indiana (Kellar 1967:435, Fig. 484). Two Morris specimens were recovered from within the village area of the site in separate locations. Other "exotic" arrowhead forms present at Angel are the Cahokia and Alba Barbed point types, besides the abundant unnotched triangular forms.

Morphological Correlates of the Morris Cluster

Additional types: Sallisaw (Brown 1968, 1976: 83; Perino 1968a:82); Sallisaw bokoshe (Brown 1968:86, Fig. 15a–g).

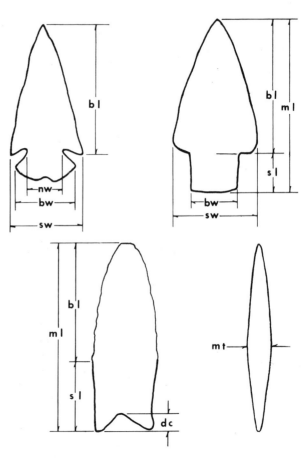

ml- MAXIMUM LENGTH
bl- BLADE LENGTH
sw- SHOULDER WIDTH
mt- MAXIMUM THICKNESS
nw- NECK WIDTH
bw- BASAL WIDTH
sl- STEM/HAFT LENGTH
dc- DEPTH OF BASAL CONCAVITY

Figure 54
Metric Attributes

APPENDIX:
Selected Projectile Point Measurements

(IN MILLIMETERS)

Metrical attributes are an important part of type descriptions. The body of metric data presented here brings together information from a wide number of sources. The measured projectile point samples are given to provide the basic dimensions of features of the blade, haft element, and other important attributes of each described type. The standard measurement procedures to obtain data on length, width, and thickness, in addition to a host of more specific measurements, are illustrated in Figure 54. Published measurement data occur in many forms. Some of the original measurements do not cover critical information of hafting elements dimensions while others do not include sample size or the standard deviation of measures which can be used for statistical tests. In these cases I have provided a broader range of measurements on additional samples whenever possible. In other cases, measurement data were exceedingly rich, which allowed for a degree of selection for pertinent measurements important for type definition and the elimination of others that specify a more select population within the range of the type. Projectile point flaking patterns, individual flake characteristics, and overall structure often have specific measurement ranges that are unique to each type. Increasingly specific attribute measurement will continue to gain importance in the analysis and classification of projectile points.

CLOVIS

A number of Clovis points have been analyzed and measured within the manufacturing and refurbishing sequences recognized at Paleo-Indian base camps in the East (Byers 1954; Ritchie 1953; McCary 1951; Dragoo 1973; Gardner 1974; Kraft 1973). These works should be consulted for site specific manufacturing and use information. For immediate purposes, three groups of measurements are provided below which cover the range of sizes for a large number of pristine and reworked specimens from three states.

Clovis projectile points from Texas (Suhm, Krieger, and Jelks 1954:412):

	range
length	60–140
width	20–40

N = 200 Clovis points from Ohio (Prufer and Baby 1963:13, Type I fluted points):

	range
length	28–132

Two groups of Clovis points from Indiana separated into length classes (Dorwin 1966:153–155):

N = 87 (Type I)

	average
length	73.2

N = 26 (Type II)

	average
length	56.4

ROSS COUNTY

N = 36 Ross County fluted points from Ohio (Prufer and Baby 1963:19):

	range	mean	median	standard deviation
length	47–160	88.1	85.5	19.1

REDSTONE

N = 7 Redstone fluted points from sites in the Tennessee River Valley in Alabama (Cambron and Hulse 1969:99):

	range	average
length	67–117	89
width		37
thickness		7
flute length	26–70	

DEBERT

N = 38 Selected metrics on both complete and basal fragments of projectile points from the Debert site in Nova Scotia (MacDonald 1968:71, Table 6):

	range	mean
length	32–109	63
width	13–26	27.4
thickness	4–11	8.1

HOLCOMBE

The following measurements were taken from an unknown number of Holcombe points from several sites along the Holcombe Beach in southeastern Michigan (Fitting, DeVisscher, and Wahla 1966; Wahla and DeVisscher 1969).

	range	mean
length	35–70	
blade width	16–28	
basal width	13–27	
thickness	3.5–6	3
depth of basal concavity	4.5 (ca. maximum)	

CUMBERLAND

N = 21 Cumberland points from Ohio (Prufer and Baby 1963:19):

	range	mean	median	standard deviation
length	46–92	69.5	71.2	7.9

FOLSOM

An unknown sample size of Folsom projectile points from Texas and other areas (Suhm, Krieger, and Jelks 1954:426):

	range	majority
length	30–80	30–50
width	16–28	

PLAINVIEW

Plainview projectile points from Texas (Suhm, Krieger, and Jelks 1954:472):

	range
length	45–80
width	18–28
basal width	20–26
depth of basal concavity	1–8

AGATE BASIN

Agate Basin projectile points from Missouri (C. Chapman 1975:241):

	range	mean
length	50–130	100
width		30

See Luchterhand (1970:26, Tables 5–6) and also Frison and Stanford (1982:Appendix) for additional measurements.

BEAVER LAKE

N = 23 Beaver Lake projectile points from the Tennessee River Valley in northern Alabama (Cambron and Hulse 1969:9):

	range	average
length	47–86	64
width		24
thickness		8

QUAD

N = 51 Quad type projectile points from the Tennessee Valley in Alabama (Cambron and Hulse 1969:98):

	range	average
length	47–86	57
width		23
thickness		7

DALTON

Selected metric data on a large sample of Dalton points from the Brand site in northeastern Arkansas (Goodyear 1974:23):

	N	range	mean
length	41	33.5–68	48
blade (body)			
length	50	22–56	33.5
stem length	102	3–21	14.4
shoulder (of stem)			
width	122	10.5–31	20.5
thickness	12	4–10	6
basal concavity	103	1.0–9.5	5.5

GREENBRIER

N = 1 Greenbrier point from Alabama (Cambron and Hulse 1969:66):

length	63
shoulder width	25
basal width	25
stem length	12
thickness	6
notch depth	4
notch width	14

HARDAWAY SIDE NOTCHED

N = 27 Hardaway Side Notched points from the Hardaway site in North Carolina (Coe 1964:67):

	range	average
length	28–50	35
width	23–35	24
thickness	3–6	4

HI-LO

N = 16 Hi-Lo projectile points from the Hi-Lo site in Michigan, plus additional length measures from other surface collections in the state (Fitting 1963b:90–91, Table 1):

	range
length	28–70
maximum width	20–35
basal width	17–32
maximum thickness	5.5–9
basal thickness	3.5–6

SCOTTSBLUFF

Scottsbluff projectile points from the Plains (Wormington 1957:267; Dick and Mountain 1960:226):

	range
length	51–127
width	25

Scottsbluff projectile points found in Texas (Suhm, Krieger, and Jelks 1954:478):

	range
length	50–150
width	25–35
stem width	20–30
stem length	12–25

EDEN

Eden projectile points from the Plains (Wormington 1957:267; Dick and Mountain 1960:226):

	range
length	71–155
width	13–19

Refer to Dick and Mountain (1960) and Wheat (1972) for additional measurements of Eden and Scottsbluff types.

HARDIN BARBED

N = 51 Hardin Barbed projectile points from central and west-central Illinois (Munson 1967:19):

	N	range	mean	standard deviation
length	34	49–135	79	18.4
width	50	28–44	36	4.0
thickness	51	7–11	8.5	1.2
blade length	45	34–115	69	20
stem length	41	13–24	17.5	3.3
stem width	40	20–30	26	2.7

THEBES

N = 41 Thebes projectile points from the lower
Illinois Valley (Luchterhand 1970:26):

	mean	standard deviation
axial length	78.5	19.5
shoulder width	47.3	7.0
thickness	9.5	1.1

N = 16 Thebes projectile points from Greene
County, Indiana (Tomak 1970:54):

	range
length	62–74
shoulder width	41–54
thickness	7–10

ST. CHARLES

N = 44 St. Charles points from the Illinois Valley
(Luchterhand 1970:26):

	mean	standard deviation
axial length	90.5	18.6
shoulder width	33.3	4.4
basal width	27.4	4.2
thickness	8.9	1.2

LOST LAKE

N = 11 Lost Lake points from Alabama (Cambron
and Hulse 1969:46):

	range	average
length	49–81	63
width	35–48	40
stem width	23–32	27
thickness	7–8	
stem length	12–15	

CALF CREEK

N = 6 Calf Creek projectile points from Calf
Creek Cave in Arkansas (Dickson 1970:71):

	N	range
length	3	37–63
width	3	39–42
thickness	6	5–9

BIG SANDY

N = 14 Big Sandy points from the Quad site in
Alabama (Cambron and Hulse 1969:13):

	range
length	35–56
width	18–20
thickness	6–8

N = 16 Big Sandy points from the LaGrange
Bluff Shelter in Alabama (DeJarnette and Knight
1976:41–42, Table 8):

	N	range
length	8	28–68
basal width	14	18–28
blade width	15	16–27
notch width	16	3–9
thickness	16	4–8

GRAHAM CAVE SIDE NOTCHED

Graham Cave Side Notched points from Missouri
(C. Chapman 1975:248):

	range
length	80–150
width	20–30

KESSELL SIDE NOTCHED

N = 9 Kessell Side Notched from the St. Albans
site in West Virginia (Broyles 1971:60):

	range
length	36–48
width	23–29
thickness	3–6

RADDATZ SIDE NOTCHED

N = 31 Raddatz points from the Raddatz Rock
Shelter in Wisconsin (Wittry 1959a:46):

	N	range	average
length	11	38–64	49.4
width	23	16–34	25.9
stem length	22	8–17	12.9
neck width	23	11–25	19.1
	19	17–21	
thickness	22	7–11	8.6

N = 31 Raddatz Side Notched points from the
Richardson site in the Illinois River Valley (Munson and Harn 1966:154, Table 1):

	range	mean
length	32–56	43
width	17–29	23
thickness	6–11	9
stem length	10–18	13
width at notches	14–21	17

OSCEOLA

Osceola projectile points from Wisconsin (Bell 1958:68):

	range	majority
length	76.2–228.6	101.6–127.0

Hemphill points from the lower Illinois River Valley in Illinois (Perino 1971a:50):

	range
length	125–230
notch depth	4–7
notch width	5–10
depth of basal concavity	2–4

KIRK CORNER NOTCHED

Kirk Corner Notched projectile points from the Hardaway site in North Carolina (Coe 1964:70):

	range	average
length	40–100	60
width	20–45	30
thickness	6–12	8

See J. Chapman (1975, 1977) and Broyles (1971) for additional measurements.

STILWELL CORNER NOTCHED

N = 6 Stilwell projectile points from Indiana:

	range
length	73–91
shoulder width	32–44
basal width	30–32
depth of basal concavity	2.5–5
thickness	7.5–9

PALMER CORNER NOTCHED

Palmer Corner Notched points from the Hardaway site in North Carolina (Coe 1964: 67):

	range	average
length	28–60	35
width	15–25	20
thickness	5–12	8

See Chapman (1975, 1977) for additional measurements.

CHARLESTON CORNER NOTCHED

N = 10 Charleston Corner Notched points from the St. Albans site in West Virginia (Broyles 1971:56):

	range	majority
length	37–53	
width	26–35	
thickness	6–9	7

PINE TREE CORNER NOTCHED

N = 7 Pine Tree Corner Notched points from Alabama (Cambron and Hulse 1969:96):

	range	average
length	40–72	54
shoulder width	23–32	27
stem width	25–30	28
stem length	10–12	11
thickness	7–8	

DECATUR

N = 17 Decatur projectile points from the Tennessee Valley in northern Alabama (Cambron and Hulse 1969:87):

	range	average
length	29–54	42
width	22–38	28
thickness	5–7	6
stem width	13–25	19

KIRK STEMMED

Kirk Stemmed projectile points from the Hardaway site in North Carolina (Coe 1964:70):

	range	average
length	70–150	100
width	30–50	35
thickness	8–15	10

KIRK SERRATED

Kirk Serrated points from the Hardaway site in North Carolina (Coe 1964:70):

	range	average
length	45–120	70
width	25–35	30
thickness	8–12	9

RICE LOBED

N = 21 Rice Lobed projectile points from the Rice Shelter in Missouri (Bray 1956:128):

	range
length	45–65
width (at shoulder)	28–32
thickness (at shoulder)	7–9

MACCORKLE STEMMED

N = 14 MacCorkle Stemmed points from West Virginia (Broyles 1971:71):

	range
length	40–63
width	22–35
stem length	12–17
stem width	18–26
thickness	3–6

ST. ALBANS SIDE NOTCHED

N = 17 Variety A points from the St. Albans site in West Virginia (Broyles 1966:23, 1971:73):

	range
length	25–37
width	17–22
thickness	5–7

N = 20 Variety B points from the St. Albans site in West Virginia (Broyles 1966:25, 1971:75):

	range
length	22–49
width	13–19
thickness	5–9

LECROY BIFURCATED STEM

N = 50 LeCroy points from the St. Albans site in West Virginia (Broyles 1971:69):

	range
length	19–35
width	16–28
thickness	4–6

LAKE ERIE BIFURCATED BASE

Lake Erie Bifurcated points from the McKibben site in Ohio (Prufer and Sofsky 1965:32):

	N	range	mean
length	12	22–38	30
width	18	16–20	
thickness	23	3–6	4.3

KANAWHA STEMMED

N = 66 Kanawha Stemmed points from the St. Albans site (Broyles 1971:59):

	range	majority
length	19–48	30–36
width	19–37	23–27
thickness	3–7	

FOX VALLEY TRUNCATED BARB

N = 31 Truncated Barb projectile points from central Illinois (Munson and Downs 1966:206):

	N	range	mean	standard deviation
length	18	24–50	36	6.6
width	29	19–35	27	3.8
thickness	31	3–7	4.5	1.0
blade length	19	14–41	27.5	6.5
stem length	29	7–10	8.5	1.0
stem width	29	10–17	14	1.8

STANLY STEMMED

N = 31 Stanly Stemmed projectile points from the Doerschuk site in western North Carolina (Coe 1964:35):

	range	average
length	40–80	55
width	25–45	35

EVA I & II

N = 10 Eva (undifferentiated) points from northern Alabama (Cambron and Hulse 1969:78):

	range	average
length	48–96	61
width	25–39	33
stem width	11–26	18
stem length	5–7	6
thickness	8–10	9

MORROW MOUNTAIN I

Morrow Mountain I points from the Doerschuk site in North Carolina (Coe 1964:37):

	range	average
length	30–70	45
width	22–45	30

N = 49 Morrow Mountain I Stemmed from the Ice House Bottom site in Tennessee (J. Chapman 1977:30):

	range	average
length	22.5–53.5	34.5
width	18.0–31.5	24.0
stem length	2.0–10.5	6.0
stem width	10.5–18.5	13.2
thickness	5.0–10.5	7.3

MORROW MOUNTAIN II

Morrow Mountain II points from the Doerschuk site in North Carolina (Coe 1964:37):

	range	average
length	30–80	60
width	18–30	20

SYKES

N = 7 Sykes points from the Westmoreland-Barber site located on the Tennessee River in southern Tennessee (Faulkner and Graham 1966:72):

	range
length	38.8–47.8
width	24.6–29
thickness	6.6–8.8

WHITE SPRINGS

N = 14 White Springs projectile points from the Tennessee River Valley in northern Alabama (Cambron and Hulse 1969:116):

	range	average
length	42–66	50
shoulder width	28–36	32
stem width	17–24	20
stem length	3–7	6
thickness	3–10	9

BENTON STEMMED

N = 5 Alabama examples of Benton Stemmed (Cambron and Hulse 1969:11):

	range	average
length	45–97	65
shoulder width	25–30	29
stem width	16–20	17
stem length	8–11	9
thickness	5–9	7

ELK RIVER STEMMED

N = 15 Elk River points from Alabama (Cambron and Hulse 1969:82):

	range	average
length	48–92	72
width	30–38	31
thickness	8–11	9
stem length	11–17	14
stem width	15–19	17
stem thickness	8–11	9

BREWERTON CORNER NOTCHED

Brewerton Corner Notched points from New York (Ritchie 1961:16):

	range	majority
length	23.88–79.45	31.75–57.15
width	31.75–38.1	
thickness	4.76–9.53	7.94

N = 7 Brewerton Corner Notched points from the Mixter site in Ohio (Shane 1975a:136):

	N	range	mean
length	5	33–37	34.6
blade length	5	24–27	25.6
width	6	22–36	27.3
haft width	6	14–19	16.3
thickness	7	7–8	7.3

BREWERTON SIDE NOTCHED

Brewerton Side Notched points from New York (Ritchie 1961:19):

	range	majority
length	20.64–98.43	31.75–57.15
thickness	6.35–12.7	7.94–9.53

N = 4 Brewerton Side Notched points from the Mixter site in Ohio (Shane 1975a:136):

	N	range	mean
length	4	22–38	31.8
blade length	4	12–29	22.5
width	4	15–24	19.5
haft width	4	11–16	13.5
thickness	4	6–8	6.8

VOSBURG CORNER NOTCHED

Vosburg Corner Notched points from New York (Ritchie 1961:55):

	range	majority
length	25.4–114.3	12.70–50.8
width	38.1 maximum	
thickness	4.77–6.35	9.525 maximum

N = 4 Vosburg Corner Notched points from the Mixter site in Ohio (Shane 1975a:135):

	N	range	mean
length	3	31–56	42.3
blade length	3	24–47	34.0
width	4	23–35	29.5
haft width	4	16–24	20.3
thickness	4	6–8	6.8

For additional measurements on Ohio specimens refer to Prufer and Sofsky (1965:32).

MATANZAS SIDE NOTCHED

N = 27 Matanzas Side Notched points from central Illinois (Munson and Harn 1966:154, Table 1):

	range	mean
length	36–53	41
width	16–22	20
thickness	5–10	8
stem length	7–10	8
width at notches	10–19	15

N = 173 Modal Matanzas points from Horizon 6 at Koster site in the lower Illinois Valley selected from Cook (1976:142, Table 43):

	N	mean	standard deviation
notch depth right	162	−1.97	0.74
notch depth left	166	−1.97	0.62
notch width right	163	8.69	2.94
notch width left	165	8.41	3.01
basal width	155	18.92	2.30

BREWERTON EARED-NOTCHED

Brewerton Eared projectile points from New York (Ritchie 1961:17–18):

Brewerton Eared-Notched

	range	majority
length	19.05–63.5	25.4–38.1
thickness	4.76–7.94	6.35

Brewerton Eared-Triangle

	range	majority
length	22.23–53.98	26.99–38.1
thickness	–	–

TABLE ROCK STEMMED

N = 10 Table Rock Stemmed points from the Rice Shelter in southwestern Missouri (Bray 1956:127):

	range
length	38–60
width at shoulder	24–32
thickness at shoulder	4–6

Table Rock Stemmed points from Missouri (C. Chapman 1975:252):

	range	usual range	average
length	40–180	40–80	50
width	15–35		
thickness	4–8		

BOTTLENECK STEMMED

N = 8 Bottleneck points from the Mixter site in Ohio (Shane 1975a:165):

	N	range	mean
length	5	29–36	32.6
blade length	5	18–28	22.8
width	7	20–25	23.1
haft width	8	9–14	12.3
thickness	8	6–8	6.9

LAMOKA

Lamoka points from New York (Ritchie 1961:29):

	range	majority
length	25.4–63.5	31.75–44.45
thickness	6.35	

N = 9 Dustin points from the Schmidt site in Michigan (Harrison 1966:58):

	N	range	mean
length	12	30–50.5	38.080
width	19	12.5–17.5	15.105
thickness	19	5–14.5	7.500

N = 4 Durst Stemmed points from Raddatz Rockshelter in Wisconsin (Wittry 1959b:48):

	N	range	average
length	3	38–47	42.6
width	4	19–23	20.5
stem length	3	12–13	12.7
thickness	4	6–7	6.2

MEROM EXPANDING STEMMED

N = 91 Merom Expanding Stemmed points from the Riverton and Robeson Hills sites (see Winters 1969:152, Table A):

	range	average
length	19–36	26
maximum width	11–20	16
maximum thickness	4–8	6
blade length	12–28	21
stem length	4–10	6
stem width, top	6–11	8
stem width, base	7–17	12
blade width, base	11–20	16

TRIMBLE SIDE NOTCHED

N = 36 Trimble Side Notched points from the Riverton, Swan Island, and Robeson Hills sites in the Wabash Valley (Winters 1969:153, Table B):

	range	average
length	21–35	27
maximum width	10–18	14
maximum thickness	5–8	6
blade length	16–32	22
stem length	3–7	5
stem width, top	5–12	8
stem width, base	9–15	12
blade width, base	10–17	14

KARNAK UNSTEMMED

N = 119 Karnak Unstemmed (Modesto) points from site 12 Mo 152, Monroe County, Indiana (Tomak 1980a:106):

	usual range	total range
length	53–72	42–95
maximum width	17–25	14–31
thickness	8–12	6–15

KARNAK STEMMED

N = 43 Karnak Stemmed projectile points from Koster site (Cook 1976:139):

	N	mean	standard deviation
length	33	75.1	11.7
width	43	24.3	2.7
thickness	43	10.4	1.7

N = 6 Karnak Stemmed points from the Patoka Reservoir area of southern Indiana (Cook 1980:387):

	N	mean	standard deviation
length	4	68.5	3.8
width	5	23.4	1.0
thickness	6	11.4	1.4

MCWHINNEY HEAVY STEMMED

Two groups of McWhinney Heavy Stemmed points from the Maple Creek site in Clermont County, Ohio (Vickery 1972:4–5):

N = 4 Non-metric attributes present in this group are basal thinning, excurvate blade shape, and well defined notching.

	range	mean
total length		
haft length	7.6–14.6	11.3
shoulder width	10.5–21.4	20.1
haft width	10.8–14.8	13.0
basal width	9.7–14.6	12.3
maximum thickness	7.5–10.3	9.1
maximum width	21.4–23.7	22.5

N = 10 Measurements of the remaining group of specimens not exhibiting the above non-metric characteristics.

	N	range	mean
total length			
haft length	10	6.4–14.5	10.0
shoulder width	9	18.8–31.1	23.0
haft width	9	10.5–15.2	13.0
basal width	10	6.9–14.0	11.5
maximum thickness	8	6.8–12.2	9.5

NEBO HILL LANCEOLATE

Nebo Hill points from Missouri (C. Chapman 1975:251):

	range
length	50–100
width	one-seventh to one-fourth the length

SEDALIA LANCEOLATE

N = 115 Sedalia points from Missouri (Seelan 1961:307):

	range
length	76–164

Sedalia points from the lower Missouri Valley in Missouri and adjacent parts of Illinois (Perino 1968a:86):

	range	average
length	102–204	152

WADLOW

Wadlow points from the Etley site (Perino 1968a:98):

	range
length	125–320
width	38–80

POMRANKY

N = 516 Pomranky points (cache blades) from the Pomranky site in Midland Co., Michigan (Binford 1963a:177):

	N	mean	standard deviation
Midland variety			
length	230	47.9	5.7
maximum width	231	25.0	3.0
basal width	231	24.0	1.7
thickness	228	5.8	1.4
Swan Creek variety			
length	68	42.3	4.1
maximum width	68	26.0	3.3
basal width	69	24.4	3.6
thickness	69	6.0	1.2
Saginaw variety			
length	209	41.0	5.1
maximum width	214	20.8	3.2
basal width	214	19.7	3.4
thickness	215	5.6	1.0

ETLEY

N = 3 Etley points with expanding stems and recurvate blade margins from the Booth site in northeastern Missouri selected from Klippel (1969:60, Table 1):

	N = 1	N = 1	N = 1
length	148.0	149.0	151.0
width	37.0	38.5	32.5
thickness	11.5	10.4	14.7

Etley Barbed points from Missouri (C. Chapman 1975:246):

	range	average
length	130–250	175

N = 23 Etley Barbed points from the Koster site in Illinois (Cook 1976:137):

	N	mean	standard deviation
length	12	83.8	131.1
width	21	36.9	4.0
thickness	23	11.4	1.5

LEDBETTER STEMMED

Ledbetter Stemmed points from the Big Bottom site in Tennessee (Sims 1971:67):

	range	average
length	76–140	127
width	35–50	45
thickness		15

	mean
length	66.3
stem length	14.4
maximum blade width	31.5
stem width	19.1

PICKWICK

N = 7 Pickwick points from Tishomingo County, Mississippi (Thorne, Broyles, and Johnson 1981:221).

	range
length	ca. 64–106
blade width	22–40
shoulder width	39–55
stem width	17–20
stem length	11–13
thickness (mid-blade)	6–13
thickness (between shoulders)	9–12

SARATOGA BROAD BLADED

N = 5 Saratoga Broad Bladed/Oak Grove projectile points from southern Indiana:

	N	range	mean
length	3	73–93	82
shoulder width	5	31–40	33.4
thickness	5	8–13	10.6
stem length	5	23–26	23.8
stem width	5	19–26	23

Oak Grove I (variants a+b) projectile points from site CH 307 in Christian County, Kentucky (Schock et al. 1977:49, Tables 8–9):

Oak Grove I,a

	range	mean
length	82–97	88
shoulder width	31–32	31
thickness	9–10	9
stem length	11–16	14
stem width	20–22	21
Oak Grove I,b N = 2		
length	83	
shoulder width	34, 38	
thickness	10, 12	
stem length	16, 19	
stem width	22, 24	

SARATOGA PARALLEL STEMMED

Saratoga Parallel Stemmed points from the Big Muddy River Basin in southern Illinois (Denny 1972:144):

SARATOGA EXPANDING STEM

Saratoga Expanding Stemmed projectile points from the Big Muddy River Basin in southern Illinois (Denny 1972:144):

	mean
width at shoulder	31.66
width of stem at point of juncture with the blade	23.2

Oak Grove II (variants a+b) projectile points from site CH 307 Christian County, Kentucky (Schock 1977:50, Tables 10–11):

Oak Grove II,a

	range	mean
length		
width	28–33	30
thickness	11–19	
stem length	12–22	17
stem width at shoulder	18–21	19
Oak Grove II,b	N = 1	
length	64	
width	36	
thickness	11	
stem length	15	
stem width at shoulder	19	

GENESEE

N = 26 Genesee points from the Mixter site in Ohio (Shane 1975a:137):

	N	range	mean
length	10	34–64	51.3
blade length	10	27–52	39.8
width	25	22–37	31.0
haft width	26	12–23	18.8
thickness	26	6–11	8.9

See Ritchie (1961:24) for additional measurements.

SNOOK KILL

Specimens from New York (Ritchie 1971a:47):

	range	majority
length	50.8–111.8	57.15–88.90
thickness	6.35–14.29	23.88–11.11

SAVANNAH RIVER STEMMED

Savannah River points from the Doerschuk site in North Carolina (Coe 1964:44):

	range	average
length	70–170	100
width	35–70	50

N = 6 Savannah River points from Alabama (Cambron and Hulse 1969:104):

	range	average
length	50–70	56
shoulder width	30–40	34
stem width	21–25	22
stem length	12–14	13
thickness	10–13	11

SUSQUEHANNA BROAD

N = 16 Susquehanna Broad points from the McKibben site in Ohio (Prufer and Sofsky 1965:33):

	N	range	mean
length	8	33–47	43
width	12	18–34	25
thickness	12	5–9	7.3

For additional measurements of exceedingly large specimens see Witthoft (1953:7) and Ritchie (1961:53).

PERKIOMEN BROAD

N = 5 Perkiomen Broad points from the McKibben site in Ohio (Prufer and Sofsky 1965:33):

	N	range	mean
length	3	31–32	31
width	3	30–31	30.5
thickness	4	6–8	6.7

Note that very large specimens of the type have been reported by Witthoft (1953:17).

MEADOWOOD

Meadowood points from New York (Ritchie 1961:35):

	range	majority
length	41.28–88.9	57.15–69.85
thickness	rarely exceeds 4.76	

TURKEY-TAIL

Metrical attributes are not available for an adequate sample of each variety of Turkey-tail. However, a few caches of the Fulton type have been measured. Measurements from one cache of Fulton (fkrs) Turkey-tails, the Conrad cache, from Berrien County, Michigan (Green and Fitting 1964:83) is shown below:

	range	mean
length	107–145	111
width	40–55	47
thickness	7–10	8
haft width (notch width)	9–18	13

A maximum length of about 200 mm. (i.e., Fulton) is noted by Bell (1960:90). A Fulton Turkey-tail cache from Clements-Brown site in Orange County, Indiana included wide-bladed specimens with maximum thickness measurements of only 5 mm. Other measurements are available in Binford (1963a:179).

DELHI

N = 80 Delhi projectile points from the Poverty Point site in Louisiana (Ford and Webb 1956:60):

	range	average
length	43–90	50–75 (78%)
blade width	28–42	ca. 34; 30–40 (80%)
thickness	5–12	ca. 8
stem length		12.6
stem width		15.3

WADE

N = 14 Wade points from Alabama (Cambron and Hulse 1969:110):

	range	average
length	39–70	40
shoulder width	27–42	34
stem width	10–17	14
stem length	9–12	11
thickness	5–9	7

BUCK CREEK BARBED

N = 28 Buck Creek Barbed points from the Ohio Valley in Indiana (Seeman 1975:108):

	N	range	mean	standard deviation
maximum length	28	79–42	60	12
maximum width	19	41–25	33	5
maximum thickness	28	9–5	7	1
blade length	28	60–27	42	11
stem length	28	19–12	17	3
stem width (distal)	28	20–14	14	2
stem width (proximal)	28	21–14	17	2

Common non-metric attributes

N = 27	frequency
basal beveling	74%
lower stem beveling	96%
basal thinning	89%
lenticular cross section	74%
straight blade edge	89%
barbed shoulders	96%

KRAMER

N = 23 Kramer points from the American Bottoms in Illinois (Munson 1966a, 1971:7), Table 3):

	N	range	average
length	13	39–71	55
max. width	22	17–28	24
max. thickness	18	5–8	7
blade length	13	22–52	37
stem length	22	16–22	18
stem width	23	13–19	16

CRESAP STEMMED

N = 5 Cresap projectile points from the Cresap Mound in West Virginia (Dragoo 1963:109):

	range	average
length	62–107	84.5
width	23–27	25
thickness		8.8

ROBBINS

N = 12 Robbins points from the Cresap Mound in West Virginia (Dragoo 1963:113):

	range	average
length	57–100	78
width	29–55	36.8
thickness	6.5–10	7.8

GARY CONTRACTING STEMMED

N = 330 Gary (typical) points from the Poverty Point site in Louisiana (Ford and Webb 1956:52):

	range
length	46–80
width	20–45
thickness	9–10

N = 10 Gary Contracting Stemmed points from the Patoka River Valley in southern Indiana (Cook 1980:385):

	N	range	mean	standard deviation
length	3	–	59.7	11
width	7	–	30.0	4.7
thickness	10	–	9.2	2.1
stem length	–	15–25	–	–

DICKSON CONTRACTING STEMMED

Selected statistics on Dickson Contracting Stemmed points from the Snyders site in Illinois (Montet-White 1968:62, Table 13a):

	N	mean	standard deviation
length	13	70.5	2.3
maximum width	16	33.7	3.5
stem length	17	19.6	2.5
stem width	18	20.4	2.0
barbs	16	6.4	2.1

ADENA STEMMED

N = 37 Ovate-base, tapered-stemmed blades from the Cresap Mound in West Virginia (Dragoo 1963:111):

	range	average
length	34–150	76.5
width	17–43	28.1
thickness	7–17	9.6

LITTLE BEAR CREEK

N = 11 Little Bear Creek points from the Little Bear Creek site in Alabama (Cambron and Hulse 1969:67):

	range	average
length	64–90	75
shoulder width	22–28	24
stem width	15–17	16
stem length	16–20	18
thickness	7–11	9

CYPRESS STEMMED

N = 5 Cypress Stemmed points from southwestern Indiana:

	range	average
length	50–59	55
shoulder width	21–28	25
stem length	24–37	29
stem width	12–20	16
maximum thickness	7–8	7

MOTLEY

N = 224 Motley points from the Poverty Point site in Louisiana (Ford and Webb 1956:57):

	range	average
length	42–120	68
width	25–46	34
thickness	5–8	

SNYDERS

N = 27 Snyders points from Illinois; selected measurements from the Aldrich collection (Deuel 1952; Montet-White 1968:68):

	N	mean	standard deviation
length	13	69.1	11.1
width	25	54.5	4.7
stem width	27	21.4	1.9
basal width	21	27.8	1.9
stem length	21	15.5	1.6

N = 13 Snyders points (Manker) from the Manker site in Illinois; selected measurements (Montet-White 1968:68):

	N	mean	standard deviation
length	11	56.6	4.9
width	11	33.6	4.9
stem width	13	18.8	1.9
basal width	13	23.2	3.2
stem length	12	14.1	1.4

AFFINIS SNYDERS

Affinis Snyders points from the Big Muddy River Basin in Southern Illinois (Denny 1972:147):

	mean
length	47
width	35.2
stem length	17.4
stem width at base	29.7

COPENA

N = 19 Copena points from the Wright village in northern Alabama (Walthall 1973:77–78):

	N	range	mean
length	9	58–94	73
width	19	20–27	23
thickness	19	6–10	7

COPENA TRIANGULAR

N = 16 Copena Triangular points from the Wright Village in northern Alabama (Walthall 1973:78–79):

	N	range	mean
length	3	45–54	49
width	16	25–30	29
thickness	16	5–10	8

STEUBEN EXPANDED STEMMED

N = 15 Steuben Expanded Stemmed points from the Illinois Valley (Montet-White 1968:80):

	N	mean	standard deviation
length	12	50.9	13.5
maximum width	15	27.1	3.6
stem width	15	16.3	2.7

BAKERS CREEK

N = 11 Bakers Creek points from Alabama (Cambron and Hulse 1969:8):

length	43–78	55
width	23–28	26
thickness	7–10	8
stem length	12–18	16
stem width	21–27	23

LOWE FLARED BASE

N = 32 Lowe Flared Base projectile points from the Wabash Valley in Illinois (Winters 1967:91):

	N	range	standard deviation
length	9	30–77	42
maximum width	21	16–28	23
maximum thickness	10	5–8	7
blade length	9	17–63	29
stem length	30	11–18	14
stem width, top	32	13–20	16
stem width, base	24	18–26	21

CHESSER NOTCHED

N = 29 Chesser Notched points from Chesser Cave in southern Ohio (Prufer 1975a:21):

	N	range	mean
length	7	33–56	
width	27	17–30	23.20
thickness	28	3–8	5

N = 10 Chesser Notched points from Raven Rocks in Ohio (Prufer 1981:26):

	N	range	mean
length	5	41–70	54.6
width	7	18–27	23.5
thickness	7	7–11	8.8

JACK'S REEF PENTAGONAL

Jack's Reef Pentagonal points from New York state (Ritchie 1961:28):

	range	majority
length	25.4–44.45	31.75–38.1
thickness	4.76 maximum	

JACK'S REEF CORNER NOTCHED

Jack's Reef Corner Notched projectile points from New York state (Ritchie 1961:26):

	range	majority
length	25.4 –57.15	44.45–50.8
width	–	–
thickness	4.76– 6.35	4.76

N = 9 Jack's Reef Corner Notched points from Alabama (Cambron and Hulse 1969:69):

	range	average
length	30–60	42
shoulder width	15–24	18
stem width	13–20	16
stem length	6–9	8
thickness	3–5	4

RACCOON NOTCHED

N = 2 Raccoon Notched points from Chesser Cave in Ohio (Prufer 1975a:22):

length	27 (single specimen)
width	22
thickness	4

N = 1 Raccoon Notched point from the Libben site in Ottawa County, Ohio (Tallan 1977:16, Fig. 1j):

length	truncated
width	19.8
thickness	5.0

SCALLORN

Scallorn points from Texas (Suhm, Krieger, and Jelks 1954:506):

	range
length	25–45
width	15–20

SEQUOYAH

N = 61 Sequoyah points from the Spiro site in Oklahoma (Brown 1976:91–92). The measurements of four separate series of Sequoyah points from different caches have been combined:

	range
total length	23.0–52.3
blade length	16.7–24.5
blade width	10.0–14.7
basal width	4.9–12.1

Examples from Missouri and elsewhere tend to average shorter in maximum length with measures of 25 to 35 mm. (C. Chapman 1980:312).

MADISON

N = 15 Madison points from northern Alabama (Cambron and Hulse 1969:53):

	range	average
length	17–33	26
width	12–21	16
thickness	3–6	4

Madison points from New York state (Roper 1970:45, Table 6):

	mean
length	17.29
width	29.43
thickness	4.43

FORT ANCIENT

Fort Ancient points from the Feurt site in Ohio (Griffin 1943:71):

	range	average
length	40–50	58
thickness	4–7	5

Fort Ancient points (Bell 1960:40):

	range
length	31.75–50.8
width	12.7 or less

LEVANNA

N = 250 Levanna points from New York (Ritchie 1961:31):

	range	majority
length	22.23–76.2	31.75–44.45
thickness		4.76

HAMILTON INCURVATE

Hamilton Incurvate points from Hiwassee Island, Tennessee (Lewis and Kneberg 1946:110):

	range
length	35–45
thickness	rarely exceeds 3

Hamilton triangular (Incurvate) points from southwest Virginia (Holland 1970:87):

	range	average
length	24–35	29
width	12–23	19
thickness	3–6	4

NODENA ELLIPTICAL

N = 75 Nodena "Willow-leaf" points from the Campbell site in southwest Missouri (C. Chapman and Anderson 1955:15):

	range
length	25.4–82.55
width	9.52–25.4
thickness	3.18–6.35

Thickness is observed to be less than 2 mm. in certain samples (see C. Chapman 1980:310).

NODENA BANKS VARIETY

Banks variety Nodena points from the Banks Village site in Arkansas (Perino 1966a:35):

	range
length	16–51

N = 7 Guntersville (Nodena Banks variety) points from northern Alabama (Cambron and Hulse 1969:50):

	N	range	average
length		33–50	35
basal width		10–18	14
blade width	4	13–21	16
thickness		6–4	5

CAHOKIA

Cahokia points from the Cahokia site in Illinois (Perino 1971b:130):

	range
length	12.7–66.68

ALBA BARBED

N = 9 Alba points from the Spiro site in Oklahoma (Brown 1976:61):

	N	range	mean
total length	8	24.9–40	31.76
blade length	8	17.5–34	24.5
blade width	9	11–22.8	16.78
basal width	6	5–8.8	7.21

MORRIS

N = 78 Morris points from the Spiro site in Oklahoma (Brown 1976:96). The following combines the ranges of five separate samples of the type from Spiro:

	range
total length	19–36
blade length	14.8–33.9
blade width	9–15.6
basal width	8.3–14.4

References

Adair, Lou C.
1976 The Sims Site: Implication for Paleo-
indian Occupation. *American Antiquity*
41(3):325–334.

Adair, L., and E. J. Sims
1970 Rockport Variety, Harpeth River Point.
Tennessee Archaeologist 26(2):23–29.

Adams, Lee M.
1950 The Table Rock Basin in Barry County,
Missouri. *Missouri Archaeological Society, Memoir* No. 1.

Adovasio, J. M., J. D. Gunn, J. Donahue, and
R. Stuckenrath
1978 Meadowcroft Rockshelter, 1977: An Overview. *American Antiquity* 43(4):632.

Adovasio, J. M., J. D. Gunn, J. Donahue, R. Stuckenrath, J. E. Guilday, and K. Volman
1980 Yes Virginia, It Really Is that Old: A Reply
to Haynes and Mead. *American Antiq-
uity* 45(3):588–595.

Adovasio, J. M., et al.
1982 The Prehistory of the Paintsville Reservoir, Johnson and Morgan Counties, Kentucky. *Department of Anthropology,
University of Pittsburgh, Ethnology Monographs* No. 6.

An AENA Project
1982 A Compilation of Fluted Points of Eastern North America by Count and Distribution. *Archaeology of Eastern North
America* 10:27–45.

Agogino, George A.
1961 A New Point Type from Hell Gap Valley,
Eastern Wyoming. *American Antiquity*
26(4):558–560.
1969 The Midland Complex: Is It Valid? *American Anthropologist* 17(6):1117–1118.

Agogino, G. A. and W. D. Frankforter
1960 A Paleo-Indian Bison Kill Site in Northwestern Iowa. *American Antiquity* 25(3):
414–415.

Ahler, Stanley A.
1971 Projectile Point Form and Function at
Rodgers Shelter, Missouri. *Missouri Archaeological Society Research Series* 8.
1976 Sedimentary Processes at Rodgers Shelter. In *Prehistoric Man and His Environments: A Case Study in the Ozark High-*

land. Edited by W. Raymond Wood and
R. Bruce McMillan, pp. 123–140. Academic Press.

Ahler, Stanley A., and R. Bruce McMillan
1976 Material Culture at Rodgers Shelter: A Re-
flection of Past Human Activities. In *Prehistoric Man and His Environments.* Edited by W. Raymond Wood and R. Bruce
McMillan, pp. 163–200. Academic Press.

Ahler, Steven A., Jon Muller, and Joel Rabinowitz
1980 Archaeological testing for the Smithland
Pool, Illinois. *Southern Illinois University at Carbondale, Center for Archaeological Investigations Research Paper* 13.

Anderson, Duane C.
1980 Stone Tool Assemblages from the Cherokee Site. In *The Cherokee Excavations:
Holocene Ecology and Human Adaptations in Northwestern Iowa.* Edited by
Duane C. Anderson and Holmes A. Semken, Jr., pp. 197–238. Academic Press.
1981 *Eastern Iowa Prehistory.* Iowa State University Press. Ames, Iowa.

Anderson, Duane C., et al.
1980 The Cherokee Sewer Site and the Cul-
tures of the Atlantic Climatic Episode. In
*The Cherokee Excavations: Holocene
Ecology and Human Adaptations in
Northwestern Iowa.* Edited by Duane C.
Anderson and Holmes A. Semken, Jr.,
pp. 257–274. Academic Press.

Apfelstadt, Gary A.
1975 Comments on a Newly Established Projectile Point Type. *Central States Archaeological Journal* 22:164–66.

Arnold, J. R., and W. F. Libby
1951 Radiocarbon Dates. *Science* 113(2927):
111–120.

Bacon, Willard S.
n.d. Middle Woodland Projectile Point Types
from the Upper Duck Valley. Manuscript
in possession of the author.
1977 Projectile Point Typology: The Basic
Base. *Archaeology of Eastern North
America* 5:107–122.

Baerreis, David A.
1951 The Preceramic Horizons of Northeastern Oklahoma. *Museum of Anthro-*

pology, University of Michigan, Anthropological Papers No. 6.

1953 Blackhawk Village Site. *Journal of Iowa Archaeological Society* 2:5–20.

1954 The Huffaker Site, Delaware County, Oklahoma. *Bulletin of the Oklahoma Anthropological Society* 2:35–48.

Baerreis, David A., Hiroshi Daifuku, and James E. Lundsted

1957 The Burial Complex of the Reigh Site, Winnebago County, Wisconsin. *The Wisconsin Archeologist*, 38(4):244–277.

Baerreis, David A., and Joan E. Freeman

1959 A Report on a Bluff Shelter in Northeastern Oklahoma (DL–47). *Archives in Archaeology* 1.

Baerreis, David A., Joan E. Freeman, and James V. Wright

1958 The Contracting Stem Projectile Point in Eastern Oklahoma. *Bulletin of the Oklahoma Anthropological Society* 5:1–20.

Baker, Charles M.

1974 Preliminary Investigations at the Mill Creek Site, 3ST12, Stone County, Arkansas. *The Arkansas Archaeologist* 15:1–17.

Barbour, E. H., and C. Bertrand Schultz

1932 The Scottsbluff Bison Quarry and its Artifacts. *Nebraska State Museum Bulletin* 34, vol. 1.

Barth, Robert J.

1979 *Preliminary Report of Excavations at the Polecat Creek Site.* Paper presented at the 1979 Midwest Archaeological Conference. Milwaukee, Wisconsin.

Bassett, John L.

1981 Chert Deposits in the Blue River Group Limestones as Lithic Raw Material Sources. In *Archaeological Data Recovery at the Mary Ann Cole Site (12 Cr 1) Crawford County, Indiana: A Prehistoric Lithic Workshop at the Confluence of the Blue and Ohio Rivers.* Edited by Jeffery A. Myers, pp. 19–26.

Bebrich, Carl A.

1968 A Supplementary Report on the Lithic Artifacts from the Sheep Rock Shelter. In a Preliminary Report of Archaeological Investigations of the Sheep Rock Shelter Site, Huntington County, Pennsylvania. Edited by Joseph W. Michels and James S. Dutt, pp. 313–452. *Department of Anthropology, Pennsylvania State University Occasional Papers in Anthropology* No. 5.

Bebrich, Carl A., and Thomas Morgan III

1968 A Preliminary Report on the Lithic Artifacts from the Workman Site (36 Bd 36), Bedford County. In Archaeological Investigations of the Workman Site, Bedford County, Pennsylvania. Edited by Joseph W. Michels and John B. Huner.

Department of Anthropology, Pennsylvania State University, Occasional Papers in Anthropology No. 4, pp. 193–282.

Beeson, William J.

1952 *An Archaeological Survey of Seven Illinois Counties in the Embarras and Adjacent Wabash River Drainages.* M.A. thesis. University of Illinois, Urbana.

Behm, Jeffery A., and William Green

1982 Collections from the Copperas Creek Site (11F100): A Multicomponent Site in the Central Illinois Valley. *Rediscovery Journal of Archaeology* No. 2, pp. 31–66.

Bell, Robert E.

1958 Guide to the Identification of Certain American Indian Projectile Points. *Oklahoma Anthropological Society, Special Bulletin* No. 1.

1960 Guide to the Identification of Certain American Indian Projectile Points. *Oklahoma Anthropological Society, Special Bulletin* No. 2.

1972 The Harlan Site, Ck–6: A Prehistoric Mound Center in Cherokee County, Eastern Oklahoma. *Oklahoma Anthropological Society Memoir* No. 2.

Bell, Robert E., and Charlene Dale

1953 The Morris Site, CK–39, Cherokee County, Oklahoma. *Bulletin of the Texas Archaeological Society* 24:69–140.

Bell, Robert E., and R. S. Hall

1953 Selected Projectile Point Types of the United States. *Bulletin of the Oklahoma Anthropological Society* 1:1–16.

Bellis, James O.

1968 *An Appraisal of the Archaeological Resources of the Lafayette and Patoka Reservoirs and a Report of Test Excavations at Hr 11 in Harrison County, Indiana.* Prepared for the National Park Service. Glenn A. Black Laboratory of Archaeology, Indiana University.

1975 The Rouch Site: A Lithic Workshop Site in Marshall County, Indiana. *Indiana Archaeological Bulletin* 1(2):27–37. Indiana Historical Society.

1982 Test Excavation Conducted at the Breeden Site, 12 Hr 11, in Harrison County, Indiana. *Proceedings of the Indiana Academy of Science* Vol. 91:78–92.

Benedict, James B., and Byron L. Olson

1978 The Mount Albion Complex: A Study of Prehistoric Man and the Altithermal. *Center for Mountain Archaeology Research Report* No. 1. Ward, Colorado.

Benmouyal, Jose

1978 La Gaspesie. In Images de la prehistoire au Quebec. Edited by Claude Chapdelaine. *Recherches Amerindiennes au Quebec* 7(1–2):55–61.

Binford, Lewis R.

 1963a The Pomranky Site: A Late Archaic Burial
 Station in Miscellaneous Studies in Typology and Classification by Anta M.
 White, Lewis R. Binford, and Mark L. Papworth. *Museum of Anthropology, University of Michigan Anthropological
 Papers* No. 19, pp. 149–192.

 1963b The Hodges Site: A Late Archaic Burial
 Station. In Miscellaneous Studies in Typology and Classification by Anta M.
 White, Lewis R. Binford, and Mark L. Papworth. *Museum of Anthropology, University of Michigan Anthropological
 Papers* No. 19:124–148.

 1963c Red Ocher Caches from the Michigan
 Area: A Possible Case of Cultural Drift.
 Southwestern Journal of Anthropology
 19(1):89–108.

Binford, Lewis R., and Mark L. Papworth

 1963 The Eastport Site, Antrim County, Michigan. In Miscellaneous Studies in Typology and Classification by Anta M.
 White, Lewis R. Binford, and Mark L. Papworth. *Museum of Anthropology, University of Michigan Anthropological
 Papers* No. 19:71–123.

Black, Glenn A.

 1933 The Archaeology of Greene County. *Indiana History Bulletin* 10(5).

 1935 Excavation of a Blackford County Site. *Indiana History Bulletin* 12(5):148–152.

 1936 Excavation of the Nowlin Mound, Dearborn County Site 7 1934–35. *Indiana
 History Bulletin* 13(7).

 1967 *Angel Site: An Archaeological, Historical,
 and Ethnological Study* 1 & 2. Indiana
 Historical Society.

Boisvert, Richard A., Boyce N. Driskell, Kenneth
W. Robinson, Steven P. Smith, and L. F. Duffield

 1979 Materials Recovered. In *Excavations at
 Four Archaic Sites in the Lower Ohio Valley, Jefferson County, Kentucky* I. Edited
 by Michael B. Collins, pp. 60–418. Department of Anthropology, University of
 Kentucky.

Bolian, Charles E.

 1980 The Early and Middle Archaic of the
 Lakes Region, New Hampshire. In Early
 and Middle Archaic Cultures in the
 Northeast. Edited by David R. Starbuck
 and Charles E. Bolian. *Occasional Publications in Northeastern Anthropology*
 No. 7, pp. 115–134.

Bottoms, Edward

 1965 The Nansemond Point. *The Chesopiean*
 3(1).

Bourn, Richard Q., Jr.

 1977 The Hammonasset Beach Site (6NH36).
 *Bulletin of the Archaeological Society of
 Connecticut* No. 40:14–38.

Bowen, William R.

 1979 The Late Archaic in the Upper Duck
 River Valley. *Tennessee Anthropologist*
 4(2):140–159.

Bradham, James F.

 1963 The Simmons Mound, 23 Ce 104: A Rock
 and Earth Fill Mound in Cedar County,
 Missouri. *The Missouri Archaeologist*
 25:69–85.

Bradley, Bruce A.

 1974 Comments on the Lithic Technology of
 the Casper Site Materials. In *The Casper
 Site: A Hell Gap Bison Kill on the High
 Plains*. Edited by George C. Frison,
 pp. 191–197. Academic Press.

 1982 Flaked Stone Technology and Typology.
 In *The Agate Basin Site: A Record of the
 Paleoindian Occupation of the Northwestern High Plains*. By George C. Frison
 and Dennis J. Stanford, pp. 181–208. Academic Press.

Brain, Jeffrey P.

 1970 Early Archaic in the Lower Mississippi Alluvial Valley. *American Antiquity* 35(1):
 104–105.

Braun, David P., James B. Griffin, and Paul F.
Titterington

 1982 The Snyders Mounds and Five other
 Mound Groups in Calhoun County, Illinois. *Museum of Anthropology, University of Michigan Technical Reports* No. 13,
 Research Reports in Archaeology Contribution 8.

Bray, Robert T.

 1956 The Culture-Complexes and Sequence at
 the Rice Site (235N200) Stone County,
 Missouri. *Missouri Archaeologist* 18
 (1–2):47–134.

 1963 The Button Cairn, 23 HI 208, Hickory
 County, Missouri. *Missouri Archaeologist*
 25:41–54.

Brennan, Louis A.

 1967 The Taconic Tradition and the Coe Ax-
 iom. *New York State Archaeological Association Bulletin* 39:1–14.

 1975 *Artifacts of Prehistoric America*. Stack-
 pole Books. Harrisburg, Pennsylvania.

 1977 The Lower Hudson: The Archaic. In
 Amerinds and Their Paleo-environments
 in Northeastern North America. Edited
 by Walter S. Newman and Bert Salwen.
 *Annals of the New York Academy of Sci-
 ences* 288:411–430.

Brooks, Samuel O., Bruce J. Gray, Byron Inmon,
and Angela Rodrigue

 1975 Greenbrier Projectile Points: A Discus-
 sion of Form and Function. *Quarterly
 Bulletin of the Archaeological Society of
 Virginia* 30(2):97–100.

Brose, David S., and Nancy M. White

 1979 Archaeological Investigation of Prehistoric Occupation in Caesar Creek Lake: Clinton, Grune, and Warren Counties, Ohio. *Cleveland Museum of Natural History Archaeological Research Report.*

Brown, James A.
1968 *Artifacts from the Spiro Site.* Unpublished manuscript.
1971 *Spiro Studies Volume 3: Pottery Vessels.* First Part of the Third Annual Report of Caddoan Archaeology–Spiro Focus Research.
1976 *Spiro Studies Volume 4: The Artifacts.* Second Part of the Third Annual Report of Caddoan Archaeology–Spiro Focus Research.

Brown, Kenneth T., and Robert J. Ziegler
1981 Nebo Hill Settlement Patterns in Northwestern Missouri. *Missouri Archaeologist* 42:43–56.

Broyles, Bettye J.
1964 Mill Pond Site 46 Me 2. *West Virginia Archaeologist* 17:10–45.
1966 Preliminary Report: The St. Albans Site (46 Ka 27), Kanawha County, West Virginia. *West Virginia Archaeologist* 19:1–43.
1969 Distribution of Southeastern Archaic Projectile Points in the Ohio Valley. *Southeastern Archaeological Conference Bulletin* No. 11:31–36.
1971 Second Preliminary Report: The St. Albans Site, Kanawha County, West Virginia. *West Virginia Geological and Economic Survey Report Archaeological Investigation* 3.

Brunett, Fel V.
1966 An Archaeological Survey of the Manistee River Basin: Sharon to Sherman, Michigan. *Michigan Archaeologist* 12(4):169–182.

Bullen, Ripley P.
1968 *A Guide to the Identification of Florida Projectile Points.* Florida State Museum. University of Florida, Gainesville.
1975 *A Guide to the Identification of Florida Projectile Points.* Revised Edition. Kendall Books.
1976 Some thoughts on Florida Projectile Points. *Florida Anthropologist* 29(1):33–38.

Bullen, Ripley P., and James B. Stoltman, eds.
1972 Fiber-tempered Pottery in the Southeastern United States and Northern Columbia: Its Origins, Context, and Significance. *Florida Anthropologist* 25:1–72.

Butler, Brian M., Glen P. Harrell, and Mary C. Hamilton
1979 An Archaeological Reconnaissance of the Illinois Portions of the Ohio River. *Southern Illinois University at Carbon-*

dale *Center for Archaeological Investigations Research Paper* No. 5.

Byers, Douglas S.
1954 Bull Brook, A Fluted Point Site in Ipswich, Massachusetts. *American Antiquity* 19(4):343–351.
1966 The Debert Archaeological Project: The Position of Debert with respect to the Paleo-Indian Tradition. *Quaternaria* 8:33–47.

Caldwell, Joseph R.
1952 The Archeology of Eastern Georgia and South Carolina. In Archeology of the Eastern United States. Edited by James B. Griffin, pp. 312–321. University of Chicago Press.
1954 The Old Quartz Industry of Piedmont Georgia and South Carolina. *Southern Indian Studies* 6:37–39.

Calkin, Parker E., and Kathleen E. Miller
1977 Late Quaternary Environment and Man in Western New York. In Amerinds and Their Paleoenvironments in Northeastern North America. Edited by Walter S. Newman and Bert Salwen. *Annals of the New York Academy of Sciences* 288:297–315.

Callahan, Errett
1979 The Basic of Biface Knapping in the Eastern Fluted Point Tradition: A Manual for Flintknappers and Lithic Analysts. *Archaeology of Eastern North America* 7(1):1–179.

Cambron, James W.
1956 The Pine Tree Site: A Paleo-Indian Habitation Locality. *Tennessee Archaeologist* 12(2):1–10.
1957 Some Early Projectile Point Types from the Tennessee Valley. *Journal of Alabama Archaeology* 3(2):17–19.
1958a Some Early Projectile Point Types from the Tennessee Valley, Part II. *Journal of Alabama Archaeology* 4(1).
1958b Projectile Point Types, Part III. *Journal of Alabama Archaeology* 4(2):10–12.
1958c Paleo Points from the Pine Tree Site. *Tennessee Archaeologist* 14(2):80–84.
1959 Projectile Point Types from the Tennessee Valley, Part V. *Journal of Alabama Archaeology* 5(3):73–75.
1970 Harpeth River Point. *Tennessee Archaeologist* 26(1):15–18.
1974 Savage Cave Site. *Journal of Alabama Archaeology* 20(2):205–216.

Cambron, James W., and David C. Hulse
1960a An Excavation on the Quad Site. *Tennessee Archaeologist* 16(1):14–26.
1960b The Transitional Paleo-Indian in Northern Alabama and South Tennessee. *Journal of Alabama Archaeology* 6(1):7–33.
1969 *Handbook of Alabama Archaeology:*

Part I Point Types. Archaeological Research Association of Alabama.

1975   *Handbook of Alabama Archaeology: Part I Point Types.* Edited by David L. DeJarnette (Revised Edition). Archaeological Research Association of Alabama.

Cambron, James W., and Spencer A. Waters

1959   Flint Creek Rock Shelter (Part 1). *Tennessee Archaeologist* 15(2):73–88.

1961   Flint Creek Rock Shelter (Part II). *Journal of Alabama Archaeology* 7(1).

Campbell, Elizabeth W. C., and William H. Campbell

1935   The Pinto Basin Site. *Southwest Museum Papers* 9.

Cantwell, Anne-Marie

1980   Dickson Camp and Pond: Two Early Havana Tradition Sites in the Central Illinois Valley. *Illinois State Museum Reports of Investigations* No. 36.

Chapman, Carl H.

1948   A Preliminary Survey of Missouri Archaeology, Part IV. *Missouri Archaeologist* 10(4):135:164.

1956   A Resume of Table Rock Archaeological Investigations. *The Missouri Archaeologist* 18(1– 2):1–45.

1975   *The Archaeology of Missouri I.* University of Missouri Press, Columbia, Missouri.

1980   *The Archaeology of Missouri II.* University of Missouri Press, Columbia, Missouri.

Chapman, Carl H., and Leo O. Anderson

1955   The Campbell Site: A Late Mississippi Town Site and Cemetery in Southeast Missouri. *Missouri Archaeologist* 17(2–3).

Chapman, Jefferson

1973   The Icehouse Bottom Site 40 MR 23. *University of Tennessee Department of Anthropology Report of Investigations* No. 13.

1975   The Rose Island Site and the Bifurcate Point Tradition. *University of Tennessee Department of Anthropology Report of Investigations* No. 14.

1976   The Archaic Period in the Lower Little Tennessee River Valley: The Radiocarbon Dates. *Tennessee Anthropologist* I (1):1–12.

1977   Archaic Period Research in the Lower Little Tennessee River Valley. *University of Tennessee Department of Anthropology Report of Investigations* No. 18.

1985   Archaeology and the Archaic Period in the Southern Ridge-Valley Province. In *Structure and Process in Southeastern Archaeology.* Edited by Roy S. Dickens Jr. and H. Trawick Ward, pp. 137–153.

Claflin, William H., Jr.

1931   The Stallings Island Mound, Columbia County, Georgia. *Papers of the Peabody Museum of American Archaeology and Ethnology* 14(1). Cambridge.

Cleland, Charles E.

1965   Barren Ground Caribou (*Rangifer arcticus*) from an Early Man Site in Southeastern Michigan. *American Antiquity* 30(3):350–351.

Cleland, Charles E., and G. Richard Peske

1968   The Spider Cave Site. In the Prehistory of the Burnt Bluff Area. Edited by James E. Fitting. *Museum of Anthropology, University of Michigan Anthropological Papers* No. 34, pp. 20–60.

Cloud, R.

1969   Cache River Side-Notched Points. *Central States Archaeological Journal* 16(3).

Clouse, Robert A., John W. Richardson, and Edward V. McMichael

1971   Interim Report of the Daugherty-Monroe Site: An Allison-LaMotte Village. *Proceedings of the Indiana Academy of Science for 1970* 80:74–83.

Coe, Joffre L.

1952   The Cultural Sequence of the Carolina Piedmont. In *Archaeology of Eastern United States.* Edited by James B. Griffin. University of Chicago Press.

1959   *Prehistoric Cultural Change and Stability in the Carolina Piedmont Area.* Unpublished thesis, University of Michigan.

1964   The Formative Cultures of the Carolina Piedmont. *Transactions of the American Philosophical Society* 54 Part 5, Philadelphia.

Cole, Fay-Cooper

1951   *Kincaid, A Prehistoric Illinois Metropolis.* The University of Chicago Press, Chicago.

Cole, Fay-Cooper, and Thorne Deuel

1937   *Rediscovering Illinois: Archaeological Explorations in and around Fulton County.* The University of Chicago Press.

Collins, Michael B.

1979   The Longworth-Gick Site (15 Jf 243). In Excavations at Four Archaic Sites in the Lower Ohio Valley, Jefferson County, Kentucky (Vol. II). Edited by Michael B. Collins. *Department of Anthropology, University of Kentucky, Occasional Papers in Anthropology* 1:471–589.

Conrad, Lawrence A.

1981   An Introduction to the Archaeology of Upland West Central Illinois: A Preliminary Archaeological Survey of the Canton to Quincy Corridor for the Proposed FAP407 Highway Project. *Archaeological Research Laboratory Reports of Investigations* No. 2. Western Illinois University, Macomb, Illinois.

Converse, Robert N.

n.d.   *The Glacial Kame Indians.* A Special

Publication of the Archaeological Society of Ohio.

1971 Fractured Base Points. *Ohio Archaeologist* 21(3):9.

1973 *Ohio Flint Types*. Revised 6th Edition. Archaeological Society of Ohio.

1981 A Basal Notched Variety. *Ohio Archaeologist* 31(1):36.

Cook, Thomas Genn

n.d. *Middle Archaic at Koster: Provisional Point Typology*. Unpublished manuscript.

1976 Koster: An Artifact Analysis of Two Archaic Phases in West-central Illinois. *Northwestern University Archaeological Program, Prehistoric Records* 1.

1980 Typology and Description of Hafted Stone Tools. In Archaeological Salvage Excavations at Patoka Lake, Indiana: Prehistoric Occupations of the Upper Patoka River Valley. Edited by Cheryl A. Munson, pp. 349–454. *Glenn A. Black Laboratory of Archaeology Research Reports* No. 6.

Corbin, James

1974 A Model for Cultural Succession for the Coastal Bend Area of Texas. *Texas State Archaeological Society* 45.

Cotter, John L., and John M. Corbett

1951 Archaeology of the Bynum Mounds, Mississippi. *National Park Service Archaeological Research Series* No. 1 Washington, D.C.

Crabtree, Donald E.

1966 A Stoneworkers Approach to Analyzing and Replicating the Lindenmeier Folsom. *Tebiwa* 9(1).

1972 An Introduction of Flintworking. *Occasional Papers of the Idaho State University Museum* No. 28.

Crane, H. R.

1956 University of Michigan Radiocarbon Dates I. *Science* 124(3224):644–672.

Crane, H. R., and James B. Griffin

1960 University of Michigan Radiocarbon Dates V. *Radiocarbon* 2:31–48.

1963 University of Michigan Radiocarbon Dates VIII. *Radiocarbon* 5:228–253.

Cremin, William M.

1975a Grammer Rockshelter 24B3 59. In Archaeological Investigations in the Cedar Creek Reservoir. Jackson County, Illinois. Edited by Michael J. McNerney, pp. 27–58. *Southern Illinois Studies Research Records* No. 12.

1975b Hidden Wagon Rockshelter. In Archaeological Investigations in the Cedar Creek Reservoir, Jackson County, Illinois. Edited by Michael J. McNerney, pp. 75–92. *Southern Illinois Studies Research Records* No. 12.

1975c Throgmorton Dam, 24B3–110. In Archaeological Investigations in the Cedar Creek Reservoir, Jackson County, Illinois. Edited by Michael J. McNerney, pp. 203–242. *Southern Illinois Studies Research Records* No. 12.

Cross, Dorothy

1941 *The Archaeology of New Jersey*. The Archaeological Society of New Jersey and the New Jersey State Museum.

Davis, Dave D., ed.

1984 Perspectives on Gulf Coast Cultural History: A Round Table Discussion. In *Perspectives on Gulf Coast Prehistory*. Edited by Dave D. Davis, pp. 315–332. University Presses of Florida.

Davis, Hester A.

1967 Paleo-Indian in Arkansas. *The Arkansas Archaeologist* 8(1):1–3.

De Camp, Darwin

1967 The Clipped Wing Point. *Central States Archaeological Journal* 14(3):109–114.

DeJarnette, David L.

1952 Alabama Archaeology: A Summary. In *Archaeology of Eastern United States*. Edited by James B. Griffin, pp. 272–284. University of Chicago Press.

DeJarnette, David L., and Vernon J. Knight Jr.

1976 LaGrange. *Journal of Alabama Archaeology* 22(17):1–60.

DeJarnette, David L., Edward B. Kurjack, and James W. Cambron

1962 Excavations at the Stanfield-Worley Bluff Shelter. *Journal of Alabama Archaeology* 8(1–2):1–124.

DeJarnette, David L., John A. Walthall, and Steve B. Wimberly

1975 Archaeological Investigations in the Buttahatchee River Valley II: Excavations at Stucks Bluff Rock Shelter. *Journal of Alabama Archaeology* 21(2):99–119.

Deller, D. Brian

1979 Paleo-Indian Reconnaissance in the Counties of Lambton and Middlesex, Ontario. *Ontario Archaeology* 32:3–20.

1983 Crowfield AFHJ–31: A Paleo-Indian Ritual Feature in Southwestern Ontario. Paper Presented at the Forty-Eighth Annual Meeting of the Society for American Archaeology. Pittsburgh, Pennsylvania.

Denny, Sidney G.

1972 The Archaeology of the Big Muddy River Basin of Southern Illinois. Ph.D. Dissertation, Southern Illinois University, Department of Anthropology.

DePratter, Chester B.

1975 The Archaic in Georgia. *Early Georgia* 3(1):1–16.

Dick, Herbert W., and Bert Mountain

1960 The Claypool Site: A Cody Complex Site

in Northeastern Colorado. *American Antiquity* 26(2):223–235.

Dickson, Donald R.
1968   Two Provisional Projectile Point Types. *The Arkansas Amateur* 7(6):5–7.
1970   Excavations at Calf Creek Cave. *Bulletin of the Arkansas Archaeological Society* 11(3–4):50–82.

Didier, Mary E.
1967   A Distributional Study of the Turkey-Tail Point. *The Wisconsin Archeologist* 48: 3–73.

Dincauze, Dena F.
1968   Cremation Cemeteries in Eastern Massachusetts. *Papers of the Peabody Museum of Archaeology and Ethnology, Harvard University* 59(1). Cambridge.
1976   The Neville Site: 8,000 Years at Amoskeag, Manchester, New Hampshire. *Peabody Museum Monographs* 4.

Dorwin, John T.
1966   Fluted Points and Late Pleistocene Geochronology in Indiana. *Indiana Historical Society Prehistory Research Series* 4(3). Indianapolis.

Dragoo, Don W.
1959   Archaic Hunters of the Upper Ohio Valley. *Annals of the Carnegie Museum* 35:139–245. Pittsburgh.
1961   An Adena Burial Site in Delaware. *Eastern States Archaeological Federation* Bulletin 20:12. Trenton.
1963   Mounds for the Dead: An Analysis of the Adena Culture. *Annals of the Carnegie Museum* 37. Pittsburgh.
1973   Wells Creek—An Early Man Site in Stewart County, Tennessee. *Archaeology of Eastern North America* 1(1):1–55. Eastern States Archaeological Federation.
1976a Some Aspects of Eastern North American Prehistory: A Review 1975. *American Antiquity* 41(1):3–28.
1976b Adena and the Eastern Burial Cult. *Archaeology of Eastern North America* 4:1–8.

Driskell, Boyce, et al.
1979   Chapter II, Background. In Excavations at Four Archaic Sites in the Lower Ohio Valley, Jefferson County, Kentucky. Volume I. Edited by Michael B. Collins, pp. 7–32. *Occasional Papers in Anthropology* No. 1, Department of Anthropology, University of Kentucky.

Duffield, Lathel
1966   *The Robert Dudgeon Site: A Stratified Archaic Site in the Green River Reservoir, South Central Kentucky*. Report submitted to National Park Service. Manuscript. Museum of Anthropology, University of Kentucky, Lexington.

Dunn, Robert A.
1984   Form and Function of the Perkiomen Broadpoint. *Pennsylvania Archaeologist* 54(3–4):11–18.

Durham, J. H., and M. K. Davis
1975   Report on Burials Found at Crenshaw Mound ""C," Miller County, Arkansas. *Bulletin of the Oklahoma Anthropological Society* 23:1–90.

Edler, Robert
1970   Benton Points in Indiana. *The Redskin* 5(2):70–71.

Ellis, C. J., and D. Brian Deller
1982   Hi-Lo Materials from Southwestern Ontario. *Ontario Archaeology* No. 38:3–22.

Elsen, J. A.
1957   Lake Agassiz and the Mankato–Valders Problem. *Science* 126(3281):999–1002.

Emerson, Thomas E.
1983   The Early Woodland Florence Phase Occupation. In The Florence-Street Site (11–S–458), by Thomas E. Emerson, George R. Milner, and Douglas K. Jackson, pp. 19–175. *American Bottom Archaeology FAI–270 Site Reports* 2.
1984   The Dyroff and Levin Sites. *American Bottom Archaeology FAI–270 Site Reports* 9.

Essenpreis, Patricia S.
1978   Fort Ancient Settlement: Differential Response at a Mississippian/Late Woodland Interface. In *Mississippian Settlement Patterns*. Edited by Bruce D. Smith, pp. 141–165.

Fairbanks, Charles H.
1942   The Taxonomic Position of Stalling's Island, Georgia. *American Antiquity* 7(3): 223–231.

Faulkner, Charles H.
1960a Walkerton: A Point Peninsula-Like Focus in Indiana. *Indiana History Bulletin* 37(10).
1960b The Red Ochre Culture: An Early Burial Complex in Northern Indiana. *The Wisconsin Archeologist* n.s. 41(2):35–49.
1968   *Archaeological Investigations in the Tims Ford Reservoir, Tennessee 1966*. Department of Anthropology, University of Tennessee, Knoxville.
1969   Comments on the Copena Point and its Distribution. *Southeastern Archaeological Conference Bulletin* 9:53–55.
1970   *The Late Prehistoric Occupation of Northwestern Indiana: A Study of the Upper Mississippi Culture of the Kankakee Valley*. Ph.D. Dissertation, Indiana University.
1978   Ceramics of the Owl Hollow Phase in South-Central Tennessee: A Preliminary Report. *Tennessee Anthropologist* 3(2): 187–202.

Faulkner, Charles H., and J. B. Graham
    1966   *The Westmoreland-Barber Site (40 Mi 11), Nickajack Reservoir, Season II*. Department of Anthropology, University of Tennessee, Knoxville.

Faulkner, Charles H., and Major C. R. McCollough
    1973   Introductory Report of the Normandy Reservoir Salvage Project: Environmental Setting, Typology, and Survey. Normandy Archaeological Project Volume 1.*University of Tennessee, Department of Anthropology, Report of Investigations* No. 11.
    1974   Excavations and Testing, Normandy Reservoir Salvage Project: 1972 Seasons. Normandy Archaeological Project Volume 2. *University of Tennessee, Department of Anthropology, Report of Investigations* No. 12.

Ferguson, Eugene S.
    1977   The Mind's Eye: Nonverbal Thought in Technology. *Science* 197(4306):827–835.

Figgins, J. D.
    1934   Folsom and Yuma Artifacts. *Proceedings of the Colorado Museum of Natural History* 13(2).

Fitting, James E.
    1963a The Hi-Lo Site: A Late Paleo-Indian Site in Western Michigan. *The Wisconsin Archeologist* 44(2):87–96.
    1963b An Early Post Fluted Point Tradition in Michigan: A Distributional Analysis. *Michigan Archaeologist* 9(2):21–24.
    1963c The Welti Site: A Multicomponent Site in Southeastern Michigan. *Michigan Archaeologist* 9(3):34–40.
    1964   Bifurcate-Stemmed Projectile Points in the Eastern United States. *American Antiquity* 30(1):92–94.
    1965   Late Woodland Cultures of Southeastern Michigan. *Museum of Anthropology, University of Michigan Anthropological Papers* No. 24. Ann Arbor.
    1970   *The Archaeology of Michigan: A Guide to the Prehistory of the Great Lakes Region*. Natural History Press. The American Museum of Natural History. Garden City, New York.
    1972a Lithic Industries of the Schultz Site. In the Schultz Site at Green Point: A Stratified Occupation Area in the Saginaw Valley of Michigan. Edited by James E. Fitting. *University of Michigan, Museum of Anthropology Memoir* No. 4:191–224.
    1972b The Schultz Site in the Valley and Beyond. In the Schultz Site at Green Point: A Stratified Occupation Area in the Saginaw Valley of Michigan. Edited by James E. Fitting. *University of Michigan, Museum of Anthropology, Memoir*, No. 4:267–272.

Fitting, James E., ed.
    1972   The Schultz Site at Green Point: A Stratified Occupation Area in the Saginaw Valley of Michigan. *University of Michigan, Museum of Anthropology. Memoir* No. 4.

Fitting, James E., J. DeVisscher, and E. J. Wahla
    1966   The Paleo-Indian Occupation of the Holcombe Beach. *University of Michigan, Museum of Anthropology, Anthropological Papers* No. 27.

Fitting, James E., Stephen R. Claggett, and Stephen R. Treichler
    n.d.   Prehistoric Projectile Points of Michigan. Great Lakes Informant. *Michigan History Division Topics in History* Series 2, Number 5.

Fitzhugh, William
    1972   The Eastern Archaic: Commentary and Northern Perspective. *Pennsylvania Archaeologist* 42(4):1–19.

Flenniken, Jeffery F.
    1978   Reevaluation of the Lindenmeier Folsom: A Replication Experiment in Lithic Technology. *American Antiquity* 43(3):473–480.

Fogel, Ira T.
    1963   Dispersal of Copper Artifacts in the Late Archaic Period of North America. *The Wisconsin Archeologist* 44(3):129–179.

Ford, James A.
    1954a The Type Concept Revisited. *American Anthropologist* 56(1):42–54.
    1954b Spaulding's Review of Ford. *American Anthropologist* 56(1):109–111.
    1961   Menard Site: The Quapaw Village of Osotouy on the Arkansas River. *American Museum of Natural History, Anthropological Papers* 48, Pt. 2.

Ford, James A., Philip Phillips, and William G. Haag
    1955   The Jaketown Site in West Central Mississippi. *American Museum of Natural History Anthropological Papers* 45(1):1–136. New York.

Ford, James A., and Clarence Webb
    1956   Poverty Point, A Late Archaic Site in Louisiana. *American Museum of Natural History Anthropological Papers* 46(1):1–136.

Fortier, Andrew C.
    1984   The Go-Kart North Site (11–MO–552N). *American Bottom Archaeology FAI–270 Site Reports* Vol. 9.

Fortier, Andrew C., Fred A. Finney, and Richard B. Lacampagne
    1983   The Mund Site. *American Bottoms Archaeology FAI–270 Site Reports* Vol. 5.
    1984   The Fish Lake Site. *American Bottoms Archaeology FAI–270 Site Reports* Vol. 8.

Fowke, G.
    1928   Archaeological Investigations II. Aborigi-

nal Flint Quarries. *Bureau of American Ethnology Annual Report* 44:399–540.

Fowler, Melvin L.
1954   Some Fluted Projectile Points from Illinois. *American Antiquity* 20(2):170–171.
1957a   Ferry Site, Hardin County, Illinois. *Illinois State Museum Scientific Papers* 8(1).
1957b   Archaic Projectile Point Styles 7000 to 2000 B.C. in the Central Mississippi Valley. *Missouri Archaeologist* 19(1–2): 7–20.
1959a   Summary Report of Modoc Rock Shelter 1952, 1953, 1955, 1956. *Illinois State Museum Report of Investigations* No. 8:1–72.
1959b   Modoc Rock Shelter: An Early Archaic Site in Southern Illinois. *American Antiquity* 24(3):257–270.
1969   The Cahokia Site. In Explorations into Cahokia Archaeology. Edited by Melvin L. Fowler. *Illinois Archaeological Survey Bulletin* No. 7, pp. 1–30.
1973   The Cahokia Site. In Explorations into Cahokia Archaeology (Revised). Edited by Melvin L. Fowler, pp. 1–30. *Illinois Archaeological Survey Bulletin* No. 7.

Fowler, Melvin L., and Robert L. Hall
1975   Archaeological Phases at Cahokia. In Perspectives in Cahokia Archaeology. *Illinois Archaeological Survey Bulletin* No. 10:1–15.

Fowler, William S.
1954   Massachusetts Fluted Points. *Massachusetts Archaeological Society Bulletin* 16:2–8.
1968   A Case for an Early Archaic in New England. *Bulletin of the Massachusetts Archaeological Society* 29(3–4):53–58.

Freeman, J. E.
1969   The Millville Site: A Middle Woodland Village in Grant County, Wisconsin. *The Wisconsin Archeologist* n.s. 50(2).

Frison, George C.
1974   *The Casper Site: A Hell Gap Bison Kill on the High Plains*. Academic Press.
1976   The Chronology of Paleo-Indian and Altithermal Cultures in the Bighorn Basin, Wyoming. In *Cultural Change and Continuity: Essays in Honor of James Bennett Griffin*. Edited by Charles E. Cleland, pp. 147–174. Academic Press.
1978   *Prehistoric Hunters of the High Plains*. Academic Press.
1986   Human Artifacts, Mammoth Procurement, and Pleistocene Extinctions as Viewed from the Colby Site. In *The Colby Mammoth Site: Taphonomy and Archaeology of a Clovis Kill in Northern Wyoming*. By George C. Frison and Lawrence C. Todd, pp. 91–96. University of New Mexico Press.

Frison, George C., and Bruce A. Bradley
1980   *Folsom Tools and Technology at the Hanson Site, Wyoming*. University of New Mexico Press, Albuquerque.
1982   Fluting of Folsom Projectile Points. In *The Agate Basin Site: A Record of the Paleoindian Occupation of the Northwestern High Plains*. By George C. Frison and Dennis J. Stanford, pp. 209–212. Academic Press.

Frison, George C., and Dennis J. Stanford
1982   *The Agate Basin Site: A Record of the Paleoindian Occupation on the Northwestern High Plains*. Academic Press.

Funk, Robert E.
1965   The Archaic of the Hudson Valley—New Evidence and New Interpretations. *Pennsylvania Archaeologist* 35(3–4): 139–160.
1977a   Early to Middle Archaic Occupations in Upstate New York. In Current Perspectives in Northeastern Archeology: Essays in Honor of William A. Ritchie. Edited by Robert E. Funk and Charles F. Hayes III, *Researches and transactions of the New York State Archaeological Association* 17(1):21–29.
1977b   Early Cultures in the Hudson Drainage Basin. In Amerinds and their Paleoenvironments in Northeastern North America. Edited by Walter S. Newman and Bert Salwen. *Annals of the New York Academy of Sciences* 288:316–332.

Funk, Robert E., and Bruce E. Rippeteau
1977   Adaptation, Continuity, and Change in Upper Susquehanna Prehistory. *Occasional Publications in Northeastern Anthropology* No. 3.

Funk, Robert E., B. E. Rippeteau, and R. M. Houck
1973   A Preliminary Framework for the Upper Susquehanna Valley. *New York State Archaeological Association Bulletin* 57: 11–27.

Funk, Robert E., and Frank F. Schambach
1964   Probable Plano Points in New York State. *Pennsylvania Archaeologist* 34(2): 90–93.

Funk, Robert E., George R. Walters, and William F. Ehlers, Jr.
1969   The Archaeology of Dutchess Quarry Cave, Orange County, New York. *Pennsylvania Archaeologist* 39(1–4):7–22.

Gagliano, Sherwood M.
1967   *Occupation Sequence at Avery Island*. Louisiana State University Press.

Gagliano, Sherwood M., and Hiram F. Gregory Jr.
1965   A Preliminary Survey of the Paleo-Indian Points from Louisiana. *Louisiana Studies* 4(1):71.

Galm, Jerry R., and Jack L. Hofman
1984   The Billy Ross Site: Analysis of a Dalton

Component from the Southern Arkansas Basin of Eastern Oklahoma. *Bulletin of the Oklahoma Anthropological Society* 33:37–74.

Gardner, William M., ed.
1974 The Flint Run Paleo-Indian Complex: A Preliminary Report 1971–73 Seasons. *Occasional Publication* No. 1. Archaeology Laboratory, Department of Anthropology, Catholic University of America.

Geistweit, Barbara Ann
1970 Archaic Manifestations in Ohio and the Ohio Valley, M.A. Thesis, Ohio State University.

George, Richard L.
1982 Blawnox: An Upper Ohio Valley Middle Woodland Site. *Annals of Carnegie Museum* 51(10):181–209. Carnegie Museum of Natural History.

Goodyear, Albert C.
1974 The Brand Site: A Techno-Functional Study of a Dalton Site in Northeast Arkansas. *Arkansas Archaeological Survey Research Series* No. 7.
1982 The Chronological Position of the Dalton Horizon in the Southeastern United States. *American Antiquity* 47(2):382–395.

Goodyear, Albert C., S. B. Upchurch, M. J. Brooks, and N. N. Goodyear
1983 Paleo-Indian Manifestations in the Tampa Bay Region, Florida. *Florida Anthropologist* 36(1):40–66.

Graham, Russell W., C. Vance Haynes, Donald L. Johnson, and Marvin Kay
1981 Kimmswick: A Clovis-Mastodon Association in Eastern Missouri. *Science* 213(4512):1115–1116.

Gramly, Richard M., and Kerry Rutledge
1981 A New Paleo-Indian site in the State of Maine. *American Antiquity* 46(2):354–360.

Granger, Joseph
1981 The Steward Site Cache and a Study of the Meadowood Phase "Cache Blade" in the Northeast. *Archaeology of Eastern North America* 9:63–102.

Graybill, Jeffery R.
1979 A Preliminary Report on Recent Archaeological Excavations in Mason County, West Virginia. *West Virginia Archaeologist* 28:1–23.

Green, Amos R., and James E. Fitting
1964 A Turkey Tail Cache from Southwestern Michigan. *Michigan Archaeologist* 10(4):83–88.

Green, Thomas J., and Cheryl A. Munson
1978 Mississippian Settlement Pattern in Southwestern Indiana. In *Mississippian Settlement Patterns*. Edited by Bruce D. Smith, pp. 293–325. Academic Press.

Greengo, Robert E.
1964 Issaquena: An Archaeological Phase in the Yazoo Basin of the Lower Mississippi Valley. *Society for American Archaeology Memoir* No. 18.

Greenman, Emerson F.
1966 Chronology of Sites at Killarney, Canada. *American Antiquity* 31(4):540–551.

Greenwell, Dale
1984 The Mississippi Gulf Coast. In *Perspectives on Gulf Coast Prehistory*. Edited by Dave D. Davis, pp. 125–155. University Presses of Florida.

Griffin, James B.
1941 Additional Hopewell Material from Illinois. *Indiana Historical Society, Prehistory Research Series* 2(3).
1943 *The Fort Ancient Aspect: Its Cultural and Chronological Position in Mississippi Valley Archaeology*. University of Michigan Press, Ann Arbor.
1964 The Northeastern Woodland Area. In *Prehistoric Man in the New World*. Edited by Jesse D. Jennings and Edward Norbeck, pp. 223–258. University of Chicago Press.
1965 Hopewell and the Dark Black Glass. *Michigan Archaeologist* 11(3–4):115–155.
1967 Eastern North American Archaeology: A Summary. *Science* 156(3772):175–191.

Griffin, James B., ed.
1952 *Archeology of Eastern United States*. The University of Chicago Press.

Griffin, James B., and Albert C. Spaulding
1951 The Central Mississippi Valley Archaeological Survey, Season 1950: A Preliminary Report. *Journal of Illinois State Archaeological Society* 1:74–82.

Griffin, James B., Richard E. Flanders, and Paul F. Titterington
1970 The Knight Mound Group Calhoun County, Illinois. In the Burial Complexes of the Knight and Norton Mounds in Illinois and Michigan. *University of Michigan, Museum of Anthropology Memoir* No. 2:11–124.

Griffin, John W.
1974 Investigations in Russell Cave. Russell Cave National Monument, Alabama. *National Park Service Publications in Archaeology* No. 13.

Guendling, Randall L., and Kevin J. Crouch
1977 *Lafayette Lake Archaeological Reconnaissance: A Preliminary Assessment of Prehistoric Cultural Resources*. Glenn A. Black Laboratory of Archaeology. Indiana University.

Guernsey, E. F.
1939 Relationship Among Various Clark County Sites. *Proceedings of the Indiana Academy of Science* 48:27–32.

1942 The Culture Sequence of the Ohio Falls Sites. *Proceedings of the Indiana Academy of Science* 51:60–67.

Guilday, John E.
1969 Faunal Remains from Dutchess Quarry Cave No. 1. In the Archaeology of Dutchess Quarry Cave, Orange County, New York. By Robert E. Funk, George R. Walters, and William F. Ehlers. *Pennsylvania Archaeologist* 39(1–4):17–19.

Gustafson, John H., and William T. Pigott
1981 A Tale of Two Sites or Big Sandy Begins to Speak. *Journal of Alabama Archaeology* 27(2):73–116.

Guthe, Alfred K.
1958 The Morrow Site. *Eastern States Archaeological Federation Bulletin* No. 17.
1964 Editor's Notes. *Tennessee Archaeologist* 20(2):82.

Haag, William G.
1942 The Pottery From the C. and O. Mounds at Paintsville. *University of Kentucky, Reports in Anthropology and Archaeology* 5(4):341–349.

Hall, Robert L.
1975 Chronology and Phases at Cahokia. In Perspectives in Cahokia Archaeology, pp. 15–31. *Illinois Archaeological Survey Bulletin* 10.

Harrison, Sidney
1966 The Schmidt Site (20 SA 192), Saginaw County, Michigan. *Michigan Archaeologist* 12(2):49–70.

Hartney, Patrick C.
1962 Peter Cave, Tennessee. *Tennessee Archaeologist* 18(1):23–45.

Harwood, C. R.
1958 The Ecusta Point. *Tennessee Archaeologist* 14(1).

Hayden, Brian, ed.
1979 *Lithic Use-Wear Analysis*. Academic Press.

Haynes, C. Vance, Jr.
1964 Fluted Projectile Points: Their Age and Dispersion. *Science* 145(3639): 1408–1413.

Hazeltine, Dan
1983 A Late Paleo-Indian Site, Cape Haze Peninsula Charlotte County, Florida. *Florida Anthropologist* 36(1–2).

Helman, Vernon R.
1952 *Archaeological Survey of Vigo County*. Indiana Historical Bureau, Indianapolis.

Hemmings, Thomas E.
1972 Early Man in the South Atlantic States. *South Carolina Antiquities* 4(2):98–106.
1978 Exploration of an Early Adena Mound at Willow Island, West Virginia. *West Virginia Geological and Economic Survey, Report of Archeological Investigations* 7.
1982 Human Adaptations in the Grand Marais

Lowland: Intensive Archaeological Survey and Testing in the Felsenthal Navigation Pool, Ouachita and Saline Rivers, Southern Arkansas, *Arkansas Archaeological Survey Research Series* No. 17.

Hester, Thomas R.
1977 The Current Status of Paleoindian Studies in Southern Texas and Northeastern Mexico. In Paleoindian Lifeways. Edited by Eileen Johnson. *The Museum Journal* 17:169–186.

Hoffman, Michael P.
1975–77 The Kinkead-Mainard Site 3PU2: A Late Prehistoric Quapaw Phase Site near Little Rock, Arkansas. *The Arkansas Archaeologist* 16–18:1–41.
1977 An Archaeological Survey of the Ozark Reservoir in West-Central Arkansas. Ozark Reservoir Papers: Archaeology in West-Central Arkansas. *Arkansas Archaeological Survey Publications on Archaeology Research Series*, No. 10.

Hofman, Jack L.
1980 Twenhafel Archaeology: The Southeastern Connection. *Tennessee Anthropologist* 5(2):185–201.

Holland, C. G.
1955 An Analysis of Projectile Points and Large Blades. In Appendix 2 of a Ceramic Study of Virginia Archaeology. By Clifford Evans. *Bureau of American Ethnology Bulletin* 160:165–191.
1960 Preceramic and Ceramic Cultural Patterns in Northwest Virginia. *Bureau of American Ethnology, Anthropological Papers*, No. 57, Bulletin 173.
1970 An Archaeological Survey of Southwest Virginia. *Smithsonian Contributions to Anthropology* No. 12.

Holland, Warren
1971 Dalton Type Cache Found. *Central States Archaeological Journal* 18(1):23–29.

Houart, Gail T.
1971 Koster: A Stratified Archaic Site in the Illinois Valley. *Illinois State Museum Report of Investigations* 22.

Hughes, Jack T.
1949 Investigations in Western South Dakota and Northeastern Wyoming. *American Antiquity* 14(4):266–277.

Hurley, William M.
1965 Archaeological Research in the Projected Kickapoo Reservoir, Vernon County, Wisconsin. *The Wisconsin Archaeologist* 46(1):1–113.

Ingmanson, John E., and John W. Griffin
1974 Material Culture, In Investigations in Russell Cave. Edited by John W. Griffin, pp. 29–62. *National Park Service Publications in Archaeology* 13.

Irwin, Henry T., and Marie Wormington
    1970   Paleo-Indian Tool Types in the Great Plains. *American Antiquity* 35(1):24–34.

Irwin-Williams, Cynthia, Henry Irwin, George Agogino, and C. Vance Haynes, Jr.
    1973   Hell Gap: Paleo-Indian Occupation on the High Plains. *Plains Anthropologist* 18(59):40–53.

Ison, Cecil R.
    1982a The Problem of Small Triangular Points as Cultural- Temporal Indicators, *Kentucky Archaeology Newsletter* 2(3):1–5.
    1982b Chronological Placement of Site 15 CK 126, *Kentucky Archaeology Newsletter* 2(1):5–6.

Janzen, Donald E.
    1971   Excavations at the Falls of the Ohio River Region. *Filson Club Quarterly* 45(4):373–380.
    1977   An Examination of Late Archaic Development in the Falls of the Ohio River Area. In For the Director: Research Essays in Honor of James B. Griffin. Edited by Charles E. Cleland. *Museum of Anthropology, University of Michigan, Anthropological Papers* No. 61:123–143.

Jefferies, Richard W.
    1976   The Tunacunnhee Site: Evidence of Hopewell Interaction in Northwest Georgia, *Anthropological Papers of the University of Georgia* No. 1.

Jelks, Edward B.
    1962   The Kyle Site, A Stratified Central Texas Aspect Site in Hill County, Texas. *Department of Anthropology, University of Texas, Archaeological Series* 5.

Jenks, Albert E.
    1937   Minnesota's Browns Valley Man and Associated Burial Artifacts. *American Anthropological Association Memoir* No. 40.

Jennings, Jesse D.
    1955   *The Archeology of the Plains: An Assessment*. Department of Anthropology, University of Utah, and the National Park Service.
    1974   *Prehistory of North America*. Second Edition. McGraw-Hill.

Jensen, Richard E.
    1970   Archeological Survey of the Rowlesburg Reservoir Area, West Virginia. *West Virginia Geological and Economic Survey, Report of Archeological Investigations* No. 2.

Johnson, Alfred E.
    1979   Kansas City Hopewell. In *Hopewell Archaeology: The Chillicothe Conference*. Edited by David S. Brose and N'omi Greber, pp.86–93.

Johnson, Eileen, Vance T. Holliday, and Raymond W. Neck
    1982   Lake Theo: Late Quaternary Paleo-environmental Data and New Plainview (Paleoindian) Data. *North American Archaeologist* 3(2):113–138.

Johnson, LeRoy, Jr.
    1964   The Devil's Mouth Site: A Stratified Campsite at Amistad Reservoir, Val Verde County, Texas. *University of Texas, Department of Anthropology, Archaeology Series* No. 6.

Johnson, W. C.
    1982   Chesser Notched Points. In the Prehistory of the Paintsville Reservoir, Johnson and Morgan Counties, Kentucky. By J. M. Adovasio et al. *Department of Anthropology, University of Pittsburgh, Ethnology Monographs* No. 6., pp. 613–614.

Jolley, Robert L.
    1979   Archaeological Reconnaissance in the Headwaters of the Caney Fork River in Middle Tennessee. *Tennessee Anthropologist* 4(1):32–62.

Jolly, Fletcher III
    1974   Notes on the Searcy Projectile Point Horizon at Renaud Cave (23 PH 16), Missouri. *Central States Archaeological Journal* 21(4):173–179.

Jolly, Fletcher III, and Ralph G. Roberts
    1974   Projectile Point Sequence at the Williams Shelter (23 Ph 34) in the South Central Ozarks of Missouri. *Central States Archaeological Journal* 21(2):59–78.

Judge, William J.
    1970   Systems Analysis and the Folsom-Midland Question, *Southwestern Journal of Anthropology* 26:40–51.
    1973   *Paleoindian Occupation of the Central Rio Grande Valley in New Mexico*. University of New Mexico Press.

Justice, Noel D.
    n.d.   The Paleo-Indian Occupation of Northeastern Indiana. Unpublished manuscript.
    1981a Quality Selection Factors in the Wyandotte chert Litho-facies. In *Archaeological Data Recovery at the Mary Ann Cole Site (12 Cr 1), Crawford County, Indiana: A Prehistoric Lithic Workshop at the Confluence of the Blue and Ohio Rivers*. Edited by Jeffery A. Myers, pp. 26–38. Prepared for the U.S. Army Corps of Engineers. Resource Analysts, Inc. Bloomington, Indiana.
    1981b Technological Analysis of the Lithic Materials. In *Archaeological Data Recovery at the Mary Ann Cole Site (12 Cr 1), Crawford County, Indiana: A Prehistoric Lithic Workshop at the Confluence of the Blue and Ohio Rivers*. Edited by Jeffery A. Myers, pp. 106–154. Prepared for the U.S. Army Corps of Engineers. Resource Analysts, Inc. Bloomington, Indiana.

Keel, Bennie C.
1972 Woodland Phases of the Appalachian Summit Area, Ph.D. Dissertation, Washington State University, University Microfilms.
1976 *Cherokee Archaeology: A Study of the Appalachian Summit*. University of Tennessee Press. Knoxville.

Keeley, Lawrence H.
1974 Technique and Methodology in Microwear Studies: A Critical Review. *World Archaeology* 5(2):323–336.

Kellar, James H.
1967 Material Remains. In *Angel Site: An Archaeological, Historical, Ethnological Study* by Glenn A. Black. II part 3, pp. 431–483. Indiana Historical Society.
1973 *An Introduction to the Prehistory of Indiana*. Indiana Historical Society.
1979 The Mann Site and Hopewell in the Lower Wabash–Ohio Valley. In *Hopewell Archaeology*. Edited by David S. Brose and N'omi Greber, pp. 100–107. Kent State University Press.

Kelley, J. Charles
1947 The Lehmann Rock Shelter: A Stratified Site of the Toyah, Uvalde, and Round Rock Foci. *Bulletin of the Texas Archaeological and Paleontological Society* 18:115–128.

Kelly, E. C.
1928 *Implement Making of the Indians*. Los Angeles.

Kenyon, Ian T.
1980a The George Davidson Site: An Archaic "Broadpoint" Component in Southwestern Ontario. *Archaeology of Eastern North America* 8:11–27.
1980b The Satchell Complex in Ontario: A Perspective from the Ausable Valley. *Ontario Archaeology* 34:17–44.

Kinsey, W. Fred, III
1959 Recent Excavations on Bare Island in Pennsylvania: The Kent-Hally Site. *Pennsylvania Archaeologist* 29(3–4):109–133.
1972 Archaeology in the Upper Delaware Valley. *Pennsylvania Historical and Museum Commission, Anthropological Series* No. 2, Harrisburg.

Kline, Gerald W., and Gary A. Apfelstadt
1975 Notes on the Lowe Flared Base Projectile Point. *Proceedings of the Indiana Academy of Science* 84. Indianapolis.

Kline, Gerald, Gary D. Crites, and Charles H. Faulkner
1982 The McFarland Project: Early Middle Woodland Settlement and Subsistence in the Upper Duck River Valley in Tennessee. *Tennessee Anthropological Association Miscellaneous Paper* No. 8.

Klippel, Walter E.
1969 The Booth Site: A Late Archaic Campsite. *Missouri Archaeological Society Research Series* No. 6.
1971 Graham Cave Revisited: A Reevaluation of its Cultural Position During the Archaic Period. *Missouri Archaeological Society Memoir* No. 9.

Kneberg, Madeline
1956 Some Important Projectile Point Types Found in the Tennessee Area. *Tennessee Archaeologist* 12(1):17–28.
1957 Chipped Stone Artifacts of the Tennessee Valley Area. *Tennessee Archaeologist* 13(1):55–66, Knoxville.

Kopper, J. S., Robert E. Funk, and Lewis Dumont
1980 Additional Paleo-Indian and Archaic Materials from the Dutchess Quarry Cave Area, Orange County, New York. *Archaeology of Eastern North America*. 8:125–137.

Kraft, Herbert C.
1970 The Miller Field Site in New Jersey. *New York State Archaeological Association Bulletin* 48:1–13.
1973 The Plenge Site: A Paleo-Indian Occupation Site in New Jersey. *Archaeology of Eastern North America* 1(1):56–117, Eastern States Archaeological Federation.
1975 *Archaeology of the Tocks Island Area*. Seton Hall University Press, South Orange.
1976 The Rosenkrans Site: An Adena-Related Mortuary Complex in the Upper Delaware Valley, New Jersey. *Archaeology of Eastern North America* 4:9–50.
1977 Paleoindians in New Jersey. In *Amerinds and their Paleoenvironments in Northeastern North America*. Edited by Walter S. Newman and Bert Salwen. *Annals of the New York Academy of Science*, 288:264–281.

Kramer, Leon G.
1947 Prehistoric Ohio Flint. *Journal of the Illinois State Archaeological Society* 5(2):32–51.
1951 Ohio Ceremonial Spears. *Ohio Archaeologist* 1(3):7–16.

Krieger, Alex D.
1944 The Typological Concept. *American Antiquity* 9(3):271–288.
1946 Culture Complexes and Chronology in Northern Texas. *University of Texas Publication* No. 4640.
1947 Certain Projectile Points of the Early American Hunters. *Bulletin of the Texas Archaeological and Paleontological Society* 18:7–27.

Kroeber, T.
1961 *Ishi in Two Worlds*. University of California Press. Berkeley.

Lavin, Lucianne
1984 Connecticut Prehistory: A Synthesis of
Current Archaeological Investigations.
*Archaeological Society of Connecticut
Bulletin* 47:5–40.
Lavin, Lucianne, and Bert Salwen
1983 The Fastener Site: A New Look at the
Archaic-Woodland Transition in the
Lower Housatonic Valley. *The Archaeological Society of Connecticut Bulletin*
46:15–44.
Lee, Sammy T., and A. Robert Parker
1972 A Preliminary Report on the Excavations
at the Cal Smoak Site. *South Carolina
Antiquities* 4(2):107–110.
Leslie, Vernon
1963 A Typology of Arrowpoints Found in
Wayne County, Pennsylvania, and Sul-
livan County, New York. *New World Antiquity* 10:70–90.
1967 The Lackawaxen Stemmed Point. *The
Chesopiean* 5(4):111–114.
Lewis, R. Berry
1975 The Hood Site: A Late Woodland Hamlet
in the Sangamon Valley of Central Illinois. *Illinois State Museum Reports of
Investigations* No. 31.
Lewis, Thomas M. N.
1954 The Cumberland Point. *Bulletin of the
Oklahoma Anthropological Society*
11:7–8.
1955 The Hamilton and Eva Point Types of
Tennessee. *Bulletin of the Oklahoma
Anthropological Society* Vol. 3. Norman.
1960 Editor's Notes: The Guinn Collection.
Tennessee Archaeologist 16(1):54–61.
Lewis, Thomas M. N., and Madeline Kneberg
1946 *Hiwassee Island: An Archaeological Account of Four Tennessee Indian Peoples.*
University of Tennessee Press. Knoxville.
1947 The Archaic Horizon in Western Tennessee. *Tennessee Anthropology Papers*
No. 2. Knoxville.
1955 The A. L. LeCroy Collection. *Tennessee
Archaeologist* 11(2):75–82.
1957 The Camp Creek Site. *Tennessee Archaeologist* 8(1):1–48.
1958 The Nuckolls Site. *Tennessee Archaeologist* 14(2):60–79.
1959 The Archaic Culture in the Middle South.
American Antiquity 25(2):161–183.
1960 Editor's Notes, Aaron B. Clement Collection. *Tennessee Archaeologist* 16(1):
49–61.
Lewis, Thomas M. N., and Madeline Kneberg
Lewis
1961 *Eva: An Archaic Site.* University of Tennessee Press, Knoxville.
Libby, Willard F.
1952 *Radiocarbon Dating.* The University of
Chicago Press.

1954 Chicago Radiocarbon Dates V. *Science*
120(3123):733–742.
Lilly, Eli
1942 A Cedar Point ""Glacial Kame" Burial.
*Proceedings of the Indiana Academy of
Science* 51:31–34.
Little, Robert M.
1970 The McKinley Site. Masters Thesis. Indiana University, Bloomington, Indiana.
Logan, Wilfred D.
1952 Graham Cave: An Archaic Site in Montgomery County, Missouri. *Missouri Archaeological Society Memoir* No. 2.
Long, A. G., Jr., and Dan Josselyn
1965 The Eva Family. *Journal of Alabama Archaeology* 11(2):43–45.
Long, Russell J.
1962 The Raisch-Smith Site near Oxford,
Ohio. *Ohio Archaeologist* 12(3–4):
58–68.
Luchterhand, Kubet
1970 Early Archaic Projectile Points, and Hunting Patterns in the Lower Illinois Valley.
*Illinois State Museum Report of Inves-
tigations* No. 19.
MacDonald, George F.
1968 Debert: A Palaeo-Indian Site in Central
Nova Scotia. National Museums of Canada. *Anthropology Papers* No. 16.
MacLean, J. Arthur
1931 Excavations of Albee Mound 1926–27.
Indiana History Bulletin 8(4).
MacNeish, Richard S.
1948 The Pre-pottery Faulkner Site of Southern Illinois. *American Antiquity* 13(3):
232–243.
1952 A Possible Early Site in Ontario. *National Museum of Canada Bulletin* No.
126:23–47. Ottawa.
Mahan, E. C.
1956 A Survey of Paleo-American and other
Early Flint Artifacts from Alabama, Part IV.
Tennessee Archaeologist 12(1):12–14.
Manley, Frank
1967 Randolph Points Redivivus. *Journal of
Alabama Archaeology* 13(2):94–98.
Manson, Carl
1948 Marcey Creek Site: An Early Manifestation in the Potomac Valley. *American Antiquity* 13(3)223–226.
Marois, Roger J. M.
1975 L'Archeologie des Provinces de Quebec
et d'Ontario. *National Museum of Man
Mercury Series. Archaeological Survey of
Canada Paper* No. 44.
Marshall, Richard A.
1958 The Use of Table Rock Reservoir Projectile Points in the Delineation of Cultural Complexes and their Distribution.
M.A. Thesis. University of Missouri. (Re-

vised as a Report to the National Park Service 1960.)

1966   *Prehistoric Indians at Meramec Spring Park: A Sketch of the Prehistory of the Meramec Spring–St. James, Missouri Area.* Edited by Carl H. Chapman.

Mason, Ronald J.

1958   Late Pleistocene Geochronology and the Paleo-Indian Penetration into the Lower Michigan Peninsula. *Museum of Anthropology, University of Michigan, Anthropological Papers* No. 11.

1962   The Paleo-Indian Tradition in Eastern North America. *Current Anthropology* 3(3):227–283.

1963   Two Late Paleo-Indian Complexes in Wisconsin. *The Wisconsin Archeologist* 44(4):199–211.

1966   Two Stratified Sites on the Door Peninsula of Wisconsin. *Museum of Anthropology, University of Michigan, Anthropological Papers* No. 26.

Mason, Ronald J., and Carol Irwin

1960   An Eden-Scottsbluff Burial in Northeastern Wisconsin. *American Antiquity* 26(1):43–57.

Maxwell, Morean S.

1951   The Woodland Cultures in Southern Illinois: Archaeological Excavations in the Carbondale Area. *Logan Museum Publications in Anthropology Bulletin* No. 7.

May, Ernest E.

1982   The Carrier Mills Projectile Point Typology, In Prehistoric Cultural Adaptation in the Carrier Mills Archaeological District, Saline County, Illinois. Edited by R. Jefferies and B. Butler, pp. 1347–1379. *Center for Archaeological Investigations Research Paper* 33. Southern Illinois University at Carbondale.

Mayer-Oakes, William J.

1951   Starved Rock Archaic, A Pre-pottery Horizon in Northern Illinois. *American Antiquity* 16(4):313–324.

1955   Prehistory of the Upper Ohio Valley. *Carnegie Museum, Annals* 34.

McCann, Catherine

1962   The Wilson Site, Bradford Co., Pennsylvania. *Pennsylvania Archaeologist* 32(2):43–55.

McCary, Ben C.

1951   A Workshop Site of Early Man in Dinwiddie County, Virginia. *American Antiquity* 17:9–17.

1955   Virginia Bifurcated Points. *Quarterly Bulletin of the Archeological Society of Virginia* 9(3):13–16.

1972   A Concentration in Virginia of the Perkiomen Broad Spearpoint. *Quarterly Bulletin of the Archeological Society of Virginia* 26(3):145–149.

1976   A Surface Collection of Indian Artifacts from the Richmond Site or Moysonec, New Dent County, Virginia. *Quarterly Bulletin of the Archeological Society of Virginia* 31(1):1–30.

McElrath, Dale L., and Andrew C. Fortier

1983   The Missouri Pacific # 2 Site. *American Bottoms Archaeology FAI–270 Site Reports* Vol. 3.

McGregor, John C.

1958   *The Pool and Irving Villages: A Study of Hopewell Occupation in the Illinois River Valley.* University of Illinois Press.

McKenzie, Douglas H.

1967   The Archaic of the Lower Scioto Valley, Ohio. *Pennsylvania Archaeologist* 37(1–2):33–51.

1975   The Graham Village Site: A Fort Ancient Site in the Hocking Valley, Ohio. In *Studies in Ohio Archaeology* (Revised Edition). Edited by Olaf H. Prufer and Douglas H. McKenzie, pp. 63–97. Western Reserve University Press. Cleveland.

McKern, W. C.

1945   Preliminary Report on the Upper Mississippi Phase in Wisconsin. *Bulletin of the Public Museum of the City of Milwaukee* 16(3). Milwaukee, Wisconsin.

McKusick, Marshall

1973   The Grant Oneota Village, *Office of the State Archaeologist Report* No. 4. Iowa City.

McMichael, Edward V.

1965   Archeological Survey of Nicholas County, West Virginia. *West Virginia Geological and Economic Survey, Archeological Series* 1.

McMichael, Edward V., and Stephen Coffing

1970   Test Excavations at the Daugherty-Monroe Site (12 Su 13). *Proceedings of the Indiana Academy of Science* 79.

McMillan, R. Bruce

1965   Gasconade Prehistory: A Survey and Evaluation of the Archaeological Resources. *Missouri Archaeologist* 27(3–4):1–114. Columbia.

1976   The Dynamics of Cultural and Environmental Change at Rodgers Shelter, Missouri. In *Prehistoric Man and His Environments: A Case Study in the Ozark Highland.* Edited by A. Raymond Wood and R. Bruce McMillan, pp. 211–232. Academic Press.

McNerney, Michael J., ed.

1975   Archaeological Investigations in the Cedar Creek Reservoir. Jackson County, Illinois. *Southern Illinois Studies, Research Records* No. 12. Southern Illinois University.

McNett, Charles W., Jr.

1985   Artifact Morphology and Chronology at

the Shawnee Minisink Site. In *Shawnee Minisink: A Stratified Paleo-Indian–Archaic Site in the Upper Delaware Valley of Pennsylvania*. Edited by Charles W. McNett, Jr., pp. 83–122. Academic Press.

McNett, Charles W., Jr., Barbara A. McMillan, and Sydne B. Marshall
1977 The Shawnee-Minisink Site. In Amerinds and their Paleo-environments in Northeastern North America. Edited by Walter S. Newman and Bert Salwen. *Annals of the New York Academy of Sciences* 288: 282–296.

McPherron, Alan
1967 The Juntunen Site and the Late Woodland Prehistory of the Upper Great Lakes Area. *Museum of Anthropology, University of Michigan, Anthropological Papers* No. 30.

Michels, Joseph W.
1968 Appendix I—Report on Dated Radiocarbon Samples. In Archaeological Investigations of the Sheep Rock Shelter Site, Huntington County, Pennsylvania. Edited by Joseph W. Michels and James S. Dutt. *Department of Anthropology, Pennsylvania State University, Occasional Papers in Anthropology* No. 5, pp. 307–312.

Michels, Joseph W., and James S. Dutt, eds.
1968 A Preliminary Report of Archaeological Investigations of the Sheep Rock Shelter Site, Huntington County, Pennsylvania. *Department of Anthropology, Pennsylvania State University, Occasional Papers in Anthropology* No. 5.

Michels, Joseph, and Ira F. Smith III, eds.
1967 *Archaeological Investigations of Sheep Rock Shelters, Huntington County, Pennsylvania*. Vols. 1 and 2. Pennsylvania State University, University Park.

Michie, James L.
1966 The Taylor Point. *The Chesopiean* 4(5&6):123.
1970a The Broad River Point. *The Chesopiean* 8(1):7.
1970b Ancient Projectile Point Types Found in South Carolina. *South Carolina Antiquities* 2(2):30–34.
1973 A Functional Interpretation of the Dalton Projectile Point in South Carolina. *South Carolina Antiquities* 5:23–36.

Miller, Carl F.
1949 The Lake Springs Site, Columbia County, Georgia. *American Antiquity* 15(1): 38–50.
1957 Radiocarbon Dates from an Early Archaic Deposit in Russel Cave, Alabama. *American Antiquity* 23(1):84.

Miller, E. O., and Edward B. Jelks
1952 Archaeological Excavations at the Belton Reservoir, Coryell County, Texas. *Bulletin of the Texas Archeological and Paleontological Society* 23:168–217.

Miller, Rex K.
1941 McCain Site, Dubois County, Indiana. *Indiana Historical Society, Prehistory Research Series* 2(1):1–60.

Mills, William C.
1907 *Certain Mounds and Village Sites in Ohio: Excavations of the Adena Mound*. Part 1, Volume 1. Columbus, Ohio.
1922 Exploration of the Mound City Group. *Ohio Archaeological and Historical Quarterly* 31(4):423–584.

Mocas, Stephen T.
1976 Excavations at Arrowhead Farm (15 Jf 237). *University of Louisville Archaeological Survey*. Louisville.
1977 Excavations at the Lawrence Site, 13 Tr 33, Trigg County, Kentucky. *University of Louisville Archaeological Survey*. Louisville.

Mocas, Stephen T., and Edward E. Smith
n.d. *Approaches to the Skeletal Biology of the Early-Middle Archaic of Eastern North America: The Utilization of Small Samples*. Manuscript in possession of the authors.

Moffett, Ross
1949 The Raisch-Smith Site. *The Ohio Archaeological and Historical Quarterly* 58(4): 428–441.

Montet-White, Anta
1968 The Lithic Industries of the Illinois Valley in the Early and Middle Woodland Period. *Museum of Anthropology, University of Michigan, Anthropological Papers* No. 35.

Moore, Clarence B.
1912 *Some Aboriginal Sites on Red River*. Reprint from the *Journal of the Academy of Natural Sciences of Philadelphia*. Vol. 14. P.C. Stockhausen. Philadelphia.

Morrow, Toby
1984 *Iowa Projectile Points*. Special Publication of the Office of the State Archaeologist. The University of Iowa.

Morse, Dan F.
1963 The Steuben Village and Mounds, A Multicomponent Late Hopewell Site in Illinois. *Museum of Anthropology, University of Michigan, Anthropological Papers* No. 21, Ann Arbor.
1969 The Schugtown Point. *Field Notes*, Newsletter of the Arkansas Archaeological Society 59.
1971a The Hawkins Cache: A Significant Dalton Find in Northeast Arkansas. *The Arkansas Archaeologist*. 12(1):9–20.
1971b Recent Indications of Dalton Settlement

Pattern in Northeast Arkansas. *Southeastern Archaeological Conference Bulletin* No. 13, pp. 5–10.

1973 Nodena: An Account of Twenty-five Years of Archeological Investigation in Southeast Mississippi County, Arkansas. *Arkansas Archeological Survey, Publications of Archeology, Research Series* No. 4.

1981 The Hickory Ridge Side-Notched Point. The Arkansas Archaeological Society, *Field Notes* 182:11.

Morse, Dan F., and Albert C. Goodyear

1973 The Significance of the Dalton Adz in Northeast Arkansas. *Plains Anthropologist* 19:316–322.

Morse, Dan F., and Phyllis A. Morse

1964 1962 Excavations at the Morse Site: A Red Ochrè Cemetery in the Illinois Valley. *The Wisconsin Archeologist* 45(2): 79–99.

1983 *Archaeology of the Central Mississippi Valley*. Academic Press.

Munson, Cheryl Ann, and Thomas Genn Cook

1980 Late Archaic French Lick Phase: A Dimensional Description. In Archaeological Salvage Excavations at Patoka Lake, Indiana: Prehistoric Occupations of the Upper Patoka River Valley. *Glenn A. Black Laboratory of Archaeology Research Reports* No. 6:721–740.

Munson, Patrick J.

1966a An Archaeological Survey of the "Wood River Terrace" and Adjacent Bottoms and Bluffs in Madison County, Illinois. *Illinois State Museum Preliminary Reports* No. 8, Springfield.

1966b The Sheets Site: A Late Archaic–Early Woodland Occupation in West-Central Illinois. *Michigan Archaeologist* 12(3): 111–120. Ann Arbor.

1967 Hardin Barbed Projectile Points: Analysis of a Central Illinois Sample. *Central States Archaeological Journal* 14(1): 16–19.

1971 An Archaeological Survey of the Wood River Terrace and Adjacent Bottoms and Bluffs in Madison County, Illinois. In An Archaeological Survey of the American Bottoms and Wood River Terrace. *Illinois State Museum Reports of Investigations* No. 21, Part 1.

1976 *Monroe Lake, Indiana, Archaeological Study: An Assessment of the Impact of Monroe Reservoir on Prehistoric Cultural Resources*. Prepared for the U.S. Army Corps of Engineers. Glenn A. Black Laboratory of Archaeology, Indiana University.

1982 Marion, Black Sand, Morton and Havana Relationships: An Illinois Valley Perspective. *The Wisconsin Archeologist* 63(1):1–17.

Munson, Patrick J., and J. P. Anderson

1973 A Preliminary Report on Kane Village, A Late Woodland Site in Madison County, Illinois. *Illinois Archaeological Survey Bulletin* 9:34–48, Urbana.

Munson, Patrick J., and N. L. Downs

1966 A Surface Collection of Truncated Barb and Bifurcated Base Projectile Points from Central Illinois. *The Wisconsin Archeologist* 47(4):203–207.

1968 A Surface Collection of Plano and Paleo-Indian Projectile Points from Central Illinois. *The Missouri Archaeologist* 30: 122–28.

Munson, Patrick J., and Alan D. Harn

1966 Surface Collections from three sites in the Central Illinois River Valley. *The Wisconsin Archeologist* 47(3):150–168.

Munson, Patrick J., and Cheryl Ann Munson

1972 Unfinished Triangular Projectile Points or "Hump-Backed" Knives. *Pennsylvania Archaeologist* 42(3):31–36.

1981 Archaeological Investigations 1980 Wyandotte Cave, Indiana: Unpublished Report. Prepared for Division of Forestry, Indiana Department of Natural Resources.

Munson, Patrick J., Paul W. Parmalee, and Richard A. Yarnell

1971 Subsistence Ecology of Scovill: A Terminal Middle Woodland Village. *American Antiquity* 36(4):410–431.

Murphy, James L.

1975 *An Archaeological History of the Hocking Valley*. Ohio University Press. Athens.

Myers, Jeffery A., ed.

1981 *Archaeological Data Recovery at the Mary Ann Cole Site (12 Cr 1), Crawford County, Indiana: A Prehistoric Lithic Workshop at the Confluence of the Blue and Ohio Rivers*. Prepared for the U.S. Army Corps of Engineers. Resource Analysts, Inc. Bloomington, Indiana.

Myers, Thomas P., and Ray Lambert

1983 Meserve Points: Evidence of a Plainsward Extension of the Dalton Horizon. *Plains Anthropologist* 28(100):109–114.

Neuman, Robert W.

1984 *An Introduction to Louisiana Archaeology*. Louisiana State University Press.

Newell, H. Perry, and Alex D. Krieger

1949 The George C. Davis Site, Cherokee County, Texas. *Memoirs of the Society for American Archaeology* No. 5.

Newton, John P.

1975–77 Paleo-Indian in the Arkansas Ozarks: A Preliminary Statement. *The Arkansas Archeologist* 16–18:85–92.

Oakley, Carey B., and Eugene M. Futato

1975 Archaeological Investigations in the Little

Bear Creek Reservoir. *Archaeology of the Bear Creek Watershed*, Volume I, Research Series No. 1.

Oliver, Billy L.
1981 The Piedmont Tradition: Refinement of the Savannah River Stemmed Point Type. Masters Thesis. Department of Anthropology, University of North Carolina, Chapel Hill.

Oplinger, Jon
1981 Wise Rockshelter: A Multicomponent Site in Jackson County, Ohio. *Kent State Research Papers in Archaeology* No. 2.

Ottesen, Ann I.
1981 *A Report on a Preliminary Study of Prehistoric Settlement Patterns in Three Counties in Northwestern Kentucky*. A Report to the Kentucky Heritage Commission, University of Louisville.

Pace, Robert E., and Gary A. Apfelstadt
1978 *Allison-LaMotte Culture of the Daugherty-Monroe Site, Sullivan County, Indiana*. Submitted to the Office of Archaeology and Historic Preservation, Interagency Archaeological Service. Atlanta, Georgia. In fulfillment of National Park Service Contracts CX 4000–4–0028 and CX 6000–5–0173.

Pace, Robert E., and Steve Coffing
1978 A Riverton Culture Gathering Site in Parke County, Indiana. *Proceedings of the Indiana Academy of Science* 87:81. Indianapolis.

Pace, Robert E., and Daniel P. Thiel
1983 Albee Component at the Cooke Site (P–5), Parke County, Late Woodland in the Central Wabash Valley. *Abstract Proceedings of the Indiana Academy of Science*. 92:78.

Palmer, Charles, and Harris Palmer
1962 Truncated Barb Points from Northeastern Illinois. *The Wisconsin Archeologist* 43(1):9–12.

Parmalee, Paul W., Andreas A. Paloumpis, and Nancy Wilson
1972 Animals Utilized by Woodland Peoples Occupying the Apple Creek Site, Illinois. *Illinois State Museum Reports of Investigations* No. 23.

Pauketat, Timothy R.
1984 A Cypress Stemmed Cache from Southern Illinois. *Illinois Antiquity* 16(2): 28–31.

Perino, Gregory
1954 The Titterington Focus-Red Ochre. *Central States Archaeological Journal* 1(1): 15–17.

1962 Review of Calhoun County, Illinois Prehistory. *The Wisconsin Archeologist* 43(2):44–51.

1963 Tentative Classification of Two Projectile Points and One Knife from West-Central Illinois. *Central States Archaeological Journal* 10(3):95–100.

1966a The Banks Village Site, Crittenden County, Arkansas. *Missouri Archaeological Society*, Memoir No. 4. Columbia.

1966b A Preliminary Report on the Peisker Site. Part 1: The Early Woodland Occupation. *Central States Archaeological Journal* 13(2):47–51.

1967 Early Projectile Points Found. *Central States Archaeological Journal* 14(3): 103–106.

1968a Guide to the Identification of Certain American Indian Projectile Points. *Special Bulletin No. 3, Oklahoma Anthropological Society*.

1968b The Pete Klunk Mound Group, Calhoun County, Illinois. In Hopewell and Woodland Site Archaeology in Illinois. Edited by James A. Brown. *Illinois Archaeological Survey Bulletin* 6:9–124.

1969 North Points or Blades. *Central States Archaeological Journal* 16(4):184–187.

1970 The Stilwell II Site, Pike County, Illinois. *Central States Archaeological Journal* 17(3):118–121.

1971a Guide to the Identification of Certain American Indian Projectile Points. *Oklahoma Anthropological Society, Special Bulletin* No. 4.

1971b The Mississippian Component at the Schild Site (No. 4), Greene County, Illinois. In Mississippian Site Archaeology in Illinois 1: Site Reports from the St. Louis and Chicago Areas. *Illinois Archaeological Survey, Inc.*, Bulletin No. 8:1–148.

1973 The Late Woodland Component at the Pete Klunk Site, Calhoun County, Illinois. *Illinois Archaeological Survey* Bulletin 9:58–59.

1975 The Apple Creek Point. *Central States Archaeological Journal* 22(2):50–51.

1976 The Cossatot River Point. *Central States Archaeological Journal* 23(3):127.

1980 The Ouachita Point: A New Type for Southwest Arkansas and Southwest Oklahoma. *Bulletin of the Oklahoma Anthropological Society*. 29:9–11.

1985 *Selected Preforms, Points, and Knives of the North American Indians* Vol. 1, Points and Barbs Press.

Perkins, George H.
1970 History and Condition of the State Cabinet: Indian Relics. In *Archaeology in Vermont, Revised Edition*. Compiled by John C. Huden, pp. 44–64. Charles Tuttle Co.

Peru, Donald V.
1965   The Distribution of Fluted Points in the Counties of Kent and Allegan, Michigan. *Michigan Archaeologist* 11(1):1–8.

Peske, G. Richard
1963   Argillite of Michigan: A Preliminary Projectile Point Classification and Temporal Placement from Surface Materials. *Papers of the Michigan Academy of Science, Arts and Letters* 48:557–566.

Peterson, D. A., Jr.
1973   The Spring Creek Site, Perry County, Tennessee: Report of the 1972–73 Excavations. *Memphis State University Anthropological Research Center, Occasional Papers* No. 7.

Pettipas, Leo
1970   Early Man in Manitoba. In *Ten Thousand Years: Archaeology in Manitoba*. Edited by Walter M. Hlady, pp. 5–28. Manitoba Archaeological Society.

Pfeiffer, John
1984   The Late and Terminal Archaic Periods of Connecticut Prehistory. *The Archaeological Society of Connecticut Bulletin* 47:73–88.

Phelps, David S.
1981   Archaeological Surveys of Four Watersheds in the North Carolina Coastal Plain. *North Carolina Archaeological Council Publication* No. 16.

Phelps, David S., and Randolph J. Widner
1981   An Archaeological Survey of the Joyce Creek Watershed, Camden County, North Carolina. In Archaeological Surveys of Four Watersheds in the North Carolina Coastal Plain. By David S. Phelps. *North Carolina Archaeological Council Publication* No. 16.

Phillips, Philip
1970   Archaeological Survey in the Lower Yazoo Basin, Mississippi, 1949–1955. *Peabody Museum of Archaeology and Ethnology Papers* 60.

Pi-Sunyer, Oriol
1965   The Flint Industry. In the McGraw Site: A Study in Hopewellian Dynamics. By Olaf H. Prufer. *Scientific Publications of the Cleveland Museum of Natural History* 3(1).

Pi-Sunyer, Oriol, John Edward Blank, and Robert Williams
1975   The Honey Run Site (33 Co–3): A Late Paleo-Indian Locality in Coshocton County, Ohio. In *Studies in Ohio Archaeology*. Revised Edition. Edited by Olaf H. Prufer and Douglas H. McKenzie, pp. 188–230. Kent State University Press.

Potter, Martha A.
1968   *Ohio's Prehistoric Peoples*. The Ohio Historical Society. Columbus.

Powers, S.
1877   Tribes of California. *Contributions to North American Ethnology* 3.

Price, James E., and James J. Krakker
1975   Dalton Occupation of the Ozark Border. *Museum Briefs* No. 20. University of Missouri, Columbia.

Prufer, Olaf H.
1963   The McConnell Site: A Late Palaeo-Indian Workshop in Coshocton County, Ohio. *Cleveland Museum of Natural History, Scientific Publications*. N. S. Vol. 2(1).

1965   The McGraw Site: A Study in Hopewellian Dynamics. *Cleveland Museum of Natural History, New Series* Vol. 3(1).

1975a Chesser Cave: A Late Woodland Phase in Southeastern Ohio. In *Studies in Ohio Archaeology*. Revised Edition. Edited by Olaf H. Prufer and Douglas H. McKenzie, pp. 1–62. Western Reserve University Press, Cleveland.

1975b The Scioto Valley Archaeological Survey. In *Studies in Ohio Archaeology*. Revised Edition. Edited by Olaf H. Prufer and Douglas H. McKenzie, pp. 267–328. Kent State University Press.

1981   Raven Rocks: A Specialized Late Woodland Rockshelter Occupation in Belmont County, Ohio. *Kent State Research Paper in Archaeology* No. 1.

Prufer, Olaf H., and Raymond S. Baby
1963   *Palaeo-Indians of Ohio*. The Ohio Historical Society. Columbus, Ohio.

Prufer, Olaf H., and Douglas H. McKenzie
1966   Peters Cave: Two Woodland Occupations in Ross County, Ohio. *Ohio Journal of Science* 66(3):333–53. Columbus.

Prufer, Olaf H., and Douglas H. McKenzie, eds.
1975   *Studies in Ohio Archaeology*. Revised Edition. Kent State University Press.

Prufer, Olaf H., and Orrin C. Shane, III
1970   *Blain Village and the Fort Ancient Tradition in Ohio*. Kent State University Press.

Prufer, Olaf H., and Charles Sofsky
1965   The McKibben Site (33 Tr 57) Trumbull Co., Ohio: A Contribution to a Late Paleo-Indian and Archaic Phase of Ohio. *Michigan Archaeologist* 11(1):9–40.

Purdy, Barbara A.
1975   The Senator Edwards Chipped Stone Workshop Site (MR–122), Marion County, Florida: A Preliminary Report of Investigations. *Florida Anthropologist* 28(4):178–192.

1981a *Florida's Prehistoric Stone Technology: A Study of the Flintworking Technique of Early Florida Stone Implement Makers*. University of Florida, Gainesville.

1981b Investigations into the Use of Chert Outcrops by Prehistoric Floridians: The Container Corporation of America Site. *Florida Anthropologist* 34(2):90–108.

Purdy, Barbara A., and Laurie M. Beach
1980 The Chipped Stone Tool Industry of Florida's Preceramic Archaic. *Archaeology of Eastern North America*. Vol. 8: 105–124.

Purrington, Burton L.
1983 Ancient Mountaineers: An Overview of Prehistoric Archaeology of North Carolina's Western Mountain Region. In *The Prehistory of North Carolina: An Archaeological Symposium*. Edited by Mark A. Mathis and Jeffrey J. Crow, pp. 83–158. North Carolina Division of Archives and History, Department of Cultural Resources.

Quimby, George I.
1959 Lanceolate Points and Fossil Beaches in the Upper Great Lakes Region. *American Antiquity* 24(4):424–426.
1960 *Indian Life in the Upper Great Lakes*. University of Chicago Press.

Reagan, Michael J.
1981 Paleo-Indian Remains from Northwest Missouri. *Missouri Archaeologist* 42: 17–26.

Redfield, Alden
1966 The Hardin Point, An Interim Analysis Report. *The Arkansas Archaeologist* 7(3):53–57.
1970 Dalton Forms from the Lower Mississippi Alluvial Valley. *Southeastern Archaeological Conference Bulletin*. No. 13. Morgantown, West Virginia.

Reeder, Robert T.
1981 Nebo Hill Occupation in a Riverine Environment. *Missouri Archaeologist* 42: 27–42.

Reichelt, David C.
1973 Clovis from Northwest Florida. *Florida Anthropologist* 26(4):165–168.

Reid, C. S.
1980 Early Man in Northwestern Ontario: New Plano Evidence. *Ontario Archaeology* No. 33:33–36.

Reid, Kenneth C.
1984 Nebo Hill: And Late Archaic Prehistory on the Southern Prairie Peninsula. *University of Kansas Publications in Anthropology* No. 15.

Reidhead, Van A., and William F. Limp
1974 The Haag Site (12 D 19): A Preliminary Report. *Indiana Archaeological Bulletin* Vol. 1(1). Indiana Historical Society.

Reinhart, Theodore R.
1975 The Artifacts from Prehistoric Kingsmill, James City County, Virginia. *Quarterly Bulletin of the Archaeological Society of Virginia* 29(3):132–161.

1979 Middle and Late Archaic Cultures in the Lower James River Area. *Quarterly Bulletin of the Archaeological Society of Virginia*. 34(2):57–82.

Ritchie, William A.
1928 An Algonkian Village Site Near Levanna, N.Y. *Research Records of Rochester Municipal Museum*, No. 1. Rochester.
1932 The Lamoka Lake Site. *Researches and Transactions of the New York State Archeological Association* 7(4).
1937 Culture Influences from Ohio in New York Archaeology. *American Antiquity* 2(3):182–94.
1940 Two Prehistoric Village Sites at Brewerton, New York: Type Components of the Brewerton, Focus, Laurentian Aspect. *Rochester Museum of Arts and Sciences Research Records* No. 5.
1944 The Pre-Iroquoian Occupations of New York State. *Rochester Museum of Arts and Sciences, Memoir* No. 1. Rochester.
1945 An Early Site in Cayuga County, New York. *Rochester Museum of Arts and Sciences, Research Records* No. 7. Rochester.
1946 A Stratified Prehistoric Site at Brewerton, New York. *Rochester Museum of Arts and Sciences, Research Records*, No. 8. Rochester.
1952 Recent Discoveries Suggesting an Early Woodland Burial Cult in the Northeast. *New York State Museum and Science Service Circular* No. 40. State University of New York, Albany.
1953 A Probable Paleo-Indian Site in Vermont. *American Antiquity* 18(3):249–258.
1955 Recent Discoveries Suggesting an Early Woodland Burial Cult in the Northeast. *New York State Museum and Science Service Circular* No. 40.
1957 Traces of Early Man in the Northeast. *New York State Museum and Science Service Bulletin* 358.
1958 An Introduction to Hudson Valley Prehistory. *New York State Museum and Science Service Bulletin* 367.
1961 A Typology and Nomenclature for New York Projectile Points. *New York State Museum and Science Service Bulletin* No. 384. Albany, New York.
1969a *The Archaeology of New York State*. Revised Edition. Natural History Press.
1969b *The Archaeology of Martha's Vineyard: A Framework for the Prehistory of Southern New England*. Natural History Press.
1971a A Typology and Nomenclature for New York Projectile Points. *New York State Museum and Science Service Bulletin* No. 384. Revised Edition.
1971b The Archaic in New York. *New York State*

Archaeological Association Bulletin 52:2–12.

1979 The Otter Creek No. 2 Site in Rutland County, Vermont. *Bulletin of the New York State Archaeological Association* No. 76:1–21.

Ritchie, William A., and Don W. Dragoo
1960 The Eastern Dispersal of Adena. *New York State Museum and Science Service Bulletin* 379.

Ritchie, William A., and Robert E. Funk
1971 Evidence for Early Archaic Occupations on Staten Island. *Pennsylvania Archaeologist* 41(3):45–59.

1973 Aboriginal Settlement Patterns in the Northeast. *New York State Museum and Science Service, Memoir* 20.

Ritzenthaler, Robert
1946 The Osceola Site: An Old Copper Site Near Potosi, Wisconsin. *Wisconsin Archeologist* 27(3):53–70.

1961a Truncated-Barb Points from Dodge County. *The Wisconsin Archeologist* 42(2):90–91.

1961b More Truncated-Barb Points from Wisconsin. *The Wisconsin Archeologist* 42(4):55–57.

1966 The Kouba Site: Paleo-Indians in Wisconsin. *The Wisconsin Archeologist* 47(4): 171–187.

1967 A Guide to Wisconsin Indian Projectile Point Types. *Popular Science Series II Milwaukee Public Museum.*

Ritzenthaler, Robert E., and Arthur Niehoff
1958 A Red Ochre Burial in Ozaukee County. *The Wisconsin Archeologist* 39(2). Milwaukee.

Ritzenthaler, Robert E., and George I. Quimby
1962 The Red Ocher Culture of the Upper Great Lakes and Adjacent Areas. *Fieldiana: Anthropology* 36(11):243–375.

Ritzenthaler, Robert E., and Warren L. Wittry
1952 The Oconto Site: An Old Copper Manifestation. *The Wisconsin Archeologist* 33(4):179–223.

Robbins, Maurice
1980 *Wapanucket: An Archaeological Report.* The Massachusetts Archaeological Society.

Roberts, Arthur
1980 A Geographic Approach to Southern Ontario Archaic. *Archaeology of Eastern North America* 8:28–44.

Roberts, Frank H. H., Jr.
1935 A Folsom Complex: Preliminary Report on Investigations at the Lindenmeier Site in Northern Colorado. *Smithsonian Institution, Miscellaneous Collections* 94(4), Washington.

1942 Archeological and Geological Investigations in the san Jon District, Eastern New Mexico. *Smithsonian Miscellaneous, Collections* 103(4).

1943 A New Site. *American Antiquity* 8(3):300.

1962 1961 Excavations at Agate Basin, Wyoming. *Plains Anthropologist* 7(16): 89–91.

Roberts, Ralph G.
1965 Tick Creek Cave: An Archaic Site in the Gasconade River Valley of Missouri. *Missouri Achaeologist* 27(2).

Rolingson, Martha Ann
1964 Paleo-Indian Culture in Kentucky. *University of Kentucky Studies in Anthropology* No. 2. University of Kentucky Press. Lexington.

1967 *Temporal Perspective on the Archaic Cultures of the Middle Green River Region, Kentucky.* Doctoral Dissertation. University of Michigan.

Rolingson, Martha A., and Michael J. Rodeffer
1968 *The Zilpo Site, Bh 37: Preliminary Excavations in the Cave Run Reservoir, Kentucky: 1968.* Museum of Anthropology, University of Kentucky, Lexington.

Rolingson, Martha Ann, and Douglas A. Schwartz
1966 Late Paleo-Indian and Early Archaic Manifestations in Western Kentucky. *Studies in Anthropology* No. 3. University of Kentucky Press. Lexington.

Roosa, William B.
1965 Some Great Lakes Fluted Point Types. *Michigan Archaeologist* 11(3–4): 89–102.

1966 The Warner School Site. *Michigan Archaeologist* 12(1):25–34.

1977a Fluted Points from the Parkhill, Ontario* Site. In For the Director: Research Essays in Honor of James B. Griffin. Edited by Charles E. Cleland, *Museum of Anthropology, University of Michigan Anthropological Papers* No. 61, pp. 87–122.

1977b Great Lakes Paleoindian: The Parkhill Site, Ontario. In Amerinds and their Paleoenvironments in Northeastern North America. Edited by Walter D. Newman and Bert Salwen. *Annals of the New York Academy of Sciences* Vol. 288, pp. 349–354.

Roosa, William B., and D. Brian Deller
1982 The Parkhill Complex and Eastern Great Lakes Paleo-Indian. *Ontario Archaeology* No. 37:3–15.

Roper, Donna C.
1970 *Statistical Analysis of New York State Projectile Points.* Masters Thesis. Indiana University.

1978 The Airport Site: A Multi-component Site in the Sangamon River Drainage. *Illinois State Museum Research Series, Papers in Anthropology* No. 4.

Rose, Edward F.
  1965 The Boats Site. Excavation No. 2. *Bulletin of the Massachusetts Archaeological Society* 26(3–4):33–39. Attleboro.
Ross, William A.
  1979 Additional Paleo-Indian Biface Variability in Northwestern Ontario. *Ontario Archaeology* No. 32:21–26.
Rouse, Irving
  1960 The Classification of Artifacts in Archaeology. *American Antiquity* 25(3): 313–323.
Salo, Lawr V., ed.
  1969 *Archaeological Investigations in the Tellico Reservoir, Tennessee, 1967–1968: An Interim Report.* Department of Anthropology, University of Tennessee, Knoxville.
Salzer, Robert J., and Mark Stock
  1961 A Fluted Point from Jefferson County. *The Wisconsin Archeologist* 42(3): 133–135.
Sanders, Thomas N.
  1980 The Church Hill Projectile Point: A Provisional Type from Christian County, Kentucky. *Kentucky Archaeological Association Bulletin* 14–15:64–66.
Sanders, Thomas N., and David R. Maynard
  1979 *A Reconnaissance and Evaluation of Archaeological Sites in Christian County, Kentucky* No. 12. Kentucky Heritage Commission.
Satterthwaite, Linton
  1957 Stone Artifacts Near the Finley Site, Near Eden, Wyoming. *University Museum, University of Pennsylvania, Museum Monographs.*
Schambach, Frank F.
  1982 An Outline of Fourche Maline Culture in Southwest Arkansas. In Arkansas Archaeology in Review. Edited by Neal L. Trubowitz and Marvin D. Jeter, pp. 132–197. *Arkansas Archaeological Survey Research Series* 15.
Schock, Jack M., and Michael Dowell
  1981 The Early Woodland Period in South-Central Kentucky. Paper presented at Kentucky Archaeological Association Annual Meeting April 11, 1981.
Schock, Jack M., William Howell, Mary L. Bowman, Richard Alvey, Dana Beasley, and Joel Stoner
  1977 A Report on the Excavations of Two Archaic Sites (Ch 302 and Ch 307) in Christian County, Kentucky. *Kentucky Archaeological Association Bulletins* 6 and 7.
Schock, Jack M., and Terry W. Langford
  1979a *An Archaeological Shoreline Reconnaissance of Barren River Lake, Allen, Barren and Monroe Counties, Kentucky.* Department of Sociology, Anthropology, and Social Welfare. Western Kentucky University, Bowling Green.
  1979b Some Projectile Point Types from Barren River Lake, Kentucky. *Kentucky Archaeological Association Bulletin* 11:1–39.
  1981 *An Archaeological Survey and Testing of a Proposed Alcohol Plant South of Franklin in Simpson County, Kentucky.* Report submitted to the Kentucky Agricultural Energy Corporation, Franklin, Kentucky.
Schoonover, Margaret
  1960 The Schoonover Point: A New Type. *Ohio Archaeologist* 10(3):102–103.
Schroedl, Gerald F.
  1978 Excavations of the Leuty and McDonald Site Mounds. *University of Tennessee Department of Anthropology, Report of Investigations* No. 22. *Tennessee Valley Authority Publications in Anthropology* No. 15.
Scully, Edward G.
  1951 *Some Central Mississippi Valley Projectile Point Types.* Museum of Anthropology, University of Michigan.
Seelan, R. M.
  1961 A Preliminary Report of the Sedalia Complex. *Newsletter of the Missouri Archaeological Society* No. 153. Columbia.
Seeman, Mark F.
  1975 The Prehistoric Chert Quarries and Workshops of Harrison County, Indiana. *Indiana Archaeological Bulletin* 1(3). Indiana Historical Society.
  1977 *The Hopewell Interaction Sphere: The Evidence for Inter-Regional Trade and Structural Complexity.* Ph.D. Dissertation. Indiana University.
  1985 Craft Specialization and Tool Kit Structure: A Systemic Perspective on the Midcontinental Flint Knapper. In Lithic Resource Procurement: Proceedings from the Second Conference on Prehistoric Chert Exploitation. Edited by Susan C. Vehik. *Center for Archaeological Investigations Occasional Paper* No. 4, pp. 7–36.
Seeman, Mark F., and Olaf H. Prufer
  1982 An Updated Distribution of Ohio Fluted Points. *Midcontinental Journal of Archaeology* 7(2):155–170.
Sellards, E. H.
  1952 *Early Man in America.* University of Texas Press. Austin.
  1955 Fossil Bison and Associated Artifacts from Milnesand, New Mexico. *American Antiquity* 20(4) Part 1:336–344.
Sellards, E. H., Glen L. Evans, and G. E. Meade
  1947 Fossil Bison and Associated Artifacts from Plainview, Texas. *Geological Society of America Bulletin* 58:927–954.

Sellers, Paul V.
1960 Vase-Shaped or Bottle-Neck Type Flint Points. *Central States Archaeological Journal* 7(3):114–115.

Semenov, Sergei A.
1964 *Prehistoric Technology* (translated by M. W. Thompson). Cory, Adams and MacKay. London.

Shane, Orrin C., III
1975a The Mixter Site: A Multicomponent Locality in Erie County, Ohio. In *Studies in Ohio Archaeology*. Revised Edition. Edited by Olaf H. Prufer and Douglas H. McKenzie, pp. 121–186. Western Reserve University Press. Cleveland.
1975b Appendix: Ohio Radiocarbon Chronology. In *Studies in Ohio Archaeology* Revised Edition. Edited by Olaf H. Prufer and Douglas H. McKenzie, pp. 357–368. Kent State University Press.

Shane, Orrin C., III, and James L. Murphy
1975 A Survey of the Hocking Valley, Ohio. In *Studies in Ohio Archaeology*. Revised Edition. Edited by Olaf H. Prufer and Douglas H. McKenzie, pp. 329–356. Kent State University Press.

Shay, C. Thomas
1971 *The Itasca Bison Kill Site: An Ecological Analysis*. Minnesota Historical Society. Minneapolis.

Shelley, Phillip H., and George Agogino
1983 Agate Basin Technology: An Insight. *Plains Anthropologist* 28(100):115–118.

Shippee, J. M.
1948 Nebo Hill: A Lithic Complex in Western Missouri. *American Antiquity* 14(1): 29–32.
1957 The Diagnostic Point Type of the Nebo Hill Complex. *Missouri Archaeologist* 19(3):43–46.

Simons, Donald B.
1972 Radiocarbon Date from a Michigan Satchell-type Site. *Michigan Archaeologist* 18(4):209–214.

Simpson, J. Clarence
1948 Folsom-like Points from Florida. *Florida Anthropologist* 1(1–2):11–15.

Sims, Ernest J.
1971 The Big Bottom Site. *Tennessee Archaeologist* 27(2):50–91.

Smith, Arthur G.
1960 The Sawmill Site, Erie County, Ohio. *Ohio Archaeologist* 10(3):84–97.

Smith, D. C., and Frank M. Hodges, Jr.
1968 The Rankin Site, Cocke County, Tennessee. *Tennessee Archaeologist* 24(2): 37–91.

Snow, Dean R.
1980 *The Archaeology of New England*. Academic Press.

Soday, Frank J.
1954 The Quad Site: A Paleo-Indian Village in Northern Alabama. *Tennessee Archaeologist* 10(1):1–20.

Sollberger, J. B.
1970 The Rockwall Point. *Newsletter of the Oklahoma Anthropological Society* 18(2).

South, Stanley
1959 A Study of the Prehistory of the Roanoke Rapids Basin. Master's Thesis. Department of Anthropology, University of North Carolina, Chapel Hill.

Speth, John D.
1972 Mechanical Basis of Percussion Flaking. *American Antiquity* 37(1):34–60.

Spiess, Arthur E., Bruce J. Bourque, and R. Michael Gramly
1983 Early and Middle Archaic Site Distribution in Western Maine. *North American Archaeologist* 4(3):225–244.

Spiess, Arthur E., and Mary Lou Curran
1985 Caribou (Rangifer Tarandus l.) Bones from New England Paleoindian Sites. *North American Archaeologist* 6(2): 145–160.

Springer, James, Claude C. Karsh, and William F. Harrison
1978 Early Archaic Stone Tools from Northern Illinois. *The Wisconsin Archeologist* 59(3):277–309.

Starbuck, David R.
1980 The Middle Archaic in Central Connecticut: The Excavation of the Lewis-Walpole Site (6–Ht–15). In Early and Middle Archaic Cultures in the Northeast. Edited by David R. Starbuck and Charles E. Bolian. *Occasional Publications in Northeastern Anthropology* No. 7, pp. 5–38.

Starbuck, David R., and Charles E. Bolian, eds.
1980 Early and Middle Archaic Cultures in the Northeast. *Occasional Publications in Northeastern Anthropology* No. 7.

Starna, William A.
1979 Late Archaic Chronology for the Middle Mohawk Valley, New York State: A Review of the Type Concept and Cross-dating. *Man in the Northeast* 17:3–18.

Steinbring, Jack
1966 A Scottsbluff Projectile Point from Manitoba. *The Wisconsin Archeologist* 47(1):1–7.

Stemle, David L.
1981 The Turkey-tail point. *Central States Archaeological Journal* 28(3):113–122.

Stephens, Denzil
1974 Excavations at the Stoner and Lowe Sites. *Illinois State Museum Research Series, Papers In Anthropology* No. 2.

Stephenson, Robert L.
1952 The Hogge Bridge Site and the Wylie Focus. *American Antiquity* 17(4): 299–312.
Stephenson, Robert L., and Alice L. Ferguson
1963 The Accokeek Creek Site: A Middle Atlantic Seaboard Culture Sequence. *Museum of Anthropology, University of Michigan, Anthropological Papers* No. 20.
Steward, Julian H.
1954 Types of types. *American Anthropologist* 56(1):54–57.
Stoltman, James B.
1972 The Late Archaic in the Savannah River Region. *Florida Anthropologist* 25: 37–62.
1974 Groton Plantation: An Archaeological Study of a South Carolina Locality. *Monographs of the Peabody Museum* No. 1. Harvard.
Storck, Peter L.
1984 Research into the Paleo-Indian Occupations of Ontario: A Review. *Ontario Archaeology* 41:3–28.
Stothers, David M.
1972 A Preliminary Report on an Archaeological Survey of Selkirk Provincial Park. Unpublished report on file, National Museums of Canada (Ottawa) and Ontario Ministry of Culture. London, Ontario.
1975 Radiocarbon Dating the Culture Chronology of Southwestern Ontario. *Man in the Northeast* 10:29–42.
1977 The Princess Point Complex. *Archaeological Survey of Canada Paper* No. 58.
Stothers, David M., and G. Michael Pratt
1981 New Perspectives on the Late Woodland Cultures of the Western Lake Erie Region. *Midcontinental Journal of Archaeology* 6(1):91–122.
Straffin, Dean
1971 The Kingston Oneota Site. *Office of the State Archaeologist Report* No. 2. Iowa City.
Suhm, Dee Ann, and Edward B. Jelks
1962 Handbook of Texas Archaeology: Type Descriptions. *Texas Memorial Museum Bulletin* No. 4 and *Texas Archaeological Society Special Publications* No. 1. Austin, Texas.
Suhm, Dee Ann, Alex D. Krieger, and Edward B. Jelks
1954 An Introductory Handbook of Texas Archaeology. *Bulletin of the Texas Archaeological Society* 25.
Swanson, Earl H., Jr., ed.
1975 *Lithic Technology*. Mouton. The Hague.
Swartz, B. K., Jr.
1973 Mound Three, White Site Hn–10 (IAS-BSU): The Final Report on a Robbins Manifestation in East Central Indiana.

Contributions to Anthropological History No. 1. Ball State University.
1982 The Commissary Site: An Early Late Woodland Cemetery in East Central Indiana. *Contributions to Anthropological History* No. 3. Ball State University.
Taggart, David W.
n.d. *The Feeheley Site: A Late Archaic Site in the Saginaw Valley*. Manuscript on file, Museum of Anthropology, University of Michigan, Ann Arbor.
1967 Seasonal Patterns in Settlement, Subsistence, and Industries in the Saginaw Late Archaic. *Michigan Archaeologist* 13(4):153–170.
Tallan, Michael L.
1977 *An Analysis of the Flint Artifacts and Debitage from the Libben Site, Ottawa County, Ohio*. Master's Thesis.
Taylor, Fayne G.
1957 Early Chipped Flint Objects from West Tennessee. *Tennessee Archaeologist* 13(2):81–87.
Taylor, Walter W.
1948 A Study of Archaeology. *Memoirs of the American Anthropological Association* No. 69.
Thomas, David Hurst, Clark S. Larsen, and Ann M. Lunsford
1979 The Cunningham Mound Group. In The Anthropology of St. Catherines Island 2. The Refuge-Deptford Mortuary Complex. By David Hurst Thomas and Clark S. Larsen. *Anthropological Papers of the American Museum of Natural History* 56(1):22–83.
Thomas, Ronald A.
1962 Projectile Point Sequence at the Breckenridge Shelter. *The Arkansas Archaeologist* 3(10).
Thomas, Ronald A., and Hester A. Davis
1966 Excavations in Prall Shelter (3 BE 187) in Beaver Reservoir, Northwest Arkansas. *The Arkansas Archaeologist* 7(4):63–79.
Thompson, David H.
1973 Preliminary Excavations at the Hopkins Site (6–LF– 1), Warren, Connecticut. *Bulletin of the Archaeological Society of Connecticut* 38:5–24.
Thorne, Robert M., Bettye J. Broyles, and Jay K. Johnson
1981 Yellow Creek Archaeological Project. Vol. 1. *Archaeological Papers of the Center for Archaeological Research* No. 1. *Tennessee Valley Authority Publications in Anthropology* No. 27.
Titterington, Paul F.
1938 *The Cahokia Mound Group and its Village Site Materials*. Private Publication, St. Louis.
1950 Some Non-Pottery Sites in the St. Louis

Area. *Illinois State Archaeological Society* 1(1):19–31.

Tomak, Curtis H.

1970   *Aboriginal Occupations in the Vicinity of Greene County, Indiana.* Master's Thesis. Indiana University, Bloomington.

1979   Jerger: An Early Archaic Mortuary Site in Southwestern Indiana. *Proceedings of the Indiana Academy of Science* 88: 63–69.

1980a   Scherchel: A Late Archaic Occupation in Southern Indiana with Appended Chert Descriptions. *Central States Archaeological Journal* 27(3):104–111.

1980b   An Outline of the Cultural Sequence of a Portion of the Valley of the West Fork of the White River in Southwestern Indiana. Paper presented at the Annual Meeting of the Indiana Historical Society. Indianapolis, Indiana.

1980c   Alton: A Paleo-Indian Site in Southern Indiana. *Proceedings of the Indiana Academy of Science* 89:84–90.

1982   A Note on the Distribution of Riverton Points. *Central States Archaeological Journal* 29(1):21–24.

Tomak, Curtis H., and Norma J. O'Conner

1978   An Early Woodland Burial from Greene County, Indiana. *Proceedings of the Indiana Academy of Science* 87:90–97.

Tomak, Curtis H., Norma J. Tomak, and Van A. Reidhead

1980   The Earlier Archaic Components at the Leonard Haag Site, Dearborn County, Indiana. *Journal of Alabama Archaeology* 26(1):28–60.

Toth, Alan

1979   The Marksville Connection. In *Hopewell Archaeology: The Chillicothe Conference.* Edited by David S. Brose and N'omi Greber, pp. 188–199. Kent State University Press.

Tringham, Ruth, et al.

1974   Experimentation in the Formation of Edge Damage: A New Approach to Lithic Analysis. *Journal of Field Archaeology* 1:171–196.

Trubowitz, Neal T.

1979   The Early Archaic in Western New York. *New York State Archaeological Association Bulletin* No. 75:52–58.

Tuck, James A.

1974   Early Archaic Horizons in Eastern North America. *Archaeology of Eastern North America* 2(1):72–80.

Tunnell, Curtis

1977   Fluted Projectile Point Production as Revealed by Lithic Specimens from the Adair-Steadman Site in Northwest Texas. In Paleoindian Lifeways. Edited by Eileen

Johnson. *The Museum Journal* No. 27: 140–168.

Turnbaugh, William A.

1975   Toward an Explanation of the Broadpoint Dispersal in Eastern North American Prehistory. *Journal of Anthropological Research* 31(1):51–68.

1980   Early and Middle Archaic Elements in Southern Rhode Island. In Early and Middle Archaic Cultures in the Northeast. Edited by David R. Starbuck and Charles E. Bolian, pp. 59–72. *Occasional Publications in Northeastern Anthropology* No. 7.

Turner, Ellen Sue, and Thomas R. Hester

1985   *A Field Guide to Stone Artifacts of Texas Indians.* Texas Monthly Press.

Van Buren, G. E.

1974   *Arrowheads and Projectile Points.* Arrowhead Publishing Company. Garden Grove, California.

Vickery, Kent

1972   Projectile Point Type Description: McWhinney Heavy Stemmed. Paper presented at the 29th Southeastern Archaeological Conference, Morgantown, West Virginia, October 13–14, 1972.

1976   *An Approach to Inferring Archaeological Site Variability.* Ph.D. Dissertation. Department of Anthropology, Indiana University.

Wachtel, H. C.

1957   Ohio Triangles. *Ohio Archaeologist* 7(4):120–121.

Wahla, Edward J., and Jerry DeVisscher

1969   The Holcombe Paleo-Point. *Michigan Archaeologist* 15(4):109–111.

Walsh, James P.

1977   Arrowhead Casino: A Middle to Late Archaic Site at Saratoga Lake, N.Y. *New York State Archaeological Association Bulletin* No. 71:29–42.

Walthall, John A.

1972   The Chronological Position of Copena in Eastern States Archaeology. *Journal of Alabama Archaeology* 18(2):137–151.

1973   A Restudy of the Wright Village (LUv65), A Middle Woodland Habitation Site in Lauderdale County, Alabama. *Tennessee Archaeologist* 29(2):69–108.

1980   *Prehistoric Indians of the Southeast: Archaeology of Alabama and the Middle South.* The University of Alabama Press.

Ward, H. Trawick

1983   A Review of Archaeology in the North Carolina Piedmont: A Study of Change. In *The Prehistory of North Carolina: An Archaeological Symposium.* Edited by Mark A. Mathis and Jeffrey J. Crow, pp. 53–80. North Carolina Division of Archives and History Department of Cultural Resources.

Waring, A. J., Jr.
1961   Fluted Points on the South Carolina Coast. *American Antiquity* 26(4): 550–552.

Warnica, James M., and Ted Williamson
1968   The Milnesand Site: Revisited. *American Antiquity* 33(1):16–24.

Wasley, William W.
1960   A Hohokam Platform Mound at the Gatlin Site, Gila Bend, Arizona. *American Antiquity* 26(2):244–262.

Waters, Spencer A.
1957   Paleo-Indian Artifacts from Collections in North Alabama. *Tennessee Archaeologist* 13(1):49–54.

Wauchope, Robert
1966   Archaeological Survey of Northern Georgia with a Test of Some Cultural Hypotheses. *Society for American Archaeology Memoir* No. 21.

Webb, Clarence H.
1946   Two Unusual Types of Chipped Stone Artifacts from Northwest Louisiana. *Bulletin of the Texas Archaeological and Paleontological Society* Vol. 17:9–17.
1948   Evidence of Pre-Pottery Cultures in Louisiana. *American Antiquity* 13(3): 227–231.
1959   The Belcher Mound, A Stratified Caddoan Site in Caddo Parish, Louisiana. *Memoirs of the Society for American Archaeology* 16.
1970   Settlement Patterns in the Poverty Point Cultural Complex. In The Poverty Point Culture. Edited by Bettye J. Broyles and Clarence H. Webb, pp. 3–12. *Southeastern Archaeological Conference Bulletin* No. 12.
1977   The Poverty Point Culture. *Geoscience and Man*. School of Geoscience, Louisiana State University, Baton Rouge.

Webb, C. H., J. L. Shiner, and E. W. Roberts
1971   The John Pearce Site (16CD 56): A San Patrice Site in Caddo Parish, Louisiana. *Bulletin of the Texas Archeological Society* 42:1–50.

Webb, William S.
1939   An Archaeological Survey of Wheeler Basin on the Tennessee River in Northern Alabama. *Bureau of American Ethnology Bulletin* No. 122.
1940   The Wright Mounds Sites 6 and 7 Montgomery County, Kentucky. *University of Kentucky Reports in Anthropology* 5(1). University of Kentucky, Lexington.
1946   Indian Knoll, Site Oh 2, Ohio County, Kentucky. *University of Kentucky Reports in Anthropology and Archaeology* 4(3), Part I.

1950a   The Carlson Annis Mound. *University of Kentucky Reports in Anthropology* 7(4).
1950b   The Read Shell Midden. *University of Kentucky Reports in Anthropology* 7(5).
1951   The Parrish Village Site, Site 45, Hopkins County, Kentucky. *University of Kentucky Reports in Anthropology* 7(6).

Webb, William S., and Raymond S. Baby
1957   *The Adena People* No. 2. The Ohio Historical Society. Ohio State University Press.

Webb, William S., and David L. DeJarnette
1942   An Archaeological Survey of Pickwick Basin in the Adjacent Portions of the States of Alabama, Mississippi and Tennessee. *Bureau of American Ethnology Bulletin* 129. Washington, D.C.
1948a   The Flint River Site, Ma 48. *Alabama Museum of Natural History, Museum Paper* 23. University of Alabama.
1948b   Little Bear Creek Site Ct 8. *Alabama Museum of Natural History, Museum Paper* 26. University of Alabama.

Webb, William, and J. Elliott
1942   The Robbins Mounds Site Be 3 and Be 14, Boone County, Kentucky. *University of Kentucky, Reports in Anthropology and Archaeology* 5(5):373–499.

Webb, William S., and William G. Haag
1947   Archaic Sites in McLean County, Kentucky. *University of Kentucky, Reports in Anthropology* 7(1).

Webb, William S., and Charles E. Snow
1945   The Adena People. *University of Kentucky Reports in Anthropology and Archaeology* 6.

Weinland, Marcia K.
1980   The Rowena Site, Russell County, Kentucky. *Kentucky Archaeological Association Bulletin* 16–17.

Weinland, Marcia K., and Jason M. Fenwick
1978   A Reconnaissance and Evaluation of Archaeological Sites in Daviess County, Kentucky. *Kentucky Heritage Commission Report* No. 6.

Weinman, Paul L., and Thomas P. Weinman
1969   A Snook-Kill Workshop. *Pennsylvania Archaeologist* 39(1–4):23–28.

Wendorf, Fred, and Alex D. Krieger
1959   New Light on the Midland Discovery. *American Antiquity* 25(1):66–78.

Whallon, Robert, and James A. Brown, eds.
1982   Essays on Archaeological Typology. *Center for American Archeology, Seminars in Archeology* 1. Kampsville, Illinois.

Wheat, Joe Ben
1972   The Olsen-Chubbuck Site: A Paleo-Indian Bison Kill. *Society for American Archaeology Memoir* No. 26.
1977   Technology, Typology, and Use Patterns at the Jurgens Site. In Paleoindian Life-

ways. Edited by Eileen Johnson. *The Museum Journal* 17:126–139.

1979   The Jurgens Site. Journal of the Plains Conference Memoir 15. *Plains Anthropologist* 24(84):Part 2.

White, Anta M.
1965   Typology of Some Middle Woodland Projectile Points from Illinois and Michigan. *Papers, Michigan Academy of Science, Arts and Letters* 50.

Willey, Gordon R.
1966   An Introduction to American Archaeology. Vol. 1 North and Middle America. Prentice-Hall.

Willey, Gordon R., and Philip Phillips
1958   *Method and Theory in American Archaeology*. The University of Chicago Press. Chicago.

Williams, Stephen, ed.
1968   The Waring Papers: The Collected Works of Antonio J. Waring, Jr., *Papers of the Peabody Museum, Harvard University* 48. Cambridge, Massachusetts.

Williams, Stephen, and Jeffrey P. Brain
1983   Excavations at the Lake George Site, Yazoo County, Mississippi, 1958–1960. *Papers of the Peabody Museum* 74.

Williamson, Ronald F.
1980   The Liahn II Site and Early Woodland Mortuary Ceremonialism. *Ontario Archaeology* 33:3–12.

Wilmeth, Roscoe
1978   Canadian Archaeological Radiocarbon Dates. Revised Version. *Archaeological Survey of Canada Paper* No. 77.

Wilmsen, Edwin N., and Frank H. H. Roberts
1978   Lindenmeier, 1934–1974: Concluding Report on Investigations. *Smithsonian Contributions to Anthropology* 24.

Winsch, John, M.D.
1971   A Further Note on Fractured Base Points. *Ohio Archaeologist* 21(4):30.

Winters, Howard D.
n.d.   *Projectile Points of the Cache River Valley*. Unpublished manuscript on file at the Illinois State Museum, Springfield.
1959   The Paleo-Indian Period. In Illinois Archaeology. *Illinois Archaeological Survey Bulletin* 1:5–9.
1962   The LaMotte Culture of the Wabash Valley. *Council for Illinois Archaeology Report* No. 9.
1963   An Archaeological Survey of the Wabash Valley in Illinois. *Illinois State Museum, Reports of Investigations* No. 10.
1967   An Archaeological Survey of the Wabash Valley in Illinois. Revised Edition. *Illinois State Museum, Reports of Investigations* No. 10. Springfield.
1969   The Riverton Culture. *Illinois State Museum, Reports of Investigations* No. 13. Springfield.

Winters, Howard D., and Nancy Hammerslough
1970   The Havana Tradition. In *Adena: The Seeking of an Identity*. Edited by B. K. Swartz Jr. pp. 138–141. Ball State University.

Witthoft, John
1952   A Paleo-Indian Site in Eastern Pennsylvania: An Early Hunting Culture. *Proceedings of the American Philosophical Society* 96(4):464–495.
1953   Broad Spearpoints and the Transitional Period Cultures. *Pennsylvania Archaeologist* 38(1):4–31.

Wittry, Warren L.
1951   A Preliminary Study of the Old Copper Complex. *The Wisconsin Archeologist* 40(4):137–267.
1959a   The Raddatz Rockshelter SK5, Wisconsin. *The Wisconsin Archeologist* 40:33–39.
1959b   Archaeological Studies of Four Wisconsin Rockshelters. *The Wisconsin Archeologist* 40(4):137–267.

Wolfal, Mark, Phil McClure, and Robert E. Pace
1978   A Riverton Culture Base Camp in Bartholomew County, Indiana. *Proceedings of the Indiana Academy of Science* 87:81. Indianapolis.

Wood, W. Raymond
1963   Two New Projectile Points: Homan and Agee Points. *The Arkansas Archaeologist* 4(2):1–6.

Wood, W. Raymond, and R. Bruce McMillan
1967   Recent Investigations at Rodgers Shelter, Missouri. *Archaeology* 20(1):52–55.

Wormington, H. M.
1957   Ancient Man in North America. *Denver Museum of Natural History Popular Series* No. 4. Peerless Printing Co., Denver, Colorado.

Wormington, H. M., and R. G. Forbis
1965   An Introduction to the Archaeology of Alberta, Canada. *Proceedings Denver Museum of Natural History* 11:1–207.

Wray, Donald E., and Richard S. MacNeish
1961   The Hopewellian and Weaver Occupations of the Weaver Site, Fulton County, Illinois. *Illinois State Museum Scientific Papers* 7(2).

Wright, Henry T., and Richard E. Morlan
1964   The Hart Site: A Dustin Complex Fishing Camp on the Shiawassee Embayment. *Michigan Archaeologist* 10(3):49–53.

Wright, Henry T., and William B. Roosa
1966   The Barnes Site: A Fluted Point Assemblage from the Great Lakes Region. *American Antiquity* 31(6):850–860.

Wright, J. V.
1976   The Grant Lake Site, Keewatin District, N.W.T. *National Museum of Man Mer-*

cury Series Archaeological Survey of Canada Paper No. 47.

1978 The Implications of Probable Early and Middle Archaic Projectile Points from Ontario. *Canadian Journal of Archaeology* 2:59–78.

Wyatt, Ronald J.

1977 The Archaic on Long Island. In Amerinds and their Paleoenvironments in North-eastern North America. Edited by Walter S. Newman and Bert Salwen. *Annals of the New York Academy of Sciences* Vol. 288, pp. 400–411.

Wyckoff, Don G.

1964 The Cultural Sequence at the Packard Site, Mayes County, Oklahoma. *Oklahoma River Basin Survey Project, Archaeological Site Report* No. 2, Norman.

Projectile Point Type Index

285

EDITORS: Terry L. Cagle and Roberta L. Diehl
BOOK AND JACKET DESIGNER: Matthew Williamson
PRODUCTION COORDINATOR: Harriet Curry
TYPEFACE: ITC Garamond, with Optima
PRINTER: Thomson-Shore
BINDER: John H. Dekker and Sons